W9-ADU-221

Angkor—Before and After:
A Cultural History of the Khmers

Angkor—Before and After:

A Cultural History of the Khmers

David Snellgrove

WEATHERHILL

David Snellgrove
ANGKOR—BEFORE AND AFTER:
A cultural history of the Khmers

Published in North America by
Weatherhill, Inc., 41 Monroe Turnpike,
Trumbull, CT 06611 USA
in cooperation with Orchid Press,
P.O. Box 19, Yuttitham Post Office,
Bangkok 10907, Thailand

Copyright © 2004 by Orchid Press. Protected by copyright under the terms of the International Copyright Union: all rights reserved. Except for fair use in book reviews, no part of this publication may be reproduced in any from or by any means, electronic or mechanical, including photocopying, recording, or by any information storage or retrieval system without prior permission in writing from the copyright holder.

All photographs by Suthep Kritsanavarin copyright © Suthep Kritsanavarin 2003.

Cover illustration: A Buddhist nun, in charge of a small stone shrine on the upper level of the Bayon, looking out at one of towering Bodhisattva images.
Photograph by Suthep Kritsanavarin.

Endpapers: Muang Tam. A view in the late evening. Photograph by Suthep Kritsanavarin.

Printed and bound in Thailand

ISBN: 0-8348-0539-1

Contents

Illustrations

Plates

Maps

Figures

Preface

Angkor reopened to visitors during the 1990s after an enforced closure of nearly thirty years, and since then university research-work relating to the Khmer empire has made rapid progress. L'École française d'Extrême Orient has resumed its tasks of research and restoration, interrupted in 1970, while many other countries have joined in this work with various reconstruction projects for the preservation of the ancient monuments on this particular site. The Phnom Penh Museum, founded in 1930 on the initiative of EFEO, which was left abandoned during the Khmer Rouge period, reopened in 1979 under the Vietnamese occupation. However it was not until 1996 on the occasion of the international exhibition, *Angkor and ten centuries of Khmer art,* which was held in Paris, New York and in Japan, that a full programme of restoration of the collections was undertake by the EFEO, supported by the Cambodian and French Ministers of Culture. Soon afterwards the Musée Guimet in Paris, totally renovated, reopened its galleries of some of the finest pieces of Khmer art. These events created a surge of new interest in Cambodia, and since 1995 an appreciable number of works on Angkor have been published, many offering magnificent photographs of Angkor Vat and of the ruins of Angkor Thom, such as the splendid work of Claude Jacques and Michael Freeman, *Angkor, Citadels and Palaces*, River Books, Bangkok 1997. I must also mention the earlier work by Smitthi Siribhadra, Elizabeth Moore and Michael Freeman, *The Palaces of the Gods* (Bangkok 1992) which illustrates the vast Khmer artistic and architectural heritage in Thailand, followed by *A Guide to Khmer Temples in Thailand and Laos* by Michael Freeman (Bangkok 1995). Although various publications have described Preah Vihear and more rarely Bantây Chmar, one looks in vain in recent works for the other great temple-complexes in Cambodia, such as Beng Mealia, Preah Khan of Kampong Svay, Chao Srei Vibol and even the historical site of Angkor Borei. In order to find some documentation relative to these major sites as well as many other important archaeological sites in Cambodia, one must return to the early pioneers such as Lunet de Lajonquière or Étienne Aymonier or to various monographs published before 1970.

Préface

Depuis qu'Angkor s'est rouvert aux visiteurs, dans les années 1990, après une clôture forcée de près de trente ans, les recherches universitaires consacrées à l'empire khmer ont connu un rapide regain. L'École française d'Extrême-Orient a repris, sur place, ses travaux de recherche et de restauration, interrompus en 1970, et plusieurs pays ont mis en œuvre, conjointement, divers projets de reconstruction afin de préserver les anciens monuments du site. Le Musée de Phnom-Penh, fondé en 1920 sous l'égide de l'EFEO, demeuré à l'abandon sous les Khmers Rouges, a rouvert dès 1979, pendant l'occupation vietnamienne. Ce n'est cependant qu'en 1996, à l'occasion de la préparation de l'exposition internationale « Angkor et dix siècles d'art khmer » qui s'est tenue à Paris, à New York et au Japon, qu'un programme complet de restauration de ses collections a été entrepris, conduit par l'EFEO avec le soutien des ministères français et cambodgien de la Culture. Peu de temps après, le Musée Guimet, entièrement rénové lui-même, rouvrait ses galeries des chefs-d'oeuvre d'art khmer. Ces événements ont suscité une véritable renaissance de l'intérêt pour le Cambodge et, depuis 1995, un nombre appréciable d'ouvrages sur Angkor ont été publiés, certains offrant de magnifiques photographies d'Angkor Vat ou des ruines d'Angkor Thom, au premier rang desquels l'ouvrage classique et solide du Pr. Claude Jacques et Michael Freeman, *Angkor, résidence des dieux,* Édition Olizane, Genève 2001. Il faut encore mentionner le livre, légèrement antérieur aux autres, de Smitti Siribhadra, Elizabeth Moore et Michael Freeman, *The Palaces of the Gods* (Bangkok, 1992) qui porte sur le vaste héritage artistique et architectural khmer de Thaïlande, bientôt suivi par *A guide to Khmer Temples in Thaïland and Laos* par Michael Freeman, (Bangkok 1995). Cependant, bien que tel ou tel ouvrage comporte une description du temple forteresse de Banteay Chmar ou plus souvent de Preah Vihear, on chercherait en vain dans ces ouvrages récents une description des autres grands complexes de temples du Cambodge que sont Beng Mealea, le Grand Preah Khan de Kompong Svay, celui de Chao Srey Vibol, ou même du site historique d'Angkor Borei. Il faut parfois, pour trouver une documentation relative à ces ensembles, ainsi qu'à

The author of this book, of which I have the honour to write the preface, has certainly done this. Since his arrival here, not only has he read exhaustively the available works on ancient Cambodia, but he has taken the trouble, often not without physical difficulty, of visiting almost all the sites mentioned in his book, be they in Cambodia, Thailand or Laos.

I met David Snellgrove in 1995 on the occasion of his first visit to Cambodia thanks to the recommendation of our joint friend Irène Martin du Gard, who was at that time Editor of the revue *Arts asiatiques* (Annales du musée national des Arts asiatiques - Guimet et du musée Cernuschi, *Cahiers de l'Ecole française d'Extrême-Orient*). She had already known him for some forty years and was well acqainted with his important work on Buddhism and the thread of his research-work in India, Nepal, the Tibetan frontier regions, then more recently turned towards Indonesia, especially the great monuments of Indian inspiration in Central and Eastern Java. It is the same interest in Indian forms of civilization based on the adoption of Sanskrit as the main literary language, which led him naturally to Cambodia in 1995. I have had the opportunity of accompanying him on his journey to Koh Ker, and then along the terrible route to Preah Khan of Kampong Svay, and also the less difficult journey to Angkor Borei, while on his several journeys around Thailand he was accompanied by a Thai photographer, Mr Suthep Kritsanuvarin, who also came with us to Preah Khan. This work of David Snellgrove covers large aspects of Khmer civilization, as much historical as geographic, from the 6th century to the present day, although he writes in greater detail of the period of Khmer 'grandeur', when the Khmer empire included vast areas situated beyond the native frontiers.

bien d'autres sites archéologiques importants du Cambodge, se tourner vers les pionniers comme Lunet de Lajonquière ou Étienne Aymonier, ou vers les monographies publiées antérieurement à 1970. C'est ce qu'a fait l'auteur de ce livre dont j'ai l'honneur d'écrire la préface. Depuis son arrivée dans ce pays, non seulement le Pr. Snellgrove, a lu de façon exhaustive tous les ouvrages disponibles sur le Cambodge ancien, mais il s'est donné la peine de visiter lui-même, parfois non sans intrépidité, presque tous les sites dont il est fait mention dans cet ouvrage, qu'ils soient au Cambodge, en Thaïlande ou au Laos.

J'ai rencontré David Snellgrove en 1995, à l'occasion de son premier séjour au Cambodge, grâce aux recommandations de notre amie commune Irène Martin du Gard, alors rédactrice de la revue des Arts asiatiques (Annales du musée national des Arts asiatiques - Guimet et du musée Cernuschi, Cahiers de l'Ecole française d'Extrême-Orient) qui le connaît depuis quarante ans. Elle était au courant de ses travaux importants sur le bouddhisme et connaissait le fil de ses recherches sur l'Inde, le Népal et surtout sur le Tibet, orientées ultérieurement vers l'Indonésie, notamment vers les grands monuments d'inspiration indienne du centre et de l'est de Java. C'est le même intérêt pour les formes indiennes de civilisation, fondées sur l'adoption du sanskrit comme principale langue littéraire, qui devait naturellement le conduire au Cambodge en 1995. J'ai eu la chance de l'accompagner moi-même à Koh Ker, puis sur la piste effroyable du Preah Khan de Kompong Svay ainsi que sur celle moins difficultueuse d'Angkor Borei, tandis que lors de ses nombreux périples en Thaïlande, il était accompagné d'un photographe thaïlandais, M. Suthep Kritsanuvarin qui était également au Preah Khan avec nous. L'ouvrage du Pr. Snellgrove aborde de larges aspects, tant dans une dimension historique que géographique, de la civilisation khmère, du VIe siècle à nos jours, même s'il s'étend avec prédilection sur la période de la grandeur khmère, lorsque l'empire angkorien structurait de vastes territoires situés bien au delà des frontières.

Olivier de Bernon,
Maître de Conférences,
École française d'Extrême Orient,
Paris

ACKNOWLEDGMENTS

The idea of producing this book derived directly from Mr Hallvard Kuløy of Orchid Press, Bangkok. In March 2001 he encouraged Mr Suthep Kritsanuvarin, a professional photographer from Bangkok, to meet me in Siem Reap, hoping that some book would emerge from our collaboration. He himself did not have time to develop any clear ideas on the subject, as unhappily he died suddenly less than two months later. Suthep had already begun to take photographs with some financial support from the Orchid Press, and I began to produce the text of this new book. Planned as 'A Cultural History of the Khmers' from the 6th century to the 20th, it was bound to include material (with notable additions and amendments) already covered in my small book *Khmer Civilization and Angkor.* During 2001 Suthep made two visits to Cambodia, and in April of that year we made a tour together of some thirty-two Khmer sites in north-west Thailand and in southern Laos. This was the most wide-ranging of other tours which I have made of ancient Khmer sites in Thailand, and by drawing on Thai sources, mainly notes from the Fine Arts Department of the Government of Thailand, Suthep introduced me to sites which I would otherwise not have seen. We made another short tour together in February 2002 adding yet a few more sites, previously unvisited. On two other short journeys around sites in Thailand in April 1988 and February 1999 I was accompanied by Peter Skilling and his admirable driver/companion Somneuk.

The first person plural pronoun when used in the text includes those who accompanied me on these many journeys; in Cambodia this was almost always Pheung Vutthy, my constant companion here, or occasionally his adopted son Ratna, especially around Bantây Chmar and the important sites within range of Battambang. On other adventurous journeys to Koh Ker, Preah Khan of Kampong Svay, and Angor Borei, Olivier de Bernon came with us. Suthep and his wife Usanee also came with us on that occasion. I accept gladly some thirty photographs from his collection, as well a few kindly offered me by Signora Giulia Anglois who accompanied us on visits to several sites in Cambodia and in Thailand. Later some were offered me by Martin Polkinghorne, a PhD student of the University of Sydney and assistant to Dr Pamela Gutman, who visited me in Siem Reap, and finally two by Tom Sarœun of the EFEO, Phnom Penh. Eight have been gratefully received from the Musée Guimet in Paris. The rest are my own.

The text of this book has been mainly written in Siem Reap, where I have been greatly helped by Monsieur Olivier de Bernon, 'Maître de Conférences' d'École française d'Extrême Orient, whose time is divided between Paris and Phnom Penh, where he still remains responsible for the finding and preservation of surviving Cambodian manuscripts, largely destroyed during the Khmer Rouge period. As on previous occasions, he has provided me not only with copies of many of the articles quoted in my sources, but also xeroxed copies of whole books, of which the most substantial is George Coedès' eight-volume collection of the Inscriptions of Cambodia. He and his close colleague in Bangkok, Mr Peter Skilling, who assists him in the elucidation of Pâli sources as relevant to the Khmer Theravâda period, have read Chapters 6 and 7 of this book, urging some amendments and making helpful suggestions. I also owe a personal word of thanks to Michel Tranet (EFEO) for the use of his material in the section concerning Sambor Prei Kuk, and to Bruno Bruguier (EFEO) for the use of two maps of major routes in ancient Cambodia.

Of the many French scholars whom I quote, a special note of appreciation is due to George Coedès for his vast erudition in the 'classical' aspects of South-East Asian cultural history and his remarkable powers of historical deduction. By 'classical' I mean primarily those sources which used Sanskrit, the classical language of India, as their medium, as for example the considerable collections of stone inscriptions, on which scholars have very largely depended for their discovery of the past of all these South-East Asian peoples. But like many of his colleagues, his erudition was not limited to the reading of Sanskrit. A large part of these inscription are written in ancient Khmer, largely incomprehensible to the people of Cambodia nowadays, and it is due entirely to the initiative of French and other foreign researchers that a number of qualified Khmer scholars are now able to read for themselves these texts relating to their past history, and to take an active part in recent planning, seminars and excavations.

The recent founding two years ago of a Khmer Cultural Centre in Siem Reap has also proved very useful to me, not only on account of its small library, now always on the increase, but also because many Khmer and foreign scholars are attracted to this new centre. Of these I might mention as examples the Indian professor Kamaleswar Bhattacharya, expert in the elucidation of the elaborate Sanskrit versification typical of the Angkor-period stone inscriptions, or Madame Madeleine Giteau, whose substantial volume on *Iconographie du Cambodge post-Ankorienne* has been of the greatest assistance in writing of the later period. As for the later history of Cambodia I owe much to Monsieur Khin Sok, 'Maître de Conférences' at the National Institute of Oriental Languages and Civilizations in Paris, and in the same context of modern Khmer scholarship I must surely mention Madame Saveros Pou (formerly Lewitz) who has worked mainly on the Khmer/Pâli inscriptions of the later period. French and other foreign scholars are so numerous for the Angkor period, that I mention no further names in particular, but turning to the earlier period of 6th to 8th centuries, where the name of George Cœdès again comes to the fore, I must surely mention the recent studies of the American scholar Michael Vickery, which have been of the great help to me in this present book.

I must certainly mention another American scholar, no longer alive, namely Lawrence Stanley Briggs, author of a comprehensive work, entitled *The Ancient Khmer Empire*, first published by the American Philosophical Society, Philadelphia in 1951. His was the first comprehensive study written in English on the history of the Khmer Empire from its beginnings in the 6th century until its demise in the 14th. In his preface, written fifty years ago, he writes: 'The excavations and studies of scholars, particularly those of the École française d'Etrême Orient during the nearly fifty years of its existence, have accumulated such a mass of historical, epigraphic, iconographic, architectural, and other data in this field that the earlier histories are completely out of date and the sheer mass of the new data has retarded their revision.' In his notes he cites about 150 scholarly writers and 750 separate references, many of them consisting of several items. More than 160 separate items come from George Coedès alone. No other author, English-speaking or French, has produced so comprehensive an account of the history of Angkor, referring to practically all the known archaeological sites and to a very large selection of stone inscriptions relating to sites where nothing remains except the inscribed stele itself. Despite the renewed interest in Khmer studies since the country came to life again after a disastrous twenty-year period of warfare, death and destruction, Brigg's monumental work has not yet been bettered as a detailed historical survey, while it remains as a tribute to the devoted labours of the many French and non-French scholars of the past. At the same time I readily acknowledge its great help to me in assembling very much the same materials in a more concise form.

Since most statues and stone-inscriptions as well as many decorative motifs, especially finely carved lintels and frontal pieces have been removed for safely to museums, primarily the National Museum in Phnom Penh and the Musée Guimet in Paris, I am grateful for the help received from Madame Irène Martin du Gard, formerly editor of *Arts Asiatiques*, the journal of this great asiatic museum, for the help that she has given me in choosing selected items. We have made several visits together to the Khmer collection there, and she and Olivier de Bernon arranged subsequently for permission to reproduce them. Permission to reproduce photographs from the Phnom Penh Museum is not so readily available, but the recent publication of the catalogue by the École française d'Extrême Orient (see Nadine Dalsheiner in the Bibliography) means that the most important items of this collection are already available in print and so easily accessible to any interested reader. For those who visit the monuments at Angkor, the only fully detailed guide-book is that by Maurice Glaize of the EFEO who was himself responsible for much or the renovation work at Angkor from the late 1930s until the mid-20th century. *Les monument du groupe d'Angkor* (first published in Paris in 1944 with revised editions up

1. (p. 17 top left) Kong Sangsara (of the Conservation d'Angkor) and Vutthy by the eastern gopura *of Bantây Thom (Angkor).*

2. (p. 17 top right) Taing Joy, Vutthy's younger brother, at the Bayon.

3. (p. 17 bottom left) Hokpheng, computer-assistant, and his wife Devi, the daughter of Vutthy, in front of the Khmer Cultural Centre at Siem Reap.

4. (p. 17 bottom right) Somneuk, Peter Skilling's Thai assistant, seated by the spout of a sûtrasoma *at Narai Jaeng Vaeng (Sakhon Nakon).*

to 2003) is the work of one who was devoted to his vocation and to these temples, as he then knew them before the neglect and looting of more recent times. It is regrettable that no English edition has so far been produced. Of various guide-books in English I would commend that of Dawn F. Rooney, *Angkor, an introduction to the temples*. Thanks are certainly due to the EFEO, that great research institution founded in 1898 and still going strong, which has been my main support in practical as well as academic affairs during the last eight years. A final word of thanks must go to David Murray of Orchid Press who has painstakingly seen this work through to publication. As in other recent publications I must surely express my thanks to the Ministry of Foreign Affairs for allowing me these long periods of residence in Cambodia.

5. (above left) Olivier de Bernon (centre) and Peter Skilling with the local priest at Phnom Baset (Kandal Province).

6. (left) Excavations at Muang Sima (Khorat). Suthep and his wife Usanee are photographing.

7. (below left) Admiring a new baby. Vutthy's wife Pang is on the right.

8. (below) Ratna, Vutthy's adopted son, by the western outer wall at Bantây Chmar.

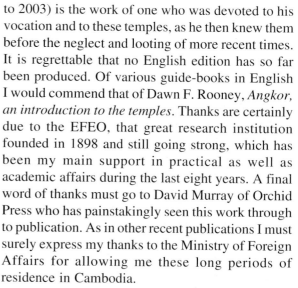

Introduction

This book attempts to cover Khmer civilization from its known origins in the early centuries AD to the present day. Thus the very important Angkor period which will occupy a major part of the book may be seen within the larger context of the earlier period and more significantly in relationship with the changed cultural developments which coincided with the gradual dissolution of the Angkor empire during the 13th to 15th centuries. The term 'empire' may seem a rather extravagant term when measured in the context of the British and French empires, but it may plausibly be used for the short period in the 11th to 13th centuries when Angkor was the major power on the South-East Asian mainland, challenged occasionally only by the Cham principalities of the eastern coastline. As is well known the downfall of this 'empire' was caused primarily by the Thai advance from the north, resulting in the gradual occupation of more and more Khmer territories, eventually even the Angkor (Siem Reap) district. Other factors, social, religious and economic, were also involved, as explained in Chapter 6. Cambodia was thus reduced to an even smaller area than it occupies on our maps today, becoming in effect a client state of the united Thai kingdom of Siam, based on Ayuthaya and then later Bangkok. At the same time the Vietnamese who descended along the coastal area, finally putting an end to Cham civilization in the 15th century, also played their part in the occupation of Khmer frontier areas, even attempting for a short and ruinous period (1834-47) to impose not only the norms of Vietnamese administration upon the country, but even to replace the Theravâda Buddhism of the Khmers with their Confucian form of Chinese Buddhism. The only salvation for Cambodia was to turn for help once again to Siam, involving warfare between these domineering neighbours, waged destructively on Cambodian soil. It was in this time of total destitution that the French appeared on the scene.

The former colonial powers, primarily Britain, France and Holland, are sometimes blamed for the ills which their former colonies have suffered since gaining independence, although they are all too often due to the misgovernment of post-colonial rulers. If there is something for which they should certainly not be blamed, this is their scholarly interest in the countries which they occupied including archaeological research and the collecting of examples of architectural pieces some of which went to their national museums in London, Paris and Amsterdam. Such collections formed part of extensive archaeological surveys and the laborious reading of ancient inscriptions in order to assist in reconstructing the earlier history and appreciating the earlier high level of culture of their occupied territories. Before the arrival of the Europeans, local peoples had the vaguest ideas of their past history, which at best survived only in quasi-historical legendary accounts. Unfortunately it must be admitted that the first Europeans, amongst whom the Portuguese and the Spanish must be included, who established trading bases in Asian countries, were interested (with very few exceptions) only in financial gain, usually involving the military occupation of foreign territory. The same primary interests motivated likewise the British and the Dutch who later arrived on the scene, and it was not until their home governments (approximately from the mid 19th century onwards) began to exercise some form of control over these militant trading ventures, that serious interest began to be taken in the history and culture of these occupied territories. It is interesting to note that the French occupation of Indochina was very late compared with British and Dutch occupation of the India and the Malay archipelago, dating precisely from the time when European scholars were beginning to take an interest in investigating and unraveling the earlier history of their colonial territories. Thus the French could claim with some justification that their occupation of Vietnam, Cambodia and Laos was a form of 'civilizing mission'. Whether Vietnam with its well-established Chinese form of administration and its Confucian ethics needed civilizing all over again, may well be considered doubtful, but Cambodia was in such a deplorable state that the establishing of a French protectorate over the country in 1853 must fairly be regarded in some important respects as ultimately beneficial. Firstly, over a period of 150 years French cultural expeditions and French scholars have succeeded in providing the people of Cambodia with detailed information concerning their earlier history, dating the reigns of their earlier kings and providing descriptions of most ancient Khmer sites with notes of their dates and purposes, all of which knowledge can only be gained by the reading of ancient inscriptions (5th to 14th century) in Sanskrit and Khmer. This book and all the other recent books that have appeared derive their knowledge of the history, architecture and culture of the Khmers mainly from French sources. Secondly, this French protectorate put an end to Siamese encroachments, and by reclaiming the provinces of Battambang and Siem Reap (Angkor), they established the boundaries of Cambodia as they exist on our maps today.

Cambodia is now a small country, covering something over 180,000 square kilometres, bordered to the west and the north by Thailand and then by Laos in the north-east, while the eastern boundary, twisting round to the south, now adjoins Vietnam. To the south-west there is a short piece of coastline, which nowadays provides the main seaport of Kampong Saom (alias Sihanoukville) and some very pleasant beaches. The range of the Dangrek Mountains, rising at the most to about 700 metres, now forms the northern boundary with Thailand, but at the western end they become low hills, so that now the Cambodian north-western plain opens out in the direction of the lower valley of the Chao Praya River and so to Bangkok. At the eastern end of the Dangrek Range, where Cambodia adjoins Laos, the mighty Mekong River makes a passage through the lower hills, thus rendering fertile this eastern section of the country. It is joined at Phnom Penh by the great watercourse, known as the Tonle Sap (= Freshwater River), which applies both to the river itself and to the great lake, extending northwards as far as the Angkor region. Such is the quantity of water descending the Mekong during the monsoon season (June to October), that it flows northwards up the Tonle Sap, raising the level of the lake by several metres. As the water descends over the winter period (temperature then about 28ºC), the lake gradually diminishes in size, leaving extensive areas of fertile soil around its borders for the planting of rice. A similar service is provided by the Mekong in the eastern part of the country thanks to the alluvial soil, which it carries down during the monsoon months. Cambodia is thus a heavily wooded country with magnificent forests and wide stretches of fertile soil in the vicinity of these well-watered areas. Tropical fruits and vegetables are plentiful and as can be well imagined there is no lack of fish. Pork, beef, chicken and duck are also available on more festive occasions. Despite such potential bounty, Cambodia remains a poor country, and if monsoon rains, or heavy floods (where transport becomes difficult even if crops are not ruined) are delayed famine is by no means unknown. Wet rice is the main crop and the staple diet, while dry rice, maize and other lesser crops can be grown in the more hilly regions in the north leading up to the Dangrek Range, in the north-east section of the country bordering on Laos and in the wild expanse of the Kravanh (Cardamom) Mountains in the south-west. Although these rise to little more that 500 metres, these relatively mountainous areas are the home of tribal peoples who may be referred to collectively as Pnong, including also the Por, the Saoch, the Chong and the Samre, all with their diverse dialects and customs. These tribes represent the original inhabitants in the country before the Khmers arrived on the scene in the prehistoric period. One may note that they provided many of the slaves referred to in Sanskrit/Khmer inscriptions of the Angkor period and in the later Pâli inscriptions. The other major source for slaves were prisoners of war.

In the Angkor period, Cambodia embraced not only the lower Mekong Valley which has gradually been absorbed into Vietnam from the 17th century onwards (see Chapter 7), but also the greater part of present-day Thailand as well as southern Laos, so some brief description must also be given of the whole of mainland South-East Asia as relevant to the history of the Khmers. When they first enter history in the 6th century AD they are known to have occupied what is now southern Laos in the Champassac region and probably also the lower valley of the Mun river which flows eastwards into the Mekong at approximately the same latitude. There were Khmer settlements all the way down the Mekong at least as far as the present Vietnamese frontier and an important historical site known as Angkor Borei. The Vietnamese had not yet appeared on the scene and the lower Mekong Valley and the whole southern coast formed part of a maritime state known by the Chinese as Funan, no local name having as yet been discovered in any inscription. During the late 6th century the Khmers succeeded in absorbing Funan, as will be explained in Chapter 2. Others sometimes write of Funan as though it represents the beginning of Khmer history and the relationship between them requires careful consideration. Economically they prove to be quite distinct entities; Funan was a maritime state depending on overseas trade with China, the Malay Peninsula and India, and even Arabia. The Khmers

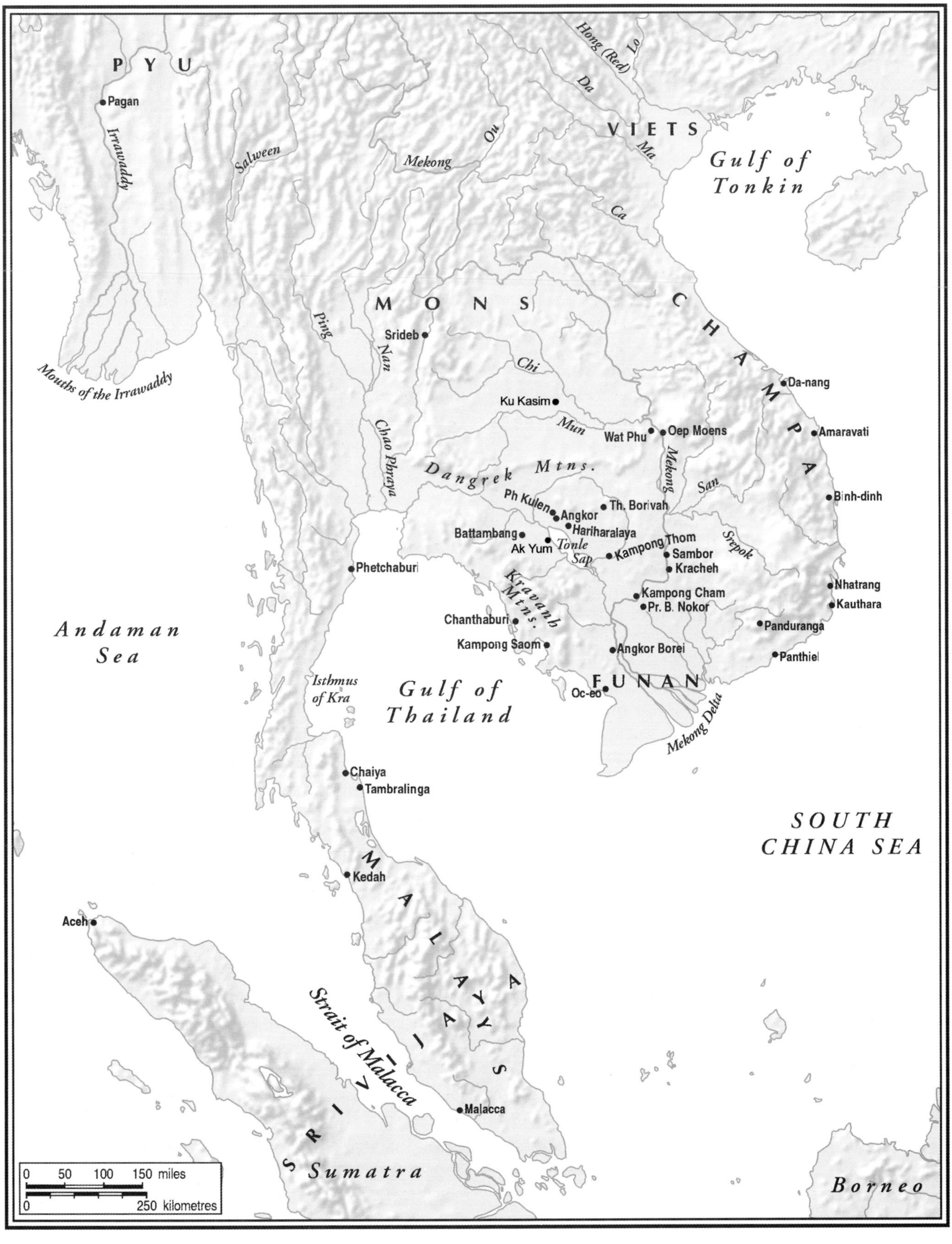

Map 1. Before Angkor.

are first known as a collection of small independent land-powers and Cambodia continued to develop as a land-power, depending on agricultural produce and the spoils of war, as more and more territory was won, mainly northwards and westwards. The coastal population of Funan was probably partly Mon and Khmer with a considerable mixture of people of Malay/Indonesian stock, who were great sea-farers and by the early centuries AD (doubtless even earlier) occupied all coastal regions (at least those suitable for trade) throughout the whole Malay archipelago. However the inland parts of Funan were surely peopled by Khmers, notably in the area around Angkor Borei, which is now assumed to have been the chief inland city of Funan. Thus the last kings of Funan in the 6th century may well have been partly Khmer or even fully Khmer, and this can explain the seeming ease with which the Khmers occupied Funan.

From the 7th century onwards Khmer settlements begin to appear not only in the Angkor region (see Chapter 2, 'Other Early Settlements') but also north of the Dangrek Range into what is now Thai territory. With the founding of Angkor itself in the late 9th century, Khmer temples begin to appear on the Khorat Plateau and also westwards where this plateau descends towards the Chao Praya valley, providing even easier access to what is now central Thailand and eventually the Thai-Malay peninsula. Northwards Khmer power extended by the 11th century as far as Sukhothai in the NW and Sakhon Nakon in the NE. Before the arrival of the Thais (12th century onwards) the inhabitants of these mainland areas, whether those of the Chao Praya Valley or the Khorat Plateau and northwards were largely Mon, a people who, as will be made clear later, were racially akin to the Khmers. Southwards along the Thai-Malay peninsula, the population was largely Malay. Westwards, Khmer power extended close to the present Thai-Burmese frontier in the neighborhood of Khanchanaburi (specifically the Khmer temple-fortress of Muang Singh, not far from the notorious 'Bridge of the River Kwai'). Eastwards the Khmers established themselves no further afield than southern Laos, as they were blocked by the Annamese mountain range, which separated them from the Cham principalities along the coast. (However this did not prevent frequent warfare with these neighbours at least up to the 13th century, when the Chams were threatened by the Vietnamese advance from the north.) All in all this is a large amount of territory to be covered in any cultural history of the Khmers, even though Cambodia appears as such a small country on present-day maps.

Although French scholars have naturally predominated in the 150 years of investigation and research (just as British scholars have predominated in the study of the cultural history of India), more and more foreign scholars are now interesting themselves in the Cambodian past, and not least of all the Thais, since so much of Khmer history is located in present-day Thailand. One gains the impression that in the middle of the 18th century the administrative and social conditions in Siam were generally similar to those prevailing in the then client state of Cambodia. However change was already underway. King Mongkut (Râma IV) attempted to reform Buddhist institutions in the country, having learned Pâli and studied the Buddhist scriptures as a monk during the reign of his brother, whom he in due course succeeded. He realized that modernization of the country was essential, if Siam was to be able to deal with the risk of encroachments from the British on one side in Burma and the French now on the other side in Cambodia. Britain and France and the USA became involved in the country as the result of various treaties, mainly concerning trade.

His successors, King Chulalongkorn (1868-1910) and Vajiravuth (1910-1925), carried the gradual process of modernization still further, while during the early reign of King Prajadhipok (1910-1935) the National Library, the National Museum, and the Fine Arts Department (which corresponds in its activities, at least on a national scale, with the École française d'Extrême Orient and with the British Archaeological Survey of India) were founded at the beginning of the 20th century. With the consent of the Government of Thailand French scholars had already been surveying some the main Khmer temples in Thailand, but from the mid-20th century onwards this responsibility became that of the newly founded Fine Arts Department of the Government of Thailand. Some major ancient Khmer temples, such as Phimai, Phnom Rung and Phnom Wan have been wonderfully restored, many more smaller sites have been discovered, listed and described, while excavations, often with foreign assistance, have revealed much of the earlier Mon period and traced the origins of civilization in Thailand back to 6,000 years BC and possibly even earlier. Most of this is relevant eventually to a cultural history of the Khmers, especially those excavations which take us back 2,000 years or more, when the Mon-Khmers were already the predominant population in mainland South-East Asia.

Of all the Khmer historical sites in Cambodia itself only Angkor remains readily accessible to visitors. More hardy travellers can also visit Sambor Prei Kuk thirty-two kilometres north of Kampong Thom, and Bantây Chmar some sixty-five kilometres north of Sisophon. Preah Vihear can be reached easily from the Thai side if one happens to be in that remote north-east corner of Thailand. Recently the Cambodian Government has constructed a new road so that access from the Khmer side has been greatly eased. The present Ministry of Tourism would like to make these sites and also a few others easily available to tourists, but the financial costs will be heavy to build decent roads and carry out necessary restoration work, thus making up for the neglect and destruction of the last fifty years. At the same time many important Khmer sites in Thailand can be reached easily and comfortably, while apart from the National Museum, Bangkok, there are several important museums on the provincial cities, such as Lopburi, Khorat, Phimai, Ubon Ratchathani and Khon Kaen. The cultural heritage of Thailand comprises the impressive remains of Mon and Khmer civilisation, namely of the two peoples who were there before the Thais arrived on the scene. So full credit must go to them for the present care taken of the great works of art that they have inherited. Such is essentially the historical background against which any history of Khmer civilisation has to be written, taking full account of French, Thai and to a less extent Vietnamese participation.

Note on Transliteration

Sanskrit names and terms are written in accordance with the normal system of transliteration except for the unvoiced palatal *c*, which is represented by *ç* as in Çaṇḍi, Çitrasena, Çola. Such words are often written in anglicized form as Chandi, Chitrasena, Chola, thus confusing *ç* with the Sanskrit voiced palatal *ch*. However a few of such better known names, such as Champa are retained here in this popular form. Literary Khmer employs the same alphabetical system as Sanskrit, but Khmer names appear here in a popular phonetic form, with very few exceptions, e.g. Çaturmukha (pronounced Çatomukh). I note that in the French transliteration of Sanskrit ç is often used to represent the letter ś, but this should cause no confusion.

Chapter 1

The Origins of Khmer Civilization

The early inhabitants of South-East Asia

The Khmers are one of the earliest historically known people of the South-East Asian mainland, conventionally referred to as Indochina. They appear to have occupied the middle and lower Mekong Valley from the lower Mun Valley southwards towards the coast. Their neighbours to the west and the north were the Mons, who occupied what is now central Thailand (around the Gulf of Siam) and the Khorat Plateau to the north of the Dangrek Range, which nowadays forms the frontier between Thailand and Cambodia. Their neighbours to the east were the Chams, who occupied the lower river-valleys along the eastern coast of Indochina.[1] Thus a present-day political map of this part of the world presents a totally different picture from the situation existing during the first millennium AD, since Thailand and Vietnam as now constituted were non-existent. The Thais and the Viets were later arrivals on the scene, pressing down from the north, in the one case on the Mons and the Khmers, and in the other case on the Chams, who have been totally displaced and now have no country to call their own. Likewise the Mons and their highly developed culture have been absorbed into the later developing Burmese and Thai civilizations. The Thais also adopted significant elements, linguistic, social and architectural, of Khmer culture, which is the main subject of this book. Despite this relentless Thai pressure the Khmers have survived as an independent country. This is much reduced in size from the period of maximum Khmer expansion (11th to 13th centuries), but is probably not so very different from the area occupied at the beginning of their recorded history in the 6th to 7th centuries.

Indochina is not a very satisfactory name for the South-East Asian mainland, as it suggests quite wrongly a cultural area which is part Indian and part Chinese with no particular characteristics of its own. Although China has had a continuing trading and political interest in the whole area from the earliest known historical period onwards, Chinese cultural influences have impressed themselves firmly only on the Viets who as noted above were later arrivals on the scene, generally from the Red River Valley basin. By contrast, Indian cultural influences have been so pervasive that some writers have referred to Indochina as 'Outer India' and the more enthusiastic Indian scholars have even suggested that Indian colonies were established throughout the many coastal areas, whence Indian culture readily spread inland. Nowadays there is a strong reaction against such an interpretation and some scholars tend to go to the other extreme, emphasizing the indigenous nature of local social organization and attempting to minimize the Indian contribution. Recent archaeological research has now revealed the social and economic bases of Mon-Khmer civilization as essentially indigenous, as will be illustrated below, but it is undeniable that the cultural impact of India has been enormous. This is inevitable because the Mons, Khmers and the Chams, all previously illiterate, adopted Indian scripts not only for writing their own languages, but also for the importation of Sanskrit and Pâli literature, which was bound to form the basis of their first literary endeavors and which laid them open at the same time to Indian cultural and religious concepts. By contrast only the Viets adopted the Chinese system of writing and with analogous results.

Indigenous Factors

But first let us summarize the little that can be known of indigenous Mon-Khmer civilization. Our information is limited largely to the Mon areas of central Thailand and the neighboring Khorat area, which the Khmers scarcely penetrated until the 9th century onwards. Because of the appalling political conditions in Cambodia during the second half of the 20th century excavations in Cambodia itself have been rare until only recently. However we may assume similarities between central Thailand and Cambodia existed, not only because the Mons and Khmers are closely related, but also because the economic and social conditions of the Khmers as known in the 7th century would be incomprehensible without the assumption of the earlier necessary phases. Excavations in Thailand have succeeded in recording the existence of many neolithic sites dating back from the 2nd to the 1st millennium BC, and also bronze-age (*c.*1500 BC onwards) and the even more significant iron-age sites (*c.*700 BC onwards) which bring us relatively close to the early historical period. Typical of the neolithic sites is the use of pottery and polished stone axes. There are also indications of primitive farming and animal husbandry. The discovery of the metallurgy, initially that of bronze (usually an alloy of copper with tin or lead), and later that of iron, might seem to lead us directly into the first known historical times. First bronze and then later iron which is so much harder, turned into agricultural implements, eased enormously the clearing of forested ground for the founding of new settlements, while turned into weapons, it gave far greater scope to the human tendency to domination and violence. Some of these sites had a long history and were sooner or later absorbed in the advance of the Khmers northwards and westwards from the 9th century onwards. One might mention in particular Srîdep (< Śrîdeva, also written as Sri Thep), which as its name suggests was a thoroughly 'Indianized' city still flourishing in the 13th century. Here there is a likely example of later Mon and Khmer cross-relations. (For references see note 2.)

In the course of my writing I have come across a short article by Dr Dougald O'Reilly and Mr Pheng Sytha of the Royal University of Phnom Penh concerning some very recent excavations in north-west Cambodia (Snay village in Bantây Meanchey Province) where the construction of a new road has uncovered fortuitously an iron-age burial site.

> *The excavation (5 m by 15 m) revealed nine prehistoric burials and over 300 artifacts including ceramic vessels, glass beads, grinding stones, carnelian beads, bronze bangles, and iron tools and weapons. Evidence of body armour was fugitive in the excavated area but one individual was interred with a cache of iron points and an iron sword. This young adult male was also buried with green glass earrings, bronze rings, glass beads and a large tiger canine around the neck. An unidentified bronze artifact was held in the man's left hand. The other burials were not as well appointed. A child, of two or three years of age, was buried with ivory bangles, glass beads and a piece of unidentified iron.*

Although the site has not been dated, it is estimated to have been occupied during the early centuries AD.[2] This brings us remarkably close to the earliest known historical sites, not yet excavated, and marked by the earliest inscriptions of the 6th to 7th century. One also reflects how very much more there remains to be discovered under the soil in Cambodia. An interesting site which we have visited personally (see the illustrations) is that of Moeng Sema to the west of Nakhon Ratchasima on the Khorat Plateau, where the quasi-circular earth fortifications are clearly visible. The graves here are about 2,000 years old, and the foundations of several Mon shrines can be seen and also the ruins of a later shrine, attributable to the Khmers, who arrived later in this area.

Charles Higham, on whom I rely generally for such relevant information, notes that the use of iron led to the formation in the early centuries BC of much larger communities covering some fifty hectares, where the emergence of social classes is clearly suggested by a minority of tombs distinguished by their wealthy paraphernalia as against a majority of much simpler burial sites.[3] The contents of the grave of a wealthy man, presumably one of the ruling elite, would contain bronze rings, bracelets and ornaments, agate and carnelian pendants and beads, as well as iron implements and weapons (*The Civilization of Angkor*, pp. 151-8). Numerous examples of such artifacts may be seen in the National Museum, Bangkok, and elsewhere in local museums already mentioned above. Soon to be added to such items would be luxuries deriving from the extensive trade which developed over established sea-routes from Arabia and India, passing across the Malay Peninsula, around the coast of Indochina and arriving finally in China. This had certainly developed by the beginning of the first millennium AD, gradually including routes that coasted the major islands of the Indonesian archipelago, especially Sumatra, Java and Borneo.

Thus while we note that the social and economic basis of Mon and Khmer settlements was largely indigenous and land-based, we note also that the other major elements of their developing civilization, namely those linguistic, architectural and religious were sea-borne, coming primarily from India. Odd luxury items such as mirrors and jewellery arrived from still further away, even from the Roman world, while high-grade pottery and other luxury items came from the other direction, from China.

The inhabitants of the coastal regions in the earliest known period were sometimes Mon or Khmer, but they were mainly people of another stock whom we may equally well refer to as Malays or Indonesians. Although it is usually assumed that all these people who now occupy not only the Indochina mainland, but also the Malay/Indonesian archipelago, arrived from regions further to the north

9. *(above) A corpse and the remains of funereal offerings.*

→ *11. (p. 9) The stone foundations of an early Khmer shrine at Muang Sima. The Khmers can scarcely have arrived here before the 8th – 9th century. See Plate 73, p. 70.*

10. (below) The surviving foundations of a Mon shrine at Muang Sima of which there are several others.

and may be generally described as Mongoloid, the Malays and Indonesians belong to a different language group from the Mon-Khmers. To complete the picture one might also add the Pyus, who together with the Mons inhabited central and lower Burma in the earliest known historical period, and who were later submerged by the arrival of the Burmese. This does not mean that the whole of South-East Asia was deprived of human inhabitants before the arrival of the Mon-Khmers or the Pyus. Traces of still earlier races, usually known as Veddoid (because of a presumed relationship with the Veddas of Ceylon) are still to be found in the remoter regions of the South-East Asian mainland and islands.

So far as this book is concerned we are interested primarily in the Khmers, but also in the Mons, the Chams and the Malay-Indonesians who occupied mainly the coastal settlements. Having developed as maritime dwellers, the last named probably played a greater part in the trade which linked India with the Malay-Indonesian archipelago, as well as with the coastal areas of Indochina and South China, as did seamen from the west and east coasts of India. However this may be, the linguistic, cultural and religious influences, which were to play so large a part in Khmer civilization, come undoubtedly from India in a form of one-way traffic. Moreover it was scarcely possible that such influences should reach the Khmers, an inland people, directly. The earliest pronounced signs of such influences are found in small city-states along the Malay Peninsula, mainly at its narrowest section, which served as a land-crossing, thus saving the longer and more dangerous voyage through the straits between Malaya and Sumatra, now known as the Straits of Malacca. At the same time an important trading emporium developed near the southern tip of the Indochina mainland, precisely at a site known as Oc Eo near present-day Rach Gia in what is now the extreme south of Vietnam. Aerial photography and recent excavations leave no doubt of its importance as the major port on the long route from India via the Malay Peninsula to China. Knowledge of all such maritime states in their 'Southern Seas' comes in the first instance from Chinese sources and the local names available to us are all in Chinese. This particular maritime state at the very south of the Indochina mainland was known by the Chinese as Funan and it seems that it had already gained a form of hegemony over certain maritime states along the Malay Peninsula. I quote from Paul Wheatley a passage preserved in the *Annals of the Liang Dynasty* (502-557) concerning the King of Funan.

Once more he used troops to attack and subdue the neighboring kingdoms, which all acknowledged themselves as his vassals. He himself adopted the title of Great King of Funan. Then he ordered the construction of great ships

and crossing right over the Chang-hai (Gulf of Siam), attacked more than ten kingdoms, including Chü-tu-k'un, Chiu-chih and Tien-sun. He extended his kingdom for 5-6,000 li. Then he attacked the kingdom of Chin-lin.[4]

Influences from India

As far as Indian influences are concerned, we might quote the extreme case of an Indian Brahman supposedly becoming King of Funan. He is said to have come via Pan-pan, another small maritime state well known to the Chinese, which flourished during the 5th and 6th centuries in the region of the Isthmus of Kra, in the area of (later) Chaiya. The earliest mention of it (in the *Annals of the Liang Dynasty*) brings it directly into relationship with Funan.

Chiao Chen-ju (Kauṇḍinya) was originally an Indian Brahman who received a divine fiat to reign over Funan. Chiao Chen-ju rejoiced in his heart. He arrived in Pan-pan to the southward. When the Funanese heard of him, they all welcomed him with delight, went before him and chose him as their king. Once more he modified all the laws to confirm with the usage of India.

Pan-Pan is described in several later Chinese compilations:

The people live mostly by the water-side, and in default of city-walls erect palisades of wood. The king reclines on a golden dragon-couch, with all his chief retainers kneeling before him, their hands crossed and resting on their shoulders. In the country are numerous Brahmans who have come from India in search of wealth. They are in high favour with the king. There are ten monasteries where Buddhist monks and nuns study their canon.[5]

These Chinese accounts are accepted with a certain reserve. Culled from earlier works, they are usually much later than the events that they describe. However there can be no doubt of the existence of Funan as the major trading emporium in the 'Southern Seas' and of the extent to which the various other maritime states were permeated by Indian culture, both Brahmanical and Buddhist already by the 3rd century AD. Funan plays an important part in the early history of the Khmers, because their more southern inland strongholds bordered on its territory, and thus it would seem that it was mainly though Funan that Indian influences gradually permeated Khmer civilization. However the Khmers were also in contact with the Chams on their eastern borders and some Indian influences probably came also from that direction.

Foremost among Indian influences on the civilizations of South-East Asia is the art of writing. From this all else inevitably followed, exerting entirely analogous secondary influences as did the introduction of Latin to the earlier illiterate peoples of Western Europe. The first literature to become prevalent throughout South-East Asia was mainly in Sanskrit, the classical language of all Brahmanical writings and also of Mahâyâna Buddhism, but also in Pâli, a composite Indian dialect, which continued to be used by some early Buddhist orders. We may note at once that the use of Pâli was mainly limited to the Pyu and Mon communities in the Irrawaddy and Chao Praya valleys (in present-day terms lower and central Burma and Thailand) and thus the Khmers scarcely came into contact with this form of Indian language until almost the end of the Angkor period. The earliest inscriptions found in Funan and in Champa were usually in Sanskrit but occasionally in Pâli. In any case Sanskrit continued to be used as the classical language of the Khmers until the 14th century and by the Chams even later, much as Latin continued to be used in Europe throughout the Middle Ages and even later. Khmer appears on inscriptions from the 7th century onwards, but it never achieved the literary prestige of Sanskrit. Thus Sanskrit remained not only the literary language of the minority of Brahmans and Buddhists of Indian descent, but of all the subsequent generations of educated Khmers, presumably that small minority of rulers and prelates, monks and courtiers, who might hold the rank of Brahmans and Kṣatriyas (princely class). Clearly, such social ranking was fundamentally an indigenous process, but as soon as Indian Brahmans arrived on the scene these ranks were readily interpreted in Indian terms. At the same time they were never imposed upon Khmer society which developed nothing resembling the Indian caste-system. In any case Buddhist monks remained outside it, although as we shall note certain leading Buddhist prelates came to be treated with the same high honours as the court-Brahmans.

We know very little of the pre-Indianized religion of the Khmers, because by the time they enter history (about the same time as the earliest relevant Sanskrit inscriptions) from the 6th century onwards, their gods tend to be conceived in Indian terms. However thanks to a recent publication of Michael Vickery, *Society, Economics and Politics in pre-Angkor Society*, certain elements begin to become clear. Thus it is interesting to note that the emergence of written Khmer in the 7th century reveals the existence of Khmer gods known as *kpoñ*, related linguistically to the human rank of *poñ*, which also occurs in these early inscriptions. The last known use of the term *kpoñ* occurs in year 715 where there is reference to a feminine protective divinity of a Queen Jayadevî in a typical mixture of Khmer and Sanskrit: *kpoñ kamratâñ añ Srî Senamukhavijayâ* = the revered divinity (Khmer) Noble Victorious-Army Vanguard (Sanskrit).[6] Another divinity appears to be named in the same inscription but lacking the Khmer honorific title, Śrî Sundarasvâmi, meaning presumably the Noble Lord (or Lady) of Beauty; 'i' may represent a root-ending for feminine –'î'.[7] It would seem that there was already a tendency to translate the names of local gods into Sanskrit, and again Vickery provides some cogent examples, such as *Aśnasaronâtha* = 'Lord of the Stone Pool', who is surely a local Khmer god *(Society, Economics and Politics,* p. 140). Also the use of the Sanskrit title *Îśvara* (Lord) for some local male divinities might easily lead to their eventual identification with the Great Lord (*Maheśvara*) Śiva. In the later period the addition of the suffix *îśvara* for male divinities and *îsvarî* for female divinities allow for the creation of divinized royalty regarded as aspects of Śiva and his consort Umâ. Once we pass to this later period, marked by the accession of Jayavarman II and the introduction of the cult of the Devarâja (Khmer: *kamraten jagad ta râja*), it may be taken for granted that most divinities with Sanskrit names are meant to represent fully their Indian prototypes, such as Śiva, Vishnu, Harihara (Śiva and Vishnu combined), Brahmâ, Sûrya, the Sun-God, Lakṣmî. spouse of Vishnu, Varuṇa, god of the water, Indra, god of war, Yama, god of death. But even such well-established Indian gods may occasionally have been associated earlier with a local divinity. A cogent example is the fierce goddess *Mahîṣâsuramardinî* = 'She who crushes the buffalo-demon'. It is possible that her popularity is associated with an early Khmer rite of buffalo-sacrifice (see below). So far as the few named Buddhist divinities are concerned, such as Prajñâpâramitâ, the Goddess of Wisdom, the Bodhisattvas Avalokiteśvara and Vajrapâṇi, we may assume that these are direct Indian borrowings. At the same time there is nothing to have prevented a popular early feminine divinity from being later associated with the 'Goddess of Wisdom' or an early popular fierce divinity being subsequently identified with Vajrapâṇi, 'Thunderbolt-in-hand'.

12. An early image of a goddess, probably mid-7th century, from Koh Klieng, one of the many small islands in the Mekong, northern Sambor. She may be identified subsequently as Umâ. (From Parmentier, vol. I, p. 270.)

A note on Indian Gods as relevant to Cambodia

The major Indian gods derive from the earliest Vedic times, especially from the 'Rig Veda' (*ṛgveda*), or 'Knowledge of the Sacred Verses', the first of the set of 'Four Vedas' which provide the basis for Brahmanical, and eventually Hindu religion in the wider sense. Mainly concerned in the earlier stage of their religion with the worship of their Indo-European gods, corresponding in origin to those of all other Indo-European peoples (notably perhaps those of Greece and Rome) they gradually develop into the cult of a single supreme Being known as Brahman. In the developing stage the earlier divinities tend to be praised by their adherents as superior to all other gods until the realization comes that there can be essentially one supreme Being.[8] The gods best known to our readers are probably Brahmâ, the personification of *brahman* the absolute, Śiva (Gentle) also known as Rudra (Fearful), and Vishnu, a Vedic god of the heavens, but also of water through association with another god Varuṇa. Śiva and Vishnu appear rarely as greater than other gods in the Vedic pantheon, but by the first century AD they had become established as the Great Gods of Hinduism, identical in essence in that they are inseparable in the absolute state of *brahman,* as symbolized by the God Brahmâ. Already by the 5th century Śiva and Vishnu are conceived as a unity, known as *Hari* (=Vishnu) *–hara* (=Śiva). One of the earliest representations appears amongst some famous rock-carvings at Mahabalipuram on the south-east coast of India, one of the main sources of Indian cultural influences in South-East Asia. Thus Harihara is already well known to the Khmers by the 7th century and doubtless still earlier in Funan. Brahmâ, Śiva and Vishnu are often treated as though they were a form of trinity, but any of the three may be given priority of place, depending upon the preferences of their devotees. A carving which one often sees is that of Vishnu lying on his back in the primaeval waters with a lotus-stalk rising from his navel, topped by a lotus-flower on which is seated Brahmâ. These major gods all have feminine partners, even Brahmâ, who is associated with Sarasvatî, the Goddess of Speech. Vishnu shows a preference for Lakṣmî, the goddess of fortune, while Śiva was enamoured of a Himalayan nymph named Aparṇâ, later identified with his better known consorts, Umâ or Gaurî. These may be referred to more generally simply as Devî, the Goddess. Together with their supposed spouses, other related divinities, and (in the case of Vishnu) manifestations in divine-human form, Hinduism has developed an enormous pantheon of supernatural beings. Of the quasi-human manifestations the best known are surely Krishna and Râma, both regarded as incarnations (*avatâra*) of Vishnu. By using this brief summary as an initial framework, it should be sufficient to explain the significance of the many other gods, as they occur in the text.

While one may take for granted the readers' general knowledge of the Indian (Hindu) pantheon, a few may be surprised by the existence of Buddhist gods and goddesses, existing seemingly in close association with the Lord Buddha himself. This comes about in India from maybe the 1st century BC onwards, as the result of the easy association of lay Buddhists with their Hindu fellow-countrymen. As is well known, a serious Buddhist monk hopes to process through a series of lives to a state of ever greater perfection, verging at last on Buddhahood itself.[9] At the same time the so-called historical Buddha Sâkyamuni who lived about the 6th century BC was never regarded as the one and only. Previous Buddhas were listed by name and although modern scholars may regard them as mythical, they were equally real for early believers, who following upon Sâkyamuni's decease, soon concentrated their faith on a future Buddha Maitreya ('Loving Kindness'). According to the traditional accounts of his life Sâkyamuni had lived through a long series of previous lives, always aiming at final perfection. As an aspirant to Buddhahood he is referred to in the stories of his earlier lives as *Bodhisattva* = 'a being who is set to gain enlightenment'. It was thus logical to assume that apart from Sâkyamuni, who had completed the long course, there were other beings who were still on the way towards Buddhahood thanks to their gradual increase in wisdom and merit. Their merit might be increased by the help they gave to other struggling beings in the cycle of existence, while devotion to them might also have a positive effect for the progress of those who prayed to them. In this way it became possible for the later Buddhism of the so called Mahâyâna (Great Way) to envisage a class of divine beings who for all practical purposes were equivalent to the great gods of Hinduism. For example there is a close parallel between Avalokiteśvara, the Lord who looks down (in compassion from the heavens) and the Lord Śiva in his tranquil aspect. Both receive the title of Maheśvara = the Great Lord. Vajrapâṇi, 'Holder of the Thunderbolt', probably derives from Indra, the Vedic god of war, who holds the same weapon. Mahâmâyâ, queen of the small Indian state of the Sâkya clan and mother of Sâkyamuni becomes idealized as Târâ, the 'Saviouress', regarded as the Mother of All Buddhas. She might well be compared with the Christian concept of Mary as 'Mother of God'. She also tends to be identified with the 'Perfection of Wisdom' (*Prajñâpâramitâ*), which is also the title of an important collection of Mahâyâna Buddhist scriptures.[10] These later developments did not efface earlier Buddhist traditions, where the only Bodhisattvas normally

13. Aparṇâ, the spouse of Śiva.
Toraṇa from Preah Pithu, Angkor,
first half of 13th century,
sandstone, h. O.87m. br. 1.34 m.
Musée Guimet MG 18912

She is the daughter of the god Himavat, symbol of the sacred Himalayas, and of Menakâ, an ancient Vedic goddess. She is known as Parvatî, the Mountain Goddess or as Devî and has many forms as the primary goddess of Śaivite tradition.

Here she is undergoing a test to prove her worthiness to become Śiva's wife. She appears twice here in two consecutive scenes:

First above, where she is closing her ears so as not to hear the blasphemies against Śiva which a Brahman on the right of the scene (in fact Śiva himself in disguise) is uttering in order to put her reactions to the test.

Secondly to the left Śiva in his true form is raising her up from a kneeling posture.

The other capped kneeling figure is a subsidiary devotee, in the first case beseeching the false Brahman to cease his blasphemies, and secondly commending Aparṇâ for having passed the test.

recognized are Sâkyamuni before his enlightenment and the future Buddha Maitreya. However so far as the Angkor period is concerned, it is only the Mahâyâna that counts, as received from Funan or from Champa. We shall note that the Khmers soon met with the earlier traditions of the Theravâda (the 'Old Way') when they extended their rule over the Mons who occupied the Khorat Plateau and the region around the Gulf of Siam. In the post-Angkor period this form of Buddhism has prevailed in Cambodia, as will be explained in the later chapters.

Chapter 2

Before Angkor

Funan

Funan is known mainly from early Chinese records, as already illustrated above. It is known to have maintained diplomatic contacts (in the form of tribute-missions) with the Chinese court from the 3rd to the first half of the 6th century and even later after it had succumbed to Chenla (Cambodia). The high esteem in which Funan was held may be illustrated by the wording of an imperial order relating to an embassy sent in AD 505:

> *The King of Funan, Kauṇḍinya Jayavarman, lives at the limits of the ocean. From generation to generation he and his people have governed the distant lands of the south. Their sincerity manifests itself afar; through their many interpreters they offer presents in homage; it is fitting to reciprocate and show them favour and accord them a glorious title. This is possible (with the title of) General of the Pacified South, King of Funan.*[1]

We note in passing that this king Jayavarman, who died in 514, is assumed to be a descendant of the Brahman Kauṇḍinya referred to above. His wife, Queen Kulaprabhâvatî, and also possibly a son named Guṇavarman (the reading of the name is uncertain) have left stone inscriptions, one referring to the Queen's founding of a hermitage, and one which celebrates the establishing of 'a realm wrested from the mud' (the reclaiming of marshy ground) and the founding of a sanctuary which contained a foot-print of Vishnu. The last king of Funan was Rudravarman who may have usurped the throne from this Guṇavarman, and who sent various embassies to China between 517 and 539.[2] Rudravarman himself seems to have been favorable to Buddhism and may have been responsible for sending Buddhist texts and Buddhist scholars including the famous Indian scholar Paramârtha to China at the special request of the emperor.

Funan must have been a small but very prosperous kingdom, its wealth being based on trade. Aerial photography has given a fair idea of the extensive layout of the great coastal trade-emporium at Oc Eo while excavations have provided some idea of its

14. Avalokiteśvara (Rach Gia)
Tân-long (ancient province of Rach-gia), Vietnam.
Mid-7th to 8th century, limestone, h. 1.88 m.
Style of Funan. Musée Guimet MA 5063

wealth in artifacts arriving both from the west and from the east.[3] The port seems to have been connected by a canal with the capital, which in the later period was probably at Angkor Borei and so was eventually taken over by the Khmers.

The Beginnings of Champa

Champa developed as a confederation of small provinces, which correspond to the various plains bordering on the major river-mouths along the eastern coast of Indochina. Especially important is present-day Quang-nam with the recorded archaeological sites of Tra-kieu, Mi-son and Dong-duong, an area then known as Amarâvati. This name suggests at once an avowed association with the renowned Indian city of the same name.[4] Then there is Vijaya in present-day Binh-dinh, Kauṭhâra in the plain of Nha-trang and Pâṇḍuranga in the region of Phan-rang. Already in the 2nd century Chinese accounts make mention of these people who lived south of Tongking in a land known rather vaguely as Lin-yi, as though they were rather troublesome neighbours.[5] It is impossible to define their racial origins clearly, although it would be surprising if they were not related to the Viets to the north, who were to become their perennial enemies. It is likely that there were strong Indonesian elements also present, namely the same seafaring people who occupied the Indonesian archipelago and probably also represented a large racial element in Funan.

Indian influences must have affected the culture of Champa simultaneously with neighbouring Funan, and it is significant to note that just as the kings of Funan were associated with an Indian royal founder, the Brahman Kauṇḍinya, so the kings of Champa claimed as theirs the Mahârṣi Bhrigu, a Brahmanical sage from the great Indian epic, the Mahâbhârata. A very early Sanskrit inscription, dated for paleographic reasons even to the 3rd century was found in the Nha-trang region. It refers to a sacrificial rite by a king named Bhadravarman, offered to Śiva under the name of Bhadreśvara (= the Worthy Lord) and transmitted by Agni, the god of fire and sacrifice.

Homage to God! By favour of the feet of the Lord Bhadreśvara I do what is right by you Agni, so that He may preserve the sons and grandsons of the Great King of the Law, Śrî Bhadravaman as long as the sun and moon shall last. May this rite succeed by favour of the Earth-Goddess.

Another inscription refers to a donation by King Bhadravarman to a shrine dedicated to Śiva under the name of Bhadreśvara in Mi-son (Quang-nam Province) It begins with acclamations to Śiva and Umâ, to Brahmâ and Vishnu, to the Earth, to the Winds, to Space and to Agni.[6]

A later inscription, much mutilated, refers to the rebuilding of the same shrine by a later king Śambhuvarman. Unfortunately the date cannot be read clearly. As many as twenty-five later inscriptions, nearly all in a ruinous state, have been found near Mi-son, giving references to later kings and their donations. These inscriptions are dedicated mainly to Śiva, usually under the title of Bhadreśvara, but the other main Brahmanical gods are also well known.[7] It is not until the year Śaka 824 (AD 902) that the first dated Cham Buddhist inscription is known. This also comes from Quang-nam Province and is dedicated to Avalokiteśvara, also referred to as Lokanâtha = 'Lord of the World'.[8]

Wat Phu

The emergence of the Khmers into recorded history has been associated with a possible early Khmer victory over the Chams in the Champassac region of present-day southern Laos. That the Chams first occupied this region is suggested by an inscription of a king Devânîka, who is described as a 'great

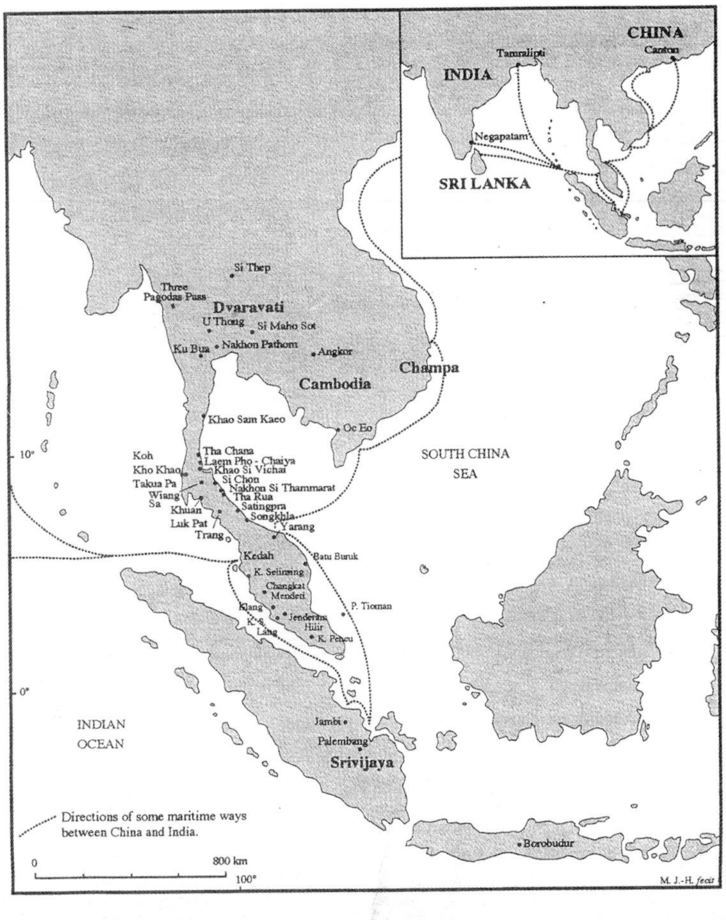

Map 2. The Malay peninsula and some of its archaeological sites. By courtesy of Michel Jacq-hergoualc'h, The Malay Peninsula.

king of kings' (*Mahârâjâdhirâja*) who 'came from a distant country' to achieve 'supreme royal overlordship' (*mahâdhirâjaiśvarya*) by the grace of Lingaparvata (the god of the sacred mountain) which rises above Wat Phu. The inscription is undated but Coedès attributes it to the first half of the 5th century and suggested that the king here referred is probably a king from Champa.[9] Furthermore, an oft-quoted passage concerning the Khmers from the *Sui Shu* (*Annals of the Sui Dynasty*, AD 581-618) states that:

> *Near the capital of the kingdom is a mountain named Ling-chia-po-p'o (= Lingaparvat), on the summit of which a temple was constructed, always guarded by a thousand soldiers and consecrated to the spirit named P'o-to-li (viz. Bhadreśvara), to whom human sacrifices are made. Each year the king himself goes to this temple to make a human sacrifice during the night.*[10]

This site is traditionally identified with the city of Śreṣṭhapura, which is thus placed in the vicinity of a sacred mountain in the Champassac region and is said to have been founded by a king named Śreṣṭhavarman, the son of Śrutavarman.[11]

In a very much later inscription the occupation of this area was still regarded as the source of the Khmer monarchy, since Jayavarman VII in an inscription of AD 1186 is praised as 'a descendent of Śrutavarman and Śreṣṭhavarman, the origins of a brilliant line of kings'.[12] Śrutavarman and seemingly his heroic companions receive praise for their valour in the oft-quoted Baksei Chamkrong inscription (early 10th century), but no connection is suggested between him and Rudravarman (the first Khmer ruler of Funan) who is the next one to receive praise.[13] Since Śreṣṭhavarman is not named in these earlier inscriptions, it has been urged that he may be regarded as quasi-historical or even mythical.[14] A historical problem exists if this presumed contact between the Khmers and Chams has to be brought into some relationship with the eventual predominance of the Khmers over Funan so much further to the south. But Cambodia (or Chenla as it was called by the Chinese) was certainly not a united country in the 6th to 7th century, and the warring of one Khmer chief in the north does not necessarily have to be brought into relationship with what was happening far to the south. Śrutavarman was probably remembered as a renowned Khmer chieftain and thus placed before Rudravarman because of his presumed earlier date.

Whatever its historical basis, the cult of Śiva as Bhadreśvara, certainly originally a Cham title, comes to be accepted as a regular part of Khmer mythology. It is also possible that the cult of Śiva as their primary divinity was adopted from the Chams. By contrast in Funan Vishnu was readily worshipped together with Śiva and other Brahmanical gods while also Buddhism flourished. It is significant that the site of Wat Phu under the shadow of this mountain in the Champassac region has come to be associated

16. *(above) Wat Phu. The main shrine is built on a platform cut into the mountain-side. The present temple dates to the 12th century, about the time of Sûryavarman II. It has long since been transformed into a Buddhist temple.*

← 15. *(p. 16) Wat Phu. A general view looking east from the main shrine.*

17. *(below) Wat Phu. Rock-carvings on the site of Avalokiteśvara flanked by Brahmâ and Vishnu, presumably of the same date as the present temple.*

traditionally with the origins of Khmer history and that its importance to later generations was never forgotten. Like all such important Khmer historical sites new construction work and improvements continued up until the 13th century. Practically nothing remains of the earliest period except some brick and stone-work at ground level and a few rock-carvings. The main stone-built shrine, now a Buddhist temple, built on its platform cut into the mountain-side, as well as the two large buildings far below, usually identified as palaces, probably date from the times of Sûryavaman II, first half of the 12th century. Despite its generally ruined state, this site remains on account of its magnificent situation one of the most impressive. The present temple of the early 12th century, modest in its dimensions, stands on a platform on a hill-slope contiguous to the Lingaparvata. It is approached first by a long causeway and then by a double set of steep steps. Looking down eastwards from the temple one sees the causeway passing between two large elegantly built stone buildings now roofless, identified as palaces. Then the causeway passes between ornamental pools, dry except in the monsoon season, and still further beyond a much larger baray of some 600 by 200 metres. A second baray of similar dimensions was later built of the south side of the earlier one. These great stretches of water represent the limit of the sacred complex, but the causeway must have extended eastwards to the ancient city presumably near the Mekong River. Around the platform of the temple there are remains of brick structures and stonework which go back to much earlier periods, associated presumably with the Khmer occupation of the site possibly in the late 6th to 7th century onwards. There are also some important rock-carvings, as shown in our illustrations. The region southwards down the Mekong shows traces of earlier Khmer occupation. We visited one site in particular, known as Oup Moens on the eastern side of the river, built above a subsidiary stream. The sanctuary and the south gopura of a temple some sixty metres long can still be distinguished. Several lintels and nâga-heads lie around.

We might note in passing that the reference to human sacrifice by the Khmers has later associations, for it was still being performed in the 19th century on the summit of Ba Phnom (some sixty kilometres south-east of Phnom Penh). The sacrifice was offered to Durgâ (consort of Śiva) in the manifestation of Slayer of the Buffalo-Demon

18. The ruins of Oup Moens, a short distance down the left bank of the Mekong from Wat Phu. These sites are now in southern Laos, but in the earlier known historical period Khmer settlements stretched downstream to Kampong Cham Province (Cambodia). The carved stone, presumably a fallen lintel, with its curling foliage, is quite different from those further south, as will be noted. (See Parmentier, vol. I, nr. p. 296. He refers to this site as Huei Thamo.)

(*Mahîṣâsuramardinî*). David Chandler's informant, an old man who witnessed the last occasion of such a sacrifice, told him that only prisoners already condemned to death for a serious crime were chosen as victims and that their consent to die as a form of sacrifice was seemingly required.[15] Ba Phnom was an important strategic and sacred site for the people of Funan before it was occupied by the Khmer. The possibility suggests itself that this was a very ancient rite, confirming their triumph over Funan, just as the earlier sacrifice on Wat Phu may well have confirmed their victory over the Chams.

Angkor Borei: Chenla replaced Funan

Present archaeological research suggests that Angkor Borei was the chief city of Funan, which was taken over by Khmer rulers during the 6th century. How this actually occurred remains obscure. According to the Chinese source (*Sui Annals*, 589-681) Funan was conquered by the Khmers whose country is named (for the first time) as Chenla:

> *The kingdom of Chenla is south-west of Lin-yi. It was originally a vassal kingdom of Funan.... The family name of the king was Ch'ali (kṣatriya): his personal name was She-to-ssu-na (Çitrasena); his ancestors had gradually increased the power of the country. Çitrasena seized Funan and subdued it.*[16]

In the same context we learn that Çitrasena's son and successor, Îśânavarman sent an embassy to the Chinese court as the recognized ruler of Chenla in 616-617.[17] Several 7th century inscriptions (Vickery, *Society, Economics and Politics*, pp. 74-75) refer to Çitrasena as the brother of a certain Bhavavarman who preceded him on the throne, while his father is named as Vîravarman. Their grandfather is named as Sarvabhauma, which is hardly a proper name. It is best interpreted as a derivative form of Sanskrit *sarvabhûmi,* meaning the 'whole world' and thus suggesting the Indian notion of a 'universal monarch'. It would seem that Bhavavarman, followed by his brother Çitrasena (who ruled as Mahendravarman) may have been Khmer usurpers of the throne of Funan. The name of their father seems to be known, but otherwise all may be make-believe as in the case of other Khmer claimed lineages. Some later royal lists suggest that the succession was more or less regular. Vickery (*Society, Economics and Politics*, p. 41) draws special attention to an inscription dated 667 (K.53), which lists four generations of a family who provided ministers to five kings, Rudravarman, Bhavavarman,

19. A mukhalinga, *square, with four faces (*mukha*) and pointed, surviving at Oep Moens. (Photograph by Suthep Kritsanuvarin.)*

Mahendravarman, Îśânavarman and his successor Jayavarman (see p. 21).

An important early temple at Angkor Borei is the massively brick-built one with a solid laterite base, which stands on the summit of Phnom Da. This is doubtless an early site dating back to the Funan period, but the present brick-built temple has the main features of other (smaller) Khmer brick-built temples. Probably because of the shape of the top of the hill on which it stands, it faces north. There are false doors on the other three sides, modelled in brick and a corbelled brick roof rising to the height of some thirteen metres. It is thus a typical Khmer temple maybe of the 10th century. Near the base of a neighbouring summit, known as Phnom Bakheng there stands a totally different kind of temple known as the Âśram Mahârosei. This is built of stone, namely of basalt, like the small temple of Kuk Preah Thiet referred to below (see Plate 40, p. 36), and of which the nearest source seems to have been north

20. Phnom Da, a hilltop at Angkor Borei, far to the south, where Khmer principalities bordered on the maritime state of Funan. The present temple on the summit, built of laterite and brick, is probably a later Khmer construction of the 10th to the 11th centuries, although the site is an early one.

of the Kampong Cham area. It is rectangular-shaped with a solid tiered stone roof, while the entrance is adorned with a toraṇa also worked in stone. It has three small windows set into the two sides, and a window on either side of the entrance. It resembles no other Khmer temple, early or late, and must probably be understood as a remarkable survival of a type of Indian shrine, as earlier introduced into South-East Asia, possibly adapted by the Chams and thus transmitted to inland Khmer territory. One can point to similarities with certain much larger 8th century Javanese temples, such as Çaṇḍi Sari and Çaṇḍi Plaosan, especially in their use of windows, but the origin of this feature need not be Javanese, but simply Indian, as at Bhuvanesvara (Orissa). Henri Mauger of the archaeological service of the EFEO, who was responsible for its reconstruction in 1935, enunciated the theory that this temple was originally built in the early 6th century further north in the 'homeland' of the Khmers in the Krachau (Kratie) area where the basalt stone was readily available, and that after the presumed capital city of Angkor

21. Âśram Maharosei at the foot of a neighbouring summit. This is one of two rare early temples built of basalt, the other being Kuk Preah Thiet. Its strange significance is explained in the text.

Borei became a Khmer citadel under Bhavavarman and Mahendravarman, it was dismantled and moved to its present position as a symbol of Khmer triumph.[18] Why this unusual shrine should have had such a symbolic importance, it is impossible for us to know, but he adduces interesting technical arguments from the actual stonework, which suggest that the shrine was indeed dismantled and then rebuilt, rather than having been newly built with stone brought from so great a distance. It contained an image of Harihara, which is now in the Musée Guimet in Paris. Henri Mauger also unearthed in the same area the eight-armed Vishnu triad with Balarâma and Râma, both regarded as incarnations (*avatâra*) of Vishnu, among the finest pieces of early Khmer sculpture, which can be seen in the Phnom Penh Museum. It seems likely that the so-called Âśram Mahârosei shrine was deliberately chosen as the sanctuary of the main image of this group, namely the great Harihara image.[19]

South of Angkor Borei there are scanty remains of early Khmer brick shrines in the lower Mekong region. A useful survey is provided by Henri Parmentier in his *L'art Khmer primitif,* pp. 93-113. The most important of these is the impressive brick-built temple-complex probably founded by Îśânavarman on the summit of Phnom Bayang, of which the foundations can still be seen.[20] On the slopes of this hill there are several other small shrines, notably Prâsâd Ta-nâng (east), as illustrated by Parmentier (pls 42-44). The importance of another site some ten kilometres south of Phnom Da, namely Kdei Ang (or Ang Chumnik), of which practically nothing remains, is revealed by several inscriptions. One dated AD 629 (K.54) refers to the foundation of the site by an *âcarya* named Vidyavinaya. A later addition notes gifts given to the shrine by Jayavarman. Another inscription, dated AD 667 (K.53) refers to the setting up of a *Śiva-linga Vijayeśvari* by Simhadatta, governor of nearby Âḍhyapura, listing four generations of the priestly family, to which he belonged. They had served successively the kings Rudravarman, Bhavavarman, Mahendravarman, Îśânavarman and Jayavarman, thus covering the period when 'Funan becomes Chenla'. A later inscription undated (K.56) of the reign of Râjendravarman (944-968) who is duly eulogized, refers to the repair and the founding of many temples in the area, mentioning incidentally pools and rice-fields as well as the usual donations of property and personnel. The text is very corrupt, but it serves to emphasize the importance to the later Angkor kings of this fertile southern region.[21] Further south one might mention another early temple, Prâsâd Prei Çek near the town of Phuoc-hung (Parmentier, *L'art Khmer primitif*, pl. XXXVIII), which has one surviving tower held in place by a tree which has grown over it. All these temples were of brick. At other sites several Buddha—and Bodhisattva—images have been unearthed, mostly to be seen at the Phnom Penh Museum or in the Saigon Museum, as mentioned below. For a survey of the few available inscriptions from this most southern region, most of them

22. Harihara from Angkor Borei,
7th century, limestone, h. 1.78 m.
Musée Guimet MG 14910

referable to the reign of Jayavarman I, one may turn to Vickery, *Society, Economics and Politics*, pp. 111-5. At the same time these inscriptions provide evidence that Khmer influence extended westwards to the Kampot coastal area, where some small cave-temples have been discovered. [22]

As for the relationship between Funan and Chenla, it is likely that Funan maintained a form of suzerainty over the neighbouring Khmer principalities, so long as it was powerful enough to do so. Intermarriage with Khmer aristocratic families was also probable, since racially there was little or no difference. I have already suggested above that the coastal area where trade flourished was probably occupied largely by people of Malay/Indonesian stock, but Mons and Khmers were also well represented, and inland they must have predominated. Thus earlier kings of Funan, even before this Khmer 'conquest', may quite possibly have been of Khmer stock. But however close their earlier relationship, Funan, as it had been, and Cambodia as it now continued to develop, were totally different entities. The one had depended for its authority and wealth on sea power. The other was a land-based power depending for its future on agriculture and warfare. Funan was cosmopolitan in population, favouring a variety of Indian religious traditions, Buddhist as well as Brahmanical. The population of Cambodia until it began to dominate people further afield was Khmer and the official royal cult remained firmly Brahmanical, primarily that of Śiva and his *linga*, but with ready acceptance of Vishnu if so preferred in royal circles. It is difficult to envisage the people of Funan becoming willingly subject to Cambodia, and this probably came about (as cogently argued by Vickery, *Society, Economics and Politics*, pp. 325-6) from their economic and political decline in the 6th to 7th centuries as the result of a major change in shipping and trading routes. At the same time they were now confronted by the growing power of the Khmers who were engaged in forging a new unity amongst themselves.

A note on Śrîvijaya

The reason for Funan's decline is not hard to find. It coincided with the growing strength of a new maritime power, namely Śrîvijaya with its main trading emporiums on the south-east coast of Sumatra. Funan's prosperity had depended upon the shorter sea-route, which made use of the land-route across the Kra Isthmus of the Malay Peninsula. Surprising little is known about the history of Śrîvijaya which developed from the 6th to the 13th century as the major sea-power in South-East Asia, over the same period that Cambodia developed as the major land-power. Based on the south-east coast of Sumatra at present-day Palembang and Muara Jambi with an important trading emporium at Kedah on the west coast of the Malay Peninsula, it dominated all trade passing through the Straits of Malacca. It included western and central Java during the 8th to 9th centuries, establishing there for a short time the line of Buddhist kings, usually known as the Śailendras, who were responsible for the massive creations of Borobudur and Çaṇḍi Sewu and other Buddhist shrines. It gained a form of suzerainty over the petty kingdoms on the coasts of the Malay Peninsula, which had formerly owed some form of allegiance to Funan, and it is interesting to note that here its frontier (never clearly defined) was eventually in contact with the extended Khmer 'empire' which advanced down the peninsula from the area around the Gulf of Siam in the 12th to 13th centuries. However this contact came about when both these 'empires' were beginning to lose their grips on their outlying territories. While Cambodia was gradually losing territory by the advance of the Thais southwards, so Śrîvijaya was weakened by the sea-power of the Çola dynasty in South India as well as by the growing maritime power of the Hindu-Buddhist kingdoms of eastern Java, eventually succumbing to the kingdom of Majapahit in the 13th century.[23]

Îśânavarman and his successors

It seems that Bhavavarman and Mahendravarman were the first declared Khmer rulers of what was once Funan, which by this time had doubtless already lost any hegemony which it exerted over the smaller states along the Malay Peninsula. Next it was Îśânavarman who in the course of the first half of the 7th century established Cambodia as a powerful federation of Khmer chiefdoms, although his control in some areas may have been more nominal than actual. Local *pura* or 'citadels', such as Bhavapura, once his own father's domain, must have continued to exert considerable local authority, and there is mention also in inscriptions of Anindapura, probably to the north of the Great Lake, Indrapura near present-day Kampong Cham, also Vyâdhapura and Âḍhyapura near Ba Phnom, and Çakrânkapura, Amoghapura and Bhîmapura of less certain location. One inscription (see Vickery, *Society, Economics and Politics*, p. 336) appears to list the last three named as subject to the ruler of Tâmrapura, a name which seems to be otherwise unknown.

Such central power as he exercised is represented by his new capital of Îśânapura of which the extensive ruins can still be seen today in the jungle (Sambor Prei Kuk) some thirty kilometres to the north of the present provincial capital of Kampong Thom. During our visits to this site, we were astounded at the ambitious layout of this ancient royal city, which prefigures the later capital on Phnom Kulen and even that of Angkor. There are innumerable brick-built temples, each a square or rectangular brick shrine on a raised platform and surmounted by a tiered brick roof. Thanks to earlier French efforts for the preservation these temples, they retain much of their original decorative brick-work, not only decorative devices, but also plaques illustrating divinities and human figures. Surviving iconography from the site reveals Îśânavarman's religious proclivity as firmly Brahmanical, primarily Śaivite. But as well as the numerous *Śiva-lingas*, there are also images of Vishnu, while Harihara (Vishnu and Śiva combined) was also represented, as well as popular Hindu divinities such as Gaṇeśa and Durgâ as Mahîṣâsuramardinî (Slayer of the Buffalo-Demon).

Although this important site in central Cambodia provides the most impressive examples of early Khmer architecture, other shrines, also dating to the mid-7th century, were already being built in the Angkor area and even close to the Dangrek mountains, which at that time seem to have represented the northern limits of Khmer influence (see below). There need be no doubt that this first Khmer city of Îśânapura of which we have substantial archaeological remains had no lack of building skills, no lack of manpower to carry out such works, and no lack of wealth, which could surely only derive from agriculture and animal husbandry. So far as Indian cultural and religious influences were concerned, Funan had been fully receptive, and such influences as reached the Khmers in their inland strongholds, presumably reached them mainly through their contacts (including inter-marriage) with Funan.[24] Îśânavarman's incursions into the coastal areas which were once part of Funan may have resulted in some temporary persecution of Buddhism, according to the notes of a famous Chinese Buddhist scholar, I-tsing, who sailed from Canton in AD 671 for India. He mentions first Lin-yi (closely associated with Champa in Chinese sources) with seeming approbation, and then mentions Funan:

> *Setting out westwards (from Lin-yi), one reaches (on foot) within a month the country (Kuo) of Poh-nan, formerly called Fu-nan. Of old it was a country, the inhabitants of which lived naked; the people were mostly worshippers of heaven (the gods or devas), but later on Buddhism flourished there, but a wicked king has now expelled and exterminated them all, and there are no members of the Buddhist brotherhood at all, while adherents of other religions (or heretics) live intermingled.*[25]

As hearsay, one need scarcely treat this as a final word on the subject, but one notes that whereas Funan was renowned for its Buddhist interests up to the time of its demise, the Khmer kings whom we now meet are primarily interested in the cult of Śiva, and there may have been some destruction of Buddhist shrines during the course of Îśânavarman's campaigns. However as we shall note, Khmer dominance soon extended northwards from what was once the centre of Funan, and the paucity of later royal foundations and Sanskrit/Khmer inscriptions south of Angkor Borei from the 9th century onwards suggests that these maritime provinces were often left to go their own way.

Îśânavarman died probably soon after 637 (Vickery, *Society, Economics and Politics,* p. 342) and was succeeded by his son Bhavavarman II who is known to have been reigning round about 640 because of an inscription (K.79), which despite an uncertain reading, is taken as 639 or 644. He is also referred to as the Mahârâja Bhavavarman in an interesting inscription (K.1150) from the Chanthaburi area (on the Gulf of Siam not far west of the present Cambodian frontier) which was administered by his elder brother Śivadatta.[26] The use of the explicit Indian title is not at all surprising from this region. He was succeeded by Jayavarman who according to the first two inscriptions which name him, was reigning from about 655 to his presumed death about 680. Despite his relatively long reign and the twenty or so inscriptions that refer to him, his origins have remained uncertain. According to Vickery's careful research, he may have been a grandson of Bhavavarman with a certain Çandravarman (who did not reign) as father. The location of his capital remains uncertain, although a fair claim might be made for the site, later known as Bantây Prei Nokor, in Kampong Cham Province, where the remains of earlier ruins are still to be seen, as described below.[27] Jayavarman's inscriptions cover a very large area from Wat Phu in the north to the area just south of Angkor Borei and coastal area near Kampot. He is praised as a great man of war and he may have been often engaged in small widespread campaigns in an effort to maintain his position of authority. He probably died some time before 680 since an inscription (K.451) of that date refers to a gift of personnel by the local ruler to a shrine of Kedârêśvara (a Śiva-image named after the shrine at Kedâra in India[28]) and seemingly treated as an offering for 'the king who had gone to Śivapura (the abode of Śiva). Despite some rather uncertain contrary evidence which would extend his reign to the early 690's, this would certainly seem to refer to his presumed identification with Śiva after his death (as in the case of so many later Khmer kings) or at least may be understood as a respectful manner of referring to his decease.[29]

He was succeeded by his daughter Queen Jayadevî, who is responsible for an inscription dated 713, already referred to above, which names her Khmer protective divinity. However the main purpose of the inscription concerns gifts by her daughter Śobhâjayâ, married to an Indian Brahman named Śakrasvâmin, to a shrine of Śiva Tripurântaka (Destroyer of the Three [Demon] Citadels) and the gifts which were bestowed by the queen upon the Brahman. It refers to Jayavarman posthumously as Śivapada (= close to Śiva). There is also a reference to difficult times, but this may be conventional.[30]

Long live Śrî Jayadevî who although afflicted with this evil age sustains
the burden of the earth as a fraction of the moon (sustains) the splendour of the night.

It is interesting to note the extent to which the main Indian divinities were already known under very specific Indian titles, which can only be due to the direct influence of Indian Brahmans. Jayadevî is known from another inscription, which confirms that she was daughter to Jayavarman.[31] From the time of Jayadevî, if not earlier, Cambodia, never a firmly centralized entity, seems to disintegrate. Already from the beginning of the 8th century, the Chinese begin to refer to a Lower ('Water') Chenla and an Upper ('Land') Chenla. Upper Chenla, probably comprising what is now northern Cambodia, the lower Mun Valley around present-day Ubon Ratchathani and southern Laos, may have held together at least until the reign of Jayadevî, who probably maintained her court in the Angkor region, since the inscriptions attributed to her are found there. At least the state of Sambor (Śambhupura) in the far north-east seems to have remained independent during the reign of Jayavarman and into the early 9th century. An inscription of 803 refers to a royal succession there, listing a king known by his posthumous title of Indraloka, followed by three queens in succession, the last one being Jyeṣṭhâryâ who was presumably still reigning at the time of the inscription. Vickery argues that this suggests a royal lineage from about 740 onwards or even earlier, thus becoming contemporary with the reign of Jayadevî.[32] Lower Chenla, presumably corresponding more or less to Funan as it once was, namely the lower Mekong valley, might have split up as the result of local dynastic feuds.

Coedès has observed that meanwhile the coastal areas from Tongking southwards, occupied by the Chams, were under assault by the Jâvakas, presumably of Śrîvijaya. Near Tongking a stone inscription of 767 records this attack and the resultant pillage, while two inscriptions in Champa, dated 774 and 787, record similar invasions. There are no such precise records of invasions on the south (Cambodian) coast, but as this was so much nearer home for the attackers, they may also have invaded here, possibly occupying limited areas. Within this context there may be some truth in a strange 'seaman's tale'. A 10th-century Arab writer, Abu Zaid Hassan, retells a story attributed to the merchant Sulaymân about how the Mahârâja of Zâbag (Śrîvijaya) retaliated against the threat of a Khmer king by sending an expedition to cut off this king's head and bring it to him on a dish.

When the news of these events reached the kings of India and China, the Mahârâja became even greater in their eyes. From that moment the Khmer kings, every morning upon rising, turned their faces in the direction of the country of Zâbag, bowed down to the ground and humbled themselves before the Mahârâja to render him homage.[33]

There may be some substance to this story, for Jayavarman II who restored unity to the Khmer kingdom in the early 9th century (see Chapter 3) considered it necessary at his consecration to perform a special Brahmanical ritual to ensure that the Khmers should be no longer be subject to this 'Java'.[34]

The cultural aspects of pre-Angkor society.

Michael Vickery (*Society, Economics and Politics*, p. 33) lists succinctly the main points which make this period of the 6th and 7th centuries distinct from all that followed:

the paucity of contemporary local records during the 8th century and the first three quarters of the ninth, until the reign of Indravarman (877-89), (thus causing a break between the two periods), a shift of political and economic center from southern and central Cambodia to north of the Tonle Sap, and the linguistic differences in pre-

Angkor and Angkor languages. The Angkor inscriptions, moreover show a quite different structure, different titles, different designations for gods, and different economic terminology. In spite of the obvious continuity from pre-Angkor to Angkor Cambodia, the latter society has become distinct from the former.

The linguistic changes are too specialized a matter to be treated here and Vickery in his short survey (pp. 83-99) lists the main features. Of wider interest are some variations in local titles, which reflect the changes taking place in society. Perhaps the most significant of these in the title *poñ* referring to a local chief who may also have had religious functions. Vickery treats it as an earlier Mon-Khmer term, possibly related with the term *fan*, used in Chinese sources as referring to local rulers in Lin-yi and Funan. Of great interest is also the corresponding Khmer term *kpoñ* referring to a local divinity and the fact that both terms no longer appear on inscriptions in the Angkor period. The concept of *poñ* as local community leaders would fit well in an agricultural society existing as extended family units free of all state control. This probably happier state of affairs preceded the time when metallurgy and especially the use of iron tools and weapons resulted not only in an increase of size of such communities, but also the subjection of a group of such communities to the leader or ruler of the one which proves to be most powerful. This resembles the situation reached in early Khmer society where the home of the ruler becomes a 'fort' (*pura*—already a Sanskrit term is thus in general use) and the ruler himself may have been generally referred to as *kurung* or some variant Khmer term. However this term, sometimes translated as 'king', seems to have become debased by the time the first inscriptions were written and Sanskrit titles such as *prabhu* (lord) and *svâmi* (chief) are preferred. The ruler, however named, receives the honorific appellation of *kamratâñ añ*, as also do the gods. This has already been noted above. The polite appellation *mratâñ* (without the prefix k-) has a wider application and Vickery argues convincingly that someone referred to as *mratâñ* usually appears as superior to a *poñ*. Presumably *mratâñ* is a more recent title, maybe used for officials who surrounded the ruler. This survives (with a slightly different spelling) into the Angkor period, while the term *poñ* relates to an earlier form of society that disappeared gradually as the new order of society prevailed. From the time of Jayavarman I onwards the king claims lordship over the whole of Khmer society and this claim was more firmly established by Jayavarman II towards the end of the 8th century.

All such local rulers, whether self-declared kings or those defined as *mratâñ* or *poñ*, represent together with the Brahmans attached to royal courts, a kind of aristocracy who exert considerable control over the 'commoners' (*kñum*) referred to in the inscriptions. This term is often translated as 'slave' and one might add that in the modern language it is a polite first person singular pronoun (namely 'I'). This term 'slave' might seem justified to some extent since such 'commoners' could be given to a temple, usually as a whole group or even one or more whole villages, or they could be sold and bestowed elsewhere as individuals. When a village is given in this way, it presumably makes little difference to the inhabitants. Their taxed produce goes to the temple instead of to the previous owner. When builders and other craftsmen are given to a place, they are presumably given individually in accordance with the required work. There seems to be no overall term to distinguish ordinary villagers (farm-workers) from craftsmen and the more cultured retainers, thus they all come under the category of 'commoners', but there is an order of superior and lower rankings with dancers and musicians coming first. Then there were the temple servants and in the case of a princely temple the maintenance staff, followed by the kitchen staff and manual workers. Surpluses of rice, silver and gold, metalwork, ritual vessels, locally woven cloth and other such items could also be bestowed. Exchanges might also be arranged so that there was also a business aspect of what might otherwise be regarded as meritorious works. Apart from farming villagers, craftsmen and temple-staff who might also form part of such transactions, there doubtless were slaves in the more usual understanding of the term, namely captives from war or from raids into out-lying areas and to them too the term *kñum* applies. The fact that all our information relates to the founding of temples or later donations gives a one-sided view of society. Thus we know nothing of how the commoners were mustered for other domestic purposes or for war, although the ruler's success in war is often a subject treated at length in the inscriptions.

Sambor Prei Kuk

Differences between the earlier period and that of Angkor relate to the temples themselves quite as much as to the actual inscriptions. Although they sometimes rise to an impressive height with their corbelled tiered pyramid-roofs, they usually consist of a single shrine-room. Many temples were built as single entities even when they are found in close proximity to one another. Occasionally they are arranged as a set of three, as in the later period. By far the largest conglomeration of such temples is Îśânavarman's new capital which can still be visited in the jungle (Sambor Prei Kuk) some thirty kilometres north of Kampong Thom, mostly dating to the latter half on the 7th century.[35] Here there are also good examples of temples laid out in a basic set of five, viz. as a form of maṇḍala, and this Indian pattern remains typical of all the great creations of the Angkor period, of which Angkor Vat is doubtless the best known. Overall there are three main groups of temples. A smaller seemingly ill-defined group of shrines lies in a west-central direction, many of which are of a later date. The group to the north, the most extensive, seems now so dispersed in the jungle that its configuration is difficult to make out. The central temple of the centre ground (C1) has been well restored, but the subsidiary shrines are now total ruins (Tranet, *vol.1*, pp. 71-110). That to the south, still standing within its square enclosure, is certainly an impressive site, although the main temple is not so well preserved as C1. One enters the enclosure from the east and immediately ahead is the central temple of Śiva with a remarkably high pinnacled roof, rising in a steep ascent of carefully corbelled brick-work; its structure can be best appreciated by gazing upwards from the empty interior. It is rectangular, approximately fifteen by ten metres, and stands within a square courtyard with ruined entrance-portals to the four directions. There are shrines of octagonal shape, which are located to the four intermediate directions, mostly in a good condition. An extra one, strangely facing west, while all the others face east, was added on the north side of the main temple. Also facing west, and logically so because it faces the main temple, is an important shrine on the east side. This contains an unusually elaborate pedestal with a stone canopy which presumably contained an image of Śiva's mount, the bull Nandin, looking in the direction of Śiva's *linga* which certainly occupied the central temple (Tranet, *vol. 2*, pp. 13-183). Several inscriptions have been found on this particular site, at least three referring specifically to Îśânavarman. One of them (K.440) which is especially fulsome in his praise, honours Śiva in the opening verses as Prahasiteśvara, the 'Laughing Lord' and mentions at the end the silver image the sacred bull (*Vṛṣabha*) which presumably was set up in the special eastern shrine facing the central one. Another inscription refers to the setting up of a *Śiva-linga* in the Śaka year 549 (AD 627) by one who served the king, a certain Pâsupâta Brahman, who was versed in grammar, the Brahmanical systems of Vaiśeṣika, Nyâya and Sâmkhya, and the doctrine of the Sugata (the Buddha, being the only known reference to Buddhism on this site). The opening verses are in praise of Śiva, referred to as Kadambeśvara (Lord of Plenty). In the northern group we note a later inscription, opening with salutations to Śiva, Vishnu and Brahmâ (K.436), which is in praise of the prowess of Râjendravarman (reigned 944-960), listing his many religious foundations, including the restoration of the cult of Gambhîresvara, which seems to have been neglected.[36]

In this early period temples are built of brick with blocks of sandstone used for the door-posts, the step and the lintel, the most decorative part of the whole building. There are normally false doors built of brickwork on the other three sides. The real door on the main side was of wood. The whole structure usually stands upon a platform of laterite and any surrounding wall is constructed of the same material. (Such brick-built temples continue into the early Angkor period, often in sets of three. In the later Angkor period the whole temple is usually built of sandstone.) The earliest temples usually consist of one cell although they may have a small antechamber consisting of little more than an enlarged doorway. The roof consists of a continuation of the walls upwards of ever decreasing dimensions in four stages, seemingly topped by a rounded disk. Unfortunately these tapering roofs have long since collapsed, but good reconstructions can be found in the Tranet volumes, e.g. *vol.1*, p. 165 for the basic design, and pp. 78-79 which illustrate the elaborations. These are usually repetitions of designs that already appear on the lower walls. The square (or rectangular) temples just mentioned above have all these features and the main central one some extra refinements. Not only does the main eastern entrance have a decorated lintel, but also do the false doors on the other three sides. In the case of C1 the platform is reached by a flight of steps guarded by seated lions, surprisingly well preserved. All these temples are decorated with plaques made of brickwork and originally covered with stucco. These plaques all represent a highly decorative pillared building with a rounded dome roof. Between the pillars there stand royal figures and in the upper section, divinities. They are nowadays often referred to as 'flying palaces' simply because usually no obvious ground-support is shown, but it is doubtful if they were thus conceived. Some of them in fact rest on decorative bands of brickwork which go

23. (above) Sambor Prei Kuk. Here one finds in the jungle some 32 km north of Kampong Thom, groups of brick-built temples, among the earliest known in Cambodia, which constituted the 7th century city of Îśânapura. Temple S1 on the right and S2 on its eastern side to the left

right about the base of the temple. These decorative devices are typical of Sambor Prei Kuk and are found on almost all the temples. A row of small effigies of *garuḍas* and winged horses may also go around the base of the building as though the *garuḍas* might be supporting it with their raised arms; see shrine N7 (Tranet, *vol. 1*, p. 171). Also small medallions, containing human-like figures, male and female, possibly minor divinities, decorate the lower walls of some temples (Tranet, *vol. 2*, pp. 175-83). A related decorative feature consists of small arched circles containing human figures, head and shoulders only, know as *kuḍu*. Good examples can be seen on shrine N 17 (Tranet, *vol. 1*, pp. 318-9). These decorative features typical of the early temples seem to disappear altogether in the later period.

In the northern group (Tranet, *vol. 1*, p. 112 ff.) there are numerous smaller temples, usually square and up to ten metres along each side. A few

24. (right) Sambor Prei Kuk. An ornamental plaque constructed in brickwork which decorates many of the outer walls of these temples. It has the form of an ornate palace with sometimes gods in the upper part and royal figures below.

hexagonal temples are also present. But such is their state of ruin that it is difficult to envisage a maṇḍala pattern amongst them. In the outlying group of Robang Romeas there are a few temples with two chambers, an anteroom leading directly to the shrine-room, but these are probably of the 10th and 11th centuries or even later (Tranet, *vol. 2*, pp. 271-377).

Apart from the decorative brickwork typical of most of these temples at Sambor Prei Kuk, special mention must be made of the decoration around and over the main east entrance to the shrine (and sometimes also over the false doors on the other sides). This is typical of all Khmer temples right through the Angkor period. We have noted that in the early period the temples were regularly built of brick throughout to the 10th century, but the step, the lintel and the door-frame and the flanking colonettes were always made of sandstone. The colonettes are decorated with floral patterns, garlands and bell-shaped designs, all suggesting Indian influence. On the top of the colonettes there is usually a small *makara* (mythological Indian creature resembling a crocodile) with small quasi-human figures (probably identifiable as the *kinnaras* of Indian tradition, impish attendants on the gods) as their riders. From the mouths of the two monsters there emerges an arched canopy stretched across the whole lintel, from which hang rows of decorative garlands. Attached to the canopy may be one, three or occasionally five small medallions. The central

25. Sambor Prei Kuk. The main temple of the central group (C1), remarkable for its well preserved lintels. (Photograph by Martin Polkinghorne.)

26. Sambor Prei Kuk. An octagonal shrine, especially typical of the south group, although also found elsewhere on this site.

27. (above) Sambor Prei Kuk. A lion-headed water spout of the somasûtra *or channel which carries the liquid of the oblations which have been poured over the linga inside the shrine, emerging from temple No. N.10. One may note also the usual stone plaque of a royal figure with attendants. (Seated around the spout are Vutthy central with our two motor-cycle companions, Heng on the right and Chok on his left. Sadly both have since died.)*

28. (below) Sambor Prei Kuk. A row of decorative medalions, showing a human figure struggling with a lion. (See Tranet, 2, p. 175 and 180 ff.) (Photograph by Suthep Kritsanuvarin.)

29. (above) Sambor Prei Kuk. A frieze of garuḍas and winged horses. (See Tranet, 1, p. 171.) (Photograph by Suthep Kritsanuvarin.)

30. (left) Sambor Prei Kuk. A decorative device known technically as a kuḍu, usually an encircled human head. (See Tranet, 2, pp. 73-76.) (Photograph by Suthep Kritsanuvarin.)

one often contains a small image of Indra, the god of the east, in that most temples face east. If there are three, the other two may contain small horse-riding figures, identifiable as the Aśvins of Indian tradition. Where there are five medallions, they may all contain images of the sacred geese of Brahmâ or other symbolic features. There are a few surviving examples of a *kâla*-mask in miniature form, for example on the lintels of temple S1. (See Tranet, *vol. 2*, pp. 35-36) This becomes quite a general feature from the ninth century onwards, beginning with the temples on Mount Kulen.[37] In many cases, for example on the main temple of the northern group (Tranet, *vol. 1*, pp. 120-126), an ornamental arched frontal piece (skr. *toraṇa*) surmounts the lintel. This is a well-known Indian device, which survives profusely in the Nepal Valley, where these toraṇas are usually made of carved and painted wood. In Cambodia the earliest ones, as at Sambor Prei Kuk, are made of brickwork, but later in the Angkor period where they become quite general, they are carved in stone.

31. (above) Sambor Prei Kuk. Although resembling a cabin, this unusual building in the northern group (N17) is built entirely of sandstone, not only the foundations and door-posts, but also the monolithic slabs of the walls and the flat stone roof. (See Tranet, 1, pp. 295-321.) (Photograph by Martin Polkinghorne.)

Figure 1. (below) Sambor Prei Kuk. Building No. C1 (from Tranet, vol. 1, p. 74).

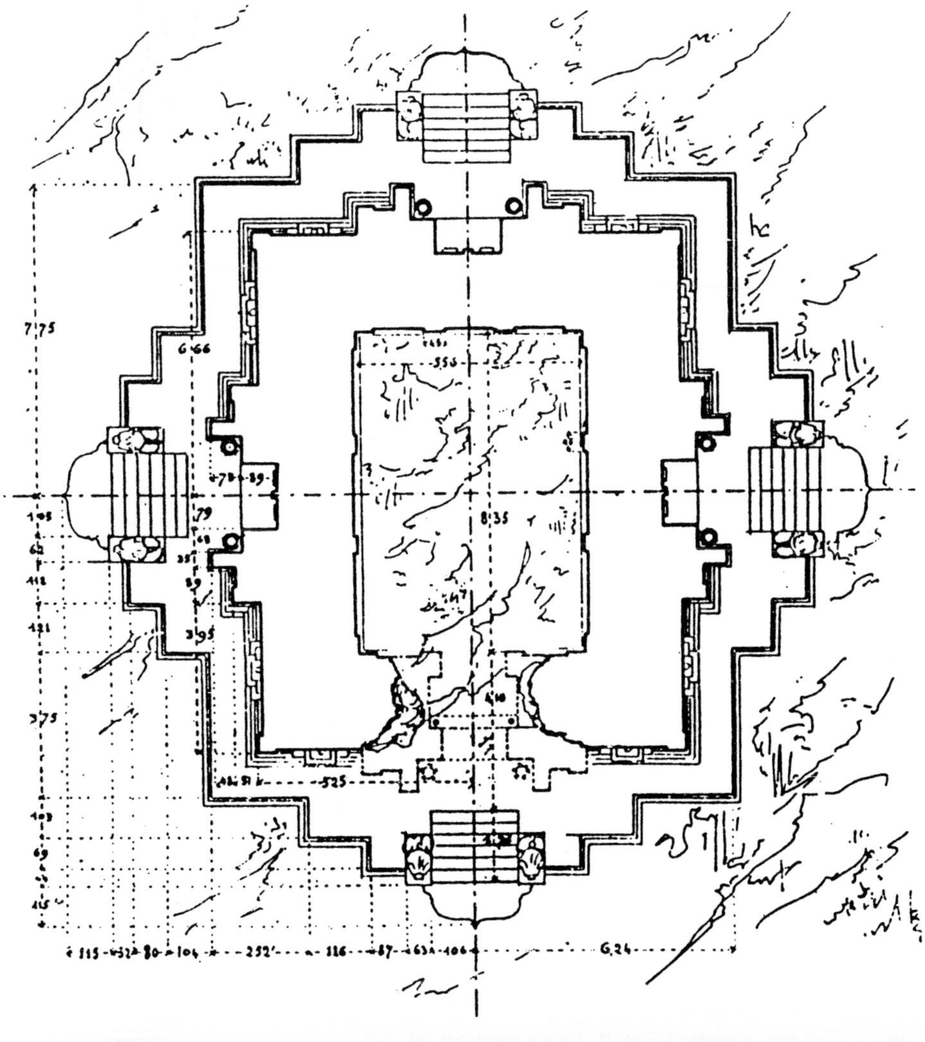

Figure 2. Sambor Prei Kuk. Façade of Building No. C1 (from Tranet,vol. 1, p. 78).

The surviving temples at Sambor Prei Kuk may number a hundred or more: 26 being accounted for in the southern group, 38 in the northern group, although those numbered 33 onwards are total ruins, and up to 12 in the central group, although the only one still standing is C1. Towards the north-west of the site there is a significant group of temples, numbered K1-17, known locally as Robang Romeas (Rinocerous Enclosure). It is reached by two kilometres of sandy cart-track, turning off from the main route leading to groups C, N and S which form the heart of the whole area. These later temples, a few of which are still standing (notably K2 ,3, 10) are all of brick, except for an unusual one which survives as a row of laterite pillars (K8). This is known specifically as the Krol Romeas (the Rhinorerous Pen), thus assumed to be a pen for animals. Tranet regards it as all that remains on a pillared hall (Vol.2, p.321-5) which seems more likely. Apart from these four major groups, one might mention some especially important temples which stand alone, all retaining local names: Prâsâd Sandân, east of the N group (also identified as N24), Prâsâd Traphieng Rophiet (Rattan Pond) along a track leading south from the C group; continuing still further one comes to Prâsâd Kuet Drung (Thumping the Chest). These three temples remain in a relatively good condition. In the far NW of the area, to the west of the K group, but quite totally separate from them, is Prâsâd Tâmum (? Grandpa Mum), once massively built, rectangular in shape but now split across its whole length, so that it will not stand for much longer. It has at least one good lintel and is decorated with the so-called 'flying palace' typical of the earlier temples. The whole area covered by these temples extends about five kilometres west to east and four north to south. On this our third visit (January 2004) we were assisted by a young man named Sunli, who had worked under Tranet and thus proved a very helpful guide. In the far SW side well beyond Prâsâd Kuet Drung, where one leaves the jungle and comes to open fields he drew our attention to a large, shaped stone which suggests the earlier existence of a landing stage. Land depression also suggests the existence of a wide water-course, once linked to the Sen River which passes by Sambor Prei Kuk and flows down to Kampong Thom.

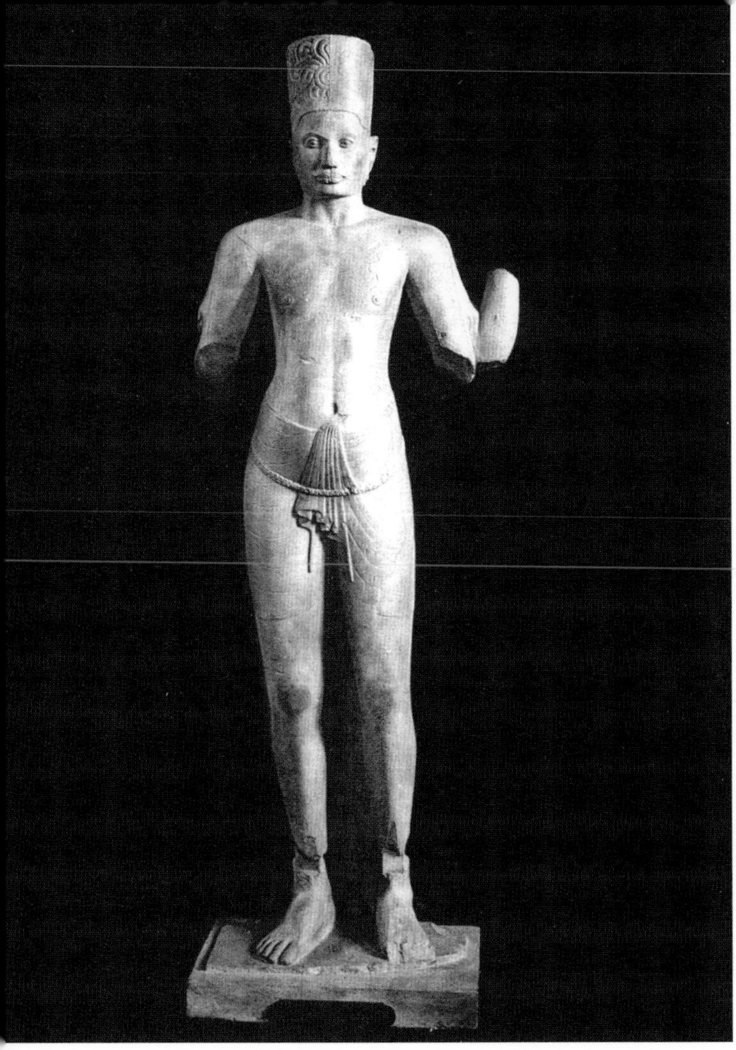

32. *(above left) The Harihara image from Prâsâd Andet (from Parmentier, vol. I, after p. 265).*

33. *(above right) Prâsâd Andet, south face. Situated some 12 kilometres west of Kampong Thom along the route from Stoung, this must have been a very important local temple, as its main image was a Harihara, 7th century, now in the Phnom Penh Museum. It was built in a similar style to the square brick-built temples of Sambor Prei Kuk. (See Tranet, 3, pp. 44-61.) (Photograph by Martin Polkinghorne.)*

34. *(right) Phum Prâsâd, a 7th century shrine surviving in the grounds of the later Theravâda monastery of the same name, in Cham province. There are many such others preserved in the same way, as will be noted below. Although the style of building resembles the temples of Sambor Prei Kuk, the decorative devices typical of there are lacking.*

Other Early Sites

Some fifteen kilometres to the west of Kampong Thom the important 7th century temple of Prâsâd Andet, once containing an image of Harihara (now in the National Museum, Phnom Penh), merits a visit although it has suffered much from neglect since its description by Henri Parmentier (*L'art Khmer primitif*, pp. 156-8). There are several other early sites in the grounds of the much later Theravâda

35. A lintel from Phum Prâsâd, typical of this early period.

36. Bantây Prei Nokor. The remains on this ancient site, some 2½ kilometres square, protected by earthen ramparts and probably formerly a palisade, can give little idea of its earlier importance as a major Khmer stronghold, dating back at least to the 6th century. All that survives now is a group of of three brick-built temples, of which the south one is a heap of rubble, and a second group, some hundred metres distant, of which now only one remains in a totally forlorn state. Nevertheless it probably represented the major centre of Khmer power in the south before the founding of Îśânapura.in the early 7th century. The best preserved temple is the central one of the major group, known as Preah Thiet Thom. With its three false doors to the three other sides and the lintel which once adorned the east side, it resembles the other early brick temples already described above.

37. (above) A lintel from Preah Thiet Thom (Parmentier, vol. I, p. 36).

monasteries southwards from here to Kampong Cham, such as Prâsâd Khna, Phnom Santuk, Phum Prâsâd and Prâsâd Thnot Chum.[38] Some fifty kilometres to the south-east of the present town of Kampong Cham there is the early and important site of Bantây Prei Nokor.[39] It is enclosed by a rampart about 2.5 kilometres each side, and originally surrounded by a wide moat. It was probably planned as a royal city, possibly by Bhavavarman I and there must have been many more buildings built of lighter materials of which no trace remains.[40] The early French sources quoted below refer to two groups of shrines, only partly standing, known respectively as Preah Thiet Thom (big) and Preah Thiet Toc (small). 'Preah Thiet' occurring in the local names of several ancient shrines, means simply 'Sacred Relics'. The major group remains much as it appears to have been the case 200 years ago, namely as just two brick-built shrines, on a platform facing east, representing the southern and the central ones, the northern one having already disappeared. Of the other group, some 200 metres distant, only one shrine now remains standing in a dilapidated state. The nearby Theravâda monastery has probably made good use of the fallen bricks for their own building purposes.

Mention must be made here of Vat Nokor, easily confused with Bantây Prei Nokor. This is a regular Khmer stone-built temple, seemingly of uncertain date, which was modified to Buddhist usage during the reign of Jayavarman VII. However this temple stands on an ancient site a few kilometres north of the town of Kampong Cham, and only excavations might reveal its significance for events in the eighth to ninth centuries. Its name Vat Nokor (the same as

38. (below) The only other forlorn temple of Bantây Preah Nokor.

Angkor Vat in reverse) suggests that it was an important citadel (Nokor) before it became a Vat (like Angkor Vat) in the 16th century by adaptation to Theravâda usage. For its later history see Chapter 5, 'Sites in the Provinces'.

Some forty kilometres directly south of Kampong Cham town where the Mekong spreads out to form subsidiary streams and islands, one particular stream of unusual length, known as the Tonle Toch, waters a fertile area centred on the small town of Tuol Svay Chrum. On this flat alluvial land stands the monastery of Preah Thiet Preah Srei, which can be reached on a motor-cycle in about an hour and a half, preferably following narrow paths which skirt the river. Far more seems to have survived of the foundations of the original Khmer temple, when Lunet de Lajonquière visited the site, but now the modern *vihara* occupies precisely the place of the central Khmer shrine. The foundations of the inner enclosure remain as well as that of the second, although much broken down, while the third and outer laterite wall encloses the whole complex just as in earlier times. There were two subsidiary shrines

39. Hanchei. This early shrine, attributable to Bhavavarman I thanks to a local inscription, formed part of a stronghold built on this imposing hill-top which overlooks the broad expanse of the Mekong River. The lintel of this temple. no longer available on the site, resembles the type of lintel already illustrated above, Plate 18, p. 18. (See Parmentier. L'art Khmer primitif, *I, p. 296). All that remains is this one temple with the foundations of a second one, enclosed within the later Theravâda monastery which now occupies the site. I note that the name Hanche, commonly used in archaeological publications, refers properly to the settlement at the foot of the hill.*

40. Kuk Preah Thiet. This remarkable little shrine, built of basalt like the Âśram Mahârosei (described above) although of a very different style, in fact a kind of windowless cell, might have served as a meditation cell or as the mausoleum of some important person. It was built close to the river near the bottom of a long flight of steps descending from the fortress above. The two following illustrations give a better idea of its strangeness. Note a basic resemblance to building N17 at Sambor Prei Kuk (Plate 31, p. 31).

on the eastern approach, represented by hillocks of earth supported by stone and brickwork. On the northern hillock a small shrine has been built of laterite blocks. Despite its present destitute condition, this was once an important site, where Jayavarman II may once have held court in the year AD 770.[41] (see below).

Also twenty kilometres north of Kampong Cham town there is another early brick-built shrine on a hilltop rising above the little town of Hanchei. An inscription clearly links this site with Bhavavarman I. It consists of long praises of Bhavavarman who has already died (gone to the abode of Śiva) and then of his son (unnamed). The author, also unnamed, announces that as supreme chief of Ugrapura he has set up a *linga* named Bhadreśvara as well as giving personnel, animals, lands etc. for its maintenance.[42] As usual, the brick-built remains are set within the grounds of the later Theravâda monastery, which occupies this magnificent site with fine views of the great Mekong River below. The name of this monastery is Jayagiri (Mountain of Victory), which probably records the earlier Khmer name for this hill, while Ugrapura may well have been the name of the Khmer citadel (*ugra* meaning 'terrible'). The foundations of a second brick-built shrine may be noted within the monastic compound, but much

41. (right) Kuk Preah Thiet. The doorway.

42. (below) Kuk Preah Thiet. One of the kuḍus which decorate the corners of the tiered roof.

more interesting is an unusual stone-built shrine near the bottom of a long flight of steps, which lead down towards the river. Its name Kuk Preah Thiet (shrine of holy relics) suggests at once that it was built as a form of mausoleum. It is constructed of blocks of basalt, a stone that is locally available, as a small shrine of simple design with no ornamentation except for the lintel and the colonettes and small kuḍus containing human faces which decorate the lower rim of the three-tiered roof.[43] It can be seen as related to the some of the simplest temples at Sambor Prei Kuk, such as N17, and its prototype is clearly Indian with possibly Cham influence.

To complete this survey of early sites in the north-east, something needs to be said of the early Khmer state of Sambor, known from scanty inscriptions to have been flourishing in the 8th and 9th centuries. We visited this small town on the banks of the Mekong, some forty kilometres north of Kratie, which is three hours by motor-launch north of Kampong Cham. Following Lunet de Lajonquière's report written now 100 years ago (*Inventaire* I, p. 186 ff.) we visited the 'Vat Tasar mo roi' (probably in more regular Khmer, *Sasar muey roi* = 'one hundred pillars') where he found ruins of a brick-sanctuary, but all traces of this seem to have now disappeared, and all local knowledge of an ancient Khmer site is absent. Ancient Sambor seemingly spread across to the nearby island of Lomieu, where there are also said to be brick remains, but none of the older inhabitants were aware of them, although they probably still exist in the jungle towards the eastern end of the island. Returning from Sambor there is a hilltop overlooking the river eleven kilometres before reaching Kratie, known as Phnom Sambok. There is a Theravâda monastery, a small religious home for old folks half way up, and a small shrine on the summit. Here there are manifest signs of old Khmer stonework and brickwork, pushed aside as mere rubbish, but nothing of special note. Twenty-five kilometres east of Kratie there are the remains of a small sanctuary, known as Preah Thiet Kvan Pi, also noted by Lunet de Lajonquière, and still existing in an ever more ruined condition according to some photographs kindly shown me by another intrepid traveller.

As noted above when writing of Wat Phu, scattered Khmer sites spread down the Mekong from what is now southern Laos to the Stung Treng district in north-east Cambodia and so link up with Sambor and the sites already described further south. Near Stung Treng there are ruins of brick temples on a Buddhist monastic site known as Vat Sophâs (Prâsâd Spheas). An inscription found on the site, dated Śaka 587 (=AD 665) refers to a shrine in which two *poñ* named Nirjitasimha and Çandrabindhu were interested as well as a high official named Śrîmad Amrîmad Amrâta.[44] The purpose of the stele was to record the donations of the mother of Nirjitasimha. At Thala Borivat just north of Stung Treng there are some other ruins mentioned by Parmentier (*L'art Khmer primitif*, p. 214). Two 7th century lintels (nos. K.1743 and 1752) from this site can be seen in the Phnom Penh Museum.

Thus the Mekong Valley represents generally the eastern limits of the Khmer 'homeland' which extended southwards and westwards to embrace the whole area around the Great Lake and the Tonle Sap.

In the Angkor region there is a group of temples built where the Western Baray was later constructed in the 11th century. Some may lie in total ruin under the bed of the eastern end of this vast artificial lake. The one important one that has survived close to the embankment of the lake is that known as Ak Yom. It consists of a solid three-tier brickwork structure, thus a form of rather flat pyramid, and thus may be the first known example of this type in Cambodia. In its present ruined condition it can give

43. A lintel from Parmentier, L'art Khmer primitif, *I, p. 278 which is so similar to the two noted from the Phnom Penh Museum that it may serve to represent them. The distinctive features are the large* makhara *heads from whole mouths of which there issues a decorated canopy. In the centre of this there is a medallion with a small image of Garuḍa holding two nâgas.*

little idea of how in looked at the time of its excavation in 1933, let alone in its original state. It has clearly been ransacked by local people in the hope of finding yet more treasures. The excavation revealed not only three inscriptions, dated 609, 704 and 1001 indicating that this shrine was dedicated to Śiva under the name of Gambhîreśvara (= the Profound Lord), but also part of the large stone *linga* which presumably once stood on the summit, also some small images, and an inner brick shrine, containing a male statue over a metre high and two elephants in gold leaf.[45] Its form anticipates the first tiered Devarâja shrine erected by Jayavarman II on the Kulen Mountain about 800. A short distance from the western end of the lake is Prâsâd Prei Kmeng, of which only a few foundation stones remain with two *yoni* (the circular stone with a lip for libations on which the *linga* stands) and the broken end of a *somasûtra*, the stone channel on which the libation flows out from the temple.[46] Other temples of this group are Phnom Run, on a small wooded hillock barely one kilometre from the northern side of the lake, of which now only a *linga* and a few stones remain, and Kok Po, of which some brick walls are still standing in a copse two kilometres further to the north.[47] Unfortunately we have no name for this very important group of early temples. Following Philippe Stern (in his article 'Hariharâlaya et Indrapuri' quoted below), I refer to it as the 'Baray Group', noting that it was the construction of the West Baray which led to their obsolescence. The early temples of the 'Ruluos group', also in the Angkor region, are discussed in the next chapter.

In the far north two of the best surviving examples

44. (left) A Śaivite ascetic (possibly Śiva as a ascetic) from the Thala Borivat area. (From Parmentier, vol. I, p. 308)

45. (below) A lintel from Sambor (from Parmentier, L'art Khmer primitif*, I, p. 212), which resembles those of Thala Borivat. The central figure in the medallion must be once again a human form of Garuḍa holding two nâgas.*

46. (above) Ak Yum. All that remains of the earliest known pyramid-temple in the Angkor area.

47. (left) Khao Noi. The central temple of a set of three built on a hill-top near Aranyaprathet (Thailand), which is just beyond the present Cambodian frontier. This temple has been recently restored by the Fine Arts Department of the Thai Government, the other two being left in their ruined state. According to the style of the early lintels, it has been dated to the 7th century and may be the earliest Khmer temple in present-day Thailand.

of early temples are just beyond the present Cambodia-Thai border where they have been the responsibility of the Fine Arts Department of the Government of Thailand. One at Khao Noi, a few miles from Aranyaprathet on the top of a steep hill, is an early example of a set of three shrines of which only the central one survives intact. It has been recently reconstructed by the Thai authorities. This site provided several examples of the earliest known style of Khmer lintel, which as mentioned above is the most decorative part of the whole building. For safety such lintels are removed and kept in a local museum, a practice that has been followed in Cambodia, where similar early lintels can be seen in the Phnom Penh Museum. It thus becomes impossible to photograph them *in situ*, although in Thailand a replica sometimes replaces the original. The second early temple of note is that of Phum Pon, a few kilometres north of a place named Kap Choeng which lies just beyond the present Thai-

Cambodia frontier along a route which crossed the frontier from Samraong on the Cambodian side. It comprises the usual brick-shrine with tapering roof. Although the whole structure remains intact, it is in a rather sorry state, especially the carved lintel over the eastern doorway. Nearby on the northern side are the bases of two other shrines, which may never have been completed or else are totally ruined. However they are too far apart to have been arranged so as to become a set of three shrines, as at Khao Noi.[48] Like so many temples that were built later to the north of the Dangrek Range, it can be approached nowadays only from the Thai side. It is interesting to reflect that such routes were used by the Khmers at least from the 7th century onwards and thus this mountain range was no obstacle to their steady advance.

Scarcity of Buddhist remains

There seem to be no known Buddhist shrines surviving from the pre-Angkor period. An inscription dated 664 from Prei Veng refers to an order by King Jayavarman that a *poñ* named Śubhakîrti should receive everything, people, farm-animals, fields and gardens of a foundation established by two Buddhist monks, who were his great-uncles. This seems to suggest the 'laicization' of a Buddhist temple or at least the estrangement of all its property to another foundation, named as Śreṣṭâśrama, which might well be Brahmanical.

Another inscription (undated) and located some fourteen kilometres along the ancient road south-eastwards from Stoung (and thus about half way from there to present-day Kampong Thom) lists donations to a shrine containing images of the Buddha, Avalokiteśvara and Maitreya.[49] Also an inscription dated 791 in the Siem Reap area refers to the erection of an image of the Bodhisattva Lokeśvara (=Avalokiteśvara).[50]

As for the surviving statues of divinities, the earliest ones come from the Angkor Borei area, as already noted. Vishnu, Śiva and Harihara (Vishnu and Śiva combined in a single figure) seem to be the most favoured in the earliest period, as are also the well-known avatars (hero-gods regarded as his manifestations in the world of men), namely Krishna, Râma and the lesser known Parasurâma and Balarâma. These latter ones were not very popular amongst the Khmers, but Krishna was well known and certainly Râma, later popularized by the introduction of the great Indian epic, the Ramâyâna. As for the earliest Buddha-images, several dating to the 6th to 7th centuries may be seen in the Phnom Penh Museum, not only from Angkor Borei, but from other scattered sites in the southern Khmer provinces of Kampong Speu and Takeo. There is one in the Musée Guimet (no.18891), also from Takeo, and this has a short inscription on the back in hybrid Sanskrit. These may reasonably be related to the Funan period, but here I must surely mention the magnificent 6th century statue of the Bodhisattva Avalokiteśvara from Funan, now in the Musée Guimet (no. MG 5063, see Plate 14, p.14). This is of a totally different style from anything later seen in Cambodia.

As already noted, the Khmers were primarily interested in the cult of Śiva. Apart from Śiva, Vishnu, Harihara (their combined form) and Brahmâ, Durgâ, the fierce manifestation of Śiva's spouse, and Gaṇeśa, the elephant-headed god, are also known to have been represented at Sambor Prei Kuk. Also found there is a set of nine gods, usually shown as a row of miniature divinities: Sûrya,

48. Buddha from Tuol Preah Theat (Kampong Speu) 7th century, limestone, h. 1 m. Musée Guimet MG 18891

49. The 7th century inscription carved on the back of this Buddha-image: 'Of those causal elemental particles of which the Buddha has spoken, he has spoken likewise of their annulment.' See also Peter Skilling, 'A Buddhist inscription'.

Çandra (the Moon), Yama (god of death), Varuṇa, (god of the water) Indra (god of war), Kuvera (god of wealth), Agni (god of fire). Rahu (god of the eclipse) and Ketu (god of brilliance). They represent the gods of the four directions, four intermediate directions and the centre. A large number of animals, real or mythological, are also represented, according to the Indian model, namely the *makara* (a kind of mythological crocodile), already mentioned above, the lion, the elephant, especially the one who served as Indra's mount, the *hamsa,* a form of mythological goose, specifically serving as Brahmâ's mount, the nâga, a form of serpent divinity, the horse, the mount of Sûrya, the Sun-God, and Garuḍa, a form of mythological eagle, and Kâla, the threatening god of time, who serves as a protective effigy, especially on many later lintels and toraṇa. All in all, the Indian contribution to the architecture, art and literature in pre-Angkor civilization is clearly considerable. However it must be emphasized that this higher culture remains the special reserve of the ruling class and their Brahman priests and mentors. The rest of the population merely subscribed to it, often enough with their enforced labour.

Chapter 3

Jayavarman II and his immediate Successors

Summary

In writing a cultural history of Cambodia one is bound by the very nature of the stone inscriptions, the sole source of our information, to arrange the text in accordance with royal reigns and the names of the leading Brahmans (no longer to be thought of as necessarily Indian) who served them. At the same time these series of reigns can also be taken as representing certain changes in architectural and artistic styles. In this chapter we are concerned with Jayavarman II who established the centre of power in the Angkor region, at Hariharâlaya (modern Ruluos) and at Mahendrapura on Mount Kulen, and a succession of five kings: his son Jayavarman III, and then the latter's cousin Indravarman, next Indravarman's son Yaśovarman, the founder of Angkor, and finally his sons, Harṣavarman and Îśânavarman II. All these reigns cover the period of 120 years between Jayavarman II's consecration on Mount Kulen in 802 and the death of Îśânavarman II in 928. It seems that even before the death of Harṣavarman in 922/3 a maternal uncle whose domain was centred at Chok Gyargar (the site now known as Koh Ker) claimed the throne as rightly his, becoming formally recognized as king in 928. His reign causes a break in the succession, mainly because he established Chok Gyargar as his capital, resulting in a significant change in architectural styles. We may note that up to the reign of this usurper, the royal succession appears as mainly patrilineal. The one exception so far is Indravarman, whose claim to the throne might have been at least partly matrilineal, in that he was the nephew of the wife of Jayavarman II, known as Dharaṇîndradevî on the Preah Ko inscription (see below).

At the same time the succession of the *purohitas* (chief Brahmanical priests) who served this succession of monarchs was strictly matrilineal, passing from uncle to nephew (sister's son). Just four chief priests served the royal succession so far, namely Śivakaivalya, followed by his nephew Sûkṣmavindu, who was succeeded by his nephew Vâmaśiva, but seemingly not with the title of *purohita*, and so followed by his son Kumârasvâmin. As will be noted below, Indravarman took a great interest in religious foundations and was surrounded by several prominent Brahmans, of whom Vâmaśiva was certainly one, having the title of 'preceptor' (*upâdhâya*). Under Yaśovarman he was known as the *Brah Guru* (Sacred Teacher), a title possibly relating to his position as *guru* to the king from his youth onwards. While it was the intention of Jayavarman II that the important position of *purohita* should remain in succession to Śivakaivalya, this becomes questionable because of the continual increase in the numbers available as one generation followed another and aristocratic families continued to proliferate. It must be noted too that there was frequent intermarriage between the royal and the priestly families, so that any distinction between *Brahman* and *Kṣatriya* in the Indian sense becomes meaningless. Members of these mixed aristocratic families might serve as officers of state or as Brahmanical priests with various titles. Thus many more priests are named in the inscriptions than it is necessary to try and work into the present text. However I mention a certain Nivâsakavi, son of the ruler (*svâmin*) of Śresṭhapura who was the guru of Jayavarman III and who erected about 857 an image of Vishnu and possibly the temple as such, namely Prâsâd Kok Po, now a total ruin just north of the Western Baray. Among these many priests only the *purohita* remained necessarily celibate, although there were certainly many celibate religious in the many ashrams which Yaśovarman founded. However it was possible, as seemingly under Yaśovarman, for a high priestly dignitary to serve effectively as *purohita* without the title. Thus the nephew of Vâmaśiva, Kumârasvâmin, continued in office during the reigns of Yaśovarman's two sons but with the title of *Hotar* ('sacrificial priest'). However while Kumârasvâmin was still in office in Angkor (Yaśodharapura), another *Hotar* named Îśânamûrti consecrated in 921 a rival Devarâja at Chok Gyargar for the benefit of the usurper Jayavarman IV.

Before proceeding further it might be helpful to explain these Sanskrit names as now universally used by the aristocracy, whether lay or religious, especially as more such names will occur from now on. Many of the royal names had already been used by Indian kings and were in no way original. The term *-varman*, which forms part of so many such names, means basically 'armour' and in compound names can be translated as 'protector'. Thus referring back to the last chapter we note that Çitrasena on becoming king took the names of Mahendravarman, which means 'Protector (such as) Great Indra'. Mahâ + Indra coalesce to form Mahendra, also one of the titles of the last king of Nepal. I note in passing that Çitrasena, meaning 'Glorious Army' is probably a sanskritized form of a Khmer name, as in the case of Queen Jayadevî's protective divinity, Senamukhavijayâ (see Chapter 2, 'Influences from India'), and that it is not a deliberately given Sanskrit title. Continuing with the title *–varman,* we may list Rudravarman, Rudra, being the name of Śiva in his fierce aspect, Jayavarman = 'Victorious Conqueror', Harṣavarman 'Exalted Protector', as of a famous Indian king of the Gupta dynasty; Îśânavarman = 'Lord Protector, Prithvîndravarman = Indra Protector of the Earth, a powerful name for a local ruler who was never king. Indra it will be recalled is the God of War. Yaśovarman = 'Famous Protector'. The name of Dharaṇîndradevî, the wife of Jayavarman II, means 'Indra Goddess of the Earth'. It is unlikely that in choosing these names any attention was given to the literal meaning. They are doubtless combinations of high-sounding terms and divine names, as bestowed upon the recipient according to the auspices performed by a priest. Turning to priestly names we note Vâmaśiva = 'Intent on Śiva', Sûkṣmavindu = 'Knowing the smallest details', Śivakaivalya = 'Unity in Śiva' and Îśânamûrti = 'Image of the Lord', Śivasoma = 'Elixir of Śiva'. Nivâsakavi means 'Court Poet', perhaps a nickname relating to this activity, and Kumârasvâmin means simply the 'young master', a title he presumably retained as son of some local ruler.

Jayavarman II

His story is known from an 11th-century stele inscription found on the site of a Khmer temple originally known as Bhadraniketana, in Aranyaprathet Province (Thailand). This is now just beyond the limits of the present western frontier of Cambodia, but in the 11th century this place lay on the main route linking Angkor to the recent Khmer acquisitions around the Gulf of Siam. This important inscription, named after the site as the Sdok Kak Thom stele, is now kept in the National Museum, Bangkok.[1] It was set up in 1052 during the reign of King Udayâdityavarman II (see below) to commemorate the foundation by a distinguished Brahman, named Sadâśiva, of a temple, containing a personal *linga* known as *Jayendravarmeśvara* (Victorious Indra Lord of Protection). Sadâśiva had been *purohita* to the previous King Sûryavarman I (1002-1050), but he had renounced his celibacy in order to marry the sister-in-law of the king himself. The text traces his priestly lineage back to the Brahman Śivakaivalya, who had been the priest of Jayavarman II and who was associated with the institution of the ritual of the Devarâja at the beginning of the 9th century. This essential ritual had been performed at that time by a specially qualified Brahman named Hiraṇyadâma. Thus this new shrine contained images of Hiraṇyadâma and of Śivakaivalya-Śivâśrama, 'equal in majesty to Brahma and Vishnu-Śiva'.[2]

The inscription is primarily interested in the new shrine and its incredibly rich endowments, as well as in the Brahmanical lineage of these privileged high-priests, solely authorized to perform the Devarâja ritual. The story of how this primary event occurred results incidentally in a brief account of Jayavarman's life story. Apart from the eulogistic language, the events are related in a strictly factual manner with no hint of explanation.

From another rather earlier inscription one gains the impression that his origin was largely unknown: 'For prosperity of the people he arose like the new blossoming of a large stemless lotus-flower in this perfectly pure lineage of kings.'[3] The Sdok Kak Thom inscription is more specific when it states; 'His Majesty came from Java to reign in the city of Indrapura.' The text suggests a triumphant return from exile, although his subsequent changes of residence suggest rather that he needed to win his way to power stage by stages. Indrapura has been identified as Bantây Prei Nokor in Kampong Cham Province, but it may be perhaps more likely the site of the present monastery of Preah Thiet Preah Srei, also in Kampong Cham Province, whence comes the inscription dated to AD 770 which actually names him.[4] He is also named in an inscription from the temple of Lobok Srot in the neighboring region of Sambor dated to AD 781. Much speculation has surrounded the significance to be attached to these two inscriptions, but nothing very cogent emerges, except that Jayavarman II may have held court at both 'Indrapura' (somewhere in the Kampong Cham area) and Sambor for a while.[5] If one accepts the account of his return from a land known as 'Java' in the inscription, then it would be reasonable to assume that he returns up the Mekong first to his homeland, namely in the Kampong Cham area. Vickery ad-

Map 3. (right) Khmer sites in the Angkor period.

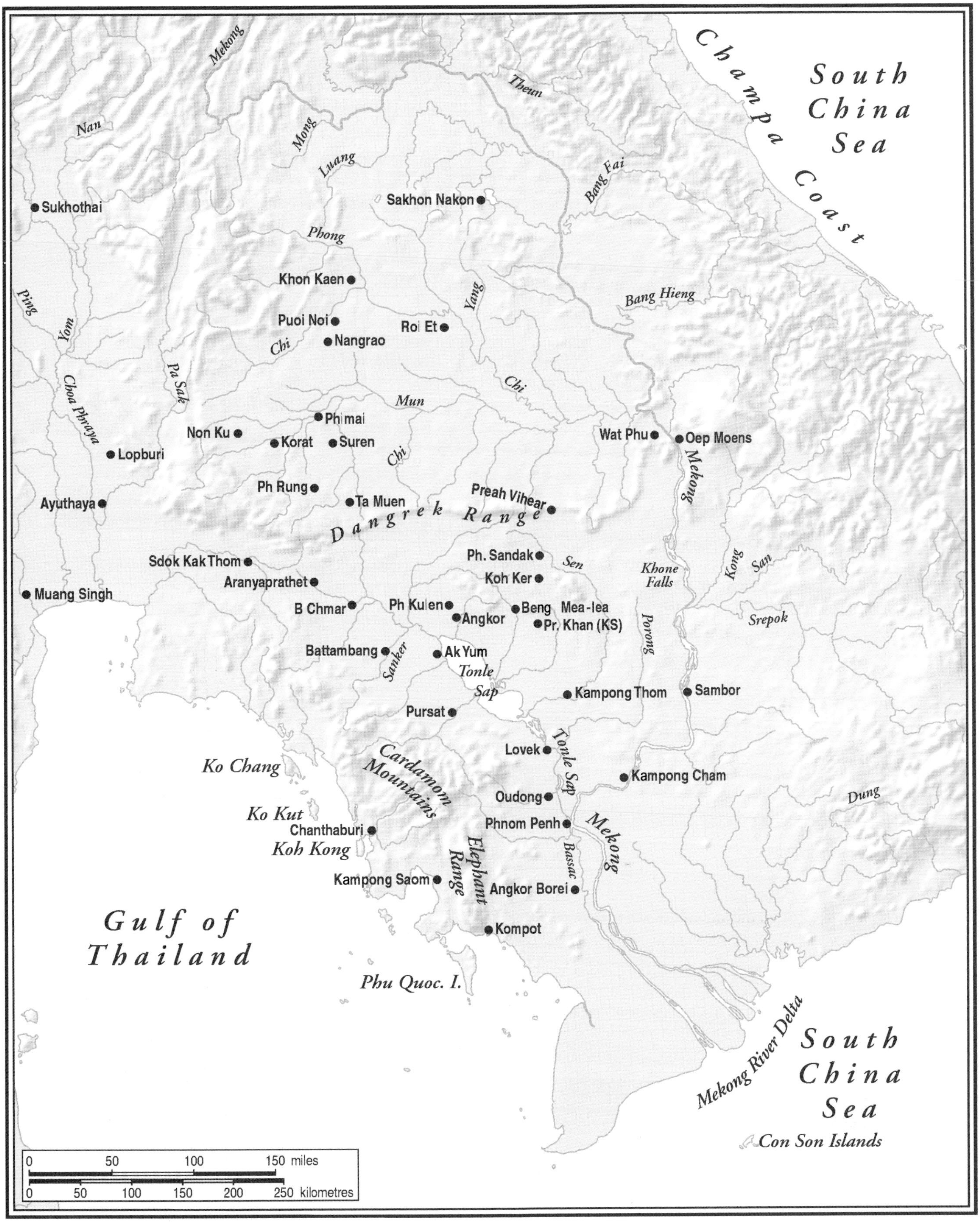
South China Sea
Champa Coast
Mekong
Theun
Nan
Mong
Luang
Bang Fai
Sakhon Nakon
Sukhothai
Phong
Khon Kaen
Ping
Yang
Bang Hieng
Yom
Puoi Noi
Roi Et
Chi
Nangrao
Choa Phraya
Pa Sak
Chi
Mun
Phimai
Non Ku
Korat
Suren
Wat Phu
Oep Moens
Lopburi
Chi
Mekong
Ph Rung
Preah Vihear
Ayuthaya
Ta Muen
Dangrek Range
Ph. Sandak
Sen
Sdok Kak Thom
Koh Ker
Khone Falls
Kong
San
Aranyaprathet
Muang Singh
B Chmar
Ph Kulen
Beng Mea-lea
Angkor
Pr. Khan (KS)
Srepok
Porong
Battambang
Sanker
Ak Yum
Tonle Sap
Kampong Thom
Sambor
Pursat
Cardamom Mountains
Tonle Sap
Lovek
Ko Chang
Kampong Cham
Dung
Oudong
Ko Kut
Phnom Penh
Mekong
Chanthaburi
Koh Kong
Elephant Range
Bassac
Kampong Saom
Angkor Borei
Gulf of Thailand
Kompot
Phu Quoc. I.
Mekong River Delta
South China Sea
Con Son Islands
0 50 100 150 miles
0 50 100 150 200 250 kilometres

duces some quite plausible arguments for associating him with Vyâdhapura further to the south. As nothing is known of his activities there, except what we learn from the Sdok Kak Thom inscription, fixing the precise location would add little to our present understanding of these events

As for his arrival from 'Java', it is sometimes readily assumed that the Central Java of the Śailendra kings is intended, where the great stûpa of Borobudur was even then in the process of construction. Thus Bernard Groslier in his study of the art and architecture of Indochina, writes: 'As the result of circumstances which are ill defined—prisoner or docile student—he resides at the court of the Śailendras. He returned to Cambodia towards 790, imbued with Javanese culture and doubtless anxious to imitate it.'[6] The name Java is known from Arab sources from the early centuries AD onwards and usually refers to the larger island of Sumatra, sometimes also including the neighbouring island of Java.[7] If one assumes logically that it was an aggressive power from which he was resolved to free his country in accordance with his later coronation ritual, it probably does not refer to the 8th-9th century kingdom of Central Java, open to the sea only on the northern coast, but more reasonably to Śrîvijaya, which was the only power at that time capable of maintaining a form of suzerainty over some part of southern Cambodia. Some confirmation of this derives from the Arab name for Śrîvijaya, namely Zâbag, a name deriving precisely from 'Jâvaka'. It may be also significant that Jayavarman arrived in Cambodia as a confirmed Śaivite, like previous Khmer kings, seemingly antagonistic to the Buddhism of Śrîvijaya and Central Java.

Thus Indrapura, which in agreement with Vickery (*Society, Economics and Politics*, p. 414) may be placed in the southern part of Kampong Cham, would have been the capital of a local ruler when Jayavarman arrived. Whatever their initial relationship, it seems certain that Jayavarman became effectively master of the place. According to the Sdok Kak Thom inscription he became associated with a Brahman scholar named Śivakaivalya, who was already established as the leading Brahman in Indrapura, responsible for a hereditary shrine containing a *Śiva-linga.* This Brahman as well as a large number of retainers followed him on his campaigns and together they moved perhaps along the east side of the Great Lake, where Jayavarman bestowed upon his Brahman companion a village and a territory known as Kuṭi. The king then proceeded to establish himself at Hariharâlaya, present-day Ruluos, some fifteen kilometres from Siem Reap, going

50. The impressive Angkor-style bridge, 80 metres long and 12 metres wide, at Kampong Kdei, a small town some 60 kilometres south of Siem Reap on the ancient route which passes east of the lake on the way to Kampong Thom. It was reconstructed in the 1960s.

south along the road east of the lake that leads eventually to Kampong Thom. Some forty-five kilometres further south of Ruluos along this same route is the town of Kampong Kdei, through which the king and his Brahman companion must have passed. This small town on the Chikreng River remains remarkable for its massive stone Angkor-style bridge with its *nâga* railings and raised nâga-hoods at both ends of the causeway.[8] This suggests that it developed as a fief of some importance; thus it may be a more likely identification for the Kuṭi bestowed upon the Brahman Śivakaivalya than the site of the ruined temple of Kuṭîśvara nowadays concealed in a copse amongst paddy-fields some 250 metres to the north of the northern *gopura* of Bantây Kdei (Angkor), as was first suggested by Coedès.[9] The Brahman continued to serve the king at Hariharâlaya until they moved on and founded the city of Amarendrapura, which has been identified (probably wrongly) as the site with ancient ruins, notably Ak Yom around the western end of Western Baray (Angkor). Jayavarman can scarcely have founded a city here, since one here already existed, as described above (in Chapter 2 'Other Early Sites'). It would seem likely that the places visited so far were former strongholds of local Khmer rulers, whom Jayavarman won over to his cause. At Amarendrapura Śivakaivalya received more territory, named Bhavalaya, and he arranged for members of his family from Kuṭi to come and take charge of these new estates. Vickery envisages a large-scale settlement of Jayavarman's followers in this place which he identifies as the Battambang area (*Society, Economics and Politics*, pp. 396-7).

Later Jayavarman with his Brahman-priest returned to the Angkor area, where he is said to have founded the city of Hariharâlaya, thus named after the joint image of Vishnu/Śiva. We have noted above that Queen Jayadevî was probably holding court in the Angkor region during the first part of the 8th century, and there are at least two now very badly ruined temples that may be dated approximately to that period. One known as Prei Monti is situated about one kilometre south of where the beautifully reconstituted Bakong now stands, and the other, Svay Pream is about four kilometres further on. They both consist of a set of three brick temples in such a state of dereliction that nothing more can be said about them. Some fifty metres from the western entrance to the Bakong there is yet another ruined shrine in a tangled copse on private property of which one lintel is remarkably well preserved. Approximately between them and quite separate from them stands the well-preserved Trapeang Phong temple, which probably belongs to the mid-9th century and is thus best considered as one of the later 'Ruluos group'. However this stands on a site where the ruined foundations of four other temples can still be seen. It must be recalled that temples as early as the two just mentioned, even earlier in the case of Ak Yom, were also standing in what is now the West Baray area when Jayavarman II first appeared on the scene. Although now very little is to be seen on these sites, enough remained during the first half of the 20th century for detailed descriptions to be possible.[10] His founding of a new city at Harahar‌âlaya may have been little more than nominal with some minimal construction, possibly including the Trapeang Phong temple. The full development of the site was the work of his successors.[11]

51. A ruined shrine with well-preserved lintel in a thicket just west of the Bakong at Ruluos. It is inserted here to emphasize that there were several temples, now all ruins, in this area, well before Jayavarman II arrived here to 'found the city of Hariharâlaya'.

Jayavarman II was primarily interested in Mahendraparvata (the Mountain of Mighty Indra), namely Phnom Kulen, about thirty kilometres north-east of Angkor (some seventy kilometres by road), where the consecration ritual, already referred to above, was performed. Phnom Kulen is the major south-eastern escarpment of a high broken sandstone plateau, its highest points ranging from 400 to 500 metres and thus dominating the Angkor plain to the south. The southern summit, which looks towards Angkor, was the centre of a large number of brick-built temples and stone shrines, resembling those at Sambor Prei Kuk, and these presumably represented the city founded by Jayavarman. Other similar shrines are located over a wide area which from the available sketch-map appears to cover a range of some twenty kilometres east to west and some thirty kilometres to the north and north-east.[12] The most thorough mapped study of the area is that by J. Boulbet and B. Dagens, which was carried out between January 1967 and June 1970. The best preserved temples which are still standing are the Prâsâd Tamri Krap, which appears to have comprised originally a set of three shrines, the Prâsâd Thma Tap and the Prâsâd Aur Phaung, which resemble in their essentials the earlier temples of Sambor Prei Kuk. They are more or less square, built of brick with stone facings for the doorways. The roof rises in the usual four stages. The corner-pieces are sometimes more ornate and the *kâla*-mask is now a common feature, surviving on other lintels where little remained of the temple itself. The imagery seems to be identical with that of Sambor Prei Kuk with the cult of the *Śiva-linga*, or of Vishnu (known from one very fine piece, (Boulbet and Dagens, 'Les sites archéologiques' p. 114), of Gaṇeśa and presumably others of whom no trace now remains. The neighboring north-western section of the plateau, which rises to about 300 metres, is the source of the Siem Reap River and its tributary, the Ruisey (Bamboo) Stream, which flow towards Angkor, supplying water for its (earlier) many artificial lakes and moats. It was regarded as a sacred river at its source, and was thus later decorated on the surrounding rocks

52. Phnom Kulen where Jayavarman II built a city in the early ninth century has suffered disastrously from military occupation over recent years. Much still remained up to the 1970s, but now except for one popular Buddhist shrine, it is hard to find the ruins lost in the jungle. Photography is also difficult when a particular site has been found. Tourists and local people go there to enjoy the scenery, but I have met only one young French researcher, namely Jean-Baptiste Chevanches, whom we accompanied on one of his expeditions into the undergrowth in February 2000.

53. One of the surviving temples, known as Prâsâd Thma Tap. As it was before 1970, (see Boulbet & Dagens, 'Les sites archéologiques', photo 108).

54. Another more impressive one, 17 metres in height, Prâsâd Aur Phaung, standing in a clearing, ('Les sites archéologiques', photo 112).

with carved figures of *lingas*, Hindu divinities, divine attendants and animal figures.

One may presume that it was already known as a sacred mountain and thus presented itself as the suitable place for Jayavarman's consecration. This was performed by a Brahman, Hiraṇyadâma, of Janapada, who instituted this ritual of the Devarâja while also initiating the Brahman priest Śivakaivalya in the same ritual for future use.[13] In order to achieve the required ritual effect, namely ensuring that Cambodia should no longer be servile to 'Java', this Brahman priest conflated four Sanskrit texts entitled *Śiraścheda* (= Decapitation), *Vinâśikha* (= Eliminating), *Sammoha* (= Illusion) and *Nayottama* (= Supreme Governance). These texts which are said to represent four 'aspects' of Śiva, have not been identified, but their titles alone may give some idea of what was involved.

Jayavarman II probably returned to Hariharâlaya only shortly before his death.

> *Next the King returned to rule in the city of Hariharâlaya and the Devarâja was also brought, while the high priest and all his relatives officiated as before. The high priest died during this reign. The King died in the city of Hariharâlaya where dwelt the Devarâja and this resides in every capital city, wherever taken by successive sovereigns as protector of the kingdom.*

This inscription seems to presume the existence of one Devarâja, which was set up in the capital wherever Jayavarman II and his successors established themselves. This practice cannot have continued for long owing to the consecration of personal royal *lingas* by later rulers, as will be seen below.

As no inscription promulgated by him has ever been found, there is little on which to elaborate a reliable account of his life, which should be one of the most interesting in the whole course of Khmer

55. 'A thousands lingas' carved under water in the sacred Ruisey (Bamboo) Stream which flows down from Phnom Kulen to circle around the temples of Angkor.

history. His career begins suddenly about 770 when he returns to his homeland known as Indrapura, presumed to be a stronghold in Kampong Cham Province. He was of recognized royal lineage and was thus able to make a base for his future operations.[14] He may have married the last of the three queens of the neighboring province of Sambor, suggested by his name appearing honorably on the inscription there (K.134).[15] In any case his first task was to consolidate his position in this general region. This achieved, he set out with a sufficient force of retainers (many from Vyâdhapura according to Vickery's reconstruction) and accompanied by his *purohita* Śivakaivalya in order to assert his authority in the north. He probably moved in a north-west direction more or less along the route which nowadays links Kampong Cham with Kampong Thom and thence to Angkor. Thus he would have kept to the east side of the Tonle Sap lake, where there were already many Khmer settlements and early temples. He may even have made the acquaintance in the Kampong Thom area of the Brahman Hiraṇyadâma of Janapada, whom he later summoned to preside over his coronation ceremony in the Kampong Thom area. He seems to have assumed authority as he advanced, giving a valuable property, known as Kuṭi 'in the eastern region' to his *purohita* Śivakaivalya.[16] He decided to found his new northern capital in present-day Ruluos, where there were already some early temples and where Queen Indradevî may have held court before him. This done, he continued his campaign around the north of the lake in the general area of Battambang Province. He gave another property here to his *purohita,* and settled his retainers there, thus occupying the region. He was then free to return to the Angkor area and establish himself on Mount Kulen, building there an extensive city on the model of Îśânapura (Sambor Prei Kuk) as founded in the first half of the 7th century by Îśânavarman. Accepting the date of 802 for his coronation, one may assume that this consolidation of his position so far had taken twenty-five or more years. We know nothing of later campaigns, although there doubtless were some. In his latter years he settled in his 'lower city' at Hariharâlaya, where eventually he was succeed by his son Jayavardhana, who took the reign title of Jayavarman III. The succession almost certainly took place in AD 834 and thus Jayavarman II may be presumed to have died in that same year and not in 850, the date which was formerly accepted.[17]

A note on the Devarâja

The Devarâja, literally 'God-King', as well as the Khmer equivalent *kamrateng jagat ta râja,* which may be translated literally as 'Lord of the World who is King', requires some elucidation. One notes that the Khmer term is a mixture of Khmer and Sanskrit, as there was no indigenous term to provide the necessary concept. The Devarâja seems to be first and foremost a *Śiva-linga* that has been consecrated as the primary national emblem, and the name applies both to the *linga* itself and to the shrine on which it was raised. It keeps Cambodia safe from any encroachments, whether from 'Java' or any other potential enemy. In this primary sense the term 'God-King' is clearly misleading in that it seems to apply to the king himself. To what extent the ruling monarch may have been identified popularly with Devarâja remains a moot point. One quotation concerning Indravarman, despite some uncertainly in the translation of the first line, suggests that the Devarâja consecration is a separate issue from his consecration as supreme ruler.

> *In that Mount Mahendra was assumed ritually as the Devarâja by the Self-Existent Lord, it follows that the noble and valiant Indravarman has received a double consecration.* (*Stèle de Bakong* A, v. 6, *ICI*, p. 20)

It is certainly assumed however that kings are normally absorbed at their demise into the supreme divinity according to the now established state-religion.[18] This is implied by their posthumous titles. Although this should normally mean Śiva, a few monarchs preferred to envisage themselves as identified with Vishnu, such as Sûryavarman II who had the Vishnuloka, now known as Angkor Vat, built with this intention. Others with Buddhist sympathies might receive the posthumous title of Nirvâṇapada, notably Sûryavarman I, and this became quite general during the later Theravâda period (14th century onwards). But it must be noted that all the Angkor monarchs, whatever their personal religious sympathies, were supposed to maintain the Devarâja state religion, even Jayavarman VII, the most famous Buddhist monarch of the Angkor period. Thus the literal translation of 'God-King' is clearly misleading, and it would seem best to leave the term untranslated. Thus this cult of the Devarâja, identified with Śiva and symbolized by a *Śiva-linga* enshrined as a 'sacred pyramid', was instituted formally by Jayavarman II. This last aspect of the cult may have been already prefigured by the earlier rites performed at Wat Phu and Ba Phnom, as referred to above, not to mention the widespread early cult of sacred mountains elsewhere.[19] The first such Devarâja was a three-tier shrine, now in a ruined condition, known locally by the inglorious nickname of Rong Chen ('Chinese vegetable-patch').[20] However, it must have been an impressive monument, even larger (the base being one hundred metres square) than the Bakong, its immediate successor at Hariharâlaya (see below). It was presumably the central monument of Jayavarman's new capital city on Mount Kulen. Leaving the term Devarâja untranslated, one applies it correctly to the specially consecrated *Śiva-linga* and by immediate association to the pyramid-shaped shrine on which it was raised.

56. Rong Chen. This ruin in the jungle was once the centre of Jayavarmam II's city. This is the upper section of the pyramid shrine that was built for the first Devarâja, consecrated on Phnom Kulen in 902. (See also Boulbet and Dagens 'Les sites archéologiques', pp. 42-43 photos 121, 122.)

57. Trapeang Phong. A mid-9th century temple which stands in the fields a few kilometres south of the more famous Bakong.

The Successors of Jayavarman II

No inscriptions and no buildings can be identified with certainty from the long reign of his son Jayavarman III (834-877). However, a shrine must surely have been built for the royal *linga* when it accompanied his father down from Phnom Kulen. The *purohita* who had succeeded Śivakaivalya under Jayavarman II, namely Sûkṣmavindu, continued to serve under Jayavarman III and probably no special significance can be attached this king's posthumous title of Vishnu. Despite their separate mythologies they were regarded one and the same, as indicated by the combined figure of Harihara, after which the capital city was named. There is one known temple that might well be attributed to Jayavarman III's reign, namely that of Trapeang Phong already mentioned above. By its style, primarily the lintels, which are well preserved, it must have been built before the Preah Ko, founded by the next king, Indravarman.

Now it stands alone (except for the nearby ruined foundations of four other earlier temples) on rising ground, surrounded by fields and clusters of trees some four kilometres south of the Bakong. It has all the features of the earlier brick-built temples as described above, being square, 6.5 metres more or less each side, with the door-frames, colonettes and lintels in stone. It is open to the east, as is usual, and there are false doors to the other three sides, all in stone. A small *kâla*-mask is set within the floral design of the lintels. These are surrounded by arched sections of brickwork as a form of toraṇa. The tiered roof rises steeply in the four storeys, probably capped by a rounded summit stone. This however is obscured by a creeping plant which covers the whole west side of the shrine. There are rounded niches to the sides of four doors (one real and three false) and miniature niches decorate the upper storeys. These all contain miniature shrines, imitating the niches below. This seems to be the only temple surviving from the long reign of Jayavarman III (834-877).

His successor Indravarman (877-889) seems to have been related to his predecessor through a maternal aunt of his wife Indradevî and thus may reasonably be described as a distant cousin. The basis for his claim to the throne is otherwise unknown. His guru was Śivasoma who was of royal descent and had studied under Śankara, who may be possibly identified as the famous Indian philosopher of that name. His fame overshadowed that of Vâmaśiva, who should have become *purohita* on the death of his uncle Sûkṣmavindu (of the Śivakaivalya line), but it is possible that Śivasoma performed this office. They founded together a religious house named Śivâśrama, which must have been a place of great importance, as the name was used as a title (viz. *Steng añ Śivâśrama*) first of Śivasoma and after of his death of Vâmaśiva.

Indravarman is best remembered for the two impressive shrines which he founded, the Preah Ko (completed in 879) and the Bakong (formally dedicated in 881) The first is dedicated to his ancestors and the second was built for the Devarâja which Jayavarman II had brought down from Mount Kulen. He is also renowned for the construction of the great artificial lake (*taṭâka*) named (after himself) as the Indrataṭâka, some four kilometres in length and rather less than one kilometre wide, aligned east-west and situated to the north of the 'city' where he was simultaneously building the Preah Ko and the Bakong.

The Bakong consists of a central shrine 2.7 metres square with a tiered roof of unusually slender proportions (probably reconstructed at a later date), raised on a fivefold square terrace, the lower one being 65 by 67 metres and the top one 20 by 12. The resulting gentle gradation from one terrace to the next allows the central shrine to be seen as one ascends the steps which lead up from all four sides. It will be noted that all the later Devarâja sacred mounds rise very steeply from one platform to the next; this not only serves to emphasize their massiveness, but also results in the summit being obscured from view as one mounts. The Bakong has a magnificent silhouette from all approaches and all angles. I have seen it suggested that it may have been inspired by Borobudur, but this seems a far fetched suggestion, the most so, as the latter's silhouette is so massive and squat. It resembles Borobudur only in being raised on a series of open terraces with four flights of steps to the four quarters with an imposing entrance arch at the foot of each flight. But one does not need the great Javanese stûpa as a model for what is effectively the basic design of any monument that affects to represent the mythical central mountain of the universe. Many temples in East Java, notably Çaṇḍi Jawi, might serve as a model, if indeed there is need to seek for one.

The five-tier mound is enshrined within an inner rectangular courtyard, 120 by 160 metres, thus allowing for increased space on the originally more ornate eastern approach. Entrance portals (*gopura*) on the four sides allowed entry into this inner courtyard, where there still stand the remains of two libraries on the east side and two subsidiary brick-built shrines on all four sides of the central monument. These eight subsidiary temples are said to represent the eight manifestations (*mûrti*) of Śiva, viz. earth, wind, fire, moon, sun, water, ethereal space and the sacrificer (*Stèle de Bakong* A, v. 25, *ICI*, p. 34). They resemble the Trapean Phong temple already described above. They have doors facing east, with false doors of stonework on the other three sides, all adorned with decorative lintels: the usual canopy with looped garlands and also with a small inset *kâla*-mask. On both sides of the doorways there are niches with inset figures, either guardians or apsaras.

Stone elephants, much dilapidated, stand on all four corners of the lower stages. On the fourth stage twelve miniature shrines, each containing originally a *linga*, are arranged around the central shrine of the summit platform The whole central complex was enclosed within a second walled enclosure of 300 by 400 metres, and this again by an outer enclosure of 700 by 900 metres with a moat and ramparts. This is the first grandiose Khmer monument of which sufficient remains to give an adequate impression of the ambitious layout of these great royal creations. As can be seen from early photographs the central section was in a disastrously

58. Trapeang Phong. One of its lintels.

59. Bakong, the pyramid-temple as built by Indravarman (877-889) at Hariharâlaya for the Devarâja which had been brought down from Phnom Kulen by Jayavarman II some time before his death in 834/5. It was found as a total ruin and its recreation under the direction of Maurice Glaize (1936-41) marks it out as one of the finest works of French conservation. Photo taken from the west.

60. The Bakong is surrounded by eight subsidiary shrines, of which one on the NW corner can be seen in the previous illustration. Its lintel is well preserved and remarkable for its intricacy. The small presiding divinity, possibly Indra, surmounts a kâla*-mask, while* gandharvas *frolic in the curling foliage. There are two to either side and six more in the series below, separated into facing groups by a three-headed nâga. The makharas at the two ends, who suspend the canopy, are mounted by small imp-like figures (*kinnara*).*

ruined state and its re-creation under the direction of Maurice Glaize during the years 1936-43 marks it out as perhaps the finest work of French conservation. All that is noticeably missing is the carved frieze-work, of which only occasional pieces could be traced amongst the ruins. Some fine pieces are set into the walls of the main central shrine.

Preah Ko consists of a set of six brick-built temples of the now traditional design (viz. a square shrine containing a small cella, surmounted by a tiered roof) standing on a rectangular platform within a double enclosure. The three front temples, facing east, intended for the male statues, are appreciably larger than the three that stand directly behind, intended for the corresponding female figures. The central shrine to the front is both taller than the other two and skilfully set back, thus emphasizing its pre-eminence, as though its companions stood forward on guard. They are remarkable for the fine decorative work, especially on the lintels over the entrances and to sides of the doorways.

The lintels on the east side have the usual canopy with hanging garlands, but above there are four miniature horse-riders and below six imps (*kinnaras*) riding nâgas. There is also a small inset *kâla*-mask. Those on the sides and back are less elaborate but all with the *kâla*-mask which might be mistaken for the head of a *garuḍa*. The stone bulls, Śiva's emblem, are set at ground level facing the temples.[21]

The six temples, all effectively dedicated to Śiva and his spouse Gaurî, were built in honour of Jayavarman II and his queen, Dharaṇîndradevî, also of Indravarmans's parents, Rudravarman and Narendradevî, and of his maternal grand-parents, Prithvîndravarman and Prithvîndradevî, all represented by suitable statues. The central temple to the fore is dedicated to Jayavarman II, divinized as Parameśvara (Supreme Lord, namely Śiva). The one on its left (north side) is dedicated to Indravarman's father as Rudreśvara, and that to its right to his maternal grandfather as Prithvîndreśvara. Thus they are both assimilated with Śiva with titles derived from their royal names. The three temples behind are dedicated to the wife of Jayavarman II, Indradevî (Dharaṇîndradevî), identified with Śiva's spouse Gaurî, Narendradevî, representing Indravarman's mother, and Prithvîndradevî, representing his maternal grand-mother. Conceived posthumously as goddesses, they become all aspects of Gaurî

Approaching the Preah Ko today along a gravel track (which leads on to the Bakong), one arrives close to the broken down eastern entrance of the second enclosure. One may therefore easily remain

61. Preah Ko, dedicated by Indravarman in honour of his parents and certain ancestors. This rather unusual double set of three shrines can be dated to an inscription of 897 which refers specifically to the three images of Śiva and three of Devî which were set up in these six shrines.

62. Preah Ko. A lintel from one of the front temples which is rather more elaborate than those of the back row in that it is decorated with horse-riders above, and by the same imp-like figures riding nâgas below.

unaware that this temple too, like the Bakong, was enclosed within this third (outer) enclosure, 500 by 400 metres, of which only traces remain. The inner enclosure of which the eastern entrance barely survives, has largely disappeared.

As we have noted above an important temple, known as Kok Po, now a total ruin, was founded in the 'Baray Group' by a certain Nivâsakavi, who had been *guru* to Jayavarman III, presumably retaining a title of honour under Indravarman. According to an inscription of Ban Bung Ke near Ubon Ratchathani, dated 886, an image was erected by a certain Somâditya during the reign of Indravarman with rich donations to 'Trailokyanâtha, master of all religious teachers'. This may have been a Buddhist shrine and one notes that the lower Mun Valley remained largely Khmer.[22]

In 889 Prince Yaśovardhana succeeded his father with the regal name of Yaśovarman, the eventual founder of the city of Angkor. Vâmaśiva who had served under Indravarman, now attended on the Devarâja with the titles of *Brah Guru* (Sacred Teacher) and 'Lord of Śivâśrama'. Early in his reign (893) Yaśovarman erected the so-called Lolei temple in the middle of the Indratațâka in honour of Śiva and his spouse, associated with his own parents and grand-parents.[23] This consists now of four tower-like brick-built shrines in a much ruined condition, two in a row facing south-east with a further two behind. Originally two sets of three shrines must have been intended exactly on the model of Preah Ko. This is suggested immediately by the fact that the two north-eastern shrines, those to the right as one faces the whole complex, are appreciably taller than the other two, and were thus clearly conceived as the central ones. Some finely worked lintels have been preserved, especially the one on the north-eastern tower, which is surmounted by a delicate frieze of Agastya figures and other divinities. The *kâla*-mask in the centre of the canopy is more prominent than on the Bakong and Preah Ko temples. The frontispieces (*torana*), unfortunately badly worn, are in stone.[24] The site of the two missing towers, possibly never completed, has been cleared as part of the courtyard of the more recent Theravâda monastery, which now presses hard upon these ancient ruins.

What one sees today can give little or no idea of this once magnificent city of Hariharapura, watered by canals from the lake which not only supplied the paddy-fields, but which also circulated through the city, around the palace, filling the great moat around the Bakong. Now there is no sign of a lake. The Lolei temple stands high and dry on a ridge, covered with lichen and encumbered with Theravâda monastery buildings which now occupy most of its former courtyard. Alone the Bakong and the Preah Ko (since its recent cleaning and repair) stand out as unusual masterpieces.[25]

The city of Yaśodharapura (Angkor)

It seems that already in the first year of his reign Yaśovarman embarked upon the construction of an artificial lake for his newly intended capital. This corresponds to the Eastern Baray, as now known in modern guide-books. Yaśovarman named it after himself as the Yaśodharataṭâka. Along the south bank of this vast reservoir of seven by two kilometres he had monasteries (*âśrama*) built for various Hindu religious communities, for Śaivas, Pâśupâtas and Tapasvins, Pañçarâtras, Bhâgavatas and Sâttvatas,[26] and also a Buddhist monastery *(Saugatâśrama)*. The stele relating to this monastery was found on the site of the much later Tep Pranam monastery in the Angkor area, suggesting that it may not have survived very long on its original site, surrounded by Śaivite and Vaiṣṇavite communities. It is also interesting to note that this Buddhist inscription is closely modeled on the non-Buddhist ones. There are so few sources available to us concerning Buddhism at Angkor, that I deal with this text in some detail. It opens with a conventional invocation to Śiva as manifest in the threefold form as Brahmâ, Vishnu and Śiva, followed by one to the Buddha:

All honour to Śiva, the Lord who originally was one alone
whom it pleased to become threefold as the Four-Faced (Brahmâ),
as Four-Armed (Vishnu) and as Śambhu,
and who became one again at the beginning of creation.
I honour with devotion the one born from a lotus-flower,
whose eyes are like lotus-flowers, whose hair-locks, adorned with the moon,
are perfumed with the juice of bunches of mandâra-flowers
and entwined with the hair of gods and demons submissive to him.

All honour to Buddha whose feet are worthy of devotion,
Who having achieved enlightenment himself, alerted the threefold world
*To the means of escape from the net of phenomenal existence (*samsâra*).*

Thereafter the following fifteen stanzas reproduce the genealogy of Yaśovarman in the same terms as the other Thnal Baray inscriptions. These are followed by twenty-eight stanzas of fervent and exaggerated praise of the king, e.g.

If the king should come here with his womenfolk,
For the good fortune of this monastery, let us ensure that he is treated as a god.
As supreme lord of the world, he is said to be the Guru of the whole earth.
Whatever he desires, let that be done, according to the words of Vyâsa:
Who fails in honoring a king, the Guru of the whole earth, gains nothing
from his offerings, his sacrifices and his services for the deceased.

After the king the Brahmans must be honoured before all others, then the heir to the throne, then ministers and the chief of the army and those who have been valiant in battle.

Then comes the verse:

*One should honour a Master of Religion (*âcârya*)*
who knows the Buddhist lore,
especially if he knows grammar as well, but rather less than a 'twice-born'
*(*Brahman*) who possesses full knowledge (*vidyâ*).*

As I shall emphasize later in commenting on other Buddhist inscriptions, the subservience of Buddhism to Brahmanism is made abundantly clear. Thus this inscription ends rather oddly for a Buddhist work, but not surprisingly in the present context:

May those who with supreme faith cause all this to prosper
come together with their family-members in the presence of the Lord of Gods(=Śiva),
that excellent untroubled pure place, for as long as sun and moon
shine down on earth.[27]

The text refers to the inmates of this monastery as 'Masters of Religion' (*âcârya*), monks (*bhikṣu*) and ascetics (*yati*). However, ignorant and ill-bred ascetics are not to be allowed entry, but only those who have overcome the desires of the senses, who observe the three times of prayer, and are devoted to the practice of virtue and of study. Together with monks who study they are entitled to daily rations. Then there are extra distributions for the 'Masters of Religion' and the older monks. There is no indication of the form of Buddhism followed, but the presence of *âcârya* suggests a Mahâyâna religious order probably of the Mûla-Sarvâstivâdins.[28] It is noteworthy that the *âcârya* or Buddhist Religious Masters, later known as *vajrâcârya* (Adamantine Masters) according to tantric tradition, were granted the status of quasi-Brahmans, while ordinary monks were not.[29]

The inscriptions refer to many other such 'religious retreats' being established elsewhere. Apart from the foundation steles, four identical ones being placed at the four corners of the lake, there is now no trace of these buildings, clearly built of less durable materials like the main buildings of the city.

An immediate requirement for the new city was a temple-complex suitable for receiving the royal *linga,* which had to be transferred in due course to its new capital city. This raises the matter of the later practice of individual rulers to set up their own particular 'Royal *linga*' which does not seem to have been envisaged in the foundation ritual of Devarâja. If indeed the Devarâja were transferred from Hariharâlaya, this would have occasioned the need for a replacement in the original shrine. However, the *linga* in its new location is referred to as Yaśodhareśvara, 'Lord Yaśodhara', suggesting that this was the king's own specially consecrated *linga,* and thus that the original Devarâja probably remained in its original home.

For the new pyramid-temple he chose the hill, known as the Bakheng, which rises steeply on the southern approach to Angkor Thom or 'Great Angkor', the new city created by Jayavarman VII in the 12th century, which one sees today. Thus it has been effectively marginalized and nowadays it is treated mainly as a fine viewpoint, where tourists gather in large numbers at sunset to see Angkor Vat to the south, the expanse of the Western Baray to the west, and in the distance the summits of Phnom Krom to the south-west and that of Phnom Bok to the north-east, on both of which Yaśovarman also built subsidiary shrines of local stone. Nowadays the ruins on the summit of Bakheng give little idea of the magnificent temple-complex as conceived by Yaśovarman and his Brahmanical advisers. The layout is clearly conceived as a maṇḍala. A fivefold terrace, gradually decreasing from 76 metres square at the base to 47 metres at the summit, supports the central terrace, on which stood the central shrine with five smaller shrines to the four intermediate quarters. Flights of steps lead up from the four main directions and these were flanked by two rows of 5 miniature shrines, making a total of 40. Similar single rows of shrines led up from the four intermediate directions, making a total of a further 20, all of these structures so far being built of local sandstone. Around each of the four angles of this enormous complex there stood seven brick-built

63. Bakheng. This was the primary pyramid-temple ever built at Angkor and for a long time remained the most impressive. It consisted of an elaborate arrangement of 108 (a sacred number) of subsidiary tower-like shrines, set at ever higher levels and surrounding the main temple on its central platform. Originally it represented the centre of Yaśovarman's new city (Angkor) and remained so until the Baphuon took pride of place in the 2nd half of the 11th century and later the Bayon, probably in the early 13th. Thereafter it was effectively marginalized until it was reconstituted as a Buddhist sanctuary in the 16th century.

tower-like shrines, making a total of 28, with a double pair of similar shrines at each of the four quarters, a further 16. The total number of these constructions was clearly calculated to arrive at a configuration of one main central shrine surrounded by the sacred number of 108 subsidiary ones. No other temple-mountain approximates to so complex a design, and although the layout of maṇḍala differs, the great complex of Çaṇḍi Sewu in Central Java occurs at once to one's mind as a similar grandiose conception.

He also built temples on the summits of Phnom Krom and Phnom Bok, prominent hills, the one some sixteen kilometres to the south-east, thus overlooking the Great Lake and the other about fourteen kilometres to the north-west with a vast view of paddy-fields and Mount Kulen in the distance. They both consist of what may now be considered the conventional Khmer temple, namely a set of three temple-shrines, of which the central one predominates. These two temples are built exclusively of local sandstone. Those on Phnom Bok are the best preserved and in both cases the views themselves merit the climb to the summit. The Theravâda monasteries, which are also there now, interfere neither with the solitude of the ruins or the view.

Enthusiastic for the construction of temples on imposing heights, Yaśovarman is also responsible for initiating the building of the great temple of Preah Vihear on a protruding escarpment in the Dangrek Mountains some 140 kilometres north-east of his new capital. Later monarchs up to the mid-12th century continued to embellish this impressive site with its magnificent views across the Cambodian plain to the south and the Khorat Plateau to the north. Also during his reign a temple was founded in 895 containing a *linga* dedicated to Bhadreśvara on Mount Sandak some forty kilometres north-west of Koh Ker. This likewise was well maintained by later monarchs.[30]

It was noted in the opening summary to this chapter that Indravarman retained his old and trusted teacher Vâmaśiva as the one responsible for the Devarâja with the title of *Brah Guru* 'Sacred Teacher'. He made him responsible for all the properties founded in the *purohita* line since Indrapura, namely the district (*sruk*) of Bhadragiri near Amarendrapura (Battambang area), the district of Kuṭi in Pûrvadiśa and the district of Bhadragiri in Jeng Bnam (Foot of the Mountain). Here the district of Bhadragiri near Amarendrapura must

64. Phnom Krom. Yaśovarman also built shrines of two hill-tops, 15-16 kilometres distant from the Bakheng, one to south-west overlooking that lake, as illustrated, and another, known as Phnom Bok, to the north-east with fine views of Phnom Kulen in the distance and of the surrounding paddy-fields. (Photograph by Giulia Anglois-Nisbet.)

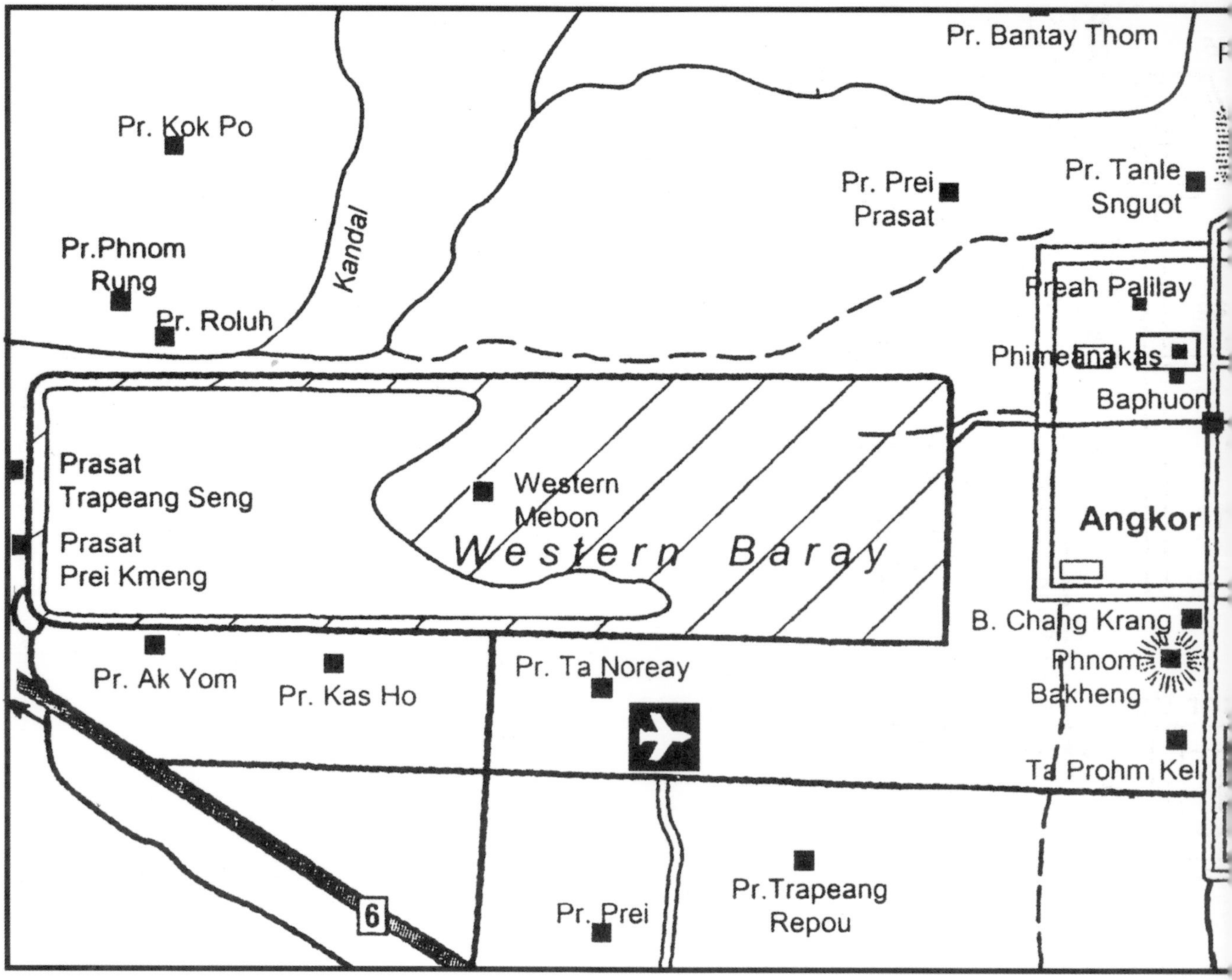

Map 4. Plan of Angkor

include the territory originally given by Jayavarman II to Śivakaivalya, known as Bhavâlaya (Amarendrapura). The other Bhadragiri of Jeng Bnam (unidentified) was founded by Śivakaivalya's younger brother on land given him by Jayavarman III. Indravarman now made further gifts of territory and precious objects to Vâmaśiva in the Amarendrapura region.[31]

It is difficult to envisage this first city of Angkor, as so much has been built on the site ever since. The two main structures were clearly the vast artificial lake to the east and the Bakheng, which logically would have stood in the centre. The western limits would therefore have extended westwards well beyond the present site of Angkor Vat. The whole area together with the lake and its religious retreats on its southern side was enclosed within a moat and earth-works of which some traces remain. The principle buildings, including the royal palace, would have been constructed of wood with tiled roofs, while the houses of the commoners, set here and there amongst paddy-fields would have been of even more fragile materials. There has been much discussion of the purpose of the vast artificial lakes of which we have so far only encountered two. It has been readily assumed that they were intended for irrigation purposes, but this has been disputed recently by other scholars who argue that they were intended for artistic and religious purposes, namely to supply water for the moats around the temples and the various canals which cut across the city.[32] When these large reservoirs were built at Hariharâlaya and certainly at Yaśodharapura, there were then very few temples standing, and it certainly would not have required a huge reservoir to supply them with decorative moats. A major purpose of these artificial lakes must surely have been irrigation. Thus I represent the more traditional view by quoting from a section from Hall, *History of S-E Asia*, pages 144-6, entitled 'The economic basis of Khmer civilization', which helps to explain how an agricultural community could attain such power and such wealth, even though this remained in the hands of a few.

The Khmers, who had inherited methods of irrigation from Funan, found the Angkor region ideal for the purpose of constructing a system of water utilization that would cause the soil to yield its utmost in the service of man. The city itself, so far from being an urban agglomeration, was

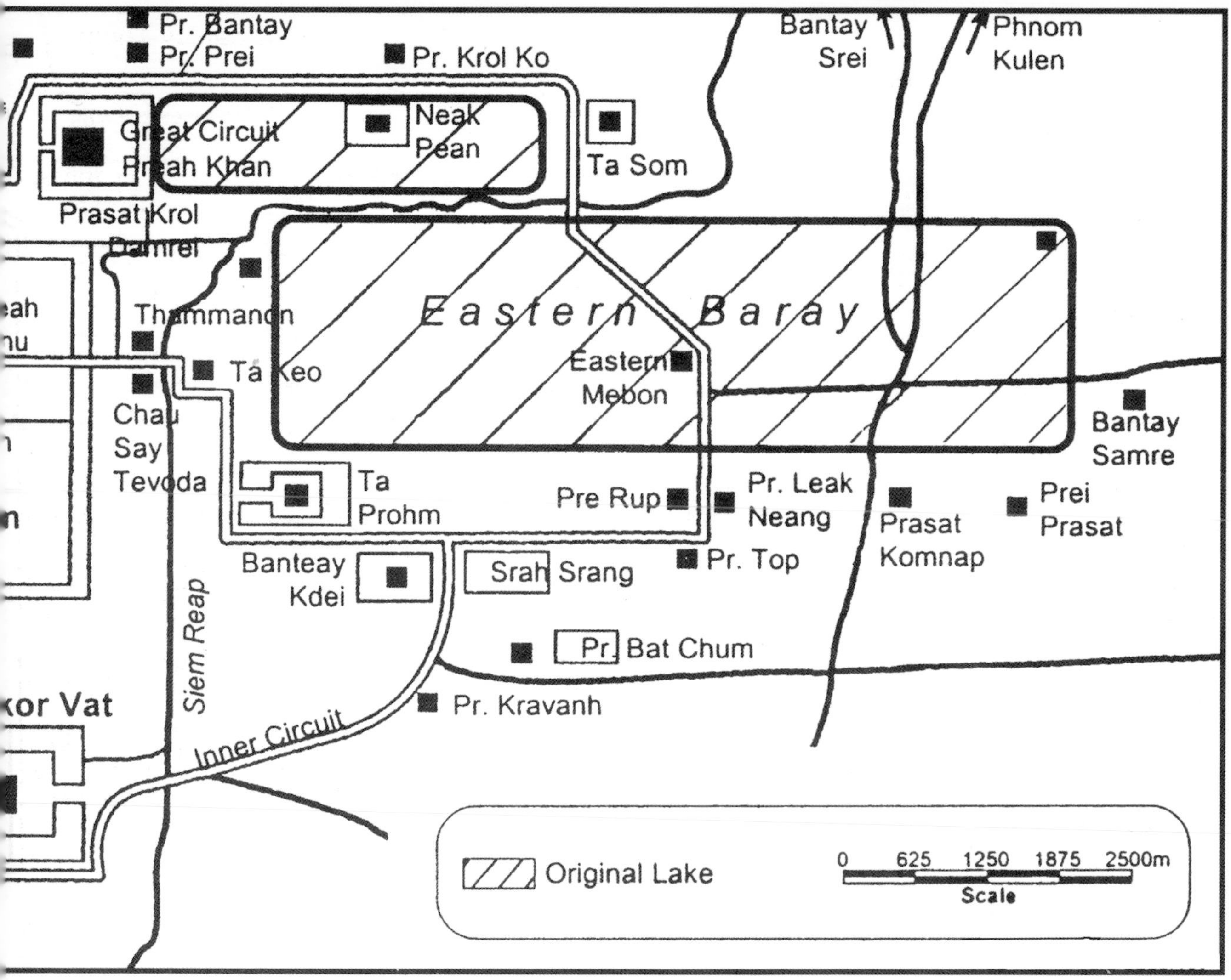

rather a collection of waterworks stretching far and wide beyond the palace and its immediate temples, with a considerable population densely settled along its causeways and canals, and much of its land cut up into cultivated holdings. In this connection modern research has established the significant fact that each Khmer king, upon taking office, was expected to carry out works 'of public interest', particularly works of irrigation. Indeed, Monsieur Groslier goes so far as to say that the labour bestowed upon the ever-developing irrigation system is far more impressive that the building of temples, which were merely chapels crowning a cyclopean undertaking.

To this I add a translated quotation from Groslier's text, in which he draws attention to the symbolic relationship between the irrigation system and the popular legendary motif of the 'Churning of the Ocean' in order to produce the elixir of life.[33]

One knows the celebrated phrase of Jayavarman VII regarding the founding of Angkor Thom: 'The city of Yaśodharapurî (here given a feminine name), adorned with palaces of precious stones, worthy and desirous, and with Jayasindhu as a garment, was married to this King for the procreation of universal happiness in a great festival under the vast awnings of his fame' (IC IV, p. 242, v. 76). The Jayasindhu, namely the moat around Angkor Thom, is effectively 'churned' by the giants on the bridges which cross it. Thus we know the rôle of the moats from the hydraulic viewpoint, and how they brought prosperity to the country by distributing the water of the barays for irrigation. What in fact is a baray and the canals which it feeds? The inscriptions inform us: It is a vast basin like a Sea of Milk (ibid., p.126, v.27). What does the king actually do in constructing such works: By his efforts the Sea of Milk itself, freed of its water content, becomes a Sea of Nectar. Thus in a general way the theme of the 'Churning of the Ocean' represents the same 'churning' by the king in order to produce the nectar which is the happiness of his subjects.[34]

Yaśovarman was succeeded in succession by his two sons, Harṣavarman who may have ruled from about 900 to 922/3, and then Îśânavarman II who seems to have held his position at Angkor until 928. Meanwhile their uncle, whose reign dates formally from 928, had set up a rival Devarâja in 921 at Chok Gargyar (Koh Ker) which was probably his personal domain. Thus they were doubtless very troubled

reigns, especially for the younger brother. Two temples of note were erected during Harṣavarman's reign, firstly the elegant brick-built shrine, known as the Baksei Chamkrong, which stands just below Phnom Bakheng, erected by the king himself, who was still reigning in 922 according to the important inscription which comes from this temple. It provides a résumé of the dynastic history of Cambodia from the beginnings until the reign of Râjendravarman (944-968), who set up this later inscription together with a golden image of Śiva in the year 948.[35]

Another temple, beautiful for its simplicity, is that known as *Kravan* (a kind of flowering tree). It consists of a set of five linked shrines, all constructed of brick, the centre one of which is decorated on its facing and side walls with images of Vishnu in incised brickwork. The one to the far right as seen from the front preserves a similar image of the goddess

65. (left) Baksei Chamkrong. This well-proportioned brick-built temple, which stands near the foot of the Bakheng, was founded by Harṣavarman I shortly before his death in 922/23. In 947 Râjendravarman set up a gold image of Śiva in this temple, as recorded in an important inscription which claims to trace the royal lineage from Śrutavarman up to his own reign.

66. (below) Baksei Chamkrong. The elaborately worked lintel incorporates Indra enthroned on his 3-headed elephant.

67. (above) Kravan. This temple, consisting of a linked set of five shrines, was founded by a high official in 921 while Harṣavarman I was still ruling, although there is no mention of the king in the relevant inscription. It was restored by B.P. Groslier in the early 1960s, being another fine piece of French reconstruction.

Lakṣmî with kneeling figures beneath her. This temple which looks as though newly built, is another fine example of French restoration work (1962-66). According to inscriptions found on the site, it was founded in the year 921 by a high official named Mahîdharavarman and dedicated to Trailokyanâtha, 'Lord of the Threefold World'.[36] There is no praise of any ruling king and nothing more is known of the two brother-kings, whose reigns at Angkor covered some twenty-eight years, while their father Yaśovarman had achieved so much in his short reign of eleven years.

68. (right) Kravan. The interior of the central shrine shows a 4-armed Vishnu on the north (left) wall, holding his conventional implements, a disc, an orb, a conch and a club, and in the process of making one of his three great strides, which encompassed the whole world. The facing wall shows an 8-armed manifestation of the same god, surrounded by devotees, arranged in series. The wall on the right, not visible in the photograph, shows him seated on Garuḍa, his preferred vehicle, set between two worshippers. (Photo by Suthep Kritsanuvarin.)

69. *Kravan. The shrine to the far right, which happens to have the best surviving lintel, contains three images of Lakṣmî, worked in brick, of which the facing one is clearly visible.*

70. *Kravan. The image of Lakṣmî, also worked in brick, on the left-side wall in the same (northern) shrine.*

Chapter 4

The Consolidation of Khmer Imperial Power

Summary

This chapter covers the period from Jayavarman IV's capital at Koh Ker seemingly founded in 921, to the beginning of the reign of Sûryavarman II in Angkor in 1113.

The Kok Ker interlude, important for the gradual extension of Khmer authority beyond the Dangrek Range, lasted only twenty-three years. Under Râjendravarman (944-968) Yaśodharapura (Angkor) was restored as the capital city. The pyramid-temples of the East Mebon and Pre Rup were built, and also probably the well known temple of Bantây Srei, although this was founded formally at the beginning of the reign of Jayavarman V (968-1001). These two kings were well disposed towards Buddhism and Râjendravarman authorized the founding of a small Buddhist temple, known as Bat Chum in the Angkor area. Jayavarman V, who built the Ta Keo and the Phimean-âkas, was served by another Buddhist prelate who had founded a monastery known as Vat Sithor in Kampong Cham Province. The inscriptions relating to these two Buddhist foundations raise again the question of the relationship between Buddhism and the Devarâja cult.

Jayavarman V, who died in 1001, was succeeded briefly by a nephew who ruled as Udayâdityavarman I, followed very soon by Jayavîravarman, whose relationship with his predecessor is uncertain. Meanwhile Sûryavarman I was already claiming the throne, which he gained by warfare about 1006. His reign, officially dated from 1002 until his death in 1050, established Khmer authority well beyond the Dangrek Range and some very impressive temples developed on the Khorat Plateau, of which the more notable are Phnom Wan, Muang Tam, Phnom Rung and Phimai. They usually developed from earlier temples on the same site, and such works of reconstruction continued under later monarchs up to Sûryavarman II and even Jayavarman VII. Some temples founded at rather earlier dates such as Wat Phu and Preah Vihear now underwent still further rebuilding. At the same time Sûryavarman ordered reconstruction work at Angkor, which had suffered from his warfare, and important sites such as Phnom Chisor in the south were refurbished. Several new temples were also built in the Battambang area and we note in particular Prâsâd Baset, which was a large domain, but of which nowadays very little remains. Also associated with Sûryavarman I is the vast domain of Preah Khan of Kampong Svay.

He was succeeded by Udayâdityavarman II who continued work on these enormous projects, also constructing another vast reservoir, known popularly nowadays as the West Baray, and founding another impressive pyramid-temple, namely the Baphuon. This effectively moved the centre of his capital well to the east and thus close to the royal palace, so that the Bakheng, the centre of Yaśovarman's first city of Yaśodharapura (late 9th century onwards) was now marginalized. There appear to have been several serious revolts during his reign as is illustrated by the various campaigns of a great general named Sangrâma. Udayadityavarman was succeeded in 1066 by his younger brother Harṣavarman III, who ruled until probably 1080. Meanwhile a pretender to the throne was already prevailing in the Khorat area, namely Jayavarman VI, whose reign dates conventionally from 1080 to 1107, when he was succeeded by an elder brother, who ruled as Dharaṇîndravarman I. But the throne was already being claimed by another pretender, who defeated his rivals after several years of warfare, reigning as Sûryavarman II, thus bringing us to Chapter 5.

Angkor abandoned for Koh Ker

King Jayavarman IV decided to build a new capital city, thus abandoning Angkor, already well established over the past 150 years. The site chosen, namely, Chok Gargyar (Koh Ker), situated some sixty kilometres in a direct line north-east of Angkor (but over one hundred by road and forest track), was probably already his personal domain. Nowadays it is difficult of access as there is a road (and even this is a simple gravel track) only as far as Svay Leu district, whence there still remain fifty-seven kilometres of rough woodland, which a 4 x 4 vehicle can manage with some difficulty in the dry season. Moreover, until 1998 it was still a 'war-zone' for Khmer Rouge and Government troops, and only since the last two to three years have the villagers returned to remake their life thereabouts.

Jayavarman's reign formally begins in 928 which was probably the date of the death of his predecessor in Angkor, but he seems to have proclaimed his right to the throne some seven years earlier according to an inscription dated 921 in Prâsâd Thom, the main temple at Koh Ker.[1] Here he declares that 'he donates with devotion to the Supreme Lord of the Threefold Word (*Tribhuvaneśvara*) everything in the essence of royalty'. The divinity was represented by an enormous *linga* raised on a pyramid thirty-seven metres high in a spacious courtyard immediately behind Prâsâd Thom. There is no doubt that it was proclaimed as *Kamrateng jagat ta râja* (Devarâja). One may deduce that Jayavarman thus proclaimed his right to the throne already in the last year of the reign of Harṣavarman I (900-922/3) even before the latter's brother, Îśânavarman II, had succeeded Harṣavarman. This act of setting up a rival Devarâja, consecrated by a Brahman named Îśânamûrti, as an effective claim to the throne, put an end to any suggestion that the original Devarâja should be transferred from one capital city to another, as was seemingly the original intention. Meanwhile Kumârasvâmin continued to serve the Devarâja at Yaśodharapura. If Chok Gargyar was already the personal domain of Jayavarman IV, who developed it as his base of operations for usurping the throne, then this change of capital city is easily explained. Whatever its real beginnings, this site seems to have developed with the construction of a large baray, *c.* 560 by 1,200 metres, known locally as the Rahal. The lie of the land caused this artificial lake to be aligned slightly west of north to east of south, and thus all the temples in its vicinity retain this alignment, facing ESE instead of due east. However all the temples built further to the south along the road from the direction of Svay Leu have the correct E-W orientation.

The centre of his new capital consisted of a series of shrines, known as Prâsâd Thom (the 'Great Temple') leading to the seven-tiered pyramid thirty-seven metres high crowned by a massive *Śiva-linga*. This major section was walled around as a single whole, while to the north of the lake a group of some ten smaller temples were gradually built. Furthermore on both sides of the approach road from the south there are more shrines and temples, all individually walled around, numbering some twenty or more. All these were built of hewn and worked stone, thus inaugurating a more massive style of architecture, very different from the brick-built temples that were then still the norm at Angkor. Other buildings, including the royal residence would have been made of local wood.

The area of Koh Ker covers an area of about five by seven kilometres through which one can drive along one central cart-track, running south to north. Thus the main temple and the great pyramid are readily accessible. The lake can be reached by walking some 500 metres through the jungle. Some of the lesser temples can be seen from the track and one can approach them relatively easily through brambles and clinging weeds. Others are not visible from the track and then one needs a local man who claims to know where they are. One follows him through jungle and brushwood, often to be disappointed by the disastrously ruined state of what remains.

The centre of interest of this whole site should be the Great Temple (Prâsâd Thom) backed by the great pyramid. This is the end of the road from Siyong village. It is now in such a ruined state that we must have recourse to the description of a French explorer, Louis Delaporte, who came here in 1868-69.

> *Let us go through quickly this whole ensemble. First there is a vast construction in the form of a cross, complicated by lateral galleries, enclosing a double courtyard. Then come two subsidiary shrines (*préasats*) between which there is a small gully, paved in sandstone. Further on there is a* gopura, *18 metres high, with eight fantastic creatures serving as guardians. This gives access to an enclosure where there is an artificial pool (*sra*) divided in two by a causeway, bordered by small colonnaded galleries and* nâgas, *while nearby there are four gigantic* garuḍas *with spread wings and standing on pedestals. The causeway leads to a chamber in the form of a cross flanked by two lateral doors. One crosses this, passing between two rows of statues, three on the right, five on the left, of which the most important is Śiva on his bull Nandin. These statues are badly mutilated and half buried. Passing through a porch, covered on the inside by inscriptions, one arrives at a sanctuary in the centre of a group of 16 tower-like shrines (tourelles) encompassed by a rectangular row of constructions which were formerly divided into cells, the whole being set within a double enclosure. A second porch on the same axis as the previous one, leads likewise to a chamber in the form of a cross, then to a causeway bordered by* nâgas *and* garuḍas, *leading to a* gopura *which is completely destroyed. Thence one enters a large courtyard with strong walls all around, where stands a seven-stage pyramid 36 metres high. On the summit there is a square pit, quite deep, surrounded by a wall two metres high which*

supports fantastic statues of lions en cariatide. *This is surrounded by a small corridor which is enclosed by yet another wall. The whole is in ruins and open to the sky.*[2]

Nowadays the whole temple from the first *gopura* to the last that opens on to vast courtyard with the pyramid, is a total wreck buried in the jungle. A narrow path, along which one stumbles, leads through these ruins where nothing as described by Louis Delaporte can be recognized. Even the double enclosure which once enclosed these precincts cannot be consistently identified. There is a small pool, roughly square in shape close to the northern side of the temple precincts with no visible sign of stonework and completely enshrouded in jungle. The one item of interest is the pyramid.

The whole area is heavily wooded and also often covered in thick jungle Some twenty temples are scattered to the north and south of the last four kilometres of the route leading up to Prâsâd Thom. The first one to the left of the route is known locally as Prâsâd Pram (Five Shrines). In fact it consists of three shrines built of brick, the central one slightly taller and larger than the other two. In front of these are two subsidiary buildings usually referred to conventionally as 'libraries', the whole being enclosed within a wall of laterite, measuring forty-eight by forty-four metres. The first shrine slightly further along the track on the right is known Prasat Neang Khmau, meaning the Shrine of the Black Maiden. We note that all these names are merely local nicknames. It consists of a single towered shrine of laterite standing on a sandstone basis. It stands within a laterite enclosure of forty-eight by forty-four metres, and is happily very easy of approach through a hole in the wall and some rough terrain. The lintel representing a four-headed Brahmâ is of special note. We passed by other shrines until we came to Prâsâd Chen ('Chinese Temple') about halfway along the route to the left side. This consists of the regular three shrines with two subsidiary buildings ('libraries') standing in

71. Koh Ker: the Great Pyramid, built in seven stages up to a height of 37 metres, and supporting the Devarâga, the 'Lord of the Threefold World', was erected by Jayavarman IV, usurper, at Koh Ker, probably his own domain, while his predecessor was still reigning at Angkor. It stands in a courtyard at the end of a series of shrine-rooms, known as the Great Temple (Prâsâd Thom), now a total ruin immersed in jungle. (Photograph by Martin Polkinghorne.)

front of them, the whole being enclosed by a high stone wall. There is broken-down *gopura* on the eastern side, and one enters the compound by climbing through a breach in the wall. The whole compound is in a ruinous condition overgrown with briars and brushwood and fallen masonry. The front of the central shrine has collapsed.

With a local man as guide we found our way to Prâsâd Pir Chan ('Two-storey Temple'), placed not far from the SW corner of the Rahal. This is so named because the central shrine appears to rise up to a second storey. It is also referred to as Prâsâd Dong Kuk according to Lunet de Lajonquière. This consists of a main shrine surrounded by eight smaller ones, set in pairs facing the four directions, with two so-called 'libraries' in front. To the north of the Rahal there is a row of about ten more temples, where we failed to penetrate. The best overall description of the whole site is that of Lunet de Lajonquière, who notes that the main characteristic of the structures at Koh Ker is a tendency to enlarge many of the main rooms and the corridors. Elsewhere the width of such structures is limited by the use of corbelled archways, since the Khmers never mastered the art of constructing a true arch in stone. Thus in order to gain extra width they had to construct upper sections in wood fixed into raised pinions. The larger scale of the buildings also results sometimes in sculptured pieces of larger size than was usual. As an unusually massive example one may refer to the image (2.78 metres in height) of the two monkey-kings in combat, which was retrieved from Prâsâd Chen and is now in the Phnom Penh Museum

Except for the pyramid and its surroundings and the one temple of Neang Khmau, much of the rest is in an advanced state of dilapidation, while it is difficult to investigate the individual buildings because of the dangerous condition of the terrain and of the buildings themselves. Thus a determined effort must be made to clear these sites, before any serious up-to-date study can be made. It would seem altogether premature to encourage tourists to come here. The intrepid French travellers who visited these sites in the second half of the 19th century and the first half of the 20th, on whose plans and drawings we still depend, came with French government support and labour forces who could clear the way, thus enabling them to produce useful reports. But since the 1950s the jungle has taken over again, while the buildings have suffered from looting by local army troops.

Important temples on the Khorat Plateau including Phnom Rung (continued under Sûryavarman I)

Jayavarman IV interested himself in further extensions to Preah Vihear, and he appears to have extended his influence well to the north of the Dangrek Range. Two of the earliest temples on the Khorat Plateau (nowadays within easy reach of the modern city of Nakhon Ratchasima (*alias* Khorat) are Prâsâd Non Ku and Prâsâd Muang Khaek, some thirty kilometres to the west of Khorat.

Of Non Ku only the massive stone base and five empty stone doorways stand void to the sky.[3] Muang Khaek is a more extensive site of which the layout of the temple can be more easily envisaged. Here too only the stone doorways are standing. Both temples were built of brick, and thus all too easily dismantled for local use when Khmer authority no longer prevailed here. Some fine lintels have been retrieved from the Muang Khaek site, now in the Phimai Museum.[4] The bare appearance of these temples might suggest that they did not arouse the interest of later monarchs, but this is probably not true. The presence of the *dharmasâla* (rest-house) of Muang Kao in the same areas (see Chapter 5) surely proves that the Khmers were still interested in this region in the 12th to 13th centuries. Certainly Phnom Wan, some ten kilometres north of Khorat, had a long and interesting history. It was probably founded on an earlier Mon site during the late 9th century and was developed further during the 11th century, when we shall refer to it again below.[5]

Likewise Phnom Rung, some 140 kilometres by road to the south-east of Khorat, remained an important Khmer stronghold from its foundation in the early 10th century until well into the 11th and 12th centuries. This area was presumably already a small Khmer state or petty-kingdom contemporary with Jayavarman II's foundation of his capital city at Hariharâlaya (Ruluos) at the beginning of the 9th century and the suzerainty of the Angkor region was probably acknowledged from the very foundation of this capital city. Such an isolated hilltop, rising to 383 metres, with a superb view of the surrounding plain, would certainly have invited early interest in the site, as in the case of Preah Vihear. Both Phnom Rung and later Prâsâd Phimai were associated with the local ruling family, the Mahîdharapura line, which occupied the throne at Angkor on some three occasions (see p. 121 below). Phnom Rung, known with certainty from the 10th century onwards, was embellished by a local ruler, named Narendrâditya,

72. Neang Khmau, one of the more accessible stone temples at Koh Ker. (Photograph by Martin Polkinghorn.)

who like Virendrâdhipativarman of Phimai, was one of the major supporters of Sûryavarman II. According to an inscription set up by his son in 1150, he received local suzerainty as a result of the armed support that he had given to his sovereign. He followed Brahmanical tradition, ending his life as a Hindu ascetic, and Phnom Rung, like the majority of important Khmer temples, was dedicated to Śiva.[6] Phnom Rung can never have been the centre of a city like Phimai, but this function was doubtless performed by the temple of Muang Tam at the foot of the hill, likewise dedicated to Śiva. In the absence of inscriptions, it is usually dated to the 11th century by the style of the carvings on its lintels.

Jayavarman IV died in 942 and was succeeded by his son Harṣavarman II, who was deposed a few years later. Thus one may calculate that this city of Chok Gargyar can have served as the capital for some twenty-three years at most, while all the time building work must have been in progress. However it may well have served subsequently as a provincial capital. An inscription dated 1001, possibly at the very beginning of the reign of Udayâdityavarman, confirms the privileges of the staff and the workers attached to Prâsâd Thom.

The rebuilding of Yaśodharapura by Râjendravarman II.

The death of Harṣavarman II brought to the throne King Râjendravarman (944-968), a nephew of Yaśovarman and therefore a cousin of his predecessor, who had ruled from Koh Ker. He was also prince of Bhavapura, a kingdom that goes back to the time of Funan (see p. 23). His ascension to the throne put an end to the short-lived capital of Koh Ker. He receives lavish but brief praise in the inscription from Baksei Chamkrong, where it may be recalled (from the end of Chapter 3) that he set up a gold image of Śiva in 948. He receives even more lavish and very lengthy praise (no less than 253 Sanskrit verses) in an inscription from the pyramid-temple,

73. Non Ku. This is one of two temples, the other being Muang Khaek, both built of stone foundations with stone door-posts and lintels, but otherwise of brick, which can be seen in this rather denuded condition on the Khorat Plateau. They are situated about 35 kilometres west of Khorat (Nakhon Ratchasima) in the Sung Noen district. They have been dated to the early 10th century, but might well be earlier than this. I draw attention to another Khmer temple, illustrated above (Plate 11, p. 9) which lies only about 20 kilometres from Khorat. Here no evidence from inscriptions is available, but Phnom Wan, even closer to Khorat (see below) was certainly in existence by the end of the 9th century.

known as Pre Rup, where he established a Devarâja, known as *Râjendrabhadreśvara*, in 861 with images of Śiva, Umâ and Vishnu. This inscription also gives his genealogy and lists several of his other religious foundations, especially the rebuilding of Yaśodharapura and his other great foundation, namely the Mebon, founded in 952 on an island in the centre of the Yaśodharataṭâka (the East Baray).[7] I quote verses 268 to 275 from the long inscription as an example of the many literary allusions involved. An obtuse reference to Mahâyâna Buddhist doctrine is also worthy of note.

To the divine sanctuaries (literally: the gods) set up by his predecessors, Indravarman, Yaśovarman and their successors, he confirmed the sacrificial arrangements instituted by these kings.

In the Yaśodharataṭâka constructed by King Yaśovarman he made manifest a sacred work (the Mebon) such as unseen (before).

In so far as this moon-like king in the splendour of his estate has made gifts at the Bhadreśvara shrine (Wat Phu), so one rejoices at the way his increase puts to shame the gradual decrease of the moon.

Having overcome the king of Champa by the force of his arms, he gave the wealth of this king to (the temple of) Vishnu, the Self-Existent, on the banks of the Vishnupadi River (? the Mekong) as though to give full meaning to the name of 'Lord of Champa' (= Çampeśvara. *the Vishnu image of this particular shrine).*

*He ordered triple portals in gold together with (other) lavish gifts for the river where a resting place (*âspada*) has been constructed on the banks of the Sîtânadi, so that in accordance with its name it should make a threefold passage.*

(Sîtânadi, the River of Sîtâ, the wife of Râma who is also identified with Lakṣmî, spouse of Vishnu, was presumably regarded as a sacred river like the Ganges, and at this point where some form of resting place had been built, it was seen as threefold probably because of the entry of a subsidiary stream, and presumably popularly named accordingly. One may compare Çaturmukha, 'Four Mouths', as the local name of the site of Phnom Penh, where the Mekong, the Bassac and the Tonle Sap, all meet as an apparent four streams of water.)

Having rebuilt the city of Yaśodharapura scarcely visible (because of so many years of neglect) he filled it with meritorious works and with pleasurable places, just as the son of Satyavatî (Vyâsa) endowed the literature of India (literally: Bharat compendium) with the Threefold Veda.

In accordance with the prayer of King Yaśovarman (that the city he founded should not be abandoned) which had become empty of meaning like (the concept of) Consciousness according to Yogaçâra doctrine, by (this king) raised high in elevation, it has been given its full meaning once more just as (the essential void of consciousness is replete with) the Triad (of Buddha, Doctrine and Community).

(The Absolute according to Yogaçâra teachings is defined as Pure Thought or Pure Consciousness. The Madhyamaka (Middle Way) school argued that all such concepts were empty of meaning in absolute terms. However whichever of these two philosophical schools might be preferred in Buddhist Mahâyâna communities no one disputed that the substance of Buddhist religion was the triad of the Buddha, the doctrine which he had taught, and the religious community which he had founded.)

As his chief priest (*purohita*) Râjendravarman chose Âtmaśiva, the nephew of Îśânamûrti who had served under his predecessor Harṣavarman II, and thus came from Koh Ker. However soon the king reverted to the traditional line stemming from Praṇavâtman who had served under Indravarman, followed by Śikhâśiva under Yaśovarman, and now Śankara, grand-nephew of Śikhâśiva, who became *hotar* (sacrificial priest) and may have effectively replaced Âtmaśiva but without the title of *purohita.* As has been noted above, these priestly families often intermarried with the royal family, were proliferating all the time, thus providing the rulers with an ever wider choice of religious dignitaries and ministers. One of his ministers was a Buddhist prelate named Kavîndrârimathana (translatable as 'Lordly Poet, Subduer of the Enemy'), who was responsible for the building of the Mebon and also a royal palace. (See p. 74.)

Two more pyramid-temples

The elegant temple-pyramid, known popularly as the East Mebon (to distinguish it from the West Mebon, built a century later) now stands high and dry. Built of mainly laterite and brick with the upper storey in sandstone, it has the regular pattern of a maṇḍala, open to the four quarters with a central shrine raised on a platform above the four surrounding shrines on the summit terrace. This in turn is raised on two lower square terraces, on the corners of which stand stone elephants. The central shrine and the four surrounding ones on the upper platform are all of brick, as are the eight small shrines (representing the eight manifestations of Śiva) on the platform below. A new feature perhaps is the covered gallery that goes around the inner enclosure, built of laterite like the rest of the main structure. The summit shrine contained the Royal *linga, Râjendreśvara,* presumably once again a newly consecrated *linga,* while among other divinities once present were Śiva and Parvatî, who represented his own divinized parents.

His other great temple, known popularity as Pre Rup, is some three kilometres due south of the East Mebon, half way along the bank of the now non-existent Eastern Baray. Although more massive, it resembles so closely its predecessor that a description is scarcely required. It consists of a triple square terrace with the now normal set of five temples on the summit. However, one notes that the upper terraces are deliberately set back towards the western side of the enclosure in order to give greater prominence to the eastern side. Moreover, an unusual feature is the row of tower-like shrines erected immediately inside the outer enclosure on the east side, intended as three to each side of the eastern entrance, although one was never finished. They are seemingly a useless addition as they spoil the symmetry of the whole maṇḍala design. On this occasion the Royal *linga* was known as *Râjendrabhadreśvara* (Royal Lord Bhadreśvara), As for the shrines in the other four corners, two contained images of Śiva representing the king himself and his predecessor Harṣavarman II, the third an image of Vishnu representing a legendary Brahman Viśvarûpa, whom the king claimed as an ancestor, the fourth an image of Umâ, representing his aunt Jayadevî, wife of Jayavarman IV.

He probably also began work on two subsidiary shrine-like palaces, all built of sandstone, the purpose of which one can only guess. They comprise a main hall forty-five metres in length, east to west with large windows and with anterooms at both ends. Early French investigators referred to them as '*kléang*' (= store-rooms) and this nickname has continued in use, although it is inconceivable that this was the purpose of these elegantly built structures. Maurice Glaize in his *Guide to Angkor* suggests that they may have been intended for royal guests. Like the other main buildings of Jayavarman V, they were completed during the early 11th century under Sûryavarman I. They stand well back on the right side of the road as one passes the palace grounds behind the row of towers known as the Suor Prat (see below), which may have been built about the same time, although they have been dated rather later.[8]

Compared with Angkor as it developed under later kings and especially Jayavarman VII, the Yaśodharapura of Râjendravarman must have appeared rather sparse so far as the major brick and stone-built temples were concerned. The impressive Phnom Bakheng surrounded by its moat and ramparts, forming a rectangle of 440 by 650 metres, clearly remained the centre of the city. Of buildings within this space the only one which remains intact is the Baksei Chamkrong on the northern side. The palace grounds lay further to the north beyond the northern ramparts, but it was not until the reign of his successor, Jayavarman V, that the great palace temple, the Phimean-âkas (the Aerial Palace) was built. To the north-east lay the expanse of the Yaśovarman's great artificial lake (Yaśodharataṭâka), with the pyramid temple of Pre Rup on its southern side probably surrounded by the several religious communities which Yaśovarman had founded. In the centre of the lake now stood the pyramid-temple known as the Mebon. Further south of the lake the Kuṭîśvara temple, possibly founded towards the end of the 8th century, now a complete ruin, would have been surrounded by other subsidiary buildings. To the south of this stood the Prâsâd Kravan, founded in the early 10th century. Far to the west of the Bakheng there was the 'Baray Group' of far earlier temples where the Western Baray was later to be built. Now all total ruins, they would have still been in operation in the late 10th century, presumably surrounded by clusters of other more fragile buildings.[9] All in all this capital city of Râjendravarman would have covered much the same area as is usually shown on present-day tourist maps of Angkor, but its centre, the Bakheng, lay well to the west of Jayavarman VII's new capital, which now dominates the scene.

We may possibly attribute to the reign of Râjendravarman the temple of Kuk Nokor near the village of Pong Ro, which is approximately half-way along the main highway from Kampong Thom to Kampong Cham. This is a fine and well preserved example of a temple constructed entirely of laterite except for the sandstone around the eastern entrance. It consists of an elongated sanctuary leading to the main shrine. The eastern *gopura* is massively built, while there is a small false western *gopura.* Thus the only entrance is from the eastern side and the only decorated lintel is the one over the eastern entrance to the sanctuary. There is a small 'library' in the south-east corner of the inner courtyard. On the eastern approach there are two barays.[10]

74. Pre Rup. Râjendravarman who restored Yaśodharapura (Angkor) as the capital city, built two pyramid-temples, one known as Pre Rup about half way along the southern side of the East Baray, and another known as East Mebon on an island which he had constructed in the middle of the lake. They are similar in design and for further details refer to the text.

75. East Mebon, façade of main shrine. Śiva on his bull Nandin surmounts the canopy with the conventional floral hangings.

76. Angkor Thom. The kléang, *probably intended as palaces for guests. A doorway on the eastern side, south end, looking through to the royal terrace.*

77. Sour Prat. One of a row of laterite towers, which stand in front of the kléang. *There is no satisfactory suggestion concerning their purpose.*

A rare Buddhist temple

Amidst this extensive range of Brahmanical temples, built at various times since the 7th century, Râjendravarman gave support to the building of the first Buddhist temple at Angkor which has survived intact to this day, namely Bat Chum. The founder was the Buddhist prelate Kâvîndrârimathana, who had served the king by building a palace and the Mebon, as already mentioned above. It is a modest building consisting of a row of three brick-built shrines of the typical Khmer pattern with brick tiered roofs, much overgrown with lichen. Two of the lintels have survived and there are traces of decorative motifs still visible on the central tower, which is slightly higher than the other two. They stand on a low laterite platform ascended by a small flight of steps, protected by two pairs of stone lions, easily reached along a small road between paddy-fields, which leads off to the right from the 'Outer Circuit' between Kravan and Sra Srang. Inscriptions on the doorways of the three towers tell us that they contained respectively images of Buddha, flanked by Vajrapâṇi and Prajñâpâramitâ ('Goddess Perfection of Wisdom'). They also provide information not only concerning this learned Buddhist who won the king's favour, but also give interesting and perhaps rather surprising information concerning the purpose of this Buddhist foundation.[11]

The three inscriptions in elegant Sanskrit verse—there is also one in Khmer—contain the same subject matter with slight variations as written by three Buddhist scholars, known as Srî Indrapaṇḍita (author of inscription A as now edited in the article referred to below), Vâp Râmabhagavat (B) and Śivacyuta- (name incomplete – C). As these texts help to reveal the relationship of Buddhism to Śaivism, as the generally established religion of the Angkor monarchs, it seems worthwhile to quote them at

78. Kuk Nokor. This most unusual temple, far from Angkor and about halfway between Kampong Thom and Kampong Cham, is built throughout of laterite except for the door-posts and lintels. The gopura *on the eastern side leads into a courtyard, containing the usual antechamber connected direct to the central shrine with its massive tower. The western* gopura, *built on the same pattern as the eastern one, is a false one in that it is built solid. The photograph is taken from the west. The only doorway is the one leading straight into the antechamber from the east, and here there is the one and only lintel, showing Indra on his three-headed elephant with the usual canopy and hangings. In the absence of any inscription nothing more precise can be known of the origins of this temple.*

79. Bat Chum. This is the only surviving Buddhist temple built at Angkor before the reign of Jayavarman VII.

80. Bat Chum. The best preserved of its lintels, a floral design surmounted by a small kâla-*mask.*

some length.

Text A opens with brief invocations to the Buddha, Lokeśvara and Vajrapâṇi, while B and C open with equally brief invocations to the Buddha, Vajrapâṇi and Prajñâpâramitâ (the Goddess Perfection of Wisdom), whose images, as we learn later in all three inscriptions, reposed in the three shrines. These invocations are followed in all cases by long exaggerated praises of the reigning monarch Râjendravarman, but also providing some factual information:

> *Just as Kuśa (son of Râma and Sîtâ) has done for Ayodhyâ, he restored the holy city of Yaśodharapurî which had remained empty for a long time, rendering it magnificent and beautiful with buildings of brilliant gold and palaces of gems like the palace of great Indra on earth. In the centre of the ocean, the sacred lake of Yaśodhara, he erected images of Brahmâ, Śiva and Vishnu as well as a* linga (A: vv. 13-14, B: v. 20 and C: v. 25).

The praises of the ruling monarch (*sine qua non*) are followed by those of Kavîndrârimathana himself, although only text C specifies that he was personally responsible for the various works mentioned above:

> *With no other concern apart from the Buddhist doctrine and although foremost amongst fellow-Buddhists, he was attached in his devotion to his king, the 'Supreme Lord'* (Parameśvara = *Śiva). Beloved of this Lord of Men, an architect like Viśvakarman (the divine architect), he was entrusted by the King to build a beautiful palace in Yaśodharapura, and by general approbation he was enjoined to create (an island of) rock and other constructions in the middle of the Yaśodhara Lake* (C: vv. 33-35).

Text B adds rather more specific details concerning his Buddhist benefactions, especially at Bat Chum itself:

> *Having united the identity of his own self with the divine self-nature of the Buddha, he acquired Yogic Knowledge* (yogijñâna) *as inherent within his own mind. Triumphantly he erected at Jayantadeśa an image of the Buddha and at Kuṭîśvara a Buddha-image flanked by two goddesses. Having erected these several shines he offered them as temples for the divinity to dwell there, just as in the lotus of his own heart* (vv. 30-32).

(I note that he set up Buddhist images at Kuṭîśvara (Angkor), known to be a Brahmanical site, where Śivâcarya, who served under Râjendravarman's successor, later set up images of Brahmâ and Vishnu. But it seems clear from a few lines in Khmer at the end of Text A that Kavîndrârimathana was already associated with a Buddhist community which existed at Kuṭîśvara quite apart from the known Brahmanical one. See Coedès, 'Inscriptions de Bat Chum', p. 229 for the transliterated text, Aymonier, *Le Cambodge*,

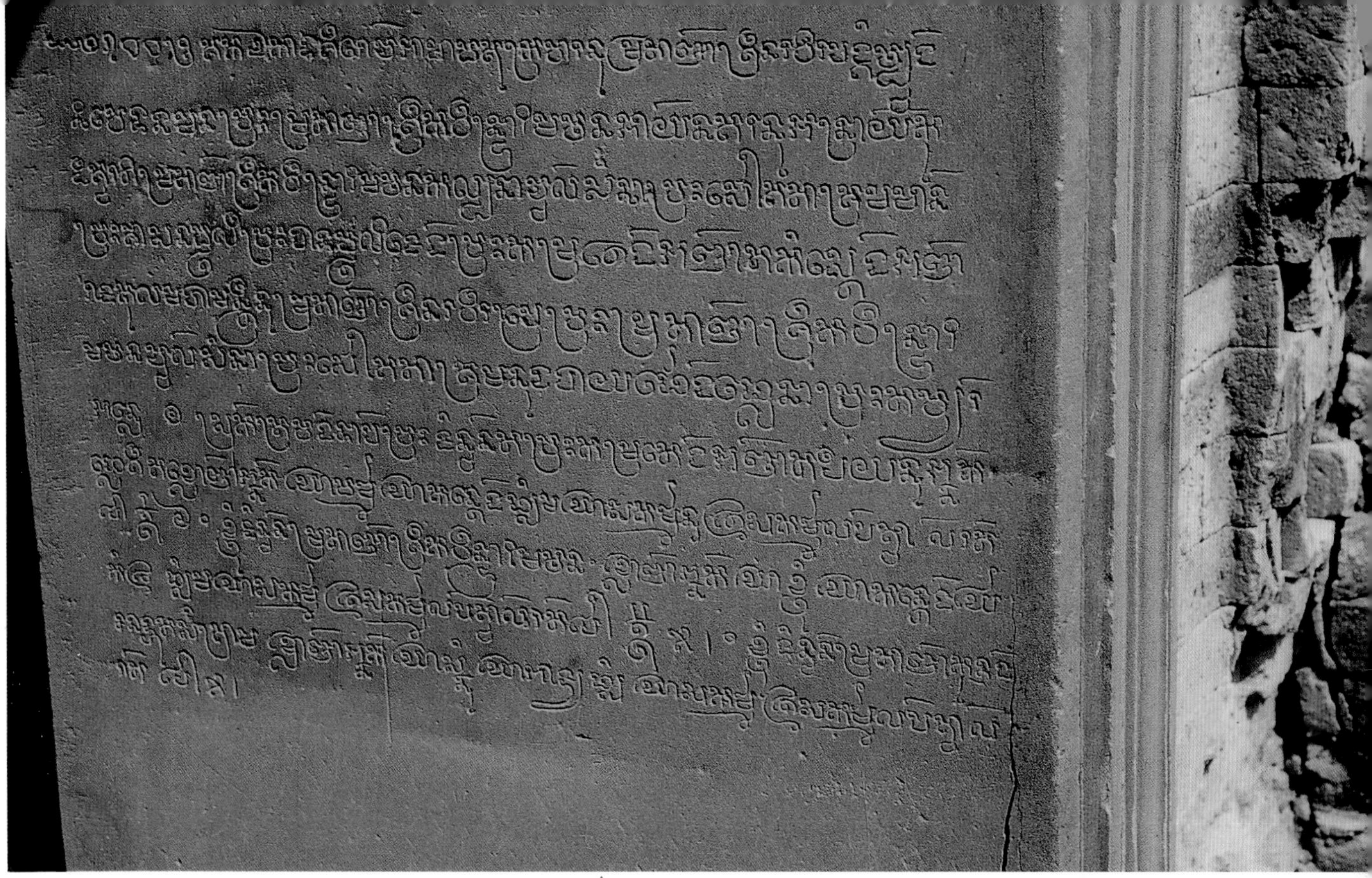

81. Bat Chum. A section of the inscription as inscribed on the lower left door-post of the southern shrine. This is the end of Inscription A, as described in the text. It is inserted as an example of the elegance of the Khmer classical script, as used for writing Sanskrit or (in this case) Khmer.

III, pp.13-14 for a suggested translation, and the section of text as illustrated. Briefly we are told that in Śaka 882 (960 AD) the King was informed of Kavîndrârimathana's beneficence at Kuṭîśvara and Bat Chum and so he himself made donations in order to ensure the revenues of both these Buddhist sites.)

> *Furthermore this ordinance of which the King in his divine palace is informed, must be carried out by wise and good men. These possessions dedicated to the gods will not be taken by honest people, and may our rulers seize evil men intent on theft! If a single tree which provides shade is not to be cut here, how much less should one cut the timbers which provide contentment for those who seek bliss. Here there dwell monks intent only upon a moral life, their minds preoccupied with the good of others, peaceful in their meditation* (C: vv. 33-37).

The rather surprising verses which follow and bring the inscription to an end are more or less the same in all three inscriptions:

> A: v.21:
> *With the exception of the sacrificial priests (*hotar*), the highest among Brahmans, no one may bathe here in this water which comes from a bathing-place on the summit of the holy mountain of Śrî Mahendragiri (Phnom Kulen); the sanctified water of this holy pool procures great merit although there is little of it.*
>
> B: v. 38:
> *With the exception of a Brahman who knows the Veda no one may bathe in the pure water of this great pool which has been dug ritually.*
>
> C: vv. 38-41:
> *(Kavîndrârimathana) has constructed this pool, which purifies with its pure water just as knowledge leads to nirvâṇa. In accordance with Buddhist ritual he has created this pool, honoured by the great and intended to bring joy to living beings, while contributing to the prosperity of the Dharma. In the sacred water of this lake, worthy of the frolics of flamingos, only the King's chief prelate (*purohita*) and Brahmans have the right to bathe. Elephants which destroy the banks of this pool must be kept away by the lion-like* sâdhus *(holy men) with the hair-style of the Dharma (presumably meaning the shaven-headed monks who live in this monastery).*

Text A ends with a further warning against those who might rob this place. It would seem that the inscriptions are primarily concerned with the dedication of the pool, which can only be used by Brahmans, and of which this small community of Buddhist monks were the appointed keepers. Other inferences will be noted below with reference to another such inscription.

The reign of Jayavarman V and the founding of Bantây Srei

Râjendravarman's reign passed peacefully into that of his son, Jayavarman V (968-1001). Towards the end of his father's reign a far better known and better endowed temple was built on the outskirts of Angkor, named popularly as Bantây Srei, presumably with reference to the many images of celestial maidens (*apsara*) inset into the walls. It was founded by the *Brah Guru* (Holy Teacher) Yajñavarâha and his brother Vishnukumâra and probably completed by 967, but the foundation stone is dated a year later, thus during the first year of the reign of Jayavarman V (968-1001).[12] It is dedicated to a *Śiva-linga* called 'Lord of the Threefold World' (*Tribhuvaneśvara*) in the central sanctuary and to Vishnu and Śiva in the side shrines.[13]

The central enclosure is set within a square courtyard, approached by an avenue, now void except for fallen boundary-stones. It is from here that one enjoys the finest view of the whole complex set against the trees of the surrounding forest. The general design is conventional in that it consists of three principal shrines on a raised terrace, enclosed in a square inner enclosure, while to the left and the right as one enters this enclosure are two subsidiary buildings, conventionally referred to as libraries. However, in front of the central shrine which is minute, there is a form of antechamber as often seen in Indian temples, and this creates perhaps an impression of over-crowding. The charm of the whole temple consists in its miniature size, the rose-coloured sandstone out of which the whole complex is constructed, the elaborately worked tiered roofs of the main shrines, and the finely worked floral decoration, which covers the walls, thus framing the deeply incised figures of apsaras and guardians. The lintels and frontal pieces (*toraṇa*), all depicting Indian mythological scenes, are exceptionally fine. One may note especially that of Râvaṇa, the evil king of Lanka, attempting vainly to overthrow the sacred Mountain Kailâsa, on which Śiva and Parvatî repose unconcerned, or another of Kâma, the god of love, in the act of shooting an arrow at Śiva, in order to disturb his meditation, while Parvatî stands by, rosary in hand, or again of the two monkey-brothers, Sugrîva and Vâlin, or of the goddess Mahîṣâsuramardinî, the Destroyer of the Buffalo-Demon. Perhaps specially noteworthy is that of Krishna killing his wicked uncle Kamṣa, depicted in a palace built of wood, thus giving some idea of the many buildings of less substantial materials which once surrounded the surviving ones of brick or stone.

I quote a few verses from one of the inscriptions relating to this temple, namely the opening

82. Bantây Srei. View from the east, taken from within the existing outer enclosure.

83. Bantây Srei. Toraṇa showing Krishna killing his wicked uncle Kamṣa.

84. Bantây Srei. Another showing Śiva and Umâ on Kailâsa with a defeated Râvana below. (Photograph by Suthep Kritsanuvarin.).

verses of the homage paid to the divinity, followed by those in praise of the two founder-brothers.

Homage to Śiva whose attribute is the resonance (of religion),
Which is beyond the power of perception and like space embraces all existence.

May the Śakti, daughter of the mountains, his ardent and faithful spouse,*
Contribute to the happiness of living beings.

(*Açalâtmajâ as here, or Himasutâ of the same meaning = Parvatî. She is in fact the mountain nymph Aparṇâ)

Descendent of the 'sanâtana tree' lineage of the resplendent Kambuja line,*
Śrî Jayavarman is the son of Srî Râjendravarman.

(*The santâna tree, symbol of longevity, is one of the trees of paradise.)

Sunk in the deep and terrible flood of the evils of time,
His subjects, having gained this high bank, draw breath again.

(His praises continue for seven more verses.)

This king of kings whose brilliance equals that of the king of the gods
Has a guru who sustains him doctrinally according to Śaivite ritual.

Son of the daughter of King Harṣavarman, the son of Yaśovarman
And grandson of Indravarman, he is one of high rank.

He is the offspring of the sage, who is expert in the Rig Veda,
Equal in knowledge and rank with the foremost of purohitas.

Confronted with the majesty (of the king), his learning already naturally lucid,
he achieved an extraordinary brilliance like the rays of the sun in a mirror.

With devotion he offered daily a garland of eight flowers to Śiva,
Making oblations on the sacrificial fire and

85. *Bantây Srei. Another showing Kâma (god of love) trying to distract Śiva by shooting an arrow of flowers.*

performing regular meditation.

Every month at the four quarters of the moon he made Brahmans recipients
Of golden articles, of clothing and of cows with full udders.

King Jayavarman who was always by his side honoured him
With parasols of peacock feathers, golden palaquins and other favours.

Together with those who encourage popular learning and so on
He undermined the foolish ideas of the simple-minded.

He was foremost in the doctrines of Patañjali, of Kanada, of Akṣapada, of Kapila, of Buddha, also in medicine, music and astronomy.

(Thus he was master in all the main Indian philosophical schools: Yoga, Vaiśeṣika, Nyâya and Sâmkhya, as well of in the Buddhist Yogaçâra school.)

The wretched, the abandoned, the blind, the feeble, children and old folk,
those sick and other unfortunates, desiring to cross the ocean of sufferings, daily filled his house.

With his literary works and his good actions he aroused the yearning
Of scholars and good men who live in various other lands (lit. continents).

In general assemblies even his enemies, under the influence of his good actions, feel a desire to be fair-minded and so find their tongues led to utter sincere praise.

He founded at Lingapura (Wat Phu) and other places many Śiva-lingas
Together with statues, religious retreats and pools.

This Yajñavarâha who surpassed all the sciences has a brother,
named Vishnukumâra, the last born of the same mother.

His knowledge grew as his mouth, like a blossoming lotus-flower, absorbed continually the ambrosiac light of the moon representing the mouth of his teacher.

All the treatises, beginning with those of grammar, all the arts and the the Śaivite yoga of his teacher,
he obtained from his elder brother.

These verses serve to emphasize the vast difference between the wealth, culture and literary accomplishments of the aristocratic class and the simple life of the common people, many of whom appear to be in desperate need of the generosity of one such as Vajravâraha. He was the personal guru of Jayavarman V, while Âtmaśiva, *purohita* under the two previous kings, continued in this position. He was later succeeded by Nâṛâyana (of the family of Praṇavâtman) who had earlier served as *hotar*. On his death he was succeeded as *hotar* by his nephew Śivâcârya, who also was a direct descendent of the priestly family of Śivakaivalya, the *purohita* of Jayavarman II in the early 9th century. On the death of Âtmaśiva, Śivâcârya became *purohita* to Jayavarman V, and became one of the most renowned of these royal religious ministers. Even if such details become tedious to the reader, it is important to emphasize the significant part played by these great functionaries in the affairs of state. We have already noticed that a Buddhist prelate, namely Kavîndrârimathana served as a kind of 'minister of works' and later he appears to have been succeeded by another Buddhist prelate, namely Kîrtipaṇḍita (see below).

More Brahmanical foundations

During his reign several other temples were founded of which little now remains apart from their inscriptions. Thus we must surely mention Preah Einkosi in Siem Reap, where the ruins now stand on the site of the present Theravâda monastery. It was founded in 968 by an Indian Brahman named Divâkarabhaṇḍa who had married the younger sister of Jayavarman V, the princess Indralakṣmî. He founded in 972 another temple known as Prâsâd Kompus in Khum Yâng (Mlu Prei) about sixteen kilometres south of Phnom Sandak and sixteen north-west of Koh Ker.[14] In addition to founding the magnificent temple of Bantây Srei, Vajñavarâha founded two other small temples at Sek Ta Tuy and Trapang Khyang,[15] near Phnom Sandak, both dedicated to Śiva as 'Lord of the Threefold World', as at Bantây Srei. It may be recalled that this was the name given to the massive *linga* set up by Jayavarman IV at Koh Ker. It should be mentioned also that during the reign of Jayavarman V further improvements were made to the great temple of Preah Vihear.

Meanwhile work was begun on two major projects, the building of yet another pyramid-temple (Ta Keo) and also of a second pyramid-temple (or possibly the reconstruction of an already existing temple) in the palace grounds, known correctly as Phimean-âkas, this being the regular Khmer pronunciation of Sanskrit *Vimâna-âkâśa,* meaning 'Aerial Palace'. The palace grounds measure 250 by 600 metres, and the only building still standing is this 'Aerial Palace'. It consists of a series of three steeply rising square terraces, the lower one in laterite and the higher ones in sandstone, on the summit of which stood originally a group of five shrines in the form of a cross-shaped tower, built of laterite and sandstone. Of these very little remains, but much of the surrounding covered gallery, such as we noted before on the East Mebon, can still be seen. It measures thirty-five by twenty-eight metres at its base and is thus rectangular in shape; except for this it resembles in its extraordinary steepness Jayavarman IV's great pyramid-temple at Koh Ker.

Viewed directly from the front, the east side, I find Ta Keo remarkably similar in appearance. It rises up as a steep three-terraced pyramid of sandstone, surmounted by the usual five summit shrines, also built of sandstone and rather box-like in their present forlorn condition. One notes that all these five summit shrines are open to all the four directions, and that every one of them has attached antechambers to each of its four sides. In the case of the central shrine, as usual appreciably larger than the others, these antechambers have a double structure. It is impressive, but perhaps massively

86. The ruins of Einkosi (Siem Reap) in the later monastery of that same name.

87. Phimean-âkas or 'Aerial Palace', the only building which still stands within the palace-grounds, 600 by 250 metres, the royal palace and other buildings being of more fragile materials.

ugly in its present denuded condition. Neither of these great works was finished during Jayavarman V's reign because of disputes regarding the succession and consequent internal wars.

A renowned Buddhist prelate and his religious foundations

It is interesting to note that this monarch also looked with favour upon a certain Buddhist prelate named Kîrtipaṇḍita, who appears to have served him at court and was responsible for quite a number of Buddhist foundations. The evidence for this derives from a stone inscription at Vat Sithor in the province of Kampong Cham.[16] After fulsome praises of the Buddha, manifest in his Self-Existent Body (*dharmakâya*), his Glorious Body (*sambhogakâya*) and his Transformation Body (*nirmâṇakâya*), followed by that of the Doctrine (*Dharma*) and of the Community *(Sangha),* conceived in Mahâyâna terms as the assembly of Bodhisattvas and their disciples, there follows the usual eulogy of the reigning monarch (Jayavarman V), where the date of Śaka 890 (AD 968) is given as the commencement of his reign. One may note that in verse forty-nine of the inscription the earlier date of Śaka 869 (AD 947) is given as referring to Kîrtipaṇḍita's major foundation at a place-name of which the first syllable is missing. This doubtless refers to Vat Sithor itself, which this great Buddhist prelate must have founded during the reign of the previous king Râjendravarman. Of primary interest however is the account of Kîrtipaṇḍita's person and of manifold activities.

Verse 27 onwards:

In him the sun of the doctrines of 'Non-Self' (nairâtmya)*, 'Mind Only'* (çittamâtra) *and the like, which have been eclipsed in the night of false teachings, shone once again in full daylight.*

On the path of the Holy Dharma he relit the torch of the 'Discourse on discrimination between the middle and the extremes' (Madyântavibhâga) *and other treatises which had been extinguished by evil winds.*

Having sought for a host of philosophical books and treatises, such as the commentary on the 'Compendium of Truth' (Tattvasamgraha)*, this sage spread wide their study.*[17]

Verse 36 onwards:

Loaded with honours by the king on account of his zeal for the protection of the circle of the realm, he was responsible for the performance within the palace of the rites of pacification, prosperity and so on.[18] *In order to save fellow-Buddhists from misfortune, he re-established the image of the Muni (Teacher, viz. Lord Buddha) fashioned with devotion, of which the throne had been broken. He provided joyously an entry-portal, enriched with gold and silver for the image of the Muni.*

In order to gain for himself as well as for others the supreme and incomparable Way of salvation, he offered the Lord Buddha two royal palanquins of gold and of silver. As residence for the Lord he dedicated a large shrine with a tiered roof of copper, adorned with gold and precious stones as well as a lion-throne. In order to gain the fruits of merit for others in the excellent field of merit, he dedicated to the Lord paddy-fields producing 4,000 khâri *(an uncertain measure of weight).*

Having established the doctrine in its normal and its hidden form, he provided religious retreats for monks and for religious laymen. He offered to the Buddha male and female elephants, horses, buffaloes and cows in great number, as well as ashrams, treasures and serving personnel, male and female.

He erected in this place for the illumination of the lineage of the Omniscient One an image of the all-saving Perfection of Wisdom, the Mother of all-saving Buddhas. He erected more than ten images of Vajrapâṇi (Vajrin) and Avalokiteśvara (Lokeśa), which had been previously consecrated on a hilltop by Śrî Satyavarman, and whose thrones were broken. On a high summit in the town of Kurârambha, also at Amarendrapura and other places, he set up images of Avalokiteśvara and so on. Having restored in great numbers in various places the images of the Buddha which had been broken, he set them up anew and installed pools and ashrams. In the year Śaka 869 (AD 947) this teacher of men, accompanied by his disciples, founded on his own initiative shrines with innumerable images of the Lord in the village of (?Dha)rmapattana for his own benefit and that of others (vv. 36-49).

As for the regulation of monastic life, it was ordained that a monthly festival be held in accordance with the twelve 'lunar mansions' (*nakṣatra*).

Verse 56 onwards:

Also in accordance with an ancient order of the Great Muni the monastery gong, placed to the south-east side of the complex, should be sounded thrice daily. Those who are attentive, even by mental reflection, to its sound, which has a purifying effect in that it announces the times for monastic ceremonies, these are the happy ones who make their way towards

88. Ta Keo. This other pyramid-temple built by Jayavarman V resembles the Phimean-âkas in its general aspect, but the summit-dispositions are rather different, as described in the text. Neither was completed during his reign.

> *heaven. May he gain great merit, who thus founds a monastery (*vihâra*) for the good of others, offering it to the Three Precious Ones!*
>
> *All the bounty intended for the Three Precious Ones should be assigned separately in three parts, and not all mixed together.*

(Presumably this means one part for the Buddha (viz. the cult of the images), one part for the Doctrine (viz. for study and copying of manuscripts) and one part for the Community (viz. the monks themselves).)

> *Unless a monastery has been properly consecrated by the monks, it is no monastery, but just a treasury* (koṣṭhâgara). *Such a foundation is made for material interests, but not for the benefit of others and for the sake of religious calm. In such a place there is no pure merit where omniscience can be obtained. Where a monastery has been founded according to the proper rule, the merit spreads everywhere at once just like space itself.*
>
> *May those evil men who destroy such merit, experience endlessly the sufferings of hell! The layfolk shall not use for their own profit the property of the monastery. This would be poison for them. Spells may cure (normal) poison, but not that deriving from (the misappropriation of) monastic property.*
>
> *Having completed with devotion this command of the Omniscient Lord, viz. the founding of this monastery in accordance with the rule, the self-controlled ones (monks) settled there permanently. The virtuous, the peaceful and the learned are superior to ordinary folk, and whoever desires merit, assigns various goods for their benefit.*
>
> *At dawn and at other proper hours the ceremonies, as ordained by the Lord for the self-controlled (monks), should be performed by the community and especially by the chief officiant. Unless specially assigned, the Buddhist community should not attend (Brahmanical) sacrificial ceremonies. Those who go on their own account, even with good intentions, are guilty of an offence.*
>
> *The prelate (*purohita*) who is expert in the homa rites with their secret hand-gestures (*mudra*), mantra and spells, and who knows the secret of Vajra and Bell, is worthy of his fees* (vv. 56-69).

Buddhism and the Devarâja cult

From these few surviving Buddhist inscriptions, that of the monastery on the shore of the Eastern Baray, that of Bat Chum and now this one from Vat Sithor, one can deduce a few ideas concerning the state of Buddhism in the developing Khmer empire of the 10th and 11th centuries. According to the Bat Cum inscription it would seem that there also was a Buddhist community at Kuṭîśvara, which was favoured by Râjendravarman. Like the numerous Brahmanical foundations, it depended upon the munificence of wealthy prelates who had won the monarch's or some local ruler's favour. The only Buddhist monastery at Angkor established by royal edict is the one founded exceptionally by Yaśovarman together with other Śaivite and Vaiṣṇavite monasteries on the banks of Yaśodharataṭâka, already discussed above. (See Chapter 3: 'The City of Yaśodharpura'.) The inscription from this site and also that of Bat Chum make it quite clear that Buddhism was treated as subservient to Brahmanical religion. At the same time the whole ethos of Buddhism as a monastic religion with its central doctrine of the renunciation of self was diametrically opposed to any notion of royal self-aggrandizement. Although several rulers are known to have had Buddhist sympathies and even some of the leading Brahmans seem to have taken an interest in Buddhist philosophical theories, there probably remained a general antagonism to the Buddhist religion in Brahmanical circles.

Although Bantây Srei in its finely restored condition may seem an exception, there was nothing exceptional in the foundation of temples and shrines by the high Brahmans of the court. Referring back to the Sdok Kak Thom inscription (see above), one notes that all the great prelates from Śivakaivalya in the 9th century to Sadâśiva in the 11th are credited with just such foundations. Two later inscriptions illustrate their continuance into the 12th century, as well the quantities of honours and gifts which were bestowed upon their chosen Brahman priests by Khmer monarchs.[19] But of a whole succession of Khmer kings up to the times of Jayavarman VII only an occasional Buddhist prelate of note seems to have won the king's favour and in two cases noted here, it would appear to have been due to architectural and building skills and with no direct relevance to religion. One certainly has the impression that Buddhism remains on the defensive, formally acknowledging that the Śaivite cult of the Devarâja represents the state religion. The inscription relating to the Buddhist community established by King Yaśovarman on the shore of the Indrataṭâka makes its subservience quite explicit. It is also written of Kavîndrârimathana that while having 'no other concern apart from the Buddhist doctrine and although foremost amongst Buddhists, he was attached in his devotion to the King, the Supreme Lord (*Parameśvara* = Śiva)'. Not only were images of the great Hindu gods often set up at Buddhist shrines, but in the case of Bat Chum, the sacred pool was primarily reserved for the use of Brahmanical prelates. This certainly does not represent an amalgamation of Hinduism and Buddhism, such as developed in eastern Java, where kings were formally identified with the great Mahâyâna and tantric Buddhist divinities, and where Buddhist prelates of the highest rank (*vajrâçârya*) eventually assumed the same rank as Brahmans, a situation which still exists in a popularized form in Nepal and in Bali. The inscription praising Sûryavarman I at Preah Khan of Kampong Svay, translated in full below, begins with a lavish invocation to Śiva followed by one to the Buddha, and some take this as an indication of the supposed amalgamation of the two religions. But the author was clearly a practising Buddhist, so why should he start his text with an elaborate invocation to Śiva, if not merely to show the necessary political respect to the dominating cult of the Devarâja?

It seems clear from these various inscriptions that Buddhism persisted in Cambodia as a religion essentially separate and generally hesitant towards Brahmanical religion, although it would have been politically disastrous to express any such hostility overtly. Meanwhile outside the capital city monastic life continued peaceably enough, probably in accordance with the *Vinaya* (monastic discipline) of the *Mûlasarvâstivâdins*, which was the one mainly followed throughout South-East Asia, as is testified by I-tsing.[20] It seems well attested that the favoured philosophical school was that of the Yogaçâra, but this was generally so in all later Mahâyâna Buddhism. I wonder what the author of the inscription has in mind when he states that a monastery that has not been properly consecrated is no more than a 'treasury' (*koṣṭhâgara*). Such is the primary meaning of the Sanskrit term, although it may also mean a storeroom or godown. It may refer to privately endowed Buddhist shrines cared for by one or two monks or religious laymen, and if so this suggests the existence of a more general Buddhist following in the country. Owing to the total lack of any surviving literature, Buddhist or otherwise, apart from the stone inscriptions (very different from the situation in East Java), it is impossible to gain any clear ideas on this subject. We may also note that Kîrtipaṇḍita 'established the Holy Doctrine in its usual (based on the Perfection of Wisdom and the Yogaçâra teachings) and its secret form', which refers to regular monastic establishments as well as the performance of tantric ritual for the gaining of enlightenment in a single lifetime. Within this same context we may note the reference to 'the priest who is expert in the *homa* rites with their secret hand-gestures, mantras and spells and who knows the secret of Vajra and Bell'. The same situation was typical of Tibet in precisely the same period, thus reproducing the forms that Mahâyâna Buddhism had already assumed in northern India. Whereas much is known concerning the part which tantric Buddhism played in Tibet, practically nothing is known of the scope of tantric Buddhism in Cambodia simply because of the total absence of the relevant literature. (For further on this subject, see pp. 172-3.)

One may note also that the range of Mahâyâna divinities, of whom the most popular are certainly Avalokiteśvara (Lokeśa), Vajrapâṇi (Vajrin) and Prajñâ, is very limited indeed compared with northern India and Tibet and even with Java. Buddhism certainly flourished in the occupied territories beyond the Dangrek Range, throughout the Khorat Plateau and westwards towards the Gulf of Siam, where Buddhism was already well established thanks to the Mon populations. However the Devarâja cult seems to have been maintained at the major Khmer temple-fortresses established throughout their occupied territories, the one notable exception being Phimai (see p. 122). However the rapidity with which Theravâda Buddhism spread once the central royal authority was weakened (13th century onwards) suggests that the general population, overtaxed by the seemingly never-ending construction of so many Brahmanical monuments, may well have been more open to the ministrations of the Buddhist communities who existed in their midst.

Sûryavarman I

This powerful king was a usurper who doubtless was resolved to gain the throne in succession to Jayavarman V. Although sons sometimes succeeded fathers, and nephews might succeed uncles, there was no stabilized order of succession. The earlier capitals such as Wat Phu, Bhavapura, Angkor Borei, Îsânapura, Śambhupura, Indrapura, and Aninditapura remained centres of local power, most of whom could claim relationship with one royal line or another, and in the event of any weakness in the centre at Angkor, any of these might make a bid for the throne.

Meanwhile Jayavarman V was succeeded in Angkor in 1001 by a nephew who ruled briefly as Udayâdityavarman I, of whom very little is known. He was suceeded by Jayavîravarman.[21] To this period of historical unceertainty, one may attribute to his reign Bantây Ampil, a temple built of the usual limestone, set within a rectangular courtyard, oriented regularly to the four directions, some forty by thirty metres The southern *gopura* is the best preserved and most of the main tower and the antechamber (*maṇḍapa*) of the central shrine is still standing, as are also two 'libraries' to north and south of the main enclosure. There are traces of a second enclosure with other ruins here and there. This

89. Bantây Ampil. This relatively small temple (inner courtyard about 40 by 30 metres) was founded by a high official in 1002 during the troubled period which led to the accession of Sûryavarman I. It consists of the usual antechamber and shrine with its tower, as well as two subsidiary buildings to north and south, thus following the usual pattern. It stands now on a remote site in the jungle more or less halfway between Damdek and Beng Mealea.

temple has remained for long buried in the jungle and has been only recently (early 2002) partly cleared. It is rather remote, but can be reached by motor-cycle following tracks (and asking the way) to Bhum Sampât (village) in Khum Knar-Por (district). One turns off the Damdek–Beng Mealea road at Po-pel village onto a small track going west. An inscription dated Śaka 924 (=AD 1002) suggests that it was founded or at least largely supported by a high official named Chok Phlâng and others who requested the royal favour for their meritorious work.[22]

Udayâdityavarman I was succeeded in 1003 by a certain Jayavîravarman, but he appears to have been immediately engaged in warfare with Sûryavarman who was approaching the capital from Sambor (Śambhupura). There may possibly have been other claimants. In the inscription from Preah Khan, translated below, he is praised for having

> *seized the kingdom in battle from a king surrounded by other kings.*

Briggs suggests that Sûryavarman came from Tâmbralinga (present-day Nakhon Si Thammarat) on the east coast of southern Thailand.[23] This important maritime state represented more or less the limits of Srîvijaya's claim to suzerainty northwards up the Malay-Thai peninsula and was thus one of the first to assert its independence. Also, thanks to close cultural and religious ties with Ceylon it was in the process of transforming its Hindu-Buddhist heritage into a Buddhist Theravâda one, just as also came about in Cambodia from the 13th century onwards. As the result of the expansionist campaigns of Sûryavarman's reign the rather vague frontier of Khmer occupied territory reached the area around the Gulf of Siam, but had not yet extended so far as to come into contact with the northern limits of Śrîvijaya. All that can be said of certainty concerning Sûryavarman's origins is that he is first mentioned in an inscription from Robang Romeas (NW group, Sambor Prei Kuk in the Kampong Thom region).[24] That he came from the south and that he demonstrated a personal preference for Buddhism seems certain, but that he came from the Thai-Malay peninsula remains doubtful. Since nothing more is heard of the ephemeral Jayavîravarman after 1006, it is assumed that by that date Sûryavarman had occupied Angkor.

An inscription of 1011, repeated eight times and written on the window-and door-posts of the eastern *gopura* of the palace grounds, gives details of an oath of allegiance taken by all those belonging to the *tamvrac,* perhaps best interpreted in the context to mean a corps of personal body-guards. The names of those who committed themselves are arranged as four groups, the different groups listed on different copies of the inscription. Since some of the copies are not clear it is impossible to be precise about the number of names. Coedès, whose translation I follow, suggests some 200 to 300 names.

> *The year Śaka 933 (AD 1002), Sunday, the 9th day of the waxing moon of the month of Bhadrapada. This is our oath: we who belong to the corps of the* tamvrac *of the first, second, third and fourth division, cut our hands at the moment of swearing in the presence of the sacred fire, the sacred jewel, the Brahmans and the (Buddhist) priests (*âcarya*), offering our lives and our due devotion faultlessly to H.M. Srî Sûryavarmadeva who enjoys absolute legitimate sovereignty from the Year Śaka 924 (AD 1002) onwards.*
>
> *We revere no other sovereign other than him. We will never oppose him or associate with his enemies. We will commit no act which is likely to harm him. We will persist in all those actions which are the result of our due devotion to King Srî Sûryavarmadeva. In the case of war we will persist in fighting courageously with no regard for our own life. In our devotion (to him) we will not flee from combat. If we die of sickness and not warfare, may we likewise gain the recompense of those who are devoted to their master.*
>
> *If we continue to live in service of the king, we will die in our devotion to him when the time of dying comes. If there is a business matter for which His Majesty the King orders us to travel afar, because something has occurred of which he has received notice, we will investigate the matter in detail while keeping to our oath. If there should be one among us who does not keep his oath (in perpetuity), we request that future monarchs may inflict royal punishment in diverse ways. If there are amongst us any traitors who do not keep this oath strictly, may they be reborn in the thirty-two places of hell for as long as the sun and moon endure. If we keep this oath faultlessly, may our Sovereign Lord who enjoys absolute legitimate royalty from the Śaka Year 924 (AD 1002) onwards, give orders for the maintenance of beneficent foundations in our villages and for the subsistence of our families. May we obtain in this world and in the world to come the recompense of those who are devoted to their master.*

Such an oath, clearly signifying an end to the prospects of any other claimant to the throne, was especially important in this particular case of a ruler whose claim to legitimacy appears to have been so weak. He claimed to have descended on the maternal side from Indravarman and to have been related through his wife Vîralakṣmî to Yaśovarman. Coming presumably from some state in southern Cambodia, he was well disposed to Buddhism, but this did not prevent him conforming to the already established order, and he retained the services of Śivâcârya who had served Jayavarman V. On Śivâcârya's death early in the new reign, he chose as *purohita* Sadâśiva, who was now head of the priestly family of Śivakaivalya, going back to the time of Jayavarman II.

Sadâśiva became a favourite of the king, who subsequently released him from his vow of celibacy (and his duties as *purohita* of the Devarâja) so as to arrange his marriage with the sister of the king's own wife. Sadâśiva thus received new titles and also the new name of Srî Jayendrapaṇḍita. At the same

90. Bantây Ampil. The doorway of the south entrance of the maṇḍapa*. The toraṇa shows Śiva on his bull Nandin. The author stands below.*

time he was appointed 'chief of works' and set about repairing the damage of the recent warfare relating to the succession.

As for the sites of Bhadrapaṭṭana and the sites of Stuk Ransi and all their establishments, completely devastated when His Majesty advanced with his forces, the Lord Srî Jayendrapaṇḍita completely rebuilt these sites and reconsecrated the images which had been set up there. At the Bhadrapaṭṭana site he set up a linga and two more images other than those belonging to the family-line. He gave all the items necessaries for these sanctuaries, he gave slaves, he built a 'watch-tower' (valabhi), he built an enclosure of laterite, he made fields and gardens, he dug a reservoir and made a dike.[25] *At the Bhadrâvasa site he consecrated the images of the gods, he reordered the site, he made a dike, an enclosure, a cattle-pen and all the sacred cows for this sanctuary. At the Ransi site, he consecrated the statues, gave the necessary items, dug a pool, made a park, dug a reservoir and made a dike.*

Apart from such repair works, the East Mebon and Ta Keo temples were completed, as well as entrance porticoes for the palace grounds. He also built or added to temples throughout the realm, such as Phnom Chisor[26] in the far south near the ancient sites of Ta Keo and Angkor Borei, as well as temples in the vicinity of Battambang.

Temples in the Battambang area

Of great archaeological importance is Prâsâd Baset, some twelve kilometres east of the city. An inscription dated 1036 lists the substantial donations made by a group of high-ranking persons to the god Jayakṣetra (= the Śiva-image of this site) with the consent of the king who agreed to the remission of taxes, possibly referring to actual founding of this temple. One dated 1043 refers to a gift of metal objects by a certain Śrîkaṇṭhapaṇḍita, as well as other gifts for the eventual purchase of more land.[27] The central shrine, with its extended antechamber, was set within three rectangular courtyards, the outer being about 200 metres square and the inner one about fifty. It was approached by a series of three *gopuras* on the east and west sides, with subsidiary towers to the north and south of the main shrine. On the eastern approach there were two large decorative reservoirs, which are now partly filled with weeds or used as paddy-fields. The ruins of the central shrine and antechamber stand on a small patch of

91. Phnom Chisor. Some 70 kilometres south of Phnom Penh such low hills presented themselves as well suited for defensive position. Sûryavarman I is known to have fortified it, and there are several references in inscriptions to Sûryaparvata (Hill of the Sun) as the god of Chisor.

92. Phnom Chisor. The temple is ruined and roofless, but it contains several well-preserved lintels. As usual there are later Buddhist additions and this hill is popular with worshippers and holiday-makers.

ground in the middle of the village. The northern tower is the only building still standing, and on this and amongst the ruins there are still some finely carved lintels and decorative doorways, The whole eastern approach is now occupied by a Theravâda monastery, where the ground is scatted with fallen pieces of stonework.

Vat Ek, about eight kilometres north of Battambang, is relatively well preserved, thanks probably in this case to the monks of the present Theravâda monastery on whose ground it now stands, more or less complete with its beautiful lotus-covered lake. It consists of the main shrine with its antechamber set within a walled enclosure of about fifty metres square, entered by *gopuras* on the east (front) and west sides. It retains some good lintels of Śiva and Parvatî on Nandin, of a dancing Śiva and of the scene of the Churning of the Ocean. It was founded by a Brahman prelate named Yogîśvarapaṇḍita, the personal guru of Sûryavarman, in 1027 AD.[28]

An inscription, of which nothing seems to be decipherable except the date of 972 Śaka (AD 1050) and the name of a prelate Kavîndrâçârya,[29] seems to associate the Buddhist temple of Banon with the end of Sûryavarman's reign, or more doubtfully with that of his successor, Udayâdityavarman II who showed no interest in Buddhism, but it has been urged upon me that the style of this group of five towers suggests the much later date of the reign of Jayavarman VII. Built on the summit of a steep hill eighty metres high, some twenty kilometres south of Battambang, it was once an impressive temple, dominating the surrounding plain and approached on the east side by a pair of artificial lakes stretching towards the Sangke River. These are now silted up and filled with weeds or used as paddy-fields. Used as a military watch-post during the recent fighting between Khmer Rouge and government troops, it has suffered the usual consequences, but when I was first there in 1998, the guardian figure who looks out over the plain, known locally as Neak-tâ Dambang-dek (local god 'Iron-Club') was still there. Since then he too has been broken off from his stone feet and stolen.[30] This hilltop temple has also become popular as a place for Sunday outings with the result that it remains strewn with discarded packets and plastic bags.

A lonely *gopura* standing by the roadside in the village of Steung, about twenty kilometres south-west of Battambang, is remarkable simply for well preserved lintels of Vishnu reposing while giving birth to Brahmâ on a lotus-stalk from his navel, a miniature scene of 'Churning the Ocean', with rishis above, one of the Pâṇḍava brothers playing dice with their Kaurava contestants, and one of a row of sages

93. (above) Baset, some twelve kilometres east of Battambang was a large and important temple-fortress, as proved by several 11th century inscriptions. It is now a total ruin, abandoned by the road-side. The ruins as seen on the north side.

supported by demonic figures. About 200 metres from the road one comes upon a row of three typical Khmer brick-built shrines standing solitarily near the more recent Theravâda monastery.[31]

Sûryavarman I made additions to Wat Phu and also further embellished Preah Vihear on the Dangrek mountains, the building initiated by Yaśovarman (see p. 59). Further work had been done there by Râjendravarman II and Jayavarman V during the 10th century. Sûryavarman I now added to the buildings in the outer court and built avenues lined with ornamental balustrades. Maybe it was during his reign that an important resthouse (*dharmasâla*) with a hospital chapel was built on the approach to Preah Vihear from the north. This is a significant change of direction, suggesting that important visitors were likely to arrive from this direction now that the whole Khorat Plateau was under Khmer administration. The main item of interest is the square tower with a slightly tapering lower section and the usual tapering summit, built mainly of sandstone on a laterite base. Some doorways and pillars of the attached building are still standing.[32] Known as Prâsât Don Tuan, this was once a far more impressive building than the later rest-houses built of laterite during the reign of Jayavarman VII.

95. (above) Baset. One of several quite well-preserved lintels.

← 94. (p. 90 bottom left) Baset. A doorway on the south side once leading into the central shrine.

96. (below) Vat Ek, some eight kilometres north of Battambang, is a small well-preserved fortress-temple in a very beautiful setting, now in the good care of the later Theravâda monastery. This view of the south side shows the entrances to the main shrine and to the maṇḍapa.

97. (above) Vat Ek. Lintel of 'churning the ocean' over entrance to the shrine from the maṇḍapa.

100. (above) Banon. The five summit-towers, taken from the west against the sun.

←*98. (p. 92 bottom left) Banon on its hilltop, 20 kilometres south of Battambang, and the steps leading up steeply to the eastern* gopura.

←*99. (p. 92 bottom right) Banon. Doorway of the eastern* gopura, *looking out over the steep descent.*

More temples across the Khorat Plateau
(continued in Chapter 5, p. 125)

He expanded the limits of Khmer interests westwards across the Khorat Plateau, and thus into the Chao Phraya Valley and the whole area around the Gulf of Siam, and thence south down the Malay Peninsula at least as far as Petchaburi. The extension of Khmer influence ever further south down the Thai-Malay peninsula was likely to create conflict with the maritime empire of Śrîvijaya, which included the southern part of the same peninsula at least as far north as Chaiya. Sûryavarman made friendly gestures (*c.*1012) to the Çola monarch of South India, Râjendraçola I, offering him the gift of a chariot, presumably anticipating conflict with Śrîvijaya on the campaign to the south on which he was about to embark.[33] In the event there was no such difficulty, as Śrîvijaya was soon involved in withstanding the Çola invasion of 1025. This invasion probably allowed the Khmers to extend their interests thus far down the peninsula.

Lopburi (then known as Lavo) to the north became a Khmer regional capital. The earliest Khmer temple, known locally as Prang Khaek, dating back to the end of the 10th century, still stands with its three brick towers in the middle of a traffic island. More impressive temples were built later, namely Wat Mahathat in a far more spacious layout, as well as Prang Sam Yod, similar to Prang Khaek, but in a more imposing setting.[34] These last two, dating to the reign of Jayavarman VII, were Buddhist foundations, but even in this Mon region, where Buddhism flourished long before and during the Khmer occupation, there are indications that they were subsequently converted into Śaivite shrines. This could only have occurred under the direct orders of the local Khmer governor of the province, indicating once again that the established religion of state was essentially Brahmanical.

The earliest temples on the Khorat Plateau, namely Non Ku and Muang Khaek, both built of brick and seemingly undergoing no further development, have already been mentioned. Phnom Wan, also dating back to that period, emerges as an impressive stone-built enclosure during the 11th century, work being completed under Sûryavarman's successor Udayâditravarman. During the 11th century other major temples were built or further developed on the Khorat Plateau. The most notable are Phnom Rung on its impressive hilltop, of which the foundation appears to go back at least to the 10th

101. Steung, view of the three wrecked towers with the new vihara *behind along the road to Pailin.*

102. Steung, one of several well preserved lintels on what must have been the eastern gopura. *It represents Vishnu, lying on a sea-monster, giving birth to Brahmâ from his navel. Joyful celestial beings are in attendance.*

103. Preah Vihear, the second courtyard.

104. Preah Vihear, the fourth courtyard.

105. (above) Preah Vihear, the summit shrine, western section, with a subsidiary windowless temple to the far side.

→107. (p. 97) Preah Vihear, the summit shrine, eastern section, overlooking the cliff.

106. (below) Lopburi, Wat Mahathat. Lopburi (Thailand) was a Khmer provincial capital from the 11th century until the late 13th century, when after a period of independence it was absorbed into the kingdom of Ayuthaya in the mid-14th century. Only the central shrine and the maṇḍapa are original Khmer. The surrounding shrines are later Ayuthaya style.

century, the nearby Muang Tam at the foot of the same hill and Prâsâd Phimai, further to the north, the only one that is overtly Buddhist, although once again Hindu motifs are present.[35] Muang Tam seems to have been completed under Udayâditravarman and thus may be credited to his reign together with Phnom Wan in its final form. Phnom Rung and Phimai are laid out on the same general design as Angkor Vat, as built a century later by Sûryavarman II, namely as a central towering shrine set within a series of square enclosures, and thus in their final form must be attributed to the 12th or 13th century. However they are of much smaller dimensions, consisting essentially of a single central tower preceded by the usual *maṇḍapa*. In the case of Phimai two subsidiary towers stand to left and right of the entry to the inner enclosure, both in a rather ruined condition. As one approaches they may give the impression a set of three shrines according to the normal Khmer pattern, as already described just above with regard to the Prang Khaek and Prang Sam Yod at Lopburi.

Sûryavarman I who dominated the Cambodian scene for half a century is clearly one of the greatest of Khmer kings. It is generally assumed that he had Buddhist sympathies, but he gave no clear outward demonstration of this, although his posthumous name Nirvâṇapada remains suggestive. Great architectural works went forward during his reign and they are all Brahmanical. Although he completed the great pyramid-temples of Ta Keo and the Phimean-âkas, there appears to be no record of his raising a Devarâja in his own name, which by now had become the regular practice of Khmer monarchs.

Udâyaditravarman II: local warfare, the founding of Bhadraniketana and the Baphuon, the construction of the Eastern Baray

Sûryavarman I was succeeded peaceably by a close relative, probably a nephew, namely Udayâdityavarman II (1050-1066), who continued the work of reconstructing the city of Angkor. However early in his reign he had to deal with trouble in the far south. We have surely noted that the Khmers from the time of Jayavarman II onwards continued to enlarge their territory northwards and the southern states, consisting of what was once ancient Funan, were neglected. No great Khmer temple-fortresses appear to have been built there, and local rulers of whom so little is known, may have been sometimes at war with the Chams of Pâṇḍuranga, the most southern of the Cham principalities which occupied the whole south-east corner of the Indochina mainland, reaching as far south as present-day Pan Thiet. In the early 1050s a Cham force even invaded Śambhupura, and having sacked the town and its sanctuaries, they offered the loot to the great shrine of Bhadreśvara at Mi-son.[36] There is no clear record of the Cambodian reply to this, but vigorous action was doubtless taken, perhaps by a great general named Sangrâma, in whose honour a special stele was erected, which was found near the Baphuon in Angkor.[37] The first part (side A) is barely legible, but it seems to trace the history of his lineage, starting from a family connection with a daughter of Jayavarman II and continuing through the major succeeding reigns up to Sûryasvarman I and Udayâdityavarman, during whose reign he carried out the heroic exploits described on the stele. Thus in the Śaka year 973 (= AD 1051) a formidable enemy, named Aravindahrada appeared in the south (*dakṣinâpatha*) and the local rulers, including that of Âḍhyapura (?) had been unable to subdue him.[38]

> *Having received the royal authority, the general Sangrâma made obeisance, and leading his army went to meet this enemy, so difficult to subdue. Having reached these terrible foes, difficult to approach like mighty mountains, this leader of our fighting force, powerful in speech, shouted with a terrible sound: 'Challenging the blazing fiery emblem of the lord of the world, which blasts his enemies' defenses, you face like a grass-hopper immediate destruction. The world must be protected by a valiant king, but you, wretched man in your folly would say (to us): You cowards are incapable of defending it. Fool, if you persist in this combat, look for a moment at this impetuous arrow of mine. It is difficult to avoid and ready to result in your death.'*
>
> *Thus addressed, this enemy leader, who never failed in combat, inflamed now with anger, replied thus to the general, who was brandishing his arms. 'Do not try to make me afraid! Understand that the issue of the combat was never in doubt and there is no doubt about (who is) the master of the world.'*
>
> *When the enemy-chief replied in this way, Sangrâma released an irresistible fire of arrows in order to consume the enemy fire-power. Aravindahrada fled in all speed to a town in Champa, and after the flight of his enemy, Sangrâma went to the temple of Śiva at Râjatîrtha (= the royal watering-place).*

Later Sangrâma was called upon to destroy a treacherous army-commander:

> *There was an illustrious leader, a competent and valiant hero named Kamvau, whom the king had appointed as an army-commander. Blinded by the splendour of his importance, and meditating in his heart the ruin of the very one to whom he owed his position, one day he issued forth from his city with his troops. With the force of his body, his armament, his prudence, his power, he was generally considered capable of conquering the whole world. His troops of great valour, with great arms, with proven heroism, innumerable, were placed to all the points of the horizon seemingly without end. With his impetuous and well armed legions, although a mere man, aspiring to conquer all the gods, he traversed the world like Râvaṇa (the evil king of Lanka) until he met (at last) with our hero. Devasrau, Vlong, Vnur, Gam, Cengsrau, Camnatt, Raññа, Khmoññ, these great military leaders and many other great captains of the king, all of great energy, were ordered by the king to vanquish this enemy, but he conquered them all, encompassing them in full battle in the glory of victory.*
>
> *The king called upon Sangrâma, who first made lavish offerings at a Śaivite temple, praying for victory. Confronting his enemy, he exchanged with him a series of insulting challenges. Then after a terrible battle Sangrâma, victorious once more, made generous offerings to Śiva.*[39]

Since the purpose of this inscription is to pay honour to this particular general, his prowess is seemingly enhanced by emphasizing the failure of others before him. Since their names are all Khmer, one assumes that they were leaders of lower rank. I have quoted the inscriptions partly for its historical value, but also as an example of the description of heroic war scenes, in which the author seems to have taken pleasure quite as much as the anonymous stone-carvers on the walls of Angkor Vat (see pp. 141-2).

It will be recalled that Sûryavarman I had 'laicised' his renowned *purohita* Sadâśiva giving him the new name of Jayendrapaṇḍita and arranging for his marriage into the royal family. Udayâdityavarman now appointed him as his own personal mentor (*Brah Guru*). He also bestowed the highest possible rank upon Jayendrapaṇḍita's old teacher, a certain Vagindrapaṇḍita, confirming him in the royal title of *dhuli jeng brah kamrateng añ* ('the sacred lord whose feet we dust'), and on his death this title passed to Sadâśiva, alias Jayendrapaṇḍita. In 1052 the King authorized the foundation of the famous temple of Bhadraniketana by Sadâśiva, where the whole lineage of royal *purohitas* back to Śivakaivalya, who had served Jayavarman II, is traced on a long inscription. (See back to Chapter 3, 'Jayavarman II', p. 44ff.)

> *In 1052 the Sacred Lord whose feet we dust founded the* kamrateng jagat Śivalinga *at Bhadraniketana. He informed H.M. Udayâditavarman of this, requesting that this establishment and serving personnel should constitute a gracious liberality in favour of the* kamrateng jagat Śivalinga *of Bhadraniketana, conferring on him the exclusive right to this*

establishment and this land.[40]

Two other major images were also installed, Brahmâ representing the Brahman Hiraṇyadâma who had devised the ritual and the joint image of Harihâra, representing Sivâkavalya and Vâmaśiva, referred to as Śivâśrama (see Endnotes, note 2 of Ch. 2) The king himself offered a second auspicious *linga* at the shrine.

> *This magnanimous king, in favor of this (guru) who wished to make a foundation on his land, installed in the place called Bhadraniketana this* linga *honoured with great offerings. Without taking into account this territory named Bhadraniketana, when making a donation to this* linga *of gold, of precious stones, of elephants, horses, etc. the king made this vow: May this* Sarvajayendravarmeśvara *(Supreme Lord who is all victorious) protect all around, its powerful brilliance dissipating all obscurity in constant splendour, honour and success up the final extinction of all being. With the zodiac in accordance with the Archer, and the sun and the other planets aligned with the Water-carrier, the Virgin, the Balance, the Water-carrier, same repeated, the Fishes and the Water-carrier, both repeated in reverse, the year accorded with the apertures (9), the mountains (7) and the Vedas (4)* [Śaka 974 = AD 1052]. *King Udayâdityavarman has given it in devotion to Śambu Jayavarmeśvara, having fixed the measurement and placed the boundaries on all sides.*[41]

Already famed as the architect for Sûryavarman's construction works, it was probably Sadâśiva who was responsible for initiating the building of yet another temple-pyramid. It followed the conventional form of an enormous three-tiered pyramid but with steeply sloping side, 120 by 90 metres at its base. It is approached by a fine stone-built avenue 200 metres long, but regrettably the Baphuon now presents itself as a rounded mass of collapsed masonry, while substantial restoration works are continually in process. A large number of bas-reliefs have survived, some of classical scenes from the Ramâyâna and the Krishna legend, and seemingly other more popular scenes such as appear later on the Bayon. Some of these have only been uncovered recently in the process of the present French programme of reconstruction. They were buried inside an enormous lying Buddha image, part of the later Buddhist readaptations, presumably of the 16th century (see Chapter 6). A linga of gold, named *Udayâdityeśvara*, was erected in a shrine on the summit and the learned Brahman Śankara who had served under Râjendravarman, served now as *purohita*. Thus the Baphuon now effectively displaced the Bakheng as the centre of Udayâdityavarman's ever-growing city of Yaśodharapura.

Udayâdityavarman II's major contribution to the beauty of the city and the cultural and economic life of the whole region was the construction of an enormous new reservoir, an artificial lake 8 by 2.2 kilometres in size. Now known as the West Baray, it is the only one of these great reservoirs to survive to the present day. It has already been noted above that this massive work, carried out in the mid-11th century marginalized entirely that group of temples and the resident community (referred to above as the 'Baray Group') dating from the 7th century onwards.

It may have been about this time that a beautiful little temple-fortress, now in a state of sad ruin, was built on a hillock some twenty kilometres east of Angkor in the vicinity of Phnom Bok. When Aymonier visited it at the end of the 19th century it was still know locally as Yos-ker (from *skr.* Yaśaṣ-kîrti), meaning 'honour and glory', which may have been its original name.[42] It is properly know as Chau Srei Vibol, maybe a regal name 'Great Renown and Glory'[skr. *Śrîvipula* (*kîrti*)]. The main shrine is set within an enclosure consisting of a covered gallery, all built in sandstone, 50 by 38 metres. The remains of two small subsidary tower-like shrines can still he identified towards the eastern end of the enclosure. On the south side one descends to a separate rectangular-shaped building with balustrades in the windows, doubtless intended as living-quarters. Nearby there are traces of a small pool. The whole complex is surrounded at the foot of the hill by a massive wall of laterite, about 200 metres each of the four sides, with *gopuras* to the four directions, built of sandstone, all ruined but still retaining some fine carving. It was certainly a Brahmical temple, serving as a strong defensive position, probably built by a local chieftain.

Phnom Wan, Phnom Rung and Muang Tam

During the reign of Udayâdityavarman II the rebuilding of Phnom Wan in grey and reddish sandstone was also completed, and thanks to the excellent reconstruction work carried out by the Thai Ministry of Fine Arts, one can see it now much as it must have looked over a thousand years ago. However it proved impracticable to rebuild the central tower. A dated inscription of which the last figure is missing—namely the Year Śaka 97—thus corresponding to any year between AD 1050 and 1057, lists substantial gifts to the temple, first by

Sûryavarman I and later by Udayâdityavarman II.[43] It is a simple lateral building, modest when compared with others on the Khorat Plateau that were then already in the process of construction (see below). It consists of ante-chamber, connecting gallery and shrine-room, aligned from east to west. A subsidiary shrine stands in the inner courtyard on the south side, and a far smaller shrine may have stood originally on the north side, which is less spacious. The courtyard is formed by a laterite wall, pierced by *gopuras* on the four sides. There are traces of a moat. It adjoins a Theravâda monastery and several Buddha images have been placed in the shrine-room which have the happy effect of giving some life to the whole building. Originally it was a Śaivite foundation and images of Brahmâ, Vishnu and Śiva are mentioned in the inscription just quoted above.

Phnom Rung also underwent reconstruction about the same time. The shape of the hill allowed for an impressive approach from the east, along an avenue marked by small lotus-topped boundary posts for a distance of 160 metres. Thence a wide terrace with *nâga*-balustrades leads into the impressive eastern *gopura,* surmounted by a toraṇa, illustrating Śiva as the lord of ascetics. The main eastern entrance of the *maṇḍapa* (antechamber) is surmounted by a lintel which figures the birth of Brahmâ from the navel of Vishnu and a toraṇa figuring a dancing Śiva. The space on the summit allows only for a single rectangular walled enclosure, in the centre of which stands the main shrine with the ante-chamber. This last contains an image of Śiva's mount, the bull Nandin, while the main shrine contains a *linga.* As is usual, the main shrine is not exactly central, being placed slightly to the west, so as to leave space for the more elaborate approach from the east. The frontal pieces (*toraṇa*) over the doorways are decorated with Hindu themes, mainly from the Râmâyana. These and the decorative patterns on the pilasters, door-frames and cornices represent the very best of Khmer sculptural art. Thanks to the excellent reconstruction work of the Thai Department of Fine Arts, it surpasses anything that can be seen at Angkor

111. (pp. 102-3 overleaf) Phnom Wan, a few kilometres just north of Khorat city, was already in existence in the late 9th century (as probably were also Non Ku and Muang Khaek further to the east). It was rebuilt on the pattern shown in this photograph by Udayâdityavarman II in the mid-11th century. It had a long and interesting history, as explained in the text. It has been restored recently by the Fine Arts Department of the Thai Government. but the stones to complete the central tower were unhappily missing. (Photograph by Suthep Kritsanuvarin.)

109. *(above) Phnom Wan. The south wall of the inner courtyard with a view of the modern* vihara.

← *108. (p. 100) Chau Srei Vibol. This beautiful little temple-fortress was built on a hill-top some 20 kilometres st of Angkor by some local chieftain probably during the reign of Udayâdityavarman II. The summit-shrine and two towers are still standing amongst the general ruin, in the grounds of a monastic site known as Vat Trâch (n. of a tree). (Photograph by Suthep Kritsanuvarin.)*

110. (below) Phnom Wan. Buddha images in the shrine, as seen from the western entrance. (Photograph by Giulia Anglois-Nisbet.)

112. (above) Phnom Rung, built on a hilltop about 95 kilometres (maybe 140 by road) south of Khorat city, has become, since its restoration by the Fine Arts Department, the most beautifully preserved Khmer temple-fortress to be seen anywhere. It was a Khmer regional capital from the early 10th to the early 13th century. View from SW corner of the inner enclosure.

113. (left) Phnom Rung. Toraṇa over the east entrance to main shrine, showing Śiva as lord of ascetics.

after the dereliction of the last thirty years.

The temple of Muang Tam was probably also constructed during the course of the 11th century. Like these other two it has been beautifully restored by the Fine Arts Department, but the main tower is missing simply because not enough remained for its reconstruction. The whole central part is enclosed within a second courtyard, comprising a moat, which is separated into four corner sections, filled with blossoming lotus-flowers, by four causeways leading in from the four outer *gopuras*. The design is quite different from Phnom Wan, since here we have a central group of five tower-like shrines. Such sets of five are usually arranged in the form of a maṇḍala with the main tower in the centre and the four others to the four intermediate quarters. Here they are arranged as a group of three, a fairly typical arrangement, but with two other shrines standing midway behind. They stand as a group on a raised platform within a courtyard that leaves room for two 'libraries' on the east side. Some very fine lintels remain *in situ*, mainly repeating the same motif of a *kâla*-mask clutching a *nâga*-like canopy in its mouth, with a small inset theme which is variable, such as a multi-armed Krishna defeating a demon, Brahmâ riding a triad of geese, or simply a rishi (ascetic) in repose. *Gopuras* pierce the four sides of this courtyard. The approach from the north is made all the more impressive by a vast baray (1,140 by 400 metres) which stretches out on that side. It is likely that this was constructed at the same time as Udayâditayarman's 'West Baray' at Angkor. Muang Tam is a very beautiful site, situated at the foot of the hill on which Phnom Rung was perhaps still in its later state of reconstruction.

Harṣavarman III, Jayavarman VI and Dharaṇîndravarman I

Udayâdityavarman II was succeeded by his younger brother Harṣavarman III. Little is known of this king, although at least three inscriptions relate to his reign. An inscription dated 1069 from Palhal village (Pursad) refers to an image of *Tribhuvaneśvara* that was set up there.[44] An inscription from Lovek refers

115. (below) Phnom Rung. Nandin the Bull in the antechamber, looking towards the Śiva-linga in the main shrine. (Photograph by Giulia Anglois-Nisbet.)

116. (pp. 106-7) A general view of Muang Tam across the moat which is divided into four angle-sections by the approaches from the four directions.(Photograph by Suthep Kritsanuvarin.)

114. (above) Phnom Rung. Lintel illustrating Vishnu giving birth to Brahmâ, and above a 10-armed Śiva.

117. Muang Tam contains some well-preserved lintels. Krishna fighting the nâga Kâliya.

118. Muang Tam. A view taken in the late evening. (Photograph by Suthep Kritsanuvarin.)

119. Muang Tam. Lintel of the main shrine, showing Brahmâ on his goose and the kâla-*mask below.*

to a Śivalinga which was set up by his *purohita* Śankarapaṇḍita.[45] At Prâsâd Sralau near Svay Chek a protégé of the king named Narapatîndravarman set up a *linga* and images of Vishnu and Śiva in recognition of the king's restoration of a village which had become deserted.[46] An inscription of Samrong (a village situated 1.5 kilometres north-east of the walls of Angkor Thom) relates that land and foundations were purchased under the direction of a certain Yogîśvarapaṇḍita, and that the king granted land mostly in the name of Bhadreśvara, god of Lingapura, and ordered the erection of a *Śivalinga*, a Nârâyana and a Bhagavatî which insurgents had destroyed at Stuk Sram.[47]

It seems that while Harshvarman III was still reigning in Angkor (at least until 1080), a prince of the Mahîdharapura family which was based in the Phimai area, started a revolt and declared himself king.[48] He is first named as King Jayavarman VI in an inscription from Phnom Wan dated 1082, where he had given instruction to senior ministers for the organization of supplies to the serving personnel of Phnom Wan and others religious houses. He was served by an ambitious young Brahman named Divâkara, to which the title paṇḍita was later added. It is assumed that this king reigned in those northern parts of the country subject to him from about 1080, but Harṣavarman III or another claimant to the throne in his name may still have been ruling from Angkor. Jayavarman VI died in 1107, receiving the posthumous name of *Paramakaivalyapada* ('Abode of Supreme Oneness') and was succeeded by an elder brother named Dharaṇîndravarman I. There are several inscriptions from his reign of which the most interesting one is that which records the setting up of an image of Trailokyavijaya in the temple at Phimai by the *Kamrateng añ* Srî Virendrâdipathivarman of Chok Vakula in 1108.

However it must have been about this time that another claimant to the throne arrived on the scene (the future Sûryavarman II). This led to the defeat and death of Dharaṇîndravarman I (holding power in the north), who received the posthumous title of *Paramaniśkalapada* ('Abode of Supreme Unity'), and also of any possible successor of Harṣavarman III at Angkor.

A note on Preah Khan of Kampong Svay

An inscription in a small chapel on this very important site associates it with Sûryavarman I, but the layout of the whole site is so similar to that of Angkor Vat that it seems best to attribute it in its finished state to Sûryavarman II, also with later additions by Jayavarman VII. It now lies in the jungle about one hundred kilometres in a direct line due east of Angkor. Since it has never been covered in any detail in other general works on Khmer civilization, it deserves rather more detailed treatment. By road and rough track the actual distance is much greater. It can be reached by a side-road going northwards from Damdek, thirty-two kilometres south-east of Siem Reap along the A6 which afterwards continues on to Kampong Kdei, Stoung and Kampong Thom, certainly an ancient Khmer route. This side-road from Damdek verges to the north-east and thus arrives at the important temple-fortress of Beng Mealea, probably founded during the reign of Sûryavarman II. From Beng Mealea a rough track continues eastwards for another fifty kilometres thus arriving at a village, named Tra Sen, on the southern side of the vast estate of Preah Khan. This track, now in a deplorable condition, presumably follows more or less what was once an ancient Khmer road, since it continues for another sixty kilometres, where, at the junction with a route which leads northwards eventually to Preah Vihear, there still stands a massive 'hospital chapel', known locally (according to a sign on the spot) as Prâsâd Neang-kra of Phum-chhoen.[49]

I insert here some relevant maps (Maps 5, 6) with the kind permission of Bruno Bruguier of the EFEO, which he has published in an important article, 'Les ponts en pierre du Cambodge ancient' (*BEFEO 87,* pp. 529-51).

Preah Khan can also be reached from Stoung, which is some one hundred kilometres along the A6 from Siem Reap towards Kampong Thom. A very rough track, possible only with a 4-wheel drive vehicle, going northwards for some fifty kilometres, connects at Preah Khan with the west-east route just described.[50] The first description of this site seems to be that of Louis Delaporte who made his way there in 1873 by this route from Stoung. Travelling wherever possible by river-routes and only of absolute necessity by land, he was supported by adequate funds thanks to the French governor-general in Saigon and by as much local assistance and labour as he might require thanks to the authorizations which he had received in Phnom Penh from King Norodom (reigned 1860-1904). It has been written of him, that like the very few other early visitors, he was more interested in creating a picturesque and romantic impression of the whole place than in describing these ruins in a rigorously scientific manner. He certainly achieves this affect with his excellent sketches of these ruined shrines, bridges and decorative causeways, bringing to life sites which have since become a mass of ruins. Nor did he neglect to make drawings of the local people, in whom he showed a sympathetic interest. Also thanks to the labour ready to hand he was able to have sites cleared of the jungle, thus making it possible to prepare ground-plans and maps. He arranged for the transport back to France of several impressively large pieces such as one of the massive stone elephants on one particular site or the magnificent stone image of the Bodhisattva Avalokiteśvara from Prâsâd Thkol. These and many other such items can still be seen today in the Musée Guimet in Paris. While these might be classed nowadays as 'archaeological thefts', one has to recognize that these pieces have been thus preserved for us, saved from the totally destructive looting of these sites, which has since taken place.

A detailed description of Preah Khan was published by Henri Mauger in the *BEFEO 1939* (2) pp. 197-220 with copious plans and drawings, of which we reproduce here plates XXXVII, showing the general plan as within the outer (fourth) enclosure, XXXVIII illustrating the central shrine in the inner (first) enclosure, and XLV showing the second and third enclosures (Maps 7-9). The outer enclosure encompasses a square with sides of 4.8 kilometres in length. It thus covers an area far larger than Angkor Thom of which the outer wall measures are 3 by 3 kilometres and of Angkor Vat, 1.5 by 1.3 kilometres. The whole complex does not face precisely east, but rather ENE, and this for no apparent reason. Maybe this happened to be the alignment of the first main temple to be built on the sites and all subsequent additions have maintained this original direction. Mauger draws attention to the existence of just one single shrine close to the SW limits of the outer enclosure that happens to be aligned accurately facing the true east. These sites must have been in use, allowing for possible periods of neglect, for a period of at least three centuries, from the 10th to the 13th. At the earlier stage it would have comprised a central shrine and subsidiary buildings of less robust materials, enclosed by the outer walls. To this early period, maybe early 10th century, also belongs the shrine in the form of a mound far to the ENE of the whole site, now known popularly as the Preah Prâsâd Damrei (Sacred Elephant Shrine) on account of the stone elephants (one is now in Paris) facing the four directions on its summit. The carved façade on the eastern side is probably 12th century work. Presumably the elephants have no more significance here than the stone elephants on the four corners of the East Mebon shrine at Angkor. The original purpose of this particular shrine remains unknown. It retains some very fine stone-carving. Developments clearly took place when Sûryavarman I acquired this property in the early 11th century and continued

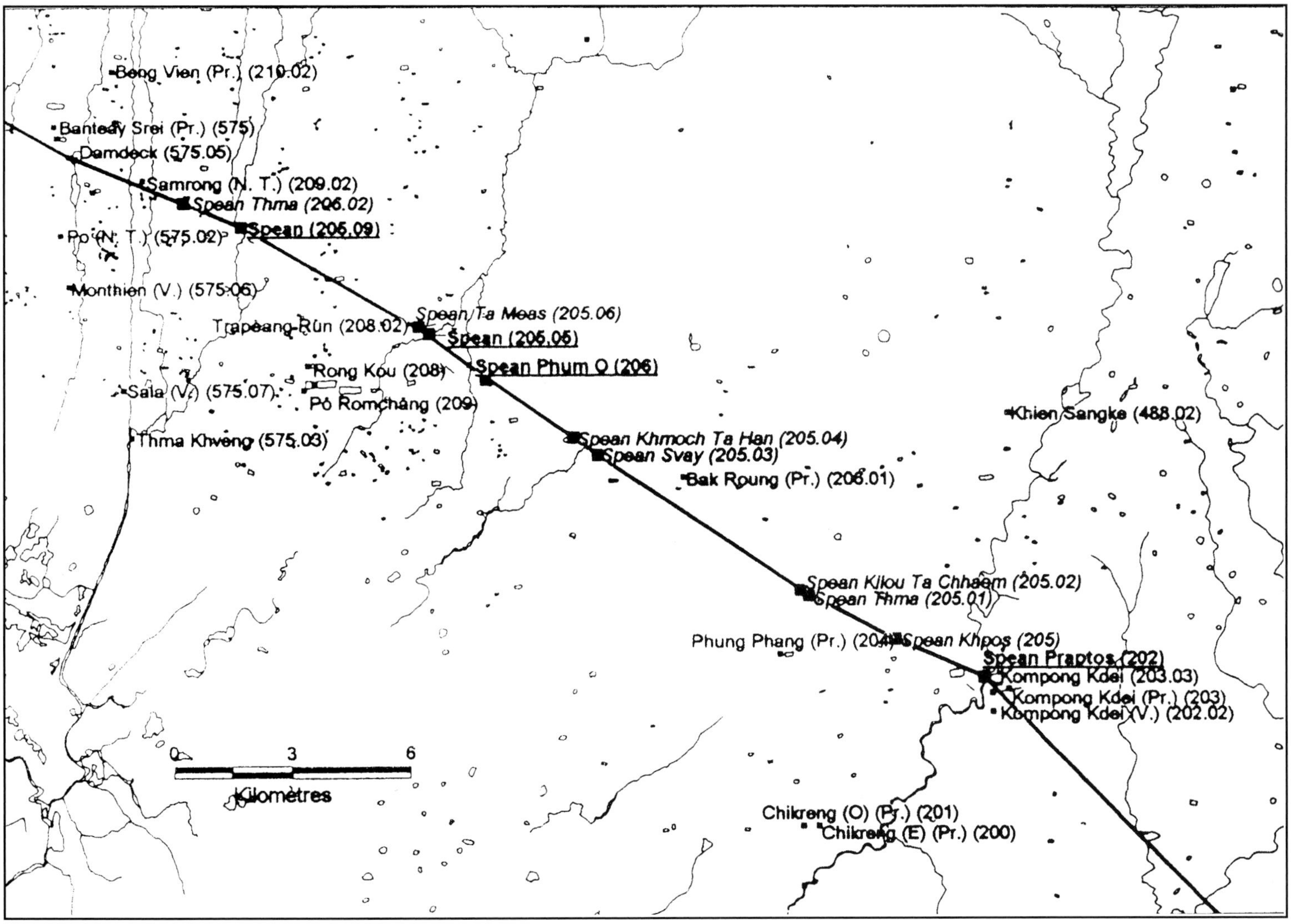

Map 5. Archaeological map of the ancient routeway between Damdek and Kompong Kdei (from Bruguier, p. 546).

Map 6. Archaeological map of the ancient routeway between Angkor and Preah Khan (from Bruguier, p. 547).

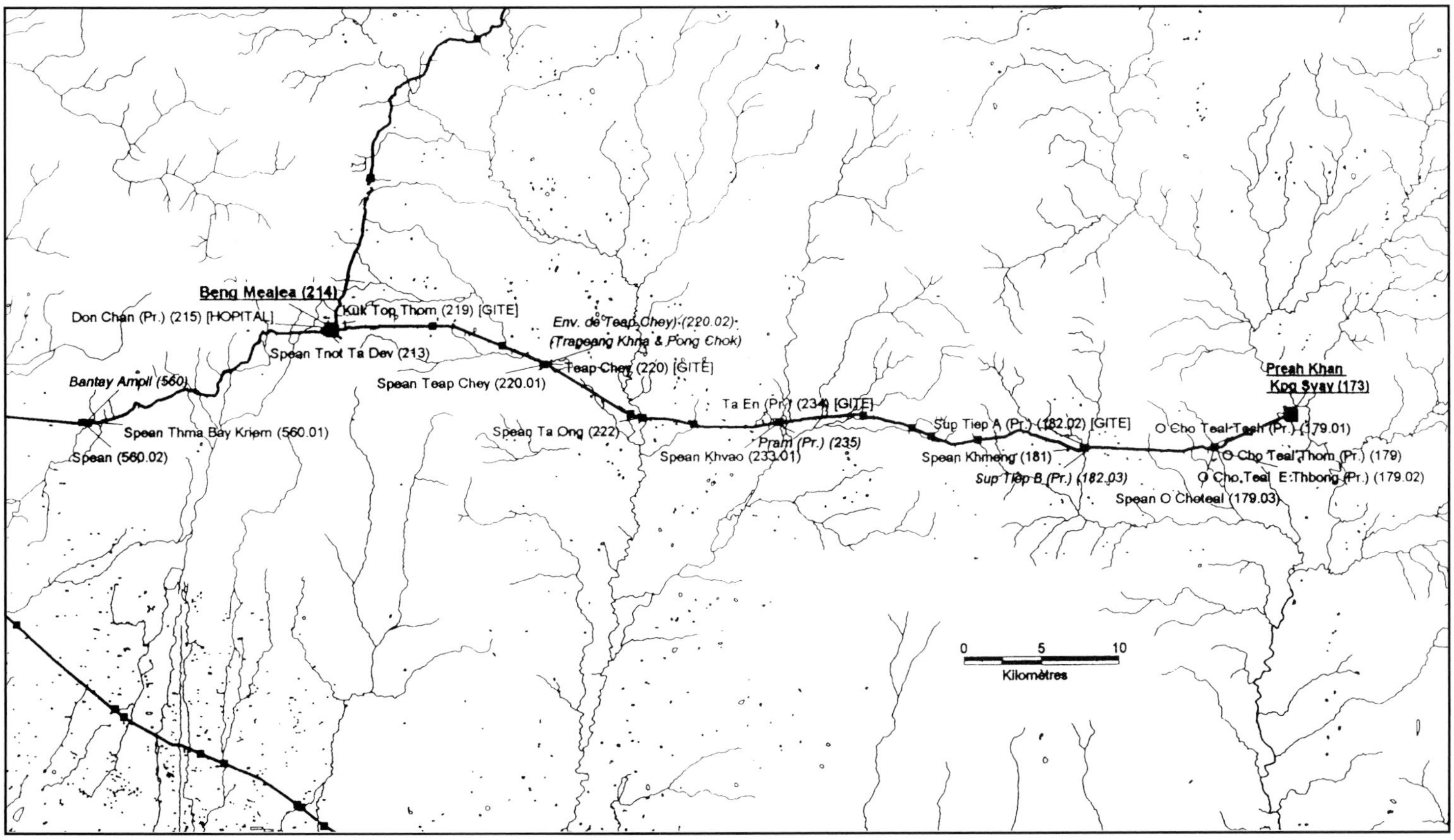

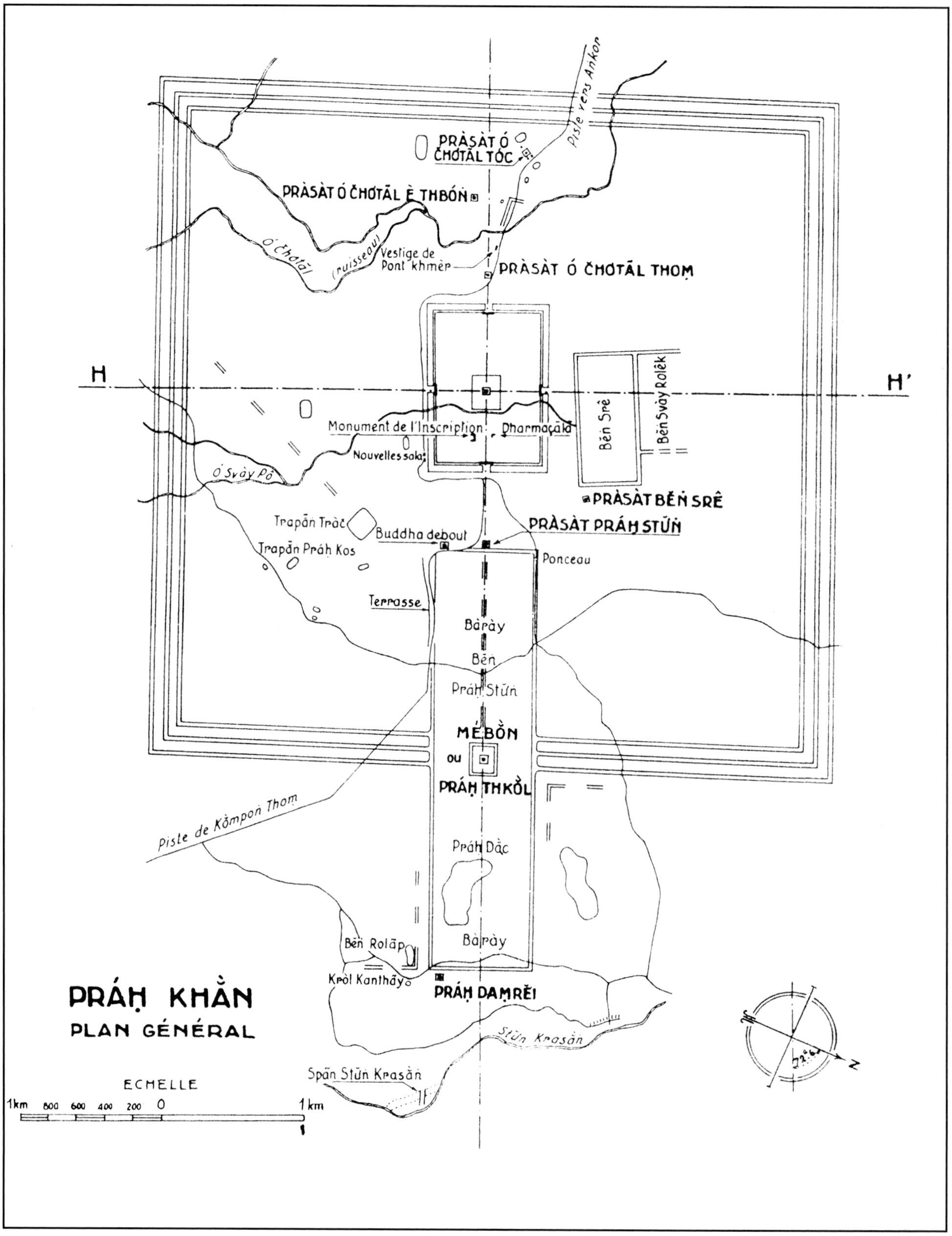

Map 7. General plan of Preah Khan (from Mauger, Pl. XXXVII).

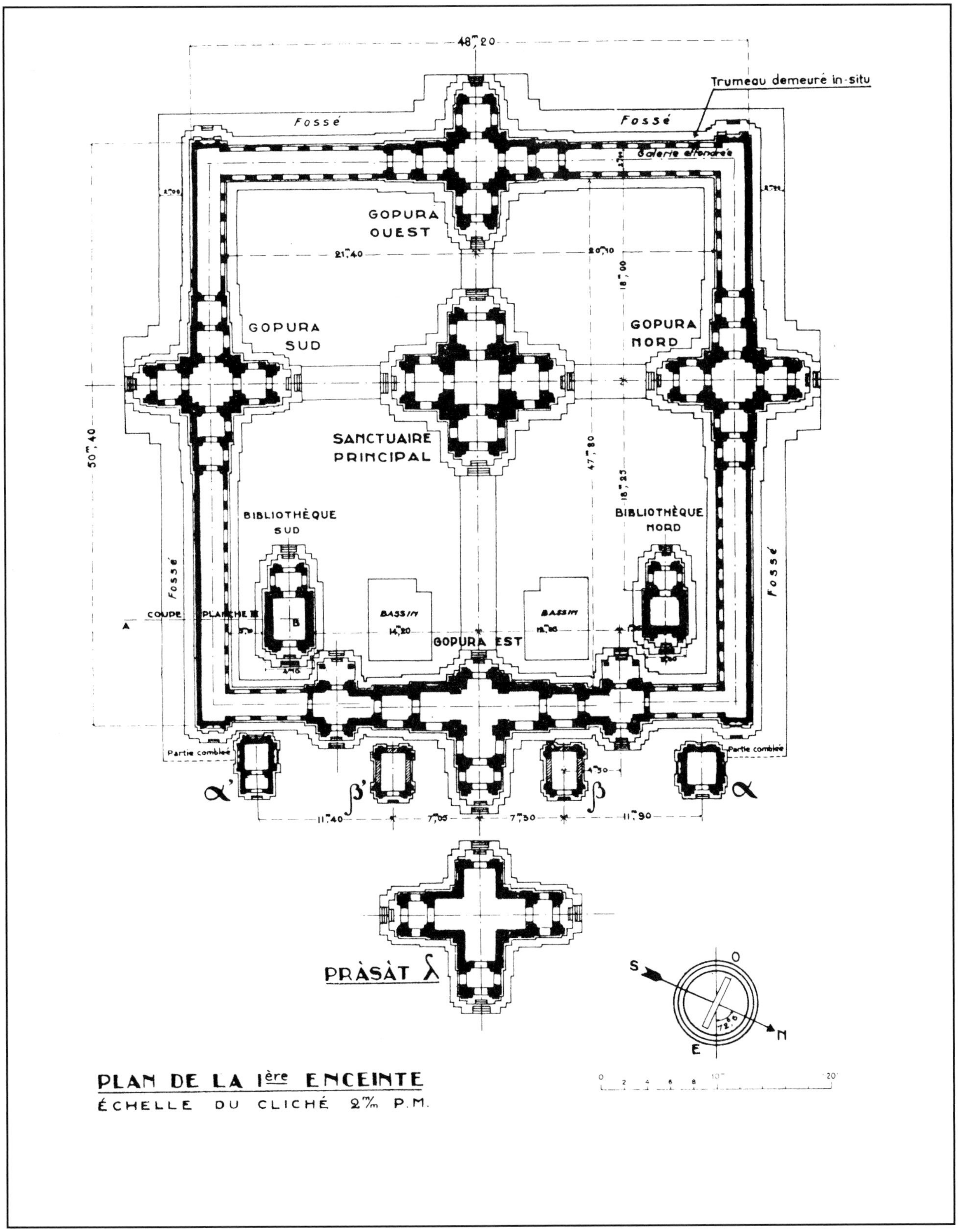

Map 8. Preah Khan. Plan of the 1st enclosure (from Mauger, Pl. XXXVIII).

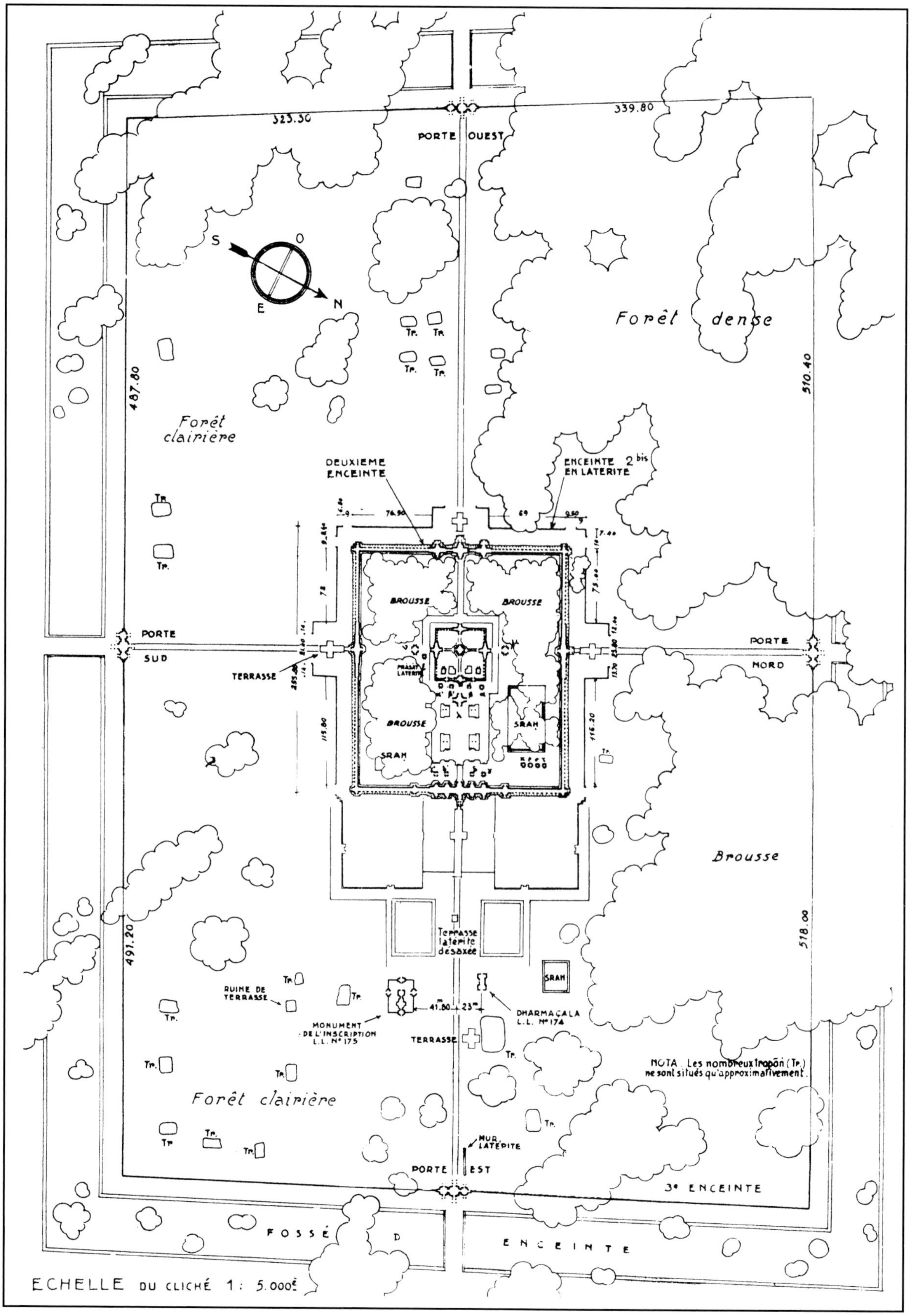

Map 9. Preah Khan. Plan of the 3rd enclosure (from Mauger, Pl. XLV).

120. (above) Preah Khan of Kampong Svay. A view of the southern side of the base of the Elephant Temple. The abandoned lintel shows effigies of five seated Buddhas, not however differentiated as the Five Buddhas of Mahâyâna tradition. There are many such similar lintels around the site. (Photograph by Suthep Kritsanuvarin.)

121. (right) Preah Khan of Kampong Svay. A well-preserved carving of a nâga by the Elephant Temple.

through to the 13th. One may speculate that he seized it from one of his several opponents whom he overcame in order to finally gain the throne about AD 1010.[51] Thus all the major developments must come well after that date, resulting in the general layout much as one sees it today. Although the site must have been cleared for Mauger to produce his precise plans and drawings, the jungle has since taken over again while the buildings have been reduced to a state of ruin even worse that when he described them. Thus it is now quite impossible to retrace his steps in anything like their entirety. Much of the area covered by the third enclosure as well as the rest of the outlying fourth enclosure is practically inaccessible. The same may well be said of the second enclosure with its ruined causeways and broken basins and pervasive undergrowth, and as for the inner enclose even the gateways (*gopura*) to the four directions which still retained their upper reaches when Mauger was there, have been reduced to the general ruinous state. It may be seen from the

122. (above) A view of the lake from the Elephant Temple, on the summit of which stand four elephants, one to each of the intermediate directions.

123. (left) Preah Thkol, now high and dry, used to stand on an island where the lake at Preah Khan passed into the third enclosure. It is very elaborately carved, probably 12th century work.

general plan that a baray, cutting through the outer (fourth) enclosure on the eastern (in fact ENE) side, was constructed from close by the 'Elephant Shrine' leading through towards the third enclosure. It is three kilometres long and some 700 metres wide. Most of it is now dried up but a good view of the lower section can be obtained from the summit of the 'Elephant Shrine'. To mark the place where this baray passes through the eastern wall, a shrine was built on a small island, known as Preah Thkol or more popularly as the Mebon (after the East and West Mebon temples at Angkor, both likewise originally built on small islands). This temple, certainly still one of the main sights of the Preah Khan complex, now stands high and dry, buried in thick jungle. It stands as a mass of intricate carvings—of elephants and human figures—near the base while enormous *makara* (mythological crocodile-like monsters) and *garuḍas* occupy the higher reaches. There are also traces of a large Buddha-mask and lintels sculptured with Buddha-images, which might seem to suggest a 12th-century date for this temple in its present form.

It is regrettable that moving around at ground

124. Preah Thkol. A section of carving, a nâga.

125. Preah Stung, built later probably under Jayavaman VII, stands guard, as it were, to the hamsa-*bridge, leading to the eastern entrance to the second enclosure.*

level one can get no visual impression of the whole or even of part of this vast site. A track leads from the Prâsâd Damrei to a substantial village (Tra Sen), which we used as our base, on the southern side of the baray, although nothing of the baray remains at this point. From here we walked some three kilometres across dry forest-tracks to reach the Preah Thkol. Thus at no point is it possible to imagine this temple as standing in the centre of a small island. Likewise to reach the central enclosure we drove eastwards through the village and then across fields and forested land, suddenly to find ourselves in the vicinity of Prâsâd Preah Stung. Moving around Angkor Thom with its large clearances and well maintained roads one can know just where one stands at any turn in the path, but within the limited travel manageable around this vast enclosure of Preah Khan, it is practically impossible to know where one is at any time without the assistance of a detailed ground plan.

Preah Stung is an impressive ruin now submerged in undergrowth except for the remaining higher walls and the central tower, which happily retains its four Bodhisattva stone masks facing the four directions, exactly as is so often seen at Angkor Thom. It is thus clearly datable to the reign of Jayavarman VII (1181-1219/20). Thus it is a later addition built at the western end (in fact WSW) of the baray on the same axis as the main temple. But here as at Preah Thkol there is no sign of any baray, but only the surrounding jungle. Following the track westwards, one crosses a bridge over the surrounding moat and so approaches the eastern gateway of the 3rd enclosure. Delaporte gives an impressionist drawing of this bridge as it must have once appeared (*Voyage au Cambodge*, pp. 20-21) but the present reality is sadly different. The moat is no more than a ditch in the jungle, where sections of the collapsed sides of the bridge can still be seen, decorated with rows of *hamsa* (sacred geese). The eastern *gopura* is relatively well preserved.

This third enclosure, some 665 by 980 metres in

extent, is now an expanse of rough grassland, some light forest and the rest jungle, the western reaches being practically inaccessible. Two buildings attract one's interest as one approaches the terrace leading to the still very impressive *gopura* to the second enclosure. These are the *dharmasâla* (chapel and rest-house complex) built in sandstone and of the kind generally associated with the works of Jayavarman VII. Nearby is another 'chapel', built in laterite and containing the important inscription, which associates the site with Sûryavarman I.

The 'terrace' leading to the *gopura* of the second enclosure is now a mass of broken rock and having made one's way over this and through one of the arches of the *gopura*, one's first impression in that of the total ruin of this whole enclosure as well as the inner enclosure at its centre. One makes one's way towards the centre along a scarcely discernible track of broken stones and undergrowth. There is no sign of any terrace such as appears on the plan, and the decorative basins once filled with water have become mere depressions in the uneven ground. The only structures immediately recognizable for their function in the centre are the four inner *gopuras* standing around the centre shrine with approaches

126. (left) Preah Stung. A section of carving on the inner wall. (Photograph by Suthep Kritsanuvarin.)

127. (below) Preah Stung. The hamsa-bridge. (Photograph by Suthep Kritsanuvarin.)

128. Preah Stung. The eastern gopura *of the outer enclosure.*

from the four directions, but of which the upper sections have totally collapsed. However enough remains to give the impression of a shrine quite plausibly constructed around the mid-11th century, although Henri Mauger suggests a later date for the gateways (*gopura*). He visited the site when it was already in a neglected and ruined state, but had not yet suffered the pillage or depredations of the last thirty years. He suggests four phases for the gradual development of the whole site: (I) the erection of the main shrine together with the inner (first) and outer (fourth) enclosures towards the beginning of the 11th century, (2) the construction of the second enclosure during the first half of the 12th century, (3) the construction of the third fortified enclosure in laterite towards the end of the 12th century, and (4) the construction of the baray together with the temples of Preah Stung and Preah Thkol last of all, perhaps towards the end of the reign of Jayavarman VII. Thus this last enterprise becomes yet one more of the many great works attributed to him. As for the three minor temples outside the third enclosure and to the north-west, only one of these is directly aligned with the rest of the complex and thus was probably constructed about the same time as the main shrine in the inner enclosure. It is known locally as the large (*thom*) Prâsâd O Chotal Thom. This is a walled temple with *gopuras* to the east (ENE) and the west (WSW), and an antechamber (*maṇḍapa*) leading to the shrine-room. It is built of sandstone and when Mauger visited it, it was already in a much-ruined state. The so-called small (*toch*) Prâsâd O Chotal Toch consists of little more than a ruined tower built of laterite and as was mentioned above it is the only shrine on the whole sites oriented correctly towards due east. The small shrine, which stands between the other two, consists of a sanctuary preceded by a vestible. With no knowledge of the intentions of the founders, they may simply be regarded as independent works of merit by donors who wished to be associated with the main shrine.

The inscription associating Sûryavarman I with this great temple reads as follows:

> *The dance of the God who has the moon for his diadem (Śiva), the play of the tips of whose glorious feet cause the earth to shake and tremble in the eight directions, a dance which causes Indra, god of the winds, to whirl and moan because of the vigorous arms which cause the palaces of the gods to sway, a dance which renders space insignificant with garlands of shooting rays from the splendour of his nine modes of dance, may his dance which brings joy and does honour to Brahmâ and the other gods, be propitious (for us).*

[The nine modes of dance are: erotic, furious, heroic, odious, comic, pathetic, marvelous, terrible and peaceful.]

> *All honour to Buddha to whom alone the title of omniscient fully applies, and whose word is true*

and expressed in due measure.

I honour the feet of my guru, the twin boats of the Perfection of Wisdom and of the Tantras, for attaining the innate knowledge of the three letters (AUM).

There is Srî Sûryavarman, endowed with royal splendour, a manifestation of Vishnu of the dynasty of the sun, whose reign began in the Śaka Year 924 (= AD 1002).

The god of love is bodiless and the moon with its rabbit (is defective), but the act of his making is free of defect, conceived of as manifest beauty.

With the learned texts as his feet, poetic writing for his hands, the six philosophical systems as his organs of sense, and with the treatise of law as his head, his thought is a living person.

As for his valour, that may be measured from the fact that he, an eminent sage, seized the kingdom in battle from a king surrounded by other kings.

129. Buddha protected by the hood of the Nâga Muçalinda from Preah Khan of Khampong Svay Limestone, 12th to 13th century, h. 1.11 m. Musée Guimet MG 18126

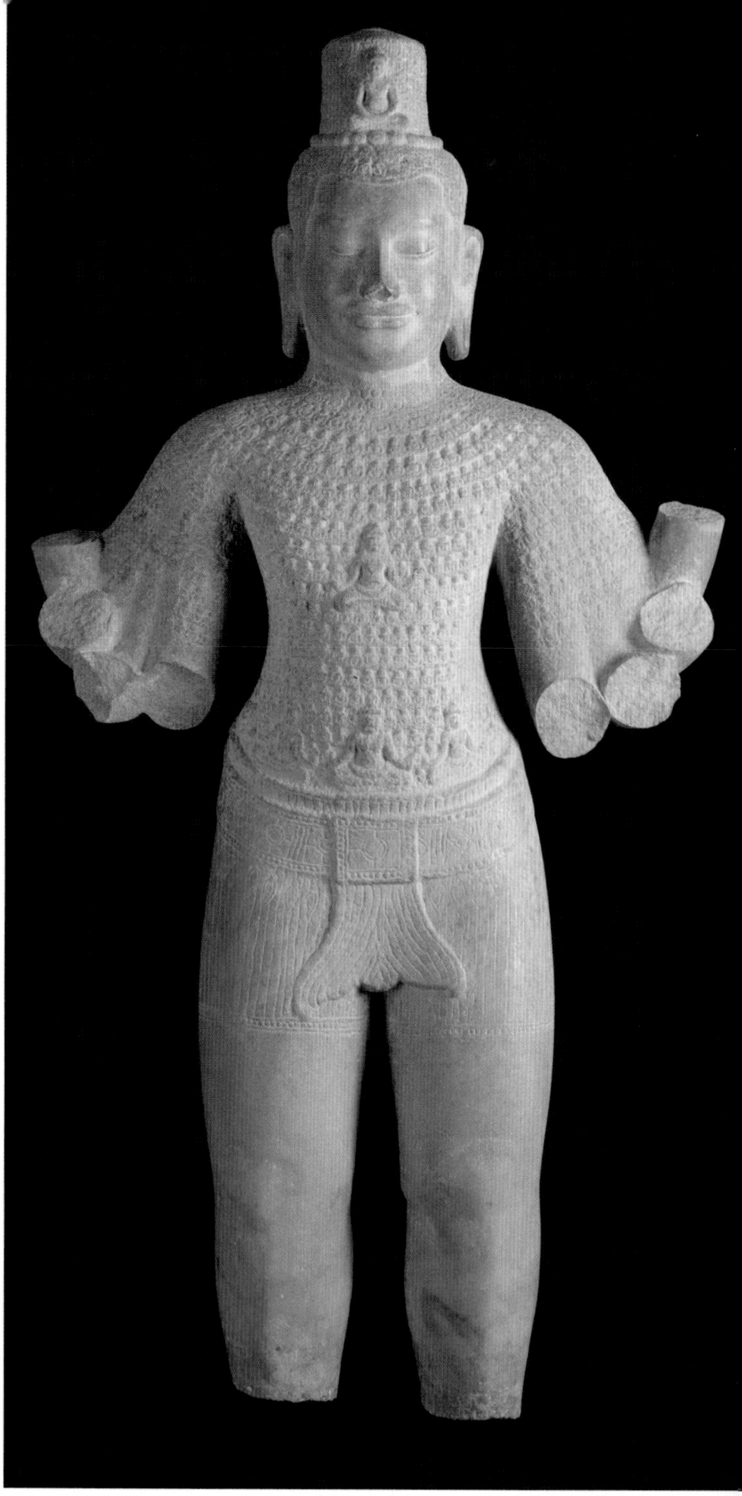

130. Avalokiteśvara from Preah Thkol, Preah Khan of Kampong Svay, 12th 13th century, h. 1.13 m. Musée Guimet MG 18139

People, overcome by the fire of the evils of (former) times, became suddenly altogether happy when it was extinguished by his libations.

Good governance (dharma) *which has lost it footing through the ages, thanks to the elixir of his rule it regains its feet and becomes youthful again.*[52]

Chapter 5

Two Great Khmer Kings

Sûryavarman II

Sûryavarman II (1113-1150) was a great warrior and the founder of many temples, of which the most famous is Angkor Vat (Vishnuloka). In the east he maintained continual campaigns against Champa by land and by sea, eventually occupying the capital of Vijaya (Binh-dinh), situated more than halfway down the east coast of Indochina. He also turned his attentions against the Vietnamese (Dai-Viet) and their capital at Nghê-an (near modern Vinh) with no apparent success, even though he was then in league with the Chams. His wars on this front served no useful purpose and three decades later the Chams took terrible vengeance. The wars in the west appear to have started when the Mons of Haripuñjaya (a kingdom centred on Lamphun) assaulted Lavo (Lopburi), already a province of the Khmer Empire. The famous frieze on the west wing of the southern gallery of Angkor Vat shows Sûryavarman in warlike procession followed by a Syam warrior and by the ruler of Lavo, both regarded as allies in this war.[1] All in all he was responsible for a vast increase of the territory which was submissive to Khmer administration, embracing most of present-day Thailand.

During his reign several temples were built or underwent extensive reconstruction on the Khorat Plateau. Phnom Wan, Phnom Rung and Muang Tam have already been mentioned, as previous rulers were responsible for their earlier development. However Phnom Rung in particular probably achieved its present magnificence during his reign. Phimai (original name Vimâya) on the Khorat Plateau, and Ta Muen Thom, built near the pass across the Dangrek Mountains on the way from Angkor to the plateau may be attributed to his reign, as well as several temples well to the north of the Khorat area extending as far as the present northern Thai city of Nakhon Sakhon (namely Prâsâd Narai Jaeng Vaeng). In the west, Khmer administration reached at least to Lopburi, and during the later 12th century to Kanchanaburi (Prâsâd Muang Singh) close to the present Burmese frontier, and thence down the peninsula at least as far as Phetchaburi, while in the east it still extended to the ancient site of Wat Phu in southern Laos.[2] Near home he was responsible for the great temple complex of Beng Mealea, and as already noted above, the vast estate of Preah Khan of Kampong Svay, as well as several modest temples in the Angkor area.

Sûryavarman II was an offspring of the 'Mahîdharapura dynasty' as so defined by George Coedès. It enters history with the usurper Jayavarman VI, seemingly son of a local ruler in the Phimai area, named as Hiraṇyavarman. As related towards the end of the previous chapter, Jayavarman VI was succeeded by his elder brother Dharaṇîndravarman I. Hiraṇyavarman had another son, Kṣitîndrâditya by another marriage, who married a daughter, named Narendralakṣmî, of Dharaṇîndravarman I, and of this marriage was born Sûryavarman II. He was thus a second cousin of Dharaṇîndravarman I, and by marriage also his grandson.[3] Although a usurper like his predecessors, the two brothers Jayavarman VI and Dharaṇîndravarman I, he had a distant claim to the throne through these Mahîdharapura family-links. Sûryavarman II continued to be served by Divâkarapaṇḍita, upon whom he bestowed the honorific royal title *dhuli jeng* 'dust of the feet'. There seems to be no mention of an official *purohita* for the Devarâja during these three reigns, and this function was probably performed by this same specially honoured Brahman.

Phimai

Situated some seventy kilometres north-east of the present-day city of Nakhon Ratchasima (known more briefly also as Khorat), this great temple was probably by far the most important Khmer administrative centre north of the Dangrek Range. It was linked by a road some 220 kilometres in length with Angkor. This crossed the Dangrek mountains at the fortress-temple of Ta Muen Thom, and passed Muang Tam and Phnom Rung direct to Phimai. Although of rather lesser dimensions, this temple-complex with its double enclosure has the same general pattern as Angkor Vat, namely a square (slightly rectangular) courtyard, entered by portals (*gopura*) to the four directions.[4] On the south (primary) side of the central towered sanctuary, preceded as usual by an antechamber (*maṇḍapa*), there stand two subsidiary shrines. This central complex is approached by a beautifully restored *nâga*-railed bridge, which leads in from the main (southern) *gopura* to the second enclosure, 274 by 220 metres. This central temple complex is set within an outer rectangular enclosure (1,020 by 580 metres) which corresponds fairly closely with the present city limits. Phimai thus presents the rare example of an outer walled enclosure of a Khmer temple-complex, still filled with the dwellings, albeit rather more modern ones, of the local population. At Angkor and elsewhere we are used to seeing Khmer temple-complexes, such as Angkor Vat, set in the midst of a vast empty park, or Preah Khan and similar foundations, standing in the midst of an outer enclosure now entirely overgrown with jungle.

Here at Phimai there once dwelt the local aristocracy, the Brahmans and Buddhist monks accredited to the main shrine, the staff and retainers, all in far less durable accommodation, which has long since disappeared. Doubtless the present population of Phimai has no great concern with the magnificent temple in their midst, except as a valuable tourist attraction, but at least they fill up the space within the outer enclosure, thus giving some idea of the vast number of people who once lived on the premises of these major Khmer fortress-temples.

The main approach was directly from the south, and a road, one of many built or consolidated by Jayavarman VII, connected Phimai with Angkor, 225 kilometres distant, covered in seventeen stages.[5] It is likely that this southern orientation was deliberately chosen by the founder so that the main shrine should face in the direction of the capital. This is an indication that the more normal eastern direction was not necessarily sacrosanct, as also in the case of Preah Vihear and Angkor Vat.

Phimai seems to be the only major surviving Buddhist temple on the Khorat Plateau, although there were probably many minor ones, as suggested by the Buddhist images and sculpture in the National Museum, Bangkok, and the provincial museums of Nakhon Ratchasima and Ubon Ratchathani. However, one gains the impression that the Brahmanical cult generally held sway throughout the provinces as the official religion, except in the far north-western parts of the empire and around the Gulf of Siam, where the Mon population was already Buddhist. One must note also that much of the decorative imagery at Phimai is Brahmanical, primarily scenes from the Râmâyana. Conventional Buddhist scenes, such as the ineffectual attack by Mâra on the Bodhisattva as he sits in meditation, the final gaining of enlightenment and his entry into nirvâṇa, decorate the upper lintels in the darkness of the inner sanctuary (now moved to the Phimai Museum). However, there are several representations of a tantric divinity in dancing pose. A clue to identification is given by an inscription

131. Phimai. A front view from the south.

132. Phimai. The nâga-balustrade, leading to the south entrance.

that records the rebuilding of this temple and the setting up of an image of Trailokyavijaya by a local ruler named Virendrâdhipativarman of Chok Vakula in 1108. Thus it seems likely that this great sanctuary was developed as a Buddhist site solely on the initiative of this presumably local governor of the province. Although this particular image referred to is no longer evident, it is likely that the ten-armed dancing figures whom we see represented, particularly on the lintel at the entrance to the main sanctuary and even more clearly reproduced on a lintel in the north-east corner of the galleries, should be identified as Trailokyavijaya ('Victory over the threefold world').[6] This title pertains to Vajrapâṇi as the result of his subduing and converting to Buddhism the major divinities of the whole (threefold) world, thus forming them into a special maṇḍala known as the *Trilokaçakramaṇḍala* (*Maṇḍala of the Circle of the Triple World*), of which he himself is the central presiding divinity.[7]

Ta Muen Thom

The actual site of this temple near the pass across the Dangrek Range seems to have been fixed by the presence of a jutting stone with a roundish base, which suggests the form of a 'self-existent' (*svayambhû*) *linga*. It was precisely over this that the central shrine with its antechamber was raised. Like Phimai, the main shrine faces south towards Angkor. Since space on the summit on which the whole complex stands is limited, this results in an unusually steep ascent up to the southern and main entrance (*gopura*). The main shrine is flanked by the ruins of subsidiary buildings to left and right, as well as (originally) two towers set back towards the northern side of the courtyard. Thus the essential plan of the temple corresponds to the typical Khmer arrangement of a central towering shrine, flanked by two others of slightly lesser height. Here though the two subsidiary tower-shrines are set rather far back. Unfortunately it has suffered wicked damage. Although it lies just inside the present Thai frontier, it was held by the Khmer Rouge after they were driven into this frontier area during the Vietnamese occupation of Cambodia (1979 onwards). All carvings, especially lintels, of value to antique dealers in Bangkok were removed or seriously damaged in the attempts at removal. Even dynamite was used, resulting in the total collapse of one of the two towers. Since 1991 the Fine Arts Department of the Thai Government has brought welcome order into the resulting chaos, but inevitably the carved stone-work remains irreplaceable.[8]

Nearby close to the gravel road which leads to Ta Muen Thom, one passes a well-preserved 'hospital chapel' and soon afterwards also a *dharmasâla* or 'rest-house' of a slightly more elaborate layout, consisting of 'chapel' and a subsidiary building in a walled enclosure. Thus the whole complex, now simply named after the nearest

133. *(above) Phimai. A lintel over a doorway in the north-east corner of the gallery, probably to be identified as Trailokyavijaya, a tantric form of Vajrapâni.*

→ 136. *(p. 125 bottom right)* *Ta Muen Thom. The main shrine of this temple seems to have been aligned over a jutting stone, which was regarded as a form of self-produced linga.*

134. *(below) Phimai. A curious carving of a form of dancing Buddha on a stone in the corner of the second enclosure.*

135. (above) Ta Muen Thom. Built just to the north of the Dangrek Range, it is now just inside the Thai border. This was formerly an important staging post of the main route from Angkor to Phimai and other places on the Khoran Plateau. This area was occupied by the Khmer Rouge during the 1980s and this particular site has suffered badly.

village, was a very important halting place on what was probably the main route crossing the Dangrek Range on the way from Angkor to Phimai.

Other temples on the Khorat Plateau and beyond

The beautiful little temple at Sikhoraphum, halfway between Surin and Sisaket on the main railway line travelling east from Khorat, has the same general design typical of Khmer pyramid-temples, viz. a major central shrine with four smaller shrines to the four corners. It is set within a square moat and a square, walled enclosure. Apart from the charm of the site, it is remarkable for the well-preserved lintel over the eastern entrance to the main shrine and for the upper parts of the towers, which represent later non-Khmer developments, as in the Wat Mahathat at Lopburi. The lintel has an elaborate pattern, showing a *kâla*-mask below, surmounted by a dancing Ïiva as well as a complicated looping of garlands, incorporating minor divinities and rishis (Hindu sages).

Prâsâd Ban Pluang stands alone as a single solid

stone square tower some forty kilometres south of Surin in the village of this name in Prathat District. It stands on an unusually high laterite platform, extending eastwards from the front of the temple as well as to the north and south, as though intended for two other constructions. This single tower with pairs of stone guardian-figures set into the four corners, has been beautifully restored. The eastern lintel shows Indra on his elephant surmounted by a toraṇa, which represents Krishna holding up Mount Govardhana. Indra appears yet again on the southern and northern lintels, suggesting perhaps a special devotion to him. However it probably remained unfinished.[9]

Prâsâd Kamphaeng Yai, now standing in a large Theravâda monastic courtyard of the same name, is within easy reach of Sisaket in Utumphon Pisai district, as marked on Thai tourist maps. It has been recently restored by the Department of Fine Arts and is generally well preserved. It consists of a walled enclosure, facing east, with entrances from all four directions, the *gopuras* to east and west being largely intact. The main building comprises three shrines standing on a high laterite platform fronted by two subsidiary shrines (or so-called libraries). The central shrine, largely of stone, resembles the tower of Prâsâd Ban Pluang, although it has a protruding portico on the east side. It stands appreciably higher than the shrines to north and south in their present limited state of repair for which bricks were mainly used. The lintel and toraṇa on the south side of the central shrine are well preserved. A scene from the Râmâyana is surmounted by Śiva and his spouse Umâ on his bull Nandin. The toraṇa of the north side shows Krishna holding up Mount Govardhana as at Ban Phluang.

Some twenty kilometres to the north is the 'hospital chapel' of Kamphaeng Noi standing in the grounds of a Theravâda monastery of the same name. It consists of a simple stone laterite tower with a walled enclosure. Although all the major temples in this area are dated generally to the 11th to 12th centuries, the building of these 'hospital chapels' and 'rest-houses' is usually attributed to the reign of Jayavarman VII, viz. late 12th to 13th century. Some forty-five kilometres south-west of Sisaket is a group of three brick-built temples, marked on the map as Prang Ku, and even nearer to the city in the village of Huai Thap Yai Than there is a similar group, of which the towers have been rebuilt in a later style resembling that of Sikhoraphum. This gives them a rather comical appearance as the new towers are out of proportion to the earlier brick-built shrines.

Some sixty kilometres south of Sisaket in Khukhan District there is good example of another *dharmasâla* or 'rest-house', consisting of the regular 'chapel' together with a smaller stone building set in the corner of the walled enclosure, known as Prâsâd Ban Samao. Still further south on the way to

138. (above) Sikhoraphum. This 12th century Khmer temple, consisting of four shines surrounding the central one, has been later modified according to Ayuthayan patterns, as was the case of the Mahathat temple at Lopburi. See Plate 106, p. 96.

← 137. (p. 126) Nearby Ta Muen Thom, in the forest there is both a dharmasâla *of the usual pattern; a shrine with tower, a subsidiary building and a* gopura*. Nearby there is a man-made pool. This is referred to locally as Ta Muen, to distinguish it from the main temple, Ta Muen Thom (Big), and the hospital chapel, Ta Muen Toch (Small), which one passes in a clearing on the left, as one approaches the other two sites. For another such chapel, see Plate 199, p. 169.*

139. (below) Another view of Sikhoraphum temple. (Photograph by Suthep Kritsanuvarin.)

140. (above) Sikhoraphum. The lintel over the main shine. This shows a ten-armed dancing Śiva on a pedestal supported by hamsa *(sacred geese) and resting on a* kâla*-mask. Just below Śiva to the left and right are four other divinities, seemingly Durgâ, Vishnu, Brahma and Gaṇeśa. Below them there is a row of attendant feminine divinities riding mythological creatures, while above* gandharvas *(heavenly musicians) are rejoicing in the sky. Altogether this temple of red sandstone has been remarkably well preserved. (Photograph by Suthep Kritsanuvarin.)*

141. (left) Prâsâd Ban Pluang. This temple of a single tower, seemingly unfinished, stands on a massive laterite platform in a village of the same name, some 40 kilometres south of Surin. It is included as one more example of careful renovoation, in this case carried out by an American archaeologist, Vance Childress. Indra on his elephant seems to be a regular motif for this temple.

the frontier town of Chong Phra Plai there is yet another 'hospital chapel' known as Prâsâd Tam-nak-srei, of which only the tower remains.

Far to the west of the plateau an unusual example of a *dharmasâla*, known as Muang Kao, can be seen just a few kilometres from the much earlier temples of Non Ku and Muang Khaek (described under Jayavarman IV in Chapter 4) some thirty kilometres west of Nakhon Ratchasima. It consists of the usual

142. Prâsâd Kamphaeng Yai. A general view across the front of the set of three shrines, looking south.

143. Prâsâd Kamphaeng Yai. The stone-facing of the northern 'library' with the main shrine on the left. (Photograph by Suthep Kritsanuvarin.)

'chapel' and separate stone building in a walled compound, but here the massive *gopura* which is built of sandstone and laterite appears as the most important part of the whole complex, the rest of which is built of laterite only, as is usually the case. Nearby there is a small stone-lined pool. Like other such structures it must probably be dated to the reign of Jayavarman VII, which suggests that Muang Khaek and Non Ku were still well maintained into the 13th century (as is politically quite likely), despite their present bare appearance. These temples are but a few examples, albeit the more spectacular ones, of the vast number that cover the Khorat Plateau and further westwards.

Travelling towards the north-east from Phimai for about fifty kilometres along Route 207 one branches off to the left well before reaching Prathai in order to reach Prâsâd Nangram close to a village of the same name. Apart from the main *vihara*, of which the walls are still standing, all built in sandstone on laterite foundations, with several well-preserved lintels *in situ,* there is also a walled *dharmasâla* consisting of a tower, a small separate chapel and a *gopura*, all built of laterite and in reasonably good condition. The *vihâra* was surrounded by a moat, of which sections still remain. Excavations carried out by the Department of Fine Arts in 1990-94 suggest that this was a Buddhist monastery, dating to the 11th-12th centuries. The *dharmasâla* was probably built later during the reign of Jayavarman VII.

To the north of Nangram in the vicinity of the village Ban Si Da (on Route 2 some forty-five kilometres north of Phimai) is the strange-looking temple of Ku Phra Ko Na, standing in a Theravâda monastery of the same name. Of the original set of three brick towers two are in a badly ruined condition, while the central one has been 'improved' by a nine-storey stone pinnacle, inset with Buddha-images.

Some sixty kilometres in a straight line north-west of Nangram is the impressive temple of Puoi Noi. This can be reached by continuing along Route 207 beyond Prathai, then turning left (northwards) into Route 207, and then into a minor road at the village of Nong Song Hong going due north towards Puoi Noi. This is a well-preserved Brahmanical temple, built of brick and red sandstone on the usual laterite base. The main temple consists of a group of three shrines on a raised platform with *gopuras* to the east and west, and two subsidiary shrines (or libraries) confronting the main set of three. Some fine lintels and toraṇa*s*, best illustrated by our photographs, remain there undamaged. This small complex is surrounded by a moat with an approach only from the east.

In the same area just beyond the village of Nong Song Hong going north is Prâsâd Ku Suan Taeng, where there is a group of three brick-built temples of which the centre one is fairly well preserved. The use of brick and the earlier conventional set of three

145. (above) Nang-ram, an 11th to 12th century Buddhist temple, occupying a solitary site some fifty kilometres north of Phimai. It consists now of little more than the foundations and the door-posts with several remarkable lintels. View across pool from the east.

← *144. (p. 130) Prâsâd Kamphaeng Yai. An ancient Buddha-image, well plastered in gold by the faithful in a new shrine on the north side of the monastic compound.*

146. (below) Nang-ram. The well-preserved dharmasâla *consisting of an enclosure with* gopura*, a shrine-tower and subsidary buildings, suggests that this lay on a major route from Phimai northwards to Khon Kaen.*

might well indicate an earlier date, but brick was still being used extensively in this northern area, and its lintels (now in the Phimai Museum) suggest a mid-12th century date.[10]

Further to the east, some fifty-five kilometres south of the pleasant city of Roy Et is the equally important temple of Prâsâd Ku Kasin, likewise built of brick and red sandstone, but not so well preserved as Puoi Noi. The central temple consists of a group of three shrines of which only the central one remains in a half-ruined condition; the door-frame still stands, surmounted by a well preserved lintel, except for the central defaced figure which may be Śiva. His throne rests on a *kâla*-mask, set within the usual garlanded canopy. One other surviving lintel on the eastern approach shows Indra on his elephant. This main temple is faced by two smaller stone-built shrines in an even more ruined condition. Only sections of the outer wall now remain.[11]

There are many other much smaller Khmer temples scattered throughout the whole region, of which only sections of stone wall remain standing, best represented by an appropriate illustration, if they are worth notice.

148. (below) Puoi Noi. This beautiful little temple of red sandstone is to be found in a village of the same name (marked on tourist maps) some 135 kilometres north-east of Khorat city. It is surrounded by a moat and approachable only from the east side.

149. (above) Puoi Noi. The frontage of the three main shrines on their laterite platform, as seen looking northwards.

← 147. (p. 132 top) Nang-ram. The lintels are all similar; they comprise a kâla-*mask with a divinity poised above it. In the two cases here, facing east, we see Indra on his three-headed elephant.*

150. (below) Puoi Noi. The toraṇa of a shine of the south-east corner of the complex, showing Śiva of his bull Nandin. On the lintel below Indra surmounts a kâla-*mask.*

151. (above) Puoi Noi. The lintel of the central shrine, showing a lying Vishnu giving birth to Brahmâ.

→ 153. (p. 135) Prâsâd Ku Kasin, indicated on the map as Suwannaphum, a temple similar in layout to Puoi Noi, but not so well preserved, is about 55 kilometres south of Roi Et.

152. (below) In the same area one finds Ku Suan Taeng, a convential set of three brick-built shrines, of which the centre is fairly well preserved.

Going some 140 kilometres further north to Nakhon Sakhon one reaches the most northerly known Khmer temple of importance in north-east Thailand. This is more or less on the same latitude as Sukhothai, which represented the limits of Khmer advance in the north-west. Prâsâd Narai Jaeng Vaeng dates probably to about the mid-11th century. All that survives is the tower of the main shrine, of which the porch has collapsed, leaving only an isolated lintel showing Indra on his elephant. However all that remains is remarkably well preserved while having the aesthetic advantage of standing in the beautiful grounds of the Theravâda monastery of the same name. The toraṇa on the eastern side over the entry to the shrine is adorned with a multi-armed figure of dancing Śiva. This surmounts a lintel showing Krishna wrestling with a pair of lions. The lintel over the false doorway on the northern side shows Krishna killing a single lion, surmounted by a lying image of Vishnu. It is this which gives this temple the popular name of 'Nâṛâyana with outstretched legs'. A double series of miniature human figures decorate the lintel over the false doorway of the south side, representing some unidentified story. Freeman has identified a monkey in the group, and so suggests a scene from the Râmâyana (*Khmer Temples*, pp.192-3). The western false doorway remains plain. The seeming remoteness of this Khmer temple far to the north probably derives from the lack of archaeological research in this area. Another ancient Khmer stone pillar remains enshrined in the great stûpa of the monastery of Phrathat Cheun Chum in the centre of Nakhon Sakhon. This can be seen through small ornamental windows, conveniently left ajar, to the four sides of this impressive 'Laos-style' shrine. The Khmer inscription on this stone has already been recorded, and although only of local interest, it confirms that this northern area was under Khmer administration, presumably in the 11th to the 12th centuries, although no satisfactory date is recorded. It tells of the division of a territory, then known as Jra-ren, part now going to the higher authority at a place then known as Vnur Vinau, and subsequent offerings made at this shrine by the ruler of Jra-reng, presumably confirming this order.[12] This short text draws our attention to the fact of how little is known to us of Khmer local history in these remote areas of their 'empire'. On the eastern limits of the town there is yet another Khmer temple, known as Prâsâd Phrathat Dum, of which only the central tower of the original three brick-built towers is still standing.

Temples at Angkor or nearby

During Sûryavarman II's reign several other small temples, all Brahmanical, were built at Angkor Thom. Thammanon and Chau-say-tevoda stand on either side of the road a short distance beyond the eastern exit from the centre of Angkor Thom.

154. (above) Prâsâd Ku Kasin. One of the surviving lintels showing Indra on his elephant.

155. (left) Narai Jaeng Vaeng at Nakon Sakhon. All that survives of this temple in the tower over the main shrine, standing in the grounds of a Theravâda monastery of the same name.

Another group of five, known as Preah Pithu, possibly later in date, is set well back from the road to the right as one leaves the palace compound towards the northern exit of Angkor Thom.

Thammanon is relatively simple, consisting of a courtyard with entrance portals east and west, a single main shrine preceded by a separate antechamber, and a small building of the kind usually described as a library. It was restored substantially during the 1920s and displays some excellent carved stonework, mainly floral designs with inset images of apsaras and guardians. It may have been dedicated to Vishnu, who rides Garuḍa on the frontal piece (*toraṇa*) on the west side of main shrine.

Chau-say-tevoda, another Śaivite temple, recently restored by a Chinese team, consists of a single main shrine preceded by a linked antechamber standing in a square courtyard with entrance portals to the four quarters. Some carvings of themes drawn from the Râmâyana still remain to be seen. Vittorio Roveda, expert in the identification of mythological scenes, has kindly drawn my attention to two toraṇas, one on each of these temples, portraying scenes from the Viśvântara-jâtaka, a popular Buddhist story concerning a previous life of Sâkyamuni Buddha. The source must be a Sanskrit literary one, well known in the Buddhist communities, to whose existence attention has already been drawn. Under later Theravâda developments (14th century onwards) this story becomes better known as the Vessantara-jâtaka.

Preah Pithu consists of a group of five temples; three of which are of similar design, namely a central shrine in a square courtyard with entrances to the four quarters. They are placed more or less in a row

156. (right) Narai Jaeng Vaeng. An image of dancing Śiva on the toraṇa surmounting the lintel of the east (front) side of this temple. Although normally 10-armed in such a pose, here there are traces of two extra arms.

157. (below) Thammonon. During the expansive reign of Sûryavarman II, building also continued at Angkor. We note here this well preserved little temple of conventional design, consisting of antechamber and main shrine with gopuras *to east and west, but with only one 'library' on the south side. It seems to have been conceived as a pair with Chau-say-tevoda on either side of the road, leading from the palace to the main eastern gateway. The latter temple was more elaborate, being provided with four* gopuras, *but was found in an advanced state of ruin. At present (2002-03) a Chinese team is working on its renovation.*

from west to east. Much ruined, they still contain some fine carvings, while other pieces lie strewn around the site. The last in the row, the furthest into the surrounding forest, is particularly interesting, in that it was later adapted as a Buddhist sanctuary and now thirty-seven small Buddha-images, arranged on a frieze, gaze down from above. They may be intended to symbolize the thirty-seven 'factors of enlightenment'.[13] The fourth temple, north of the other three, had no enclosure but is approached by a fine causeway with *nâga* railings, now in a very dilapidated condition. The fifth temple, the smallest of all, consists of a single shrine with an entrance-hall, linked to the shrine by a vestibule or covered hall, the typical design, one may note, of so many simple Indian shrines. With no inscriptions available, the circumstances relevant to the founding of these shrines are totally unknown. Certain features might associate them with Angkor

158. (left) Preah Pithu. This is the name given to a group of five temples seemingly built at various times during the 12th century and maybe even into the 13th. Shown here is the innermost of the row of three shrines, which contains the frieze of Buddhas shown below.

159. (below) Preah Pithu. Section of a frieze of 37 Buddhas. This illustration belongs properly to Chapter 6, where such adaptatons of earlier Brahmanical shrines to Buddhist usage is discussed.

Vat while others might suggest a dating closer to the Bayon. That they were all in origin Brahmanical foundations is certain.

Another important fortress-temple, Bantây Samre, may be attributed to the end of the reign of Sûryavarman II or to that of his successor Udayâdityavarman II. No inscription relating to its foundation is known. A local legend attributes it to a cucumber-grower of the Samre clan, who was so jealous of his stupendous cucumbers that he did not hesitate to kill any intruders. One day the king himself came and was duly killed. Subsequently the Samre cucumber-grower was recognized as king, when one of the royal elephants knelt before him. He is said to have built Bantây Samre as his residence. Worthless as historical material, it may reflect the uncertainties concerning the disappearance of Sûryavarman II about 1150, suggesting some palace upheaval. Bantây Samre, on the eastern limits of Angkor, is one of the best preserved and the best maintained of temple-fortresses. Consisting of the usual components, a central towered shrine preceded on the eastern side by a long rectangular hall, enclosed within an inner courtyard thirty-five by forty-four metres, with four impressive *gopuras* to the four directions, and containing two subsidiary buildings or libraries placed regularly to north and south, it represents the 'classical style' of Khmer architecture at its best. It is in fact the miniature of the great temple-complexes of Beng Mealea and Preah Khan of Kampong Svay. The outer enclosure consists of a massive gallery built of laterite, eighty by eighty-five metres, pierced by four *gopuras*, built of the usual sandstone. The whole building contains a large number of well-preserved lintels and toraṇas, where Brahmanical themes relating to Vishnu and Śiva predominate, and where there are also several scenes from the Râmâyana. On some of the toraṇas of the upper stages, scenes from the Viśvântara-jâtaka can be distinguished, as at Thammanon and Chau-say-tevoda. The carvers are clearly working within the same repertoire of subject matter. The temple is approached on the eastern side by a long promenade ending with a terrace with nâga-railing. It is interesting to note that the outer western *gopura* is more impressively built than the eastern one, possibly because this temple may have been normally approached from this direction by another promenade leading directly from the eastern end of the East Baray and thus from the direction of Angkor.

160. Bantây Samre, approach from the east. This is certainly the best-preserved of the fortress-temples in the Angkor area. There is no relevant inscription and thus no sure information about its founding, possibly during the uncertain period which followed the end of Sûryavarman's II's reign.

Angkor Vat

Angkor Vat, presumed to be the major wonder of the whole Angkor area, impresses by its enormous size. Viewed from a distance it appears at its best, and doubtless at its very best if viewed from the air, when its precise maṇḍala layout set within its square moat can be fully appreciated. Once inside its massive walls, one may well have a feeling of dull monotony. The intricate floral designs which cover the stone-work, a vast labour indeed, lighten one's feelings in no way, and the celestial maidens (*apsaras*), all looking so much the same, whom one meets at every corner, do little to gladden the heart. In so far as this vast temple may be considered as the mausoleum of Sûryavarman II, gloomy sentiments of such a kind may not be unsuitable.

Like other pyramid-temples more modest in design, it is laid out like a maṇḍala. It rises on three levels, each terrace more or less identical with towers at the four corners and portals piercing the four sides. Five towers with the central one higher than the others crown the top terrace, which is square. The lower terraces protrude westwards in order to make room for the grandiose western entrance and the two libraries to left (north) and right (south) on the second terrace, and for a further hall of approach on the lowest platform. A long causeway crossing the moat and passing between two subsidiary buildings, likewise referred to as libraries, finally brings one to this grand entrance, after which gloom prevails until one has climbed to the highest pinnacles to appreciate the truly magnificent views.

This great temple is renowned for its numerous carvings, all on Brahmanical themes. A recent and very through work on this subject has been made by Vittorio Roveda to which any interested visitor should refer.[14] The large bas-reliefs of the 3rd enclosure present eight major subjects, two to each side of the four major entrance portals, while a large number of small individual scenes decorate the walls of the corner towers. All these smaller scenes and most of the main subjects are drawn from the Indian epics, the Mahâbhârata and the Râmâyana, either directly or from later sectarian compilations. Most

161. (p. 140 top left) Bantây Samre contains many unspoiled carvings, such as this interior section of the western gopura. *This shows Skanda, leader of of the hosts of heaven on his peacock, and below scenes in honour of the sun and moon.*

162. (p. 140 top right) Bantây Samre. An inner entrance from the east, north doorway, showing the 'Churning of the Ocean'.

163. (p. 140 bottom) Bantây Samre. The toraṇa above the corresponding south doorway shows Śiva destroying Kâla, the demon of time.

164. (below) Angkor Vat as seen from NW corner.

165. Angkor Vat. A view of the main southern court-yard taken from the central tower.

166. Apsaras on the south-west corner of the central tower.

of the main scenes treat of war, individual contest and the triumph of battle, the main exceptions being the large carvings of the 'Churning of the Ocean', and the illustration of the paths to Heaven and Hell. Even in the case of these paths, one cannot but have the impression that those on the way to Heaven (even riding horses) are the victors of war, while those being cudgelled on the way to future sufferings are the wretched losers who are being driven into captivity.

Going round in anti-clockwise direction from the western entrance we see: (1) the great war between the Pâṇḍavas and the Kauravas from the Mahâbhârata, (2) Sûryavarman II triumphant and in military array, (3) Heaven and Hell scenes, (4) the Churning of the Ocean, (5) the crushing victory of Vishnu over the demons, (6) the victory of Krishna over the demon Bana, (7) the war of the victorious gods over the demons, and (8) the battle of Lanka from the Râmâyana.

167 & 168. (right) Angkor Vat. Scenes from the carved stone-panels of the south gallery, west side:
167. (top) Sûryavarman II .
168. (bottom) The entourage of the Syam (Thai) ruler.
(Photographs by Suthep Kritsanuvarin.)

A few interesting details may be added. No. 6 consists of a series of scenes in which Krishna in an eight-headed and eight-armed manifestation, mounted on Garuḍa, appears several times in the course of defeating the demon-king Bâna, whose citadel is encompassed by fire, represented by Agni, who rides a rhinoceros, a rare animal to see on these panels.[15] No.7 presents the major gods of Hindu mythology, each riding his appropriate mount while subduing one of the demons. From left to right one may recognize Kubera, god of wealth, riding a *yakṣa,* Skanda, god of war, riding a peacock, Indra, riding his elephant, then the centre-piece, namely Vishnu

on Garuḍa battling with the Demon Kâlanemi, next Yama, god of death, in a chariot drawn by bulls, Śiva drawing his bow, Brahma on his sacred goose, Sûrya, god of the sun, issuing from the sun-disk, and Varuṇa, god of the waters, riding a *nâga*.

This vast temple was dedicated as Paramavishnuloka, the 'Supreme World of Vishnu', this serving as the posthumous name of Sûryavarman II. It is assumed that his remains were entombed here with the result that Angkor Vat may also be regarded as a mausoleum. This may explain why it faces west instead of east. One may compare Çaṇḍi Jago in East Java, which was also intended as a mausoleum and thus faces west.[16]

169. Beng Mealea. This great fortress-temple, lying some 50 kilometres east of Angkor, was probably the major creation of Sûryavarman II, although there is no inscription to give confirmation of this. It is now a total ruin buried in jungle, and significant photographs are hard to obtain. This is a view of the east entrance to the inner walled enclosure, where entry can be gained to see the results of long neglect and the more recent destruction caused by marauding soldiers.

Beng Mealea (literary spelling: Bĕng Mâlâ)[17]

The great temple-fortress of Beng Mealea was built some forty kilometres to the east of Angkor on the eastern flank of Phnom Kulen, almost certainly (judging by style) during the reign of Sûryavarman II, although there is no inscription available in confirmation. Close to the village of the same name, presumably originally embraced within this enormous complex, stands the central temple-fortress, a massive structure of three enclosed courtyards, a rectangle measuring about 181 by 152 metres. The interior is in such an advanced state of dilapidation that one clambers over blocks of fallen sandstone, while the whole structure is buried in jungle. This was set within a moated enclosure that measured more that four kilometres in circumference. However now it is in such an advanced state of ruin and wanton destruction that it is difficult to make out its main features. The French authorities cleared it in the early 20th century and a plan and description will be found in Maurice Glaize, *Angkor*, 4th ed. Paris 1993, pp. 277-80. Louis Delaporte gives a description of how he found it in 1873, approaching from the vast artificial lake on the eastern approach of which he made an impressionist drawing (see his *Voyage en Cambodge*, pp. 276-7).

> *Thence one passes along a causeway, of which the point of departure was an immense esplanade or terrace with eight sets of steps, on the summit of which sixteen enormous lions with their paws raised in a menacing manner, served as fantastic sentinels guarding the sacred enclosure. One then crosses the moat which together with a surrounding causeway on the inner side encompasses the whole main structure. The bridge which is guarded by enormous dragons (*nâga*), is decorated with arching columns. Beyond the bridge another esplanade and an approach-walk, decorated with nâgas and other images and set between two groups of six basins of water, lead to the terrace in the form of a cross (*gopura*) which precedes the main building. This whole approach with the bridge etc. is repeated to the other directions north, west and south. Around the temple itself there was once a tall gallery with double colonnade surmounted by a two-stage vaulted arch, topped by a light crest. Above this ten towers reared above this enormous sanctuary in the centre of a mass of structures now in a state of ruined chaos. The doorways and the galleries are decorated with more than four hundred richly sculptured frontal pieces (fronton), of which barely ten remain in place and*

170. Beng Mealea. Another view of ornamental stonework amidst jungle on the south side.

not one of them intact. Such is the state of dereliction of this grandiose monument, that even in its very presence, it is difficult to gain any clear idea of its former magnificence. (pp. 108-10)

Such sculptured pieces as remained before recent devastations reveal the usual Brahmanical divinities, Indra on his elephant, Vishnu on Garuḍa, or a dancing image of Śiva. Krishna also appears holding aloft Mount Govardhana. The Râmâyana is also present, especially scenes relating to the Battle of Lanka.[18]

A period of uncertainly and warfare

Returning to our historical survey, we note that Sûryavarman II disappears from the scene *c.*1150. Much of the building attributed to him at Angkor (p. 136ff) and probably also at Beng Mealea must have been completed by his effective successor, Yaśovarman II. In the meantime a cousin, known as Dharaṇîndravarman II, may have claimed the throne, possibly as the result of a palace revolution. Little seems to be known of him except that he was a fervent Buddhist according to the inscription which his son, Javavarman VII, later set up in the great temple-palace of Ta Prohm in Angkor:

Finding satisfaction in the nectar of the moon of Sâkya(muni), employing the substance of his wealth for the benefit of Buddhist monks, Brahmans and needy subjects, (thus) desirous of extracting true worth from impure matter, which has no true worth, he honoured without ceasing the feet of the Buddha (vv. 16-17).

All these rulers of the Mahîdharapura dynasty were favourable to Buddhism, if not avowed practising Buddhists, and one gains the impression that from the early 11th century onwards and the succession of Sûryavarman II the cult of the Devarâja had lost much of its earlier significance for the ruling monarchs despite its continuing importance in Brahmanical circles.

Dharaṇîndravarman II, if he ruled at all, was succeed by Yaśovarman II, whose identity is uncertain, but his right to the throne was accepted by Prince Indrakumâra (possibly the future Jayavarman VII), who was engaged in a campaign against the Chams at that time. There is the curious story of Yaśovarman being attacked by Daitya Râhu (some form of demon if not a real person) when this Prince came to his assistance.[19] In the fighting the Prince was assisted by two *sanjaks* (presumably body-guards) who were killed even while the Prince prevailed against the Daitya Râhu. Later two other *sanjaks* saved the life of the Prince in fighting against the Chams. Subsequently images of the Prince were set up together with those of the four *sanjaks* in Bantây Chmar, the great temple fortress dedicated by Jayavarman VII to his son Indravarman. When a few years later he heard that a usurper named

Tribhuvanâdityadeva was plotting for the throne, Indrakumâra returned to Angkor to save Yaśovarman, but arriving too late for this, he returned to his urgent campaigning against the Chams. Probably it was his long absence that provoked the lamentations in an inscription of Queen Indradevî, who succeeded her younger sister Queen Jayarâjadevî as the wife of Jayavarman VII.[20] The text is imbued with the devotion of Mahâyâna Buddhism. It opens with salutations to the Buddha in his manifestation as *Dharmakâya* (Body of the Doctrine), *Sambhogakâya* (Glorious Body) and his *Nirmânakaya* (Transformation Body). The following verses praise the Bodhisattva Avalokiteśvara. Thereafter comes a genealogy of Jayavarman VII and his due praises, and then those of his first wife Jayarâjadevî, of whom we learn that:

> *Instructed by her elder sister Indradevî and considering the Buddha as her beloved for the future, she followed the calm way of the Blessed One through a fire of torments and a sea of suffering' (v. 59).*

During the following years Angkor was subjected to continual assaults by the Chams, culminating with the great sea invasion of 1177. Except for the fortuitous removal of the usurper, this was the greatest calamity that befell Angkor until the Siamese invasions two centuries later. On this occasion the Chams attacked by sea, sailing round the coast, then up the Mekong River, the Tonle Sap and the Great Lake, thus taking Angkor by surprise. They burned and pillaged the city, carrying off vast booty and herding prisoners into slavery. It may well be said that Sûryavarman and his successors brought this retribution upon themselves by their continual harassing of the Chams. Now however it fell to Prince Indrakumâra to restore order in the kingdom, and for the next few years he waged war by land and on sea against the Chams. The successful sea-battles were later depicted on the walls of his major architectural creation, the Bayon.

Jayavarman VII

If one assumes that he was about twenty years old in 1165 when Yaśovarman II was under attack, thus also being old enough for his campaigning against the Chams, he would have been forty-three when he was crowned king in 1181. In the course of the thirty-eight years or so of his reign he did more for the greater glory of Angkor than any previous ruler. Apart from the ruins of the Baphuon and the Phimean-âkas, and a few lesser temples, Angkor Thom (Great Angkor) as we see it in its ruined state today, is essentially the city as recreated by Jayavarman VII, while the great Buddhist temple-complexes outside the walls, such as Bantây Kdei, Ta Prohm and Preah Khan, as well as the smaller ones such as Preah Palilay, Ta Nei, Ta Som, and Neak Poen, even the lesser known Krol Ko, Bantây Prei and Prâsâd Prei, are all attributable in one way or another to his reign.

Angkor Thom

A major task was to redefine the area of the city and to this purpose new city walls were built, forming a square three kilometres on each side, protected by a moat one hundred metres across. Four roads radiated from the centre of his reconstructed city, now marked by his pyramid-temple, the Bayon, while the earlier road eastwards from the palace towards Ta Keo was retained, thus resulting in five great gateways, each surmounted by the benevolent gaze of the Bodhisattva Avalokiteśvara, facing in all four directions and presumably identified with the king himself. They are approached from outside by a causeway, of which the stone railings consist of *nâgas*, held as if in a tug-of-war between giant figures, the gods to one side and the demons (*asura*) to the other. Whatever other significance may be attached to this formation, it is scarcely possible to dissociate it from the well-known story of the Churning of the Ocean by the gods and the demons, especially as both 'teams' are represented here. Jayavarman VII also built corner shrines (Prâsâd Chrung) dedicated to Avalokiteśvara at the four angles (SE, NE, NW, SW) of the massive city-walls and also a fifth isolated one on a hilltop just to the south-east. The best preserved, i.e. the one on the SE corner, is easily reached by walking along the top of the wall, wide as a carriage-way, either from the south or the east gateway.[21]

In front of the palace grounds he constructed the imposing terrace, 300 metres long, presumably a royal vantage point for parades and formal receptions. The whole length is decorated with carved scenes of elephant riders, with *garuḍas* and rampant lions and even scenes of sport. At the far side of the parade-ground, overlooked by the terrace, there is a row of twelve towers built of laterite They stand just in front of the two supposed palaces for foreign dignitaries (known as the *kléang*) and already attributed to the reign of Jayavarman V. Thus these towers may also have been put at the disposal of royal guests. They are known popularly as the *Suor Prat*, viz. for 'cord-dancers', who presumably were supposed to perform on cords stretched between the

171. Angkor Thom. The royal terrace in front of the palace grounds.

172. Angkor Thom. An entrance to the palace grounds on the east side, recently beautifully restored.

row of towers! (See Plates 60, 61, p. 74)

The northern end of this terrace may have served as the basis for government buildings constructed of lighter materials. Beyond the northern end of the terrace there is a massive seven-storey structure (as recently restored), each storey being lined with quasi-human figures, some male with elaborate necklaces and bearing clubs or swords, also many women wearing necklaces and bangles, all seated in solemn postures. Among them, probably intended as the centrepiece, is the now well-known figure of the supposed 'Leper-King' according to local popular interpretation. This naked figure, seated with the right knee drawn up, is now well known because of the many copies that have been made of it, one being placed as a shrine, where offerings are made, in the centre of the road just south of the royal palace The one *in situ* is a copy, as the original now presides in front of the National Museum, Phnom Penh. The name inscribed on it, dated stylistically to the 15th century, states clearly that it is *Dharmarâja* (= King of the Law) which is the usual polite title for Yama, the Lord of the Dead. There seems no reason to doubt this intention, but it does not explain who are all these other quasi-human figures. The male ones with clubs and swords might well be Yama's henchmen, while the others might possibly be the denizens of a kind of underworld. George Coedès suggested that this whole massive structure might represent a form of Mount Meru, but it seems ill-conceived for such an interpretation (viz. the central mountain of the universe and the realm of the thirty-three gods of Indian tradition), and also that it served as a place for royal cremations, which is a more likely possibility. I would simply interpret it as the Realm of Yama.

The Bayon and other temples within the walls

Among the last of Jayavarman VII's great works and unusually complex in its final form, the Bayon conforms to the normal maṇḍala pattern of the earlier pyramid-temples. There is the central tower-like shrine, open to the four directions, on a circular raised terrace, surrounded by similar but lower tower-like shrines to the four directions. These lower shrines appear as duplicated on the eastern side (the main side of approach) because of the elaborate *loggia,* which leads up to the main shrine. Similar tower-like shrines stand in the four intermediate directions. From the summit of all these towers Avalokiteśvara gazes benevolently in all four directions. This main complex lies within a square enclosure, adorned by sixteen tower-like shrines, one

173. Angkor Thom. Figures on the wall of Yama. Note the monstrous many-armed figure in the upper range. It has been suggested to me that this may be intended as Hevajra, but iconographically this seems impossible, unless a deliberate distortion was intended.

174. The Bayon. A general view.

at each corner and three on each side, each tower surmounted by four-faced Avalokiteśvara. We thus approximate closely enough to the regular maṇḍala design: the main divinity emanates as four, then eight, and then sixteen. This essential design is then enclosed in a rectangle of 140 by 160 metres, certainly modest in size compared with Angkor Vat. Unfortunately, inside the main enclosure a seeming maze of stone corridors, due to later changes in the design, surround the steps of ascent to the main shrine, and here for a short while one stumbles in gloom. However, once on the summit terrace and in brilliant sunlight again, one stands entranced with the benevolent gazes of Avalokiteśvara, which surround one on all sides.[22]

Bas-reliefs cover most of the exterior walls of the outer and the inner enclosure. They are more deeply cut that those of Angkor Vat and thus far easier to photograph successfully. They are also more varied in content, as though the artisans at work had been given a space to fill with the minimum of instructions. Surprisingly, on these external carved panels of a self-proclaimed Buddhist monument, there is not one single Buddhist theme. Is it possible that all artisans were so used to reproducing Hindu themes that they had no Buddhist themes in their repertoire? Traces of carvings of small Buddha-images can still be seen within the dark galleries of the Bayon and there are a few toraṇas, representing seated Buddha-figures, usually defaced, occasionally Avalokiteśvara, and also stray scenes from Buddhist *jâtakas*, to which Vittorio Roveda has kindly drawn my attention. Together with these there are also the regular Brahmanical scenes, Śiva in ascetic guise, Indra and Krishna as well as scenes from the Râmâyana.[23] Many of these are now scarcely visible because of changes made to the general plan of the whole building and the darkness of the resulting narrow passages. In its earlier phase Buddhist imagery may well have predominated. When the later changes were made, deliberate attempts must have been made to efface the Buddhist repertoire. The outer bas-reliefs were completed presumably after the end of Jayavarman VII's reign, when Brahmanical hostility to Jayavarman's enthusiasm for Buddhism was given freedom of expression. However one may note that there was a far greater repertoire of Brahmancial imagery available at Angkor and the carvers may have been free to work many of the scenes on the outer walls in accordance with the fancy of those in charge. Meanwhile elaborate Buddhist stone carvings were certainly in vogue in the north-western provinces, as is evident from the exhibits of Khmer workmanship in the National Museum, Bangkok as well as in the main sanctuary at Phimai.

As at Angkor Vat, scenes of war and military parades tend to dominate on the outer walls, interspersed with scenes of daily life, in the palace, in the forest, even ordinary people at work and at

175. The Bayon. Carvings of the upper terrace. (Photograph by Suthep Kritsanuvarin.)

play. Beginning at the eastern entrance and going round in the regular clockwise direction, I give a summary of the various themes. Thus we begin on the outer eastern wall (south side) with military parades as the main subject but also with some princesses in a palace and next some ascetics depicted above. The outer southern wall depicts (to the right) the great sea-battle between the Khmers and the Chams, as already mentioned above, and (to the left) military elephant parades, but between these two major scenes we see men engaged in fishing and cock-fighting, a bull-fight and then palace scenes. The outer western wall (starting always from the right) depicts warriors on elephants once again, with scenes of temple-building and life of ascetics above. We then see scenes of fighting and chase with elephants in front, and finally the king returning from a visit (to ascetics) in the forest. The outer northern wall illustrates again scenes of combat with the Chams, while above we see athletes and jugglers, a defile of animals and ascetics in a forest by a river. Finally the eastern wall (north side) shows Khmers and Chams still at war.

The walls of the inner enclosure have far more varied, constantly changing scenes, of which it is difficult to give a coherent account. Here scenes of everyday life and religious scenes predominate. Śiva and Vishnu appear frequently. I give a condensed survey, beginning at the eastern entrance and going in a clockwise direction. First we see a scene of ascetics and animals in a forest, Brahmans presumably performing a ceremony around a brazier, palace scenes and also a procession of soldiers. The southern wall has again a procession of soldiers and palace scenes. There is a fight between a lion and an elephant, presumably for royal entertainment. There is a large Garuḍa and a gigantic fish, representing the ocean out of which rises Mount Meru with its ascetics and animals. There are musicians and a procession of men carrying an empty throne, a child being put into a coffin, a fisherman in his boat and a large lotus in a pool. These several scenes have been identified as referring to the story of Krishna's son Pradyumna, who was stolen by a demon, thrown into the sea, then swallowed by a large fish which was caught by a fisherman, who cut open the fish and found the child. Presumably the artisans at work on this section happened to know these scenes well and so introduced them after their

176. (right top) Stone carving from the outer wall of the Bayon, illustrating the war between the Khmers and the Chams towards the end of the 12th century. (Photograph by Giulia Anglois-Nisbet.)

177. (right bottom) A related scene from the Bayon, showing food and refreshment brought for the advancing troops. (Photograph by Giulia Anglois-Nisbet.)

178. The Bayon. A religious ceremony.

own fashion. The southern wall, left side, has scenes of Śiva and Vishnu, a pool with ascetics and animals, palace scenes and possibly a royal pilgrimage. The western wall again has scenes of Vishnu and Śiva, yet more ascetics, but also scenes of men at work and the building of a temple. This western wall to the left illustrates the Churning of the Ocean, but it is so badly worn that little can be distinguished in detail except for the vase of elixir itself and a few effigies of the gods tugging their *nâga* churning-rope. The northern wall shows more palace scenes, a mountain with the usual animals, a sanctuary with closed door near a pool, a procession, and effigies of Śiva, Brahmâ, Vishnu, Gaṇeśa and Rahu. The eastern side of this northern wall is devoted to Śiva: Śiva on his bull Nandin, the dual between Śiva and Arjuna, Śiva on his mountain crushing Râvaṇa, Śiva blessing adorers, and more palace scenes and ascetics. The eastern wall (north side) has again a variety of themes: a military parade with musicians, a prince (or king) at the feet of Śiva beside an empty throne, then a pool with two boats and divers at work, next possibly scenes illustrating the legend of how a prince rescued a maiden imprisoned in the rocks, and lastly the story interpreted as that of 'Leper-King'. Here one sees a king in his palace wrestling with a snake, which bites him. Servants hasten to consult ascetics in the forest. Women surround the sick king, and then he is seen lying with an ascetic by his side.

These scenes provide the only insight into courtly life, religious preoccupations and the life of the ordinary people of Angkor until we come to the account of Chou Ta-kuan, member of a Chinese mission to Angkor at the end of the 13th century (see pp. 176-7). Among such an array of activities depicted on these outer walls, it is noteworthy that not one Buddhist scene appears despite the impetus to the spread of Buddhism that Jayavarman VII gave throughout his nearly forty years of reign.

Of the smaller but none the less significant temples within the walls we must note Preah Palilay and the one now named as Prâsâd Top West (previously simply listed as Monument 486). Preah Palilay, which is found amongst the trees just north of the palace grounds, is now so dilapidated that its original form as a single tower-like shrine, open to all four directions and raised on a multi-tiered terrace, is scarcely recognizable. However, some finely carved Buddhist scenes can still be seen on the upper sections of the sides of the sole eastern portico (*gopura*). Still clearly visible are the scenes of Sâkyamuni receiving the dish of curds offered him by the village-girl Sujatâ, and the scene where he tames the fierce elephant sent to destroy him by his jealous cousin Devadatta. Another scene, less clear, illustrates the offerings of animals of the forests, monkeys, elephants and peacocks.[24]

Prâsâd Top West stands in a clearing on the left side of the path that leads from the Bayon to the western gateway. This is a Buddhist shrine probably dating from the 13th century built on the foundations of an earlier Śaivite temple. It is in a very dilapidated condition and seemingly has suffered much from the predatory operations of the Khmer Rouge, since several artifacts mentioned in earlier accounts are no longer there.[25] The only lintel *in situ* shows a Buddha-figure held aloft by a form of manikin or, maybe intended as garuḍa. Strangely this is not mentioned in earlier accounts. A much-damaged seated Buddha-image stands nearby under the trees. The earlier sources mention a toraṇa (fronton) of Buddha seated under the bo-tree (*Figus religiosa)* on the eastern side, and well-preserved lintels showing Śiva on the bull Nandin to the east and Indra on his elephant to the north.

A later Śaivite temple, now known as Prâsâd Top

179. Preah Pralilay. The nâga-railings of approach to the Pralilay, A Buddhist shrine built by Jayavarman VII on the north side of the palace grounds, where there are many traces of later Buddhist activity from the 16th century onwards. It is interesting to note that the inscription referring to Yaśovarman's earlier Buddhist foundation by the shore of the Eastern Baray was found here on a site known as Tep Pranam, of which nâga-railings survive together with a reconstituted standing Buddha image.

180. A repaired Buddha image in a new shrine in front of the gopura *of the Preah Palilay. These two scenes relate to the later Buddhist developments at Angkor when the old sites were brought to life again, as described in Chapter 6, and to more recent repairs.*

East (previously Monument 487), built during the reign of Jayavarman VIII, is described in the next chapter.

Three great temple-palaces and other temples outside the walls

It was within this context of outright war on the eastern front and holding operations to the west that the various building works of Jayavarman VII proceeded. We may consider first the major monastic complexes of Preah Khan, outside the walls of the city and slightly to the north-east, Ta Prohm and its close neighbour Bantây Kdei, both outside the walls towards the south-east, and other associated temples. At that time there were lakes on all sides. To the east of Bantây Kdei there is still the very beautiful Sra Srang, a rectangular pool approximately 700 by 300 metres, probably constructed during an earlier reign. Ta Prohm on its northern side abutted onto the already existing Eastern Baray. Preah Khan was newly provided with a large artificial lake, known as the Jayataṭâka, on its eastern side, nearly half the length of the Eastern Baray, and also a smaller lake on its western side. The main eastern entrance of Preah Khan would have been reached by boat, and the foundations of the landing-stage are still there to be seen.

In the middle of the Jayataṭâka, Jayavarman later built the delightful little shrine known as Neak Poen, and on its far eastern shore the smaller monastery of Ta Som. Close to the northern shores of this lake the small monastic compound of Bantây Prei was founded together with the nearby temple of Prâsâd Prei, while further eastwards, still close to the shore of the lake, the monastic compound of Krol Ko was built. As one drives around these various ruined sites nowadays, it is difficult to recreate in one's mind the charm and splendour of these various magnificent buildings, surrounded by vast stretches of water and interconnected by a network of canals. One reads of the wonder of Angkor, but with the disappearance of these vast water-works, not only was the prosperity of the city lost for ever, but also much of that wonder.

The grounds of the temple-complex of Preah Khan ('Sacred Sword') form a rectangle of 700 by 800 metres, presumably filled originally with lesser buildings for its population of about 14,000 persons. Now all is forest except for the central rectangle (175 by 200 metres) of the second enclosure. This too before its clearance in the early 20th century was likewise buried in jungle. The main complex is now cleared of undergrowth and the passage through it is easy. Preah Khan differs from the other Buddhist temple-complexes in that the entrances from all four directions are preceded by causeways with stone railings consisting of *nâgas* pulled by giant figures, on exactly the same pattern as already described for the main city of Angkor Thom itself. This suggests that Jayavarman himself may have used it, perhaps in the earlier part of his reign, as his private residence. An important inscription found in 1939

182. *(above) Sra Srang, a beautiful articial lake immediately east of Bantây Kdei.*

← 181. *(p. 154) Buddha in the earth-witness posture of the east side of the* gopura, *leading directly to the tower-like shrine of Preah Palilay, still standing but in a ruined condition.*

183. *(below) The bridge with its rows of gods and demons leading over the moat to the south gateway of Angkor Thom.*

provided much detailed information concerning the foundation of this royal abode.[26]

In this place of victory in combat, which was a receptacle of enemy blood, he established this citadel of which the stones and the golden lotus-flowers vary the colour of the soil, which shines still today as though glazed with blood.

If Prayâga (the Indian city of Allahabad) is worthy of respect because of the proximity of two holy rivers (the Ganges and the Jumna) which provide means for the purification for living beings, what should be said of this city of Jayasrî with its watering places (tîrtha) where Buddha, Śiva and the Lotus-Eyed One are invoked.

This King Jayavarman has consecrated here in the Year Śaka 1113 (= AD 1192) this Lokeśa *(Lord of the World) named Lord Jayavarman, who is the image of his father. Around this sacred Avalokiteśvara who is central, the King has placed 283 divine images.*

This certainly suggests that this temple was built on the site of a battle, presumably when the invading Chams were being driven from the capital by Jayavarman himself, hence its construction as both a vast Buddhist temple in honour of his father and himself and also as a city of 'Glorious Victory' (*Jayaśrî*), as remembered by the more popular name of the 'Sacred Sword', which survives to this day.

The general layout resembles that of a maṇḍala. It consists of a central tower-like shrine with similar but slightly lower towers to the four quarters, enclosed within a double inner courtyard, which is again enclosed within the more spacious outer courtyard with elaborate towered porticoes and antechambers. In layout it resembles the earlier pyramid-temples, but whereas these soar upwards, these temple-palaces spread out on a horizontal plane, thus conforming closely to the regular maṇḍala pattern. The inner enclosure is a maze of small shrines connected by the usual narrow covered galleries, as typical of all these massive Khmer buildings. On account of their exclusive use of corbelled archways, the overbearing weight inevitably limits the span available. In this respect one should mention the antechamber on the eastern side, nicknamed the Dancers' Hall because of the frieze of dancing apsaras which decorate the upper

184. Preah Khan, frontal view across the moat by the northern gopura *of this great palace-fortress built by Jayavarman VII. (Photograph by Suthep Kritsanuvarin.)*

walls. This is the widest spanned hall with corbelled roof in the whole of Angkor.[27]

There was no difference in architectural design of these vast temples, whether Śaivite, Vaiṣṇavite or as now nominally Buddhist. The cult would have been identical, but one assumes that Buddhist monks would have co-operated with Brahman priests at the various shrines, living in their separate communities on the vast estate enclosed by the outer walls. The items required for the cult are all listed, such as rice, sesame, milk, honey, molasses, and the quantities expected, followed by the numbers of animals and people attached to the temple:

423 goats, 360 pigeons, as many peacocks and yellow-green pigeons (Colomba hurriyala). In his devotion the King has given 5,324 villages with their inhabitants, totalling 978,840 men and women, among whom there are 444 officials, 4,006 attendants, cooks and others, 2,298 of the servile class, including 1,000 dancers, and 7,436 persons responsible for the temple-oblations.

The total number of residents seems to amount to about 14,000. One may well wonder how much practical Buddhism was involved amongst this vast concourse, but at least the inscription in its conventional opening verses is generally Buddhist Mahâyâna in its worthy intentions. It treats in turn the Buddha (in his three phases of manifestation according to Mahâyâna theory), the Body of the Dharma, the Glorious Body (understood here as the Way of the Bodhisattva) and the Sangha (the community of monks). These are the three pillars of Buddhism.

The Lord who by his accumulations (of knowledge and merit) produces on a vast scale bodily forms of the Dharma-Body, the Glorious Body and the Transformation Body, let him be adored, he who is the harbour of Buddhas and those who embody the nature of Buddhas (viz. Bodhisattvas), to Buddha who is the refuge of living beings be praise!

I honour the Way of the incomparable Supreme Enlightenment, the one and only untrammelled doctrine for the elucidation of absolute being, the Dharma, worthy of praise as the praiseworthy immortality known throughout the Threefold World, like a sword which cuts away the obscurity of the six internal foes (of desire, wrath, greed, delusion, pride and envy).

May the Sangha (community of monks), outstanding in their intent upon the good, lead you! (The Sangha) is freed from attachment since this obstructs final deliverance, but it is always intent on the advantage of others, whom they instruct in the Buddha's teachings, which they themselves recite together.

These identical Sanskrit verses serve as opening to the inscription on the stone which records details concerning the great Buddhist temple of Ta Prohm, so maybe they are largely conventional.

The outer walls of Ta Prohm, enclosing an area of one kilometre by 600 metres, once contained a population of 12,640 persons. This included 418 chief officials, with a further 2,740 on their staff, 2,232 retainers of the serving class including 615 female dancers. Furthermore, 66,625 men and women (presumably the supporting villagers) provide the services for the gods, totalling 79,365, with the Burmese and Chams presumably pressed into service. The inscription, dated AD 1186, records that Jayavarman founded this temple-complex as the citadel of Râjavibhâra, setting up here an image named Śrî Jayarâjaçûḍamaṇi, representing his mother as the Mother of the Buddhas (namely *Prajñâpâramitâ*, the Perfection of Wisdom), as well as two other images to left and right, representing his revered teachers (*guru*), surrounded by an entourage of 260 divinities.[28] No special features attach to the approaches to this temple-complex, except that the entrance portals to all four quarters are surmounted by the four-faced gaze of Avalokiteśvara, just like the main city portals, but on a smaller scale. The layout of the Ta Prohm temple-complex itself generally resembles that of Preah Khan, but the large number of fig-trees that intertwine amongst the walls make it more difficult to penetrate the inner courtyards and corridors. All this provides, however, an idealized impression of 'ancient Angkor lost in the jungle'.

Despite its large enclosure of 700 by 500 metres, the temple-complex of Bantây Kdei is appreciably smaller, being only 63 by 50 metres. Also no attempt has been made here to maintain a symmetrical maṇḍala pattern. Within this inner enclosure we find a generally rectangular arrangements of tower-like shrines positioned rather towards the east, as the normal direction of approach. Although described by Maurice Glaize as the least engaging of these three temple-complexes, I have always found it the most attractive. It is impossible to appreciate the others from ground-level because of the density of jungle that surrounds them, but one can view Bantây Kdei from its southern side, where the trees are far

185. (pp. 158-9) Preah Khan. A view from above of the towers of the inner enclosure. (Photograph by Suthep Kritsanuvarin.)

186. *(above) The Great Goddess Prajñâpâramitâ, 'Perfection of Wisdom' with whom Jayavarman VII identified his mother in the fortress–temple of Ta Prohm (Angkor). (From Maurice Glaize,* Les monuments d'Angkor, *first edition, 1944.)*

187. A toraṇa showing a dancing Śiva placed together with other pieces along the way east to west through Preah Khan. One wonders if it was part of the original structure or part the latter process of replacing Buddhist iconography with a Brahmanical one.

less dense, and admire the series of towers which rise in harmony beyond the walls of the inner enclosure. The twisting floral designs and pairs of dancing apsaras that decorate the walls and the pillars also seem to relate closely to the Bayon. Inset deeply cut figures of guardians and apsaras are now a general feature of all these later temples.

Mention must be made of the shrines closely associated with Preah Khan, all easily reached in earlier times by boat from the eastern pier. The temple known popularly as Neak Poen, because of the two *nâgas* which encircle the base of the circular shrine, is set in the centre of its own square lake, the whole complex forming an island in the middle of the much larger Jayataṭâka. It seems to have been conceived in imitation of the quasi-mythical Anavatapta Lake in the high Himalayas, renowned for its pure cool (*anavatapta*) waters. It is famous in Tibetan tradition and closely associated with Avalokiteśvara, who appears depicted on the sides of this small shrine. Thus the colophon of the *Blue Annals*, a major 15th-century Tibetan historical work by the Scholar gZhon-nu-dpal, refers to:

> *the Land of Snows (Tibet), resting on the golden foundation of the blessing of the Great Merciful Lord (Avalokiteśvara), surrounded by majestic snow mountains, where eternal streams of monks*

from the Anavatapta Lake of Morality, which removes the heat of defilement, make it replete with the jewels of preaching and meditation.

Despite the mixed metaphors, this expresses admirably the religious and the healing associations of this lake, which in the case of Neak Poen has four subsidiary shrines to the four sides of this inner pool, where the faithful might take the beneficial waters, and indeed still do today. Upper panels on three sides of the central shrine depict main scenes from the life of Sâkyamuni Buddha: his flight from the palace, the cutting of his hair as a sign of renouncing a worldly life (the only one which remains clearly distinguishable), and his mediation under the Tree of Enlightenment. The southern panel, entirely defaced, probably illustrated his entry into final nirvâṇa. The statue of the horse Balâha on the eastern side of the shrine is said to represent Avalokiteśvara carrying sufferers to salvation.[29]

The temple of Ta Som, near the eastern shore of the Jayataṭâka, resembles a small version of Bantây

188. (right) Ta Prohm. A view illustrating the picturesque effect of stones and trees interlaced. This one temple was deliberately left like this by the earlier French administration of Angkor in order to give visitors a better impression of the state of all these overgrown temples before they were cleared.

189. (below) Bantây Kdei. A view of the towers taken across the moat.

Kdei. It stands within a double enclosure and the main entrance portals are crowned with the four-faced glance of Avalokiteśvara. Although ruined in its interior it retains some fine detailed carving on the towers of the various shrines, primarily a miniature row of devotees in the act of supplication. A fine image of Avalokiteśvara, typical of all these temples attributable to Jayavarman VII, has recently been unearthed.

On the northern side of the lake in close proximity to Preah Khan one should visit Prâsâd Prei (the 'Forest Sanctuary') and just behind it Bantây Prei (the 'Forest Citadel'), and also Krol Ko (nicknamed now the 'Cow Enclosure') further along the same northern side of the lake, for despite their much ruined condition, the total tranquility of these sites urges one to linger. The ruined towers stand solitary amongst the broken walls and collapsed masonry, interspersed with carved plaques which have been set in position to form ordered rows. One is thus totally released from the gloom of the interiors of better preserved temples.

Similar in layout to Ta Som but rather different in atmosphere, the temple known as Ta Nei was built in proximity to the western shore of the Eastern Baray. It is now reached by a footpath, nearly one kilometre from the main road of the so called 'Inner Circuit' between Ta Keo and Ta Prohm. Ta Nei stands abandoned in the jungle with its walls reasonably cleared of vegetation. Like Ta Som it retains some fine carvings, including a plaque of the Bodhisattva, the future Buddha Sâkyamuni, fleeing from the palace on his horse. (This has now disappeared, one hopes into safe keeping, since renovation work began.) Penetrating deeper amongst the trees towards the east one comes upon the well preserved eastern portal with a defaced carving of Avalokiteśvara, standing on a lotus-flower.

Another seldom-visited temple-fortress, presumably built under the orders of Jayavarman VII, is Bantây Thom (Great Temple-Fortress), situated about three kilometres north-west of the city. It is reached by a narrow sandy track leading off from the 'Outer Circuit', just beyond the northern gateway of Angkor Thom. Quite possibly it was conceived as an outpost as part of the new defensive arrangements instituted by Jayavarman VII, able to give warning of any hostile approach from this direction. Much dilapidated, its three central towers still stand, although not for much longer unless urgent restoration work begins soon. These stand in an inner rectangular courtyard of 34 by 43 metres, enclosed within an outer courtyard of 104 by 116 metres. Two so-called libraries, much ruined, stood in the usual position just inside the eastern gateway to the inner courtyard. Apart from the expected decoration of apsaras and guardian-divinities set in their individual niches, there is some exquisitely

190. There are many picturesque sights nearby the Jayataṭâka, such as the western gopura *of Ta Som.*

decorative stonework on the towers. Especially noteworthy are several well-preserved lintels, one of the Bodhisattva (the future Sâkyamuni) fleeing from his palace at night, as already noticed at Ta Nei, and another of Mahâmâyâ, his mother, honoured by a pair of elephant-riders and attendant divinities. Situated on a slight eminence in desolate open bushland, this site would remain impressive for this reason alone.

Sites in the Provinces

There are two remarkably well preserved Buddhist temple-fortresses attributable to the reign of Jayavarman VII, but they soon developed as Theravâda establishments, undergoing later changes up to the 16th century and beyond. The more interesting of these is on the northern side of the town of Kampong Cham. One notes that its present name, Vat Nokor, is effectively identical with Angkor Vat, the appellation Vat being later Theravâda usage. Thus this site was probably an important Śaivite foundation, possibly going back to the time of Jayavarman II. (See 'Other Early Sites' in Chapter 3.) Whatever its earlier history, it was rebuilt as a Buddhist temple in the 13th century. The plan is relatively simple. The main shrine, approached through an antechamber, is set within two walled enclosures, which one enters through *gopuras* from the four cardinal directions. However in the 16th century or maybe even earlier, the antechamber was dismantled and rebuilt as an open *vihara*, directly adjoining the central shrine, of which the eastern face now serves as altar. This intrusion has been very skillfully achieved, far more so than the intrusion of a Christian church in the centre of the great Cordova mosque. Seen from outside, both the colourful roof of the *vihara* as well the restructured stûpa-like roof of the central shrine give this great walled temple an unusual but by no means unpleasing appearance. As might be expected, the iconography is entirely Buddhist. The main toraṇas around the central shrine illustrate the Bodhisattva's flight from the palace on his horse Kaṇṭhaka, the cutting of his hair (sign of his decision to assume a religious life) while his horse with attendants waits below, and the scene of his victory over Mâra and his consequent enlightenment. These are probably all later works and must be seen within the context of other such Theravâda works, as discussed in Chapter 6, noting however that such scenes are also typical of Mahâyâna art. Other carvings on the toraṇas of the outer walls may go back to the 13th century, especially two standing images of the Bodhisattva Avalokiteśvara, carved on the upper walls on the two sides of the western *gopura*. This same standing image appears on the frontals of many

191. Bantây Thom on the northern outskirts of Angkor Thom, as approached from the east.

192. Bantây Thom. The torana which may be seen on the previous illustration over the small entry to the left of the gopura. As this is a Buddhist temple, it may be safely identified as an illustration of Queen Mahâmâya, standing under the tree where she is said to have given birth to the future Sâkyamuni. According to the traditional account two elephants came to spray the new-born child, and the two gods, Brahmâ and Indra were in attendance. Here they appear in serving attire with strange conical hats. Still there in early 1999, it was stolen soon afterwards.

193. Bantây Thom. Another torana over a doorway in the main courtyard, showing the Bodhisattva's escape on his horse Kanthaka.

194. (above) Vat Nokor, general view from the west. One notes the roof and the new spire of the Theravâda vihara *which has been skillfully built into the ancient structure*

195. (right) Vat Nokor. One of several well-preserved toraṇas in this impressive fortress temple. This shows on the top range the Bodhisattva cutting off his hair as a sign of renouncing the world, having just descended from his horse Kaṇṭhaka who waits below with the syce.

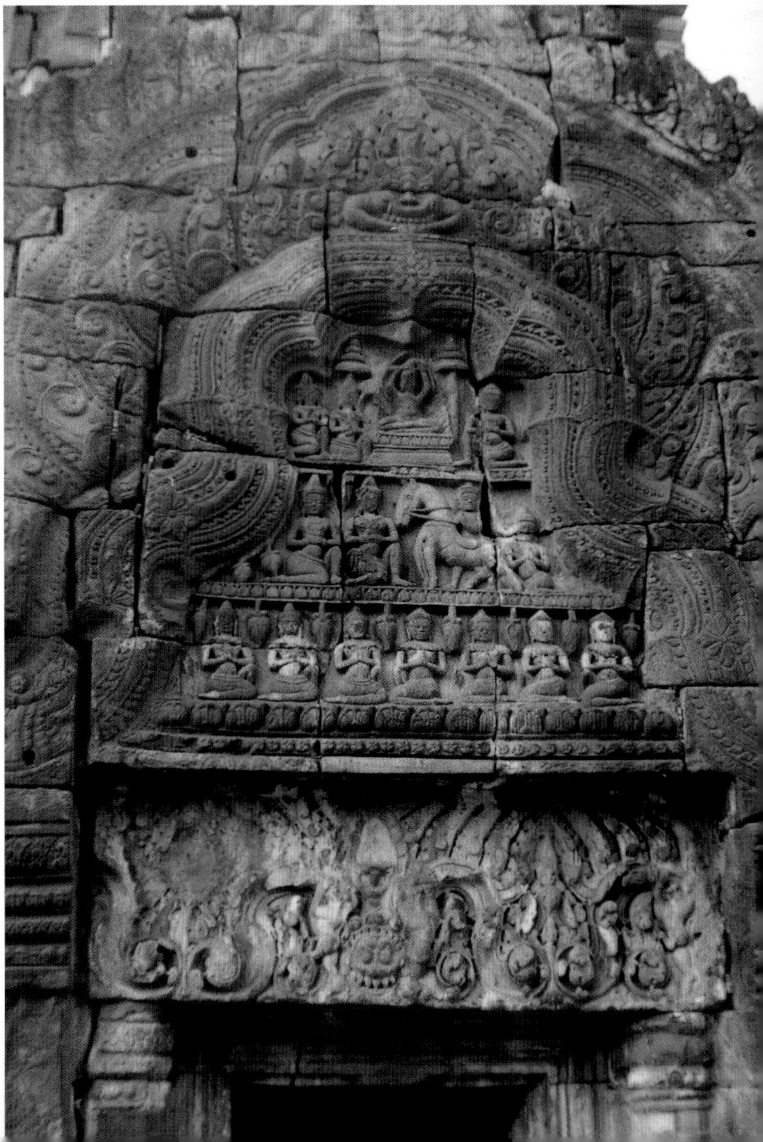

Buddhist temples attributed to Jayavarman VII, e.g. Ta Som, Ta Nei and on the little that remain of the four corner-temples on the walls of Angkor. Vat Nokor is unhappily not so well maintained, as it attracts many visitors from the town. Thus there are stalls serving drinks and refreshments in the second enclosure and the inevitable surrounding paper and plastic litter over the whole area.

The other important site is Bantây Ta Prohm (Kandal Province) some thirty kilometres south of Phnom Penh. The local name Bati refers to a nearby artificial lake, which attracts many local visitors at weekends. They scarcely visit the temple, which remains a peaceful sanctuary well cared for by a few monks and nuns. It contains some remarkable sculptures that probably date back to the 13th century. One may note particularly that of Sâkyamuni, seated in the posture of meditation, which adorns the main eastern entrance. The lintel over the main shrine portrays him lying on his right side in the position

196. Vat Nokor. A view of the inside of the later vihara, *which was built so that the ancient shrine of the original temple should serve as altar-piece for the new building with its enthroned Buddha-image. (Photograph by Suthep Kritsanuvarin.)*

of entering final nirvâṇa. The shrine-entrance has some beautifully sculptured guardian figures surmounted by small stûpas. However the most impressive sculptures of all are those of the four-armed Bodhisattva Avalokiteśvara, which adorn the toraṇa*s* above the false doors on the north and south side of the central shrine. Both these Buddhist temples have remained in use up to present times, as certified by the later inscriptions recording the visits and offerings of the faithful. As will be noted below, many Khmer Brahmanical temples (notably Vishnuloka which becomes Angkor Vat) were adapted to Theravâda usage, but the new monastery was usually built in the immediate vicinity with little or no interference with iconography of the original temple. However here we have good examples of Khmer temple-fortresses, which were actually built as Mahâyâna shrines and easily adapted to Theravâda use.

Still further afield Jayavarman VII was also engaged in works at Beng Mealea and Preah Khan of Kampong Svay, both initiated by his great predecessor. He also built the great temple-fortress of Bantây Chmar, discussed just below.

More Warfare

During his manifold building operations in the reconstructed city, roads linking Angkor to other major centres throughout the 'empire', rest-houses along these same roads, hospitals and religious foundations, and probably lastly his own pyramid-temple, the Bayon, he was also engaged in a war of revenge against Champa. Jayavarman employed as his 'commanding general' in this campaign a refugee Cham prince, named Vidyânandanda, to whose education and training he gave special care and who first served him in an internal campaign in the Battambang area. The story of this prince comes from Cham sources.

> *There is one king Srî Sûryavarmadeva, who practised the Mahâyâna religion, following the teaching of genuine knowledge. When he was young as Prince Srî Vidyânandana, he went to Cambodia in the year 1104. Noting that he had the 32 marks of perfection complete, the King of Cambodia (Jayavarman VII) felt affection for him and taught him, as suitable for a prince, all the sciences and military theory. While he was in Cambodia a city named Malyang, which was occupied by a lot of bad people and which had already been taken by the Cambodians, rose in revolt against the King of Cambodia. Seeing that the Prince was competent in all warfare, the King put him in charge of the Cambodian troops against the city of Malyang. He subdued this city according to the wishes of the King of Cambodia. Recognizing his valour, the King conferred upon him the dignity of 'crown-prince'* (yuvarâja) *and gave him all the luxuries and befits which are to be found in Cambodia. In the year 1112 the King (of Champa) Srî Jaya Indravarmadeva ong Vatou made war against the King of Cambodia, who sent the Prince to take (the city) of Vijaya and seize King Srî Jaya Indravarmadeva ong Vatou. He captured him and had him brought to Cambodia. He proclaimed Prince In, the brother-in-law of the King of Cambodia as King Sûryajayavar-mandeva in Vijaya.*[30]

The rest of the story is told more succinctly in another inscription:

197. Ta Prohm of Bati (Kandal Province). This temple-fortress some 30 kilometres south of Phnom Penh was entirely restructured by Jayavarman VII as a Buddhist temple. In this respect it resembles Vat Nokor at Kampong Cham. Since the 16th century, if not earlier, it has become a regular Theravâda estalishment, alhough no further changes have been made to the building.

198. Ta Prohm of Bati. A carving of 4-armed Avalokiteśvara on the south upper wall of the main shrine.

> *The Prince himself at the head of his army made for himself a kingdom at Râjapura (Panrâng) and took the royal name of Sûryavarman. The (new) king of Vijaya did not enjoy power for long. He was expelled by another pretender, Prince Rashupati. In 1114 Indravarman-Vatuv, who as we have seen, lived as a captive in Cambodia and had doubtless regained the favour of the King of this country, reappeared with a Cambodian army to reconquer his throne. He applied to Sûryavarman-Vidyânandana, now King of Râjapura. He joined in the campaign but having conquered Vijaya and put Prince Rashupati to death, he kept the conquest for himself. Indravarman-Vatuv withdrew to Amarâvati (Quang-nam) where he raised an army with which he tried to retake Vijaya, but he was finally beaten and killed by Sûryavarman-Vidyânandana. In 1116 he suffered another attack by the Cambodians, which he repulsed victoriously. He then went to Amarâvati where he rebuilt the temples and palaces.*[31]

Thereafter this treacherous prince, so favoured by Jayavarman VII, disappears from the scene in the internal wars of Champa, which however seems to have remained generally subject to Cambodia throughout the rest of Jayavarman VII's reign.

The outer territories

Apart from the new or reconstructed buildings in Angkor itself, many other sites throughout the empire were renovated and new temples initiated. Angkor's hold on the western provinces, on what is now southern Thailand and on the upper Thai-Malay peninsula, was maintained and even extended. More Buddhist shrines were built in Lopburi, of which the most imposing is Wat Mahathat, consisting of a central shrine set within two square walled enclosures. The central shrine with its 'corncob' profile is purely Khmer of this late period, similar to other great shrines on the Khorat Plateau, but the surrounding shrines are mainly later reconstructions. The Prang Sam Yod consists of the typical Khmer arrangement of three shrines of which the centre one predominates. Although the temples built during the reign of Jayavarman VII, when Buddhism at long last becomes the proclaimed religion of the state, were often Buddhist in intention, Brahmanical influences do not disappear either at the court or in the decorations of these temples, where Hindu motifs continue to intrude.

Mention has already been made of those at Phimai, Phnom Rung and Sikhoraphum, as well as Ku Suan Taeng and Prâsâd Kamphaeng Yai with the 'hospital chapel', known as Kamphaeng Noi, which are among the most northerly of the Khmer shrines remaining on the Khorat Plateau. As already mentioned above in the case of Phimai, many of these sites were connected by roads with hospitals and rest-houses at various places. Clearly these were all constructed of less robust materials, but the attached chapels built of stone have survived. At Preah Khan of Kampong Svay to where additions were made during Jayavarman VII's reign, there is both a *dharmasâla* (rest-house) and the separate 'chapel' containing the inscription of Sûryavarman I (see p. 109ff). A good example of a 'hospital chapel' in Angkor itself may be seen just inside the eastern precincts of Preah Khan. Another one of easy access if visiting Phnom Rung is to be found at the foot of a hill a few hundred metres from Muang Tam. A well preserved one is found at Bantây Chmar, and another in a beautiful forest setting on the way to Ta Muen Thom. The rather more complex *dharmasâla* consisting of the chapel and another stone-built building in a stone enclosure, often with an impressive *gopura*, was presumably not needed in the Angkor area. Foundation steles, wherever present, show that these beneficent works were dedicated to the Buddha Master of Medicine (*Bhaiṣajyaguru),* also well known in Nepal and Tibet.

The extreme limit westwards of the Khmer Empire at this time is indicated by the Buddhist temple of Muang Singh (in full *Śrîjayasimhapura* = City of the Victorious Lion). Situated near modern Kanchanaburi not far from the present Burmese border and some 120 kilometres west of present-day Bangkok, it was clearly conceived as a walled citadel.[32] Built solidly of sandstone and laterite, lacking all the fine decorative details of Phimai and the other earlier great Khmer temples, and probably built hastily, it has recently been reconstructed by the Fine Arts Department. The surrounding enclosure, originally 1,400 by 800 metres as indicated by the remains of the outer laterite wall, have now been turned into a public park, much frequented at weekends by local tourists. There is a small museum nearby containing several images of the Bodhisattva Avalokiteśvara, such as were produced in profusion during the reign of Jayavarman VII.

The limit eastwards of the empire was, as always, Wat Phu. The limit to the north-west was Sukhothai (until about 1220) and in the north-east Nakhon Sakhon as under Sûryavarman I. Southwards down the Thai-Malay peninsula we reach the last of Khmer

199. A good example of a hospital chapel at Preah Khan (Angkor).

200. The eastern entrance of Muang Singh, the furthest western Khmer fortress near the Thai/Burmese border. It has been recently restored by The Fine Arts Department. (Photograph by Peter Skilling.)

temple buildings at Phetchaburi, where substantial temple-ruins of the 11th to 12th centuries bear witness to earlier Khmer suzerainty. Khmer influence eventually reached as far south as Chaiya near Ligor (Nakhon Si Thammarat), where the population was doubtless Malay. The inscription on an image set up there in 1183 by the Governor of Chaiya in the name of the Mahârâja of Śrîvijaya was written in Khmer, possibly intended as a declaration, to be clearly understood by the Khmers, that this was properly a Śrîvijayan domain.

Bantây Chmar

One of the last important temples surrounded by massive walls is Bantây Chmar, dedicated to Jayavarman VII's son Indravarman. Originally built on the main route from Angkor towards the western provinces of the Khmer Empire around the Gulf of Siam, it still lies just within the present Cambodian frontier, some sixty kilometres north of the town of Sisophon, almost a three-hour journey because of the condition of the road. As this region has been

201. (left) Bantây Chmar, which has suffered the neglect of centuries and the more recent looting by army units: one tower still stands amidst collapsed masonry.

202. (below) Bantây Chmar. A frieze of dancing figures decorating the east end of the main building, leading into the antechamber.

under military occupation of one kind or another for the last two decades and more, it has suffered much depredation.[33] Apart from its obvious strategic and military importance in the past, it is especially interesting as one of the few great enclaves outside Jayavarman VII's recreated city of Angkor that was Buddhist in intention. The central enclave, a rectangle of 250 by 200 metres, stood originally at the centre of a far larger area of which the ramparts can be identified, thus enclosing the neat little hospital chapel, remarkably well preserved, as at Preah Khan (Angkor). The outer walls of this central enclave are covered with bas-reliefs, mainly of marches and battle-scenes as on many of the walls of the Bayon, but there was also a remarkable row of full-sized images of a multi-armed Avalokiteśvara, although other Buddhist scenes seem to be absent (again as on the Bayon). Many are so worn and blackened with lichen that to study them in detail is a laborious undertaking, rendered even more difficult by the dense undergrowth which surrounds the whole enclosure. Having penetrated inside these walls, the main structures are now in such a state of ruin that even the main outlines are scarcely discernable, while progress is hampered by the accumulations of fallen sandstone blocks over which one must clamber and the obstructing undergrowth through which one must force or cut one's way. In effect the central shrine is a long narrow structure, perhaps resembling that of Bantây Kdei at Angkor, with subsidiary buildings linking this to the *gopuras* (ornate entrances) at the four quarters. The eastern one corresponds to the so-called 'dancers' hall' at Preah Khan in that its upper level is decorated with a row of dancing female figures which here adopt the rather grotesque pose of a row of *garuḍas*. One notes the absence of any specifically Buddhist imagery except possibly on the well-preserved frontal piece, which leads into this particular chamber. Here I would happily have identified the central seated figure as the four-headed image of Vairoçana Buddha, but if so, he is manifestly conceived as a four-headed Brahmâ with a rishi playing a lute on his right and a pair of geese on his left. Some of the towers that are still standing retain their Bodhisattva heads, as at the Bayon and Preah Khan.

An estimate of Jayavarman VII's reign

With good reason, doubts have been raised whether Jayavarman VII within the course of a reign of some thirty-eight years could possibly have been responsible for such a vast building programme. He must have operated with enormous work-forces, completely overtaxing the economy of the country, which suffered accordingly. It is generally agreed that his last great work was that of his own pyramid-temple, the Bayon, intended as the supreme manifestation of Buddhahood. The Preah Khan

203. Bantây Chmar. A lintel of 4-headed Brahmâ.

204. Bantây Chmar. A row of life-size carvings of 'thousand-armed' Avalokiteśvara adorned the wall of the inner enclosure on the west side. Professional looters dismantled a whole section as may be seen from the break in the wall, but fortunately the trucks with the numbered piece were stopped by the Thai police. These reassembled sections of the wall may now be seen in the Phnom Penh Museum.

inscription of 1191 (vv. 116-21) mentions the setting up in various places in the empire of twenty-three images (which might be taken as representing Jayavarman VII) with the name of Jayabuddhamahânâtha (= Great Saviour Victorious Buddha). This might suggest that he claims the Buddha-nature during his life, which according to the teachings of Mahâyâna Buddhism would be quite unacceptable. At most he might reasonably regard himself as a Bodhisattva, one destined to Buddhahood as suggested by his posthumous name Mahâparamasaugata (= the Great and Supreme State of Blessedness), noting however the Sugata (the Blessed One) is the normal title of the Buddha. Thus we must envisage him as absorbed into Buddhahood at his death, just as other Khmer monarchs were envisaged as being absorbed into Śiva or Vishnu in accordance with their posthumous names.

The absence of any liturgical literature leaves unsolved the question concerning the practice of tantric rites of initiation, such as were common in royal circles in East Java. So far as iconography is concerned, the cult of the great Mahâyâna divinities seems to be limited to the ever popular Avalokiteśvara (Lokeśvara), the Goddess Perfection of Wisdom (Prajñâpâramitâ), Vajrapâṇi, who at Phimai seemingly appears in a multi-armed tantric form, with few others scarcely mentioned. Among tantric divinities we seem to know only of Vajrasattva, who represents ritually the self-identification of the tantric yogin in the absolute (*vajra* or adamantine) essence. He is thus identical with Vajrapâṇi in his supreme rôle as Lord of the *Trilokaçakramaṇḍala* (see p. 123). To what extent Khmers were interested in such ritual practices, we can have no knowledge in the absence of the relevant texts.

Judging from the several images of Hevajra which have been found, both in Angkor and at unidentified Buddhist sites elsewhere on the Khorat Plateau, of which many examples can be seen in the National Museum, Bangkok, one is led to assume that the cult of Hevajra was fairly widely practised. But here once again there is no surviving literature to clarify this interesting problem. I note however that these images always show him as a single male divinity, bereft of his feminine partner, Nairâtmyâ, with whom he is always associated in Tibetan tradition. Perhaps the cult of Hevajra was introduced exceptionally, for whatever reason we cannot know.[34]

205. Bantây Chmar. Other carvings on the wall resemble those already described at the Bayon; viz., scenes of war with the Chams and incidental scenes of daily life. Here one sees a sporting scene of a man fighting with a lion.

It is often assumed nowadays that tantric yoga necessarily involves sexual yoga, but this is by no means the case. Do we also assume from this that Khmer practisers of tantric rituals eschewed all forms of sexual yoga? It would appear so. It seems that apart from Vajrasattva no other great tantric divinities have been firmly identified in museum collections. That there may well have been others is suggested by the discovery of a rare inscription some twenty-five kilometres south of Nakhon Ratchasima in a village named Sab Bâk, dated Śaka 988 (AD 1066), corresponding to the end of the reign of King Udayâdityavarman II. This inscription records the setting up of a shrine in honour of the Five Buddhas, seemingly with Vajrasattva supreme as Âdibuddha, at a place then named Tempâsnaga, by a learned monk Dhanus. It is especially interesting to note that he followed a religious tradition of devotion to the tantric cycle known as *Guhyasamâja* ('Secret Concourse'), which centres upon Vajradhara *(alias* Vajrasattva) as supreme Buddha.[35]

By means of tantric ritual might a practiser claim to achieve Buddhahood through the process of self-identification with one of the major tantric divinities. This ritual in known to have been practised by the kings of East Java in the 13th and 14th centuries. King Kritanagara of the Singhasâri dynasty was identified ritually with Vajra-Bhairava in 1275. Likewise Âdityavarman, the last king of Śrîvijaya, who had been brought up at the Majapahit court in East Java, went through the same ritual, recorded in an inscription of 1375. A stone image of him in this manifestation can be seen in the Jakarta Museum.[36] Since Vajra-Bhairava, also well represented in Nepal and Tibet, represents the fearful aspect of Buddha Akṣobhya, Buddha-rank is certainly implied. The presence of a number of images of Hevajra in all Khmer museum collections certainly suggests a cult of this major tantric divinity. However there are no literary sources in Cambodia (as in East Java) which might confirm this likelihood, nor is Hevajra mentioned in any known stone inscription. Thus the question remains entirely open as to whether such a ritual was performed for Jayavarman VII. What he really envisaged was probably the identification of the Devarâja as the 'Victorious Buddha', but Brahmanical opposition to any such idea prevented any such explicit definition. No *purohita* for the Devarâja seems to have been appointed during his reign, or for that manner during the previous reigns of kings of the Mahîdharapura dynasty. The Ta Prohm inscription names a guru who received the title of Mangalârthadeva as well as wealth and honours, which were also bestowed upon his family, and especially a brother named Jayakîrtideva. Jayavarman VII even erected images of these two gurus.

There is also another Brahmanical family, closely associated with Jayavarman VII. This was distinguished by three great scholars (paṇḍita) who all bore the name of Bhûpatendra (= Lord of the World). They are known from a stele, set up by the youngest of the three in 1189 at Prâsâd Tor, a temple which once stood near the north-east corner of the East Baray.[37] The inscription is dedicated to Śiva, Vishnu, Brahmâ, the Goddess Gangâ and also to the first member of the family, known as Bhûpatîdrapaṇḍita I, who had served under kings Jayavarman VI, Indravarman II and Sûryavarman II. A long eulogy is dedicated to the king and to the important ancestor. Then we learn that the second so-named, Bhûpatîdrapaṇḍita II, was 'Chief of Council' *(sabhâpati)* under Jayavarman VII who bestowed the further titles of Râjendrapaṇḍita and Sûryapaṇḍita upon him, and who also set up, according to this inscription (v. 25), a statue in gold representing his own grand-father Harṣavarman III. It may be interesting to note that it is said of Bhûpatîndrapaṇḍita I in the opening dedications (v. 5) that 'he emptied the realm of death by means of a secret commentary (*guhyaṭîkâ*) so as to save the world from the ocean of transmigration'. Here we have a direct reference to tantric ritual as performed by a Brahmanical family who served Jayavarman VII.

206. Hevajra, bronze, 12th – 13th century. Musée Guimet, MA 849.

Coedès draws attention to another unusual Brahman scholar closely associated with the King. I quote:

> *An inscription from Angkor Thom tells us about the curious figure of a Brahman scholar who 'having heard that Cambodia was full of eminent experts on the Veda, came here to manifest his knowledge'. His name was Hṛṣikeśa; he belonged to the Brahmanic clan of Bhâradvâja and came from Narapatidesa, 'which can be identified with some probability with Burma, where King Narapathisithu was reigning at precisely this time.' Jayavarman VII made him his chief priest and conferred on him the title of Jayamahâpradhâna. He continued to serve under the two successors of Jayavarman VII.* [38]

Thus whereas one might expect to find Jayavarman VII surrounded by Buddhist prelates, this does seem to have been the case at all. He seems to have preferred the company of some rather unusual Brahman advisers. Yet at the same time all the inscriptions issued in own his name attest to his personal Mahâyâna Buddhist faith, and this same faith manifestly aroused violent opposition in influential Brahmanical circles soon after his death. Maybe this was because it was assumed that he was effectively replacing the cult of the Devarâja with that of the 'Victorious Buddha', which no Khmer monarch had dared to do previously, however strong their Buddhist sympathies may have been. He is now usually regarded as the greatest of Khmer kings, since during his reign the Khmer 'empire' reached its greatest extent. But at the same time this was mainly a holding operation, as the 'empire' had already reached its effective limits under the reign of Sûryavarman II. Moreover it was precisely from the end of Jayavarman VII's reign that the 'empire' began to decline, and one of the reasons for this was surely the large costs in wealth and enforced human labour that his vast construction works, mainly around Angkor, had entailed. These far exceeded those of any previous monarch, and after him sufficient funds and labour could scarcely be found to build only a very occasional stone temple.

Chapter 6

THE 13TH TO THE 16TH CENTURY

The last kings of the 'old order' (13th to early 14th century)

Jayavarman VII died about 1219 and was succeeded probably by one of his sons who reigned as Indravarman II. Little is known of this king except that he was responsible for structural changes at Bantây Srei, as recorded in inscriptions there. His death is mentioned in another inscription of 1295, where it is written that in the year Śaka 1165 (=AD 1243) the Brahman Jaya Mahâpradhâna, who as a young man named Hṛṣikeśa had served under Jayavarman VII and presumably under Indravarman II, went to Bhîmapura to make offerings on behalf of this deceased king.[1] Indravarman II was succeeded by Jayavarman VIII, whose connection with his predecessor is unknown. However he was served by the same Brahman Mahâpradhâna and by Jaya Mangalârtha, presumably from the same family as the Mangalârthadeva who had been greatly honoured by Jayavarman VII. The inscription dated 1295, just mentioned above, was set up by Jayavarman VIII to celebrate the founding of a temple (seemingly the last Angkor stone temple ever built) in honour of this Jaya Mangalârtha, deified as Jaya Trivikramamahânâtha (= Great Lord of the Three Strides) and to his mother as Trivikramadeveśvarî (= Divine Lady of the Three Strides). *Trivikrama* relates to Vishnu, who is said to have bestrode the world in three strides. This temple still stands in the forest between the two roads that lead to the great gateways on the east side of the wall of Angkor Thom.[2]

Jayavarman VIII, who reigned for fifty-two years, is generally held responsible for the defacement of the great Buddhist foundations of Jayavarman VII, notably the Bayon and Preah Khan, presumably under the influence of his Brahmanical prelates. The Buddhist images were replaced by *Śiva-lingas,* and Buddhist images in bas-reliefs transformed into Brahmanical ascetics. Recent excavations carried out by Japanese archaeologists at Bantây Kdei led to the discovery of a large collection of Buddha images, mostly broken, but some still whole, buried in a deep pit.[3] There are doubtless other such discoveries still to be made. The main Buddha-image seated in meditation under the hood of the Nâga Muçilinda, previously occupying the central shrine of the Bayon, was found during excavations in 1933 broken in pieces and buried fourteen metres deep under the central tower. It proved possible to piece it together again, thus reconstituting an image 3.60 metres in height. It has since been enthroned in a small modern shrine erected in an ancient walled enclosure amongst the trees on the right side of the royal route leading from the Phimean-âkas to the main eastern gateway of Angkor Thom.

It seems that Jayavarman VIII was forced to

207. The last Khmer stone temple built at Angkor, Mangalârtha Temple, dated 1295.

abdicate in his old age by a son-in-law who ruled as Indravarman III. The latter is praised in an inscription from Bantây Srei, referring to him as a vigorous young king who has replaced an old one, incapable of protecting the country.[4] In 1307 he retired, possibly to a Buddhist monastery which he himself had founded (see below) and was succeeded by Śrîndrajayavarman, who ruled until 1327. He in turn was succeeded by a Jayavarman Parameśvara according to Coedès' interpretation of an inscription, which must be therefore of a later date than 1327.[5] This king might well be referred to as Jayavarman IX, as Parameśvara must be a posthumous addition. This last Sanskrit inscription was composed by a Brahman scholar Vidhyeśadhîman, who acknowledges himself as servant to the three kings who succeeded Jayavarman VIII (1243-1295), namely Srîndravarman (1295-1307), Śrîndrajayavarman (1307-1327) and Jayavarman Parameśvara (1327-?). Although these kings were probably already self-proclaimed Buddhists, this statement is not suprising, as there were still Brahmans at court. From this point on with the last of these stone inscriptions there is scarcely any more firm dating of the kings of Cambodia until recent times.

As has now been well illustrated, such knowledge as is available concerning the history and religious interests of the Angkor rulers derives almost entirely from surviving stone inscriptions, which have been discovered and patiently worked on mainly by French scholars over the last 150 years. Thanks to these inscriptions it has been possible to produce a fairly reliable list of successive reigns of Khmer kings from Jayavarman II (*c*.770-834) to Śrîndrajayavarman 1307-1327). The first Pâli inscription in Cambodia which is dated 1309 comes from a Theravâda monastery named Kok Svay Cheh in Puek District near Siem Reap.[6] According to this, King Srîndravarman who abdicated and went into retreat in 1307, erected a Buddha statue and gave land to a senior Theravâda monk for the maintenance of a monastery. At the same time we know from the Mangalârtha inscription that this same king had also made gifts at this Brahmanical temple. Thus although well disposed to Buddhism, he reasonably enough made this last gesture to the old 'established religion'. Despite the deliberate defacing of Jayavarman VII's great Buddhist monuments soon after his death and the continuing influence of great Brahman officials at court, there is enough evidence to show that Buddhism was already fast becoming the accepted religion of the majority of the people of the Angkor region. Buddhism was favoured by Khmer kings from Srîndravarman onwards, and there is also no indication that this form of Buddhism suffered any persecution whatsoever. The evidence for this as well as other much interesting information derives from the observations noted down by Chou Ta-kuan, who accompanied a Chinese envoy in 1296-97 to Cambodia, presumably sent by the successor of Kubhai Khan (died 1294) in order to retrieve an embarrassing situation caused by the disappearance of a mission earlier sent to the Khmer court to demand submission. Chou Ta-kuan's descriptions of life in Angkor were included in later more compendious works and have probably suffered considerable abbreviation.[7] There are forty 'chapters', the longest about one and a half pages in length and the shortest consisting of only a few lines. The subjects covered include the royal centre of Angkor, houses in general, clothing, functionaries, religious groups, the Cambodian people, childbirth, maidenhood, slaves, language, aborigines (a few lines only), writing (a few lines only), New Year and the season, justice, sickness and leprosy (a few lines only), the dead, agriculture, configuration of the land (very few lines), products, trade (very few lines), Chinese goods (a brief list). Except for the last chapter the rest are all very brief, namely: trees and flowers, birds, animals, vegetables, fish and reptiles, fermented drinks, salt, vinegar and soy, silkworms, utensils, chariots and palanquins, boats, the provinces, the villages, collecting the gall, a prodigy, bathing, immigrants, the army, and finally a public audience given by the king.

Even in some of the very brief 'chapters' interesting facts emerge. Thus quoting *in toto* the one on villages we read that:

> *Each village has its temple or at least a pagoda. No matter how small the village, it has a local mandarin, called the mai-chieh. Along the highways there are resting places like our post-halts; these are called sen-mu (Khmer: samnak). Only recently, during the war with Siam, whole villages have been laid waste.*

The statement that Buddhism is represented so widely is interesting. The reference to resting-places along the highways relates to some of the prodigious works of Jayavarman VII already mentioned above. This and the following excerpt may represent the only source for so early an attack by the Thais, which would have had to come through Lopburi and could scarcely have reached anywhere near Angkor.[8] In any case this can only be hearsay. Concerning the Army we read:

Soldiers also move about unclothed and barefoot. In the right hand is carried a lance, in the left a shield. They have no bows, no arrows, no slings, no missiles, no breastplates, no helmets. I have heard it said that in war with the Siamese, universal military service was required. Generally speaking, these people have neither discipline nor strategy.

It seems doubtful that soldiers went unclothed. On the carvings around the Bayon many of them are wearing short coats.[9]

More substantial information comes from the 'chapter on the three religious groups':

There are three religious groups, the pan-k'i (= pandits), the chao-ku (= the noble ones) and the pa-ssu-wei (for Skr. tapasvin = ascetics). As for the pandits (the Brahmans) I am unable to say what inherited creed lies behind them, as they have no school of ceremony for training. It is equally difficult to find out what are their sacred books. I have only observed that they dress like men of the people, except that all their lives they wear round their neck a white thread that marks them as men of learning. They often rise to high position. The chao-ku (polite term of address for monks) shave the head, wear yellow robes, bare the right shoulder, knot a strip of yellow cloth around the waist and go barefoot. Their temples, which are often roofed with tiles, contain only one statue in the likeness of Sâkyamuni Buddha, which is called Po-lai (for Khmer: Preah = Lord). Moulded from clay, it is painted in various colours and draped in red. On the other hand the Buddhas on the towers are of bronze. There are no bells, no drums, no cymbals, no banners. The food of the monks is universally fish or meat, which is also set as an offering before the Buddhas, but no wine may be drunk. They content themselves with one meal a day, which is partaken at the house of a patron, no cooking being done in the monasteries. The numerous holy books that they scan are made of strips of palm-leaf, neatly bound together. These strips are covered with black characters, but no brush or ink is used; their manner of writing is a mystery. To certain monks is given the right to use palanquins with golden shafts and parasols with gold or silver handles. These men are consulted by the King on matters of serious import. There are no Buddhist nuns.

The pa-ssu-wei (ascetics, presumably followers of Śiva) are clothed like men of the people, save that on their head they wear a white or red hood. They too have monasteries but smaller than the Buddhist ones, for they do not attain the prosperity of the Buddhist group. They worship nothing but a block of stone (linga).

Lest this text should suggest that these ascetics are well clad, I quote from the chapter on clothing, most of which is otherwise concerned with the royal attire:

Round the waist they wear a small strip of cloth, over which a larger piece is worn when they leave their houses.

Although we have records of the desecration of Buddhist royal foundations, it seems most unlikely that this ever represented a persecution of the religion as such. Thus in the chapter on the 'People' we read that: 'The worship of the Buddha is universal.' Even if this is an exaggeration, it seems clear that by the end of the 13th century Buddhism in its Theravâda form pervades most of the country, as well as enjoying royal favour. This is confirmed by the 'chapter' on the New Year and the seasons, where there is reference to the ceremony of 'bringing water to the Buddhas' in which the king takes part. The reference to monks who reach high status at court, being allowed the use of palanquins and parasols, must surely be associated with the accounts we have read above of high Buddhist dignitaries gaining royal favour. It is surely likely that Theravâda Buddhism only gradually absorbed the earlier monastic establishments of Mahâyâna persuasion and for a while the Buddhist dignitaries at court continued to represent the earlier traditions.

Chou Ta-kuan reports that 'During my stay of over a year in the country I saw the King (Srîndravarman) emerge four or five times.' Having given a description of the magnificent royal procession, he continues:

The king was proceeding to a nearby destination where golden palanquins, borne by girls of the palace, were waiting to receive him. For the most part, his objective was a little golden pagoda in front of which stood a golden statue of the Buddha.

Before attempting to explain how the change from Mahâyâna Buddhism to forms of Theravâda Buddhism occurred, I must surely finish my brief survey of Chou Ta-kuan's report. Since he expresses ignorance concerning the method of writing in his section on the monks, I quote also the section devoted to 'Writing in Cambodia'.

For ordinary correspondence, as well as official documents, deer-skin or similar parchment is used, which is dyed black. The parchment is cut by the scribe in sizes to suit his needs. A sort of powder resembling Chinese chalk is moulded into small sticks called so *(corresponding to a Thai word for 'pencil'), which are used to inscribe the parchment with lasting characters.*

The chapter on agriculture, with special reference to the rise and fall of the water level in the Great Lake, corresponds closely to the situation with which we are familiar today. As for the products of the country, Chou Ta-kuan lists feathers of the king-fisher, elephant tusks (noting that the best quality is obtained from an elephant hunted and slain for the purpose), rhinoceros horns and beeswax, lacquer-wood, cardamom, gum-resin and 'chaulmoogra oil which comes from the seeds of a large tree, the pod resembling that of cocoa but round and containing several score seeds'.

Regrettably, the short chapter on trade deals only with small dealings at market level, but we learn from the equally short chapter concerning desirable Chinese goods that the Cambodians were anxious to import Chinese gold and silver, silks, tinware, lacquered trays, green porcelain, mercury, vermilion, paper, sulphur, saltpetre, sandalwood, angelica-root, musk, linen and other forms of cloth, umbrellas, iron pots, copper trays, fresh-water pearls, tung oil, bamboo nets, basketry, wooden combs and needles. Chou Ta-kuan adds: What the Cambodians most urgently need are beans and wheat, but the export of these from China is forbidden.

Chou Ta-kuan is certainly impressed with the city of Angkor. He refers to the city wall with its five gateways, the wide surrounding moat and the massive causeways. He notes the gigantic heads of Buddhas that adorn the gateways, and at the centre of the city the Golden Tower (Bayon) and the Tower of Bronze (Baphuon), 'a truly astonishing spectacle'. He mentions the 'eastern lake' which lies four kilometres from the walled city, at the centre of which there stands a stone tower, and in it there lies a recumbent bronze Buddha, from whose navel flows a steady stream of water. Here he may be referring to the famous massive bronze image of Vishnu, which was in fact found in the Western Baray and can still be seen in the Phnom Penh Museum. 'These are the monuments', he exclaims, 'which have caused merchants from overseas to speak so often of Cambodia, the rich and the noble.'

The spread of Theravâda Buddhism

The conversion of Cambodia to Theravâda Buddhism probably came about because of the ever-increasing pressure from within its boundaries as well as from without. Buddhism is a missionary religion carried peaceably by zealous monks across national boundaries even when the rulers are at war with one another. Furthermore conquest of a Buddhist land causes an exodus of Buddhist monks who can so easily rebuild their lives elsewhere. During the 11th to the early 13th century the Khmers controlled populations (mainly Mons) beyond their original frontiers who were largely Buddhist in religion. Rather further afield the city of Pagan had been built up into a powerful Burmese state by King Anuruddha who reigned from 1044 onwards and later by Kyanzittha (*c.*1086-1112). The Theravâda canon was collected and re-edited and this form of Buddhism was established as the state religion, close contacts being maintained with Ceylon. The fall of Pagan in 1287, resulting from Mongol incursions, led inevitably to an exodus of monks who reinforced missionary zeal amongst the Mons who were still subject (but not for much longer) to the Khmers. It also left the way open for the Thais, who thus inherited and gradually absorbed all the fruits of these Buddhist labours, whether literary or architectural. Moreover the Thais developed close contact with Nakhon Si Thammarat on the Malay Peninsula, which had gained its independence from Śrîvijaya, while maintaining close relations with Ceylon. It had thus become an important centre for the promulgation of Theravâda teachings.[10]

The northern Thai state of Lan Na, with its capital eventually at Chiang Mai, was established in the mid-13th century, while a central state based on the city of Sukhothai, whence the last Khmer garrison was expelled about 1220, was well established by the end of the century. Lan Na was built up into a powerful independent Thai state by Mangrai, chief of a small principality at Chiang Saen (now on the far northern Thai border with Laos), by first subduing the neighbouring Thai principalities and then by conquering the ancient Mon kingdom of Haripuñjaya in the upper Mae Ping Valley in 1281. In 1296 Mangrai founded Chiang Mai as his capital, which became a great centre of Theravâda Buddhism, thanks to the many local monks at his disposal.[11] During the same period, about 1279, Râma Khamhaeng succeeded his brother as king of Sukhothai, then still quite a small state. He seems to have extended it into a small empire, more by persuasion and alliances than by military means, while avoiding conflict with the more powerful neighbouring Thai states such as Lan Na and Phayao to the north and Lopburi to the south. He claims to have ruled with justice over a population that included Mons and Khmers as well as Thais. He is also credited with having invented a script modeled on the Khmer one and adapted to the Thai language, then certainly needed for administration.

While Brahmanical ritual was maintained for court purposes, perhaps following the Khmer practice, Buddhism was richly endowed as the state religion.

> *Above all else, Sukhothai was a Buddhist state, lavishly supporting a monastic community newly reinforced and invigorated by a celebrated patriarch who had come from Nakhon Si Thammarat. The people of Sukhothai observed the Buddhist precepts and celebrated with exuberance the ceremonies of the religious calendar. The king shared the very throne from which he heard his subjects' complaints and petitions, weekly giving it up that learned monks there might preach the Dharma of the Buddha* (David Wyatt, *Thailand*, pp. 54-55).

Whoever visits Sukhothai nowadays, maintained as a magnificent archaeological park, gains some moving impressions of the greatness of this particular Thai ruler. Regrettably, on his death the empire of Râma Khamhaeng disintegrated into petty states, maintaining a precarious existence, until in 1438 it was finally incorporated as a province of the rising power of Ayuthaya (named after the famous Indian city of Ayodhya).

This period of the 13th to 14th centuries might well be referred to as 'The Decline of Khmer Empire', but it was primarily a decline at the centre of Khmer power which led to the conversion of Cambodia to Buddhism. There is no doubt that from the 9th to the 12th centuries the royal cult of the Devarâja gave coherence and continuity to Khmer imperial policy. Mahâyâna Buddhism continued to hold its own, but it could not long survive the pressure of Theravâda Buddhism, once the implicit protection of Khmer rulers was lost, namely when the rulers themselves from Jayavarman VI onwards seem to have lost interest in the Devarâja concept. It is significant that he and his successors, mainly of the Mahîdharapura dynasty, do not seem to have appointed a special Devarâja *purohita*. When Jayavarman VII instituted

208. When the Khmers were driven from Sukhothai by the Thais in 1220, Wat Sri Sawi was probably already in the process of being built. The Khmer tradition of building this form of tower continued at Sukhotai and at Ayuthaya.

his form of Mahâyâna Buddhism in Brahmanical guise, both Brahmanical religion and Mahâyâna Buddhism were bound to lose against the pressures of Theravâda Buddhism, which seems to have already permeated his realm.

Moreover, due to the intolerable exactions that he demanded of his subjects, he seems to have effectively broken their will to submit to such tyranny thereafter. The proof of this is surely that after his reign only one king, Jayavarman VIII succeeded in rallying the few Brahmanical faithful, and getting just one more stone temple built in honour of his revered guru. At the same time the seeming rapidity of this cultural and religious change requires some further comment. According to the accounts of Chou Ta-kuan, it already had its shrines and temples in every village by the end of the 13th century. This may well be an exaggeration, and some of these temples may still have been Mahâyâna ones in accordance with the earlier traditions. In any case, the change can only have been gradual and it was bound to come about as a result of the momentum given to Theravâda teachings by the pressures mentioned above, in actual practice by Mon, Khmer and perhaps even Burmese monks who moved freely within the Khmer 'empire'. As will be shown later the Buddhist traditions imported by these monks, although generally described as Theravâda must have been largely oral, supported by texts deriving from Pâli of religious instructions relating to moral precepts, the ordering of the community and the ritual of ordination. Only in a later period, perhaps from the 17th century onwards, did Siamese influences from Ayuthaya become predominant.

The interesting question arises as to what extent Jayavarman VII was personally responsible for the rapidity of the transition. As monarch he was necessarily constrained by court tradition. We must surely assume that his attachment to the Buddhist doctrine was genuine, and architecturally he could only express it in the traditional Mahâyâna form while not neglecting the Brahmanical demands of his court circle. At the same time the numerous 'hospitals' and 'rest-houses' along his many new highways were dedicated to the Buddha Master of Medicine (*Bhaiṣajyaguru*). This Buddha-image is usually regarded as a Mahâyâna manifestation, but iconographically it presents nothing which might be regarded as heterodox by a non-Mahâyânist. He appears as a typical image of the seated Buddha Sâkyamuni, making the gesture of generosity with his right palm turned outwards, while holding his begging bowl with the sole addition of a myrobalan fruit as a typical medicinal plant. These shrines would have required monks in attendance and Theravâda monks, whether Mon or recently converted Khmer, were surely already available, serving the purpose quite as readily as Mahâyâna ones. If Jayavarman VII had any serious interest in encouraging Buddhism as the religion of his subjects, he may have known that the Theravâda form was the one that held promise for the future. There is the interesting report of one of his sons, named Tâmalinda, receiving ordination as a monk in Ceylon about the year 1180 among a group, mainly Mon it seems, sent there from Pagan.[12]

It must also be observed that the sources which led to the establishment of the 'old order' in Cambodia (namely Brahmanical and Mahâyâna religious traditions), had now dried up. Trade continued along the ancient sea-routes of the 'southern seas', but it was now rarely in the hands of Hindu-Buddhist merchants. Buddhism throughout India, the source of these traditions, was on the verge of suffering a devastating reversal. From the 9th to 10th centuries onwards no great missionary endeavours emanate from India except northwards across the Himalayas to Tibet, and even these come to an end by the year 1300. By contrast the major extension of Buddhism across mainland South-East Asia takes place from the 11th century onwards at a time when Theravâda Buddhism is becoming firmly established in Ceylon under royal decree. Thus the early forms of Buddhism, planted in the lower Irrawaddy and Chao Phraya valleys from the 5th century onwards, mainly but not exclusively *Hînayâna,* were greatly enforced. By the time later rulers, such as the Burmese kings of Pagan and later the Thai principalities began to deliberately sponsor Buddhism as their state religions, the Theravâda Buddhism of Ceylon readily presented itself as the one still active and proselytizing form of Buddhism.

Cambodia, through the medium of its 'empire' which was in direct contact with these developments, seems to have been quickly absorbed. Its earlier

211. (right) Effigy of a Buddhist religious teacher portrayed as a forest-hermit. At a monastery site near Ban Sida, Thailand, where there are also ruins of a Khmer temple. The tradition of hermit-life in the forest was strong in earlier centuries in the wild countryside of NW Thailand which then included the whole Angkor region and Battambang province. Such wandering monks as these were also responsible for introducing Buddhist teachings into Cambodia.

209 & 210. (above and right) Sima (Buddhist boundary stones) carved in Mon style, from a set of eight which have survived intact on Phnom Kulen. They suggest the presence of a Mon community of monks who may have arrived here maybe in the 16th or later centuries; 209. (above) Mahâmâya and the elephants who have come to refresh the birth of the Bodhisattva. 210. (above right) a lotus-flower after Boulbet & Degans, *photos 132 and 127.*

212. Effigy of an arhat *at the hilltop monastery (Vat Choat-nyien) in Kampong Saom. The term appears rarely in my text (see the Glossary) but as representing the highest spiritual attainment short of Buddhahood, it is an important concept in Theravâda tradition, although maybe rarely represented. Figures of such* arhats, *all recent work, stand around the picturesque grounds of this monastery with its fine views of the surrounding sea.*

Brahmanical and Mahâyâna traditions were easily overrun by this Theravâda deluge, just as the earlier Brahmanical and Mahâyâna traditions of whole Malay archipelago were later (from the 15th century onwards) overrun by Islam, imported along sea-faring routes by traders who were now largely Muslim.

Retreat to the South

The decline of the Khmer Empire is marked by the forced withdrawal from Champa, which henceforth went its own way, unhindered by attacks from Angkor. The main enemies of the Chams however remained the Vietnamese, who pressed continually south from their earlier home in the Red River Valley until by the 15th century, despite continual resistance, Champa was effectively absorbed into Vietnam. At the same time the Thais, previously known mainly as barbarians and 'slaves' (*syam*), were actively establishing themselves in small independent kingdoms in the upper Chao Phraya and Mekong valleys, gradually displacing or absorbing the earlier Mon population as well as the more remote Khmer settlements. Thus further south Khmer regional capitals such as Lopburi were able to detach themselves from the Khmer Empire, becoming effectively independent, until they were in turn overrun by the gradual Thai advance southwards. It is interesting to note that Lopburi, claiming independence for a short while, sent embassies to the Mongol (Chinese) Court between 1289 and 1299. Meanwhile in the course of the 13th century the two major kingdoms of Chiang Mai and Sukhothai were founded by successful Thai chieftains, Mangrai and Râma Khamhaeng, while holding their own against Mongol invasions.[13] The importance of Sukhothai as a Buddhist kingdom under Râma Khamhaeng has been mentioned above, but on his death this kingdom disintegrated into petty states, maintaining a precarious existence, until in 1438 it was finally incorporated as a province of the rising power of Ayuthaya. This city is said to have been founded in 1351 by a Chinese merchant adventurer named U Thong, who had married into the ruling family of Suphanburi, the main city on the western side of the Chao Phraya plain, and maybe also that of Lopburi on the eastern side. Both these Mon cities, which had been Khmer regional capitals, became subject to Ayuthaya, which now drew its strength from Khmer administrative efficiency, Chinese trading enthusiasm and Thai military power.[14] U Thong took the royal name of Râmâdhipati and from now on Ayuthaya becomes effectively Siam, and Ayuthaya and Angkor, two rival powers, were inevitably soon at war with one another.

It will be recalled that the last Khmer king of the 'old order' for whom a reliable date from a stone inscription can be given was Jayavarman Parameśvara, who reigned from 1327 onwards. From now on the only sources of information are the Royal Chronicles of Cambodia, known in several recensions, but generally regarded as unreliable; they are supposed to date from 1346 and were drawn up as lists of kings with details of the main events of each king's reign. However written on perishable palm-leaf, they were often rewritten and re-edited to suit later reigns. Thus continuity is unreliable and events are easily moved from one reign to another. Events were inserted from the *Annals of Ayuthaya,* ever more readily as Cambodia gradually became a client-state of Siam. However these too were destroyed when the Burmese sacked Ayuthaya in 1767, and were rewritten towards the end of the 18th century. The Cambodian versions are no older than 19th century.[15] The first king named in these chronicles is referred to as Nippeanbât, a phonetic spelling of Sanskrit: *nirvâṇapada* (='gone to nirvâṇa') and thus a suitable posthumous name for any Buddhist king, and we can certainly assume that all kings from now on were Buddhist (except for one who decided to become a Muslim). In 1352 during the reign of his successor, possibly named Lampongrâja, Râmâdhipati, the founder and first king of Ayuthaya, is said to have captured Angkor, installing one of his sons on the throne there. It was eventually regained by a Khmer ruler referred to in later chronicles as Râjâdhirâja of the Sun Dynasty, a title rather than a name. From now on the city had to be defended against continual attacks by the Siamese, and in 1394, Angkor is said to have been occupied yet again and a Siamese prince installed on the throne, but he was soon assassinated and the Khmers once again regained their capital.[16]

Both Chinese and Cambodian sources confirm the name of the last king who ruled in Angkor as Chao Poñea Yat who took the distinguished name of Sûryavarman on his accession.[17] In the course of his long reign of fifty years, the decision was taken in 1431 to abandon Angkor and transfer the capital first to Srei Santhor on the eastern side of the Mekong and for a while to Phnom Penh (known traditionally as *Çaturmukha* [pronounced Çatomukh], referring to the apparent 'four facing' rivers, where the waters of the Tonle Sap merge with those of the Mekong and the Bassac). Phnom Penh in this strategic position must have already served as an important commercial centre, and certainly continued to do so, although it did not become formally capital of Cambodia until 1883. In the meantime alternative capitals were Lovek, some sixty-five kilometres further north, and Oudong, in the same direction but nearer Phnom Penh. It is usually assumed that this decision arose primarily from the difficulty of defending Angkor against continuing Siamese assaults, as well as damage done to the whole irrigation system by such constant warfare. These were doubtless the initial compelling reasons, but one has to take into account that the social and economic life of the city had already changed considerably since the days of Jayavarman VII, who could command massive bands of labourers to work on his stupendous monuments. The days of such autocratic kings had passed, simultaneously it might seem with the introduction of Theravâda Buddhism. While there may be no direct relationship between the two, they were both signs of a great change in the times. Foreign trade would eventually be of more importance to the Cambodian economy than reliance upon massive home rice-production, and the ultimate move to Phnom Penh suggests immediately removal to a site ideally suited for commerce.[18] But these were considerations for the future. Throughout the 15th and 16th centuries Khmer kings were mainly

213. Ayuthaya, founded in 1351, absorbed the two Khmer regional headquarters of Suphanburi and Lopburi, and thus continued to develop Khmer styles of architecture. A typical 14th century shrine with tower in Ayuthaya.

occupied with holding their positions against attacks from Ayuthaya and regaining territory wherever they could.

The reasons given in the Royal Chronicles are surely the primary reason for the retreat from Angkor, as attributed to King Poñea Yat:

> *The kingdom of Cambodia has the Kingdom of Siam as its enemy. Previously the western provinces of the kingdom were well populated, but much of them has been taken from us by the Siamese. Moreover they have carried off a far larger proportion the population than that which remains to us, while we do not have enough people to repopulate these areas. Even if we wish to retake the provinces which the Siamese have taken from us, we cannot because on our side we are not in a condition to restart the war. The provinces which separate us from the frontier, could not provide the army required for the defense of our country, if the enemy attacks again. Our capital city is large with solid ramparts, but the inhabitants are insufficient for its defense.* (Moura, *Le Royaume du Cambodge*, vol. 2, p. 43 ff; Khin Sok,*Chroniques royales du Cambodge*, p. 66.)

This is surely sound reasoning, since levying sufficient troops appears as a major preoccupation in waging war on the frontiers and during the continual internal wars which from now on will ravish the country.

Kings of the Theravâda period

King Râma-thipdey Srei-reachea (=Lord Râma Śrîrâja), the grandson of Poñea Yat, resolved to regain some the Siamese-occupied territories, namely Khorat, Angkor and Chanthaburi. He achieved some success but returning through Battambang he learned that his brother Prince Thommo, whom he had left in charge at Çatomukh (later known as Phnom Penh) had assumed control over the area to the west of the Mekong/Tonle Sap, while his nephew has occupied the eastern side based on Srei Santhor. Thus for six years there were three effective kings, typical of so much more trouble which was yet to come. As so often, the King of Siam resolved the matter by another invasion, thus regaining any territory that might have been lost, and setting Prince Thommo on the throne, while his brother and cousin were taken to Ayuthaya.

The chronicles speak well of King Thommo-Reachea, saying that he knew the Buddhist scriptures (*Tripiṭika*) and that he lectured his administrators according to the *Dhammacakra-pravattanasutta* (Treatise of Turning the Wheel of the Doctrine), a basic sûtra attributed to the Buddha himself (cp. Khin Sok, *Chroniques royales*, p. 95 ff.). He is also said to have built a temple with bas-reliefs and a stûpa on Phnom Santuk (just south of Kampong Thom). During a later festival when a Buddha-relic was enshrined in the stûpa, the King was ordained a monk for two weeks, and on renouncing the robes, he gave the monastery 21 villages, 21 paddy-fields, 21 male personnel and 21 female, 21 carts with bulls and their harnesses, 21 buffalo-carts, 21 horses, 21 elephants, musicians and male and female slaves for the upkeep of the temple. After his death his ashes were placed in the same stûpa.

His son and successor Sokonthor did not enjoy so peaceful a reign as he was soon engaged in a long-term war with a son-in-law who set himself up as King Kân, a rare case of a commoner claiming such a title. The story merits telling in some detail. The king was struck by the beauty of a girl, offspring of an official and a temple-slave. He placed her in the first rank of concubines while bestowing honour and wealth on her parents and her brother Kân, who became one of his personal body-guards. Such was his presumption that the court dignitaries resolved to discredit him. On the first of the new year (usually in April) 1508 the King had a terrible dream of a fearful dragon with flaming mouth who set fire to the city and then seized the royal parasol and disappeared. The soothsayers interpreted this as pointing to Kân who had been born in a Dragon Year. A plot was made to drown him the following day, but his sister, whose suspicions were aroused, warned him in time. Thus he escaped and having lain quiet for a while, he reappeared claming to be an emissary of Prince Chan, the son of King Sokonthor, who acted as viceroy at Çatomukh, who had authorized him, he claimed, to raise an army in his name. Claiming that the local governor was a rebel to the king, he killed him and took charge of the army that he had raised. One presumes that Kân appeared to his new followers as an inspired 'man of destiny', who have often gained adherents to their cause in Cambodia. Hearing of this rebellion, the King, as well as the father and sister of Kân, sent messages begging him to return, assuring him of a royal pardon. He asked for a month to disband his following, but used this delay to increase it, saying that now Prince Chan was the rebel, and that the army was being raised against him by the King's orders. This rumour reached Prince Chan, only twenty-three years old, and believing it be true that his father, the King, was raising an army against him, he fled to Ayuthaya. Gradually the King realized his danger and began to levy forces, and Kân's father supporting him, went to defend Çatomukh. Here he was overwhelmed and retreated to a monastery. The aged abbot urged upon them a peaceful meeting, but he seems to have become so convinced of Kân's destiny as King of Cambodia, that Kân's father finally consented to join his son's rebellion. The King's advancing army was driven back to Lovek and Kân thus became effective king of the whole of southern Cambodia. Despite an unsuccessful campaign northwards, the kingdom was now divided into two, north and south. King Kân, rejecting any command to submit to the true king, seemed content with part of the kingdom and established a new capital city at a place named Srâlâp. seemingly about twenty-two kilometres east of Prei Veng, in a square enclave protected by earthworks, about 2,000 metres each side. Since water was scarce he had an artificial lake also constructed. According to Leclère, p. 253, whose text I am following here, this lake was still there in the early 20th century (cp. Khin Sok, *Chroniques royales*, p. 120.)

Prince Chan, who had been kept at the court of Ayuthaya all this time, now entered the fray. He succeeded in raising enthusiasm for his cause in the northern part of the country, but a general stalemate seems to have existed. Meanwhile the country was being ruined by the continual levying of forces and the neglect of all agricultural work. King Kân thus proposed to the Prince a truce during the monsoon season, so that men could return to their fields. He agreed to this despite the objections of his followers, concerning mainly the crucial necessity of raising levies. They said:

> *Kân holds tenfold more provinces than you do. If he raises an army in all those which are his, from the sea in the south to Laos in the north and to the frontier (in the east) which separates us from the Kingdom of Champa, he could put several 100,000 men in the field, while we can only oppose him with the men whom you have been able to raise from the six or seven provinces which are loyal to us.*

The Prince decided that his army was too weak to continue, and that he needed time to win reinforcements. It was to his advantage that King Kân was content with his half of the kingdom and had no great interest in continuing the war, although Prince Chan was determined to prevail. His forces were able to gain the coastal province of Kampot and Kampong Saom, and thus trade with Java in order to purchase weapons. King Kân was doing the same, but his ships, returning with 150 cannons and 3,000 arquebuses, were caught in a storm. Some ships were lost, but the rest were retrieved by Prince Chan's followers. This added 50 canons and 1,000 arquebuses to their own trading venture of 150 canons and 3,000 arquebuses. Thus reinforced, their side prevailed and King Kân was finally forced to retreat to the citadel of Samrong Prei Nokor, where after a siege of three months he was finally overcome. Kân was executed and his followers became slaves of the state. Thus the kingdom was reunited. Prince Chan established his capital at Lovek, where he built a citadel and a palace, being crowned king of a united Cambodia in 1528/9.

While walking in the nearby forest, King Chan noticed a rock which was entirely enveloped by the wood of a branch of a *gagî*-tree (*Hopea odorata* according to Khin Sok, *Chroniques royales*, p. 149 ff.). Struck by this strange sight, he resolved to use the stone and the tree in order to make four statues of the Buddha, set back to back. The stone formed the basis for the images that stood facing the four directions. This fourfold image of Sâkyamuni was presented to the adoration of the faithful in 1530 after the ceremony of 'opening the eyes' and three days of prayers. About the same time the king established a camp at the foot of a hill close to Oudong in order to watch over the construction of a monastery and an enormous statue of the Buddha in brick. He also arranged for a pagoda to be built on the eastern summit of the hill in order to enclose the image of a lying Buddha (*parinirvâṇa*). He also had two artificial pools dug, one to the north and one to the west, and later a third to the north-east. In another place he made a dam with high palisades to hold back the monsoon rains, thus creating a large expanse of water. This was later known as the 'Lake of the Iron Market' on account of the exploitation of iron-ore on its banks and the industries that subsequently developed. When these works were finished, he cleared the forest all around and turned them into immense paddy-fields, so as to produce the rice necessary for the personnel who served these temples. Special corvées were engaged on this work.

In 1534 the King of Siam organized an army of 90,000 men, putting it in charge of a refugee Prince Ong, who had been held in Siam for just such a purpose. This prince received the order to attack Cambodia, his own country, while a Siamese officer debarked 5,000 men on the Gulf of Siam. The King of Cambodia sent his naval commander to deal with the troops debarking, and went himself to confront the invading army which had already reached Pursat. On the way be noticed buds growing on an old bo-tree which was said locally to be already dead. His Majesty took this to be a favourable omen and stopped to make offerings to the local spirit who had made this possible. After that he approached the enemy. At the first engagement, Prince Ong, general of the Siamese army, was shot dead on his elephant by an arrow. Besides him many military leaders were killed and the Siamese army lost half its effective force, as well as many elephants and weapons of all kinds. It dispersed after this set-back and could undertake nothing more. The commander of the naval detachment was also repulsed and returned to Siam.

After this campaign the King of Cambodia organized funereal honours for Prince Ong, his relative, whose corpse had now fallen into his hands. Then in accordance with a vow made before the battle, he had a temple built near the old bo-tree which had foretold his great victory. The golden utensils of the slain prince and all the gold and silver which had been taken from the enemy was melted down in order to make images to place in the temple, which was named 'Temple of the all-powerful Bo-tree'.

King Chan may have died in 1567 and was succeeded the next year by one of his sons, Bâraminda Reachea, also referred to by the general title of Barom-reachea I. One notes that this is simply a phonetic spelling of Sanskrit (or Pâli) *Parama-râja* = 'Supreme King'. He organized army and navel forces to attack the Siamese once more, and despite heavy loses, they prevailed in the coastal region north of Chanthaburi. According to the Siamese account this was the result of treachery. Ayuthaya was engaged in a war with Pegu and the Cambodians took this occasion to mount their attack. Encouraged by this success the Cambodians organized another campaign, basing themselves at a village named Kampong Krasang at Angkor, and succeeded in regaining part of the Khorat Plateau. There followed a short war with Laos in which the King of Cambodia prevailed with the co-optation of his son Satha. The following year the Siamese mounted fresh attacks in order to regain the coastal provinces and the part of the Khorat Plateau that had been lost. Both sides seem to have exhausted themselves in these wars on large fronts. Following another short war with Laos, the King of Cambodia sent a mission to Ayuthaya in 1567 (according to Moura) to initiate a treaty of peace. However he died in the same year and was succeeded by Prince Satha, crowned as Mohinda Reachea but conveniently known as simply King Satha.

In 1568 Siam was again attacked by Pegu and asked for the support of the King of Cambodia, who sent a hundred elephants, a hundred horses and 20,000 soldiers under the command of Prince Srei-Sopor. When they arrived at the camp after this expedition, the King of Siam observed that the commander of the Cambodian army remained seated in his presence, and did not prostrate himself in the usual manner. In order to intimidate the young prince, some Siamese officers had some Laotian captives beheaded and hung their heads around his general quarters. Either frightened or indignant at such provocations he left for home and reported the whole matter to the King. Such was the indignation of all concerned that a campaign against the Siamese was organized under the leadership of the First Minister. However he attacked with too few forces and was repulsed.

In 1574, for no given reason, King Satha abdicated in favour of his six-year-old son, at the same time raising the rank of the present crown prince to that of acting king. This encouraged rivalry in the royal family, leading eventually to various disasters. The Siamese seem to have already reoccupied the regions of Chanthaburi and Khorat, thus reducing Cambodia more or less to its present boundaries.

It seems that in 1576 the King of Siam, Phra Naret (Naresuan), anxious because of the continual attacks by the Mons on his western front, proposed peace-terms to the Khmers and the fixing of an agreed frontier, marked by boundary-posts. This is a unique event in the history of the two countries. Whether mutually recognized or not, this marked frontier was still in place in 1883, as noted by A. Pavie, who was responsible for the fixing of a telegraphic line between Cambodia and Thailand.[19]

In 1581 the King of Siam launched an enormous attack on Cambodia. He himself advanced with 100,000 men, 800 elephants and 1,850 horses. A vanguard of 50,000 men preceded him. Although he had abdicated, the old king took charge of the situation. One minister was stationed at Battambang with 20,000 men. Another went to reinforce the garrison at Pursat with 10,000 men. One of the princes was responsible for protecting the province of Angkor with 30,000 men, and the 'acting king' remained in reserve with 3,000 men. However the Siamese overran the whole country and then laid siege to Lovek. Here at last they were beaten back for a while by fresh Khmer troops which arrived on the scene, but the Siamese returned to the assault and Lovek was taken in 1594.[20]

It is about this time that the Portuguese (established in Malacca since 1511) and the Spaniards (who had finally captured Manila in 1571) became involved in Cambodia's internal affairs.[21] The initial contacts date at least from the mid-16th century, involving trade and missionary endeavours. They were doubtless preceded by Malays, Chinese and Japanese traders, as well as the neighbouring Chams. However these fellow-Asians had no wish to subvert the Buddhist religion of the inhabitants, which was always a primary interest of the Portuguese and the Spanish. In this they were generally unsuccessful, but one at least, Father Sylvester d'Azevedo, a Dominican from Malacca, succeeded in establishing a small Christian community in Phnom Penh, consisting of foreigners such as Chams, Malays, Chinese and Portuguese. His hopes were soon raised by his association with a trading adventurer in his early twenties, the Portuguese Diogo Veloso, who arrived some time about 1583-84 with a band of other similar companions. All foreign trade was in any case the special preserve of the king, and as well as serving him in these affairs, Diogo and d'Azevedo encouraged him to apply to Malacca for military aid, desperately needed against the continuing Siamese attacks. No such help came from Malacca, but a few years later in the early 1590s another adventurer, namely the Spaniard Blas Ruiz arrived together with the owner, named Gregorio Vargas, of a merchant-ship, wrecked on the coast. Blas Ruiz, like Diogo Veloso, soon won the special favour of King Satha, who treated them like adopted sons. It was now decided to seek help from Manila and Veloso made the journey there bearing a letter from the King. When he returned bearing a favourable reply (a letter dated 8 February 1594) but no reinforcements, the Siamese had already captured Lovek and he was carried off as a prisoner together with Blas Ruiz, a number of missionaries and the royal family, except for 'King Satha' and the young heir who had fled to Srei Santhor. In the ensuing chaos a usurper, named Reamea Chung Prei, declared himself king, and so they fled still further to Laos.

Veloso won the favour of the King of Siam and was allowed to leave (presumably with his companions) on a trading venture to Manila. Gaining control of the vessel due to the death of the Siamese ambassador on board, who was properly in charge, he reached Manila and then made his way back to Phnom Penh with reinforcements in order to come to the aid of 'King Satha'. Here he found a usurper on the throne and uncertain of his fate while being kept under guard, he and his companions, like desperados, assaulted the palace and killed the usurper. Then he made his way to Vientiane to find 'King Satha', to whom he and Blas Ruiz had remained faithful all these years. But both the 'king' and the crown-prince Chettha had died, leaving the second son, Poñea Tân as legitimate heir They brought him back to Srei Santhor and he was eventually crowned king as Barom Reachea (V).[22] Despite the favours that he bestowed upon Veloso and Blas Ruiz, he proved a useless character and the country remained in disorder. Efforts urged by these two heroes and the interested missionaries to establish a form of Spanish protectorate over Cambodia came to nothing. A terrible massacre of the Europeans, initiated by a quarrel between the Spaniards and the resident Malays, occurred seemingly in 1599, and finally put an end to such a prospect for the country. Barom Reachea V died soon afterwards and was succeeded by an uncle, Poñea An (Barom Reachea VI), the younger brother of Satha and of Soryopor who was still held in Ayuthaya. Poñea An was soon murdered and succeeded by a nephew, Poñea Ñom (? 1600-1602), the youngest son of Satha who was never crowned. A cordial letter from him addressed to the head of the Franciscan Order in Manila proves that missionary priests still came to Cambodia and that the European community in Phnom Penh had been revived.[23] Poñea Ñom also welcomed in 1603 a group of missionaries from Manila who had been requested earlier, and he seems to have authorized the building of a church in Phnom Penh.

As a result of court intrigues with Ayuthaya, Soryopor was freed, and raising an army declared himself the legitimate king (1602-1618), doubtless with support from King Naresuan of Ayuthaya. Poñea Ñom resisted and thanks to Siamese intervention was overcome and put to death.[24] See below in Chapter 7 for the continuation of the story, noting that the dates given have a relative value and may not be strictly accurate.

Religious and Cultural developments

At least up to the end of the 16th century and beyond Cambodia strove to defend itself against loss of further territory. Despite frequent warfare, possibly with rather less troops than the records boastfully claim, temples were built, images were cast in precious metals or carved in wood and stone. The temples were presumably built in far lighter materials than during the Angkor period, probably of brick and wood with tiled roofs and foundations of stone. The earlier traditions of wood-carving and painting certainly continued and have done so up to the present day, although practically nothing survives of painting styles from this earlier period.

As for literature, popular stories associated with the life of the Buddha, some already found on the earlier stone carvings, were doubtless now supplemented with yet other stories of his previous lives, of which large collections had been made by the earlier Buddhist schools. Recitations of extracts from the Râmâyana must have circulated, and these were sometimes modified to accommodate other local story-telling traditions or combined with tales from the other great Indian epic, the Mahâbhârata, scenes from which, like the Râmâyana decorate the walls of Angkor Vat. Meanwhile the great Brahmanical gods and the Bodhisattvas and goddesses of the Mahâyâna disappeared from general memory, the more easily in that they had represented previously the interests of a wealthy minority of rulers and prelates. However there is one remarkable exception to this general statement. It seems that King Chan, maybe in order to celebrate his victory over the Siamese forces, led by Prince Ong (as described above) decided to complete the row of carved plaques on the northern side, eastern section, of Angkor Vat. These are primarily concerned with the story of Krishna's contest with the demon king Bâna (Bânâsura), who had overpowered and imprisoned Prince Aniruddha, a grandson of Krishna. However Śiva came to Bânâsura's final rescue. These have long been regarded as later less skilful work and thanks to inscriptions *in situ* have been dated to the period 1546-66. For a detailed account with good illustrations see Vittorio Roveda, *Sacred Angkor*, p. 67 ff.[25]

Madelaine Giteau (*Iconographie du Cambodge post-Ankorienne*) observes that few works in stone have survived intact from the earlier period, mainly because an inferior type of sandstone was increasingly used, which was presumably easier to carve, but not so durable. Protruding parts of a sculptured body, such as the outstretched arms and raised palms of a Buddha image in the *abhayamudra* (sign of no fear), were carved as separate pieces and then fixed in place. A few notable images, made of stone, such as the famous Buddha lying in the state of entering final enlightenment (*parinirvâṇa*) on Phnom Kulen (probably of the 16th century), have survived, but such images were often constructed of brickwork and stucco, duly covered with lacquer and gold. Images were also cast in various metals, bronze, other alloys, even silver and gold. We read above how King Chan had all the gold and silver vessels of Prince Ong melted down to make images for the new temple that he was building. One can scarcely expect many such images from this earlier period to survive, and the later ones inevitably show Thai influence. The favoured material for Buddha-images from the 14th century onwards seems to have been wood, which was easily available and easily worked. Parts could be sculptured separately and then fixed together. Various coatings could then be added in order to produce the desired effect. Some of the inscription, which will be quoted below, refer to just such images and just such kinds of coating, of which lacquer and gold were favourite ones.

The sites for research into the little that remains from the early Theravâda period are primarily the citadels with their royal courts, namely Srei Santhor, Lovek, Oudong, Angkor and Phnom Penh. Madelaine Giteau surveys all these sites, adding also the lesser sites of Babor and Pursad further to the north. In none of these places are any traces of royal palaces, built of fragile materials and long since disappeared. However the monasteries associated with these sites, some of them known from the Chronicles to be royal foundations, have enjoyed a much longer life. The buildings have been rebuilt again and again, and it would be difficult to find in Cambodia any monastic structure that is more than a hundred years old. But these ever-changing establishments, usually retaining their original name and essential identity, often preserve much older images and traces of earlier workmanship. Thus at Srei Santhor the Vat Srei Sar Chhor (alias Vat Srei Santhor) preserves an old sanctuary containing a number of early images, several Buddha-figures and probably also a royal figure (photo no.1, statue A of Madelaine Giteau's illustrations). According to Lajonquière's earlier account (*Inventaire, I*, pp. 167-8) there was a group of early stûpas of laterite and brick. Likewise Vat Vihear Sour, also described by Lajonquière, is of special note. The *vihâra,* which is inevitably new, contains an old shrine in brick in the gloomy space behind the altar. It has a stone lintel and false door to the three sides, suggesting a survival from the Angkor period. The pyramid roof is crowned with a four-faced head of Brahmâ. The main figure on the altar is a standing crowned Buddha in wood; below this there is an image of Sâkyamuni enthroned on a *nâga*, presumably of lacquered wood except for the stone base, which reproduces a typical Buddha-image of the earlier Angkor period (Giteau, *Iconographie*, photo 17).

As for Lovek, we read above in an extract from the Chronicles, that King Chan, crowned probably in 1528/9, founded a city here, building a palace and a citadel. This remained the capital of his successors, Baraminda Reachea and King Satha, although other places of residence were Oudong, Pursat (on the route towards Battambang) and Angkor, often serving as a base in campaigns against the Siamese. Nothing substantial remains at Lovek except for traces of the original earthen ramparts, and a few monasteries, continually rebuilt but which sometimes have preserved pieces from the earlier period. Vat Traleng Keng, which is in the centre of the town, preserves the stone found in the jungle by King Chan which served as the base for the four-faced Buddha image (carved of wood) which he set up for general veneration in 1530. (See p. 185.) This served as a palladium of the kingdom until Lovek was captured and destroyed by the Siamese in 1594. Presumably everything in wood was burned, and metal images carried off and often smelted down. Likewise at Pursat, where Khmer kings often resided, nothing remains except perhaps the name of an ancient fortress, preserved as the name of Vat Bantây Dei (= 'the monastery of the citadel of earth'). However Madelaine Giteau draws attention to several pieces older than the 17th century found in the north-western area. She mentions the existence of a stûpa built of stone with four inset Buddha-images, now ruined and eroded, at the monastery of Bakan somewhat beyond Pursad. Also Babor well to the east (now in Kampong Chnang Province) and lying on the route from Lovek to Ayuthaya, was the site of an important shrine founded by King Chan after his victory over the usurper Kân. This shrine still exists and some ancient wood-carving and Buddha-images were found there, as noted by Moura (*Le Royaume du Cambodge*, vol. 2, p. 42). Some of these items can be seen in the National Museum, Phnom Penh.

Another important site is Oudong, where King Chan founded a temple with a large image of the Buddha in stone and masonry and various sacred pools, as described in Moura's account, already quoted above. From the 17th century onwards with the demise of Lovek it became the effective northern

214. Some good examples of Buddhas carved in wood can be seen in the Phnom Penh Museum. Here two such Buddhas carved in wood are kept in a repository in Vat Bo (Siem Reap) together with other accumulated items, some many centuries old, some quite recent.

215. This seated Buddha, making the hand-gesture of preaching ('turning the Wheel of the Dharma') would be identified as the Buddha Vairoçana according to Mahâyâna usage. It is hollow and made of a copper-alloy, known as samrit *in Khmer, which is much prized as it usually contains also silver and gold and retains its freshness longer than other alloys. This image is certainly well preserved and showing no sign of Thai influence; it is probably even earlier that the two standing Buddhas, and may possibly be dated to the late Angkor period. However there is nothing against a later dating except that this hand-gesture of preaching becomes rare during the Theravâda period.*

capital city of Cambodia, but kings might still build palaces or seek refuge at Srei Santhor or in the Phnom Penh area in time of trouble. Like Lovek it has been devastated by earlier warfare and more recently by the Khmer Rouge. Although still a royal city, the many elegant stûpas that adorn the hilltops are modern replacements. However there is one hilltop site where Olivier de Bernon once conducted me. Here there are the ruins of a massive lying Buddha image, built of stone and masonry that might conceivably relate to the 16th century foundation of King Chan.

An interesting development that takes place by the 16th century is the adaptation of ancient Khmer temples as Buddhist shrines. Thus to start with the primary example the great 'Abode of Vishnu' of Sûryavarman II became Angkor Vat, viz. the great 'Angkor Monastery'. 'King Satha' may have initiated this process, since during his reign repairs were carried out on this building, still known under its old name. Thus an inscription dated July 1577 expresses joy that the king, her son, repairs the ancient temple of Vishnuloka, restoring it to its original condition. This queen Śrîsujâtâ 'possessed of great virtue' (*mahâkalyanavatî*) declares herself a lay Buddhist (*upâsakâ)* who has come to Angkor to offer Buddha-images and to sacrifice her splendid coiffure to be burned as ashes to make lacquer.

Another inscription of 1579 records that His Majesty Noble Great Victorious Supreme King, Lord Râma (viz. King Satha) recalls that at the time of his coronation, having in mind the glorification of Buddhism, he repaired the great towers of the Sacred Vishnuloka, had stones brought for the reconstruction of the nine summits of these fine towers, covering them with gold, and placed there a reliquary in honour of his ancestors and the Great Noble King, his father.' [26] From this time on a large number of inscriptions appear on the walls of Angkor Vat (still named as Vishnuloka) and other monastic sites, recording donations or bearing witness to other meritorious actions, especially it seems the freeing slaves. These are written in Khmer introducing also a number of religious terms in Pâli, and the interpretation of lay titles seems to cause some difficulty. They have been worked on mainly by Saveros Lewitz, who has produced translations entirely adequate for giving the general sense, but inevitably introducing terms of uncertain definition.

She stresses that these inscriptions, representing the religious devotion not only of royal persons, but also of administrators of all ranks, of members of the Buddhist clergy and of quite simple people, shed light on the state of society during this period.[27] Amongst the more frequent titles of these people, one may note *uk ña* as referring to high officials and governors of provinces. The term *cau baña* refers to other high-ranking dignitaries. The heads of monasteries are known as *sangharâj* and may be addressed as *anak brah, samtec* (princely title) or *anak samtec brah.* Senior monks (*mahâthera)* may be addressed simply as *brah*. Polite terms for laymen are *cau* or *anak jâ*, with variants such as *anak tâ* (grandfather). Women may be addressed as *me*, *nâng* or *anak nâng*. Slaves, often mentioned as being freed in these inscriptions, are known generally as *khñum*, names of males being distinguished by the prefix *â* and females by the prefix *me*.

The primary purpose of these acts of devotion or of beneficence (e.g. freeing slaves, building shrines or rest-houses, or sanctifying images) is the accumulation of merit, as is also the case in other Buddhist lands. Increase in personal merit is thought to counteract the adverse effects of evil actions, and thus to save one from the terrors of hell (often taken very seriously) and to ensure a favourable form of rebirth. Such hopes are often expressed specifically in prayer, such as the wish to be reborn in a family of good standing, or simply to be wealthy, or intelligent, or better still to be born in circumstances suitable for entering the religious life. The highest aspirations are those concerning the religious life and the accumulation of merit and knowledge, which are conducive to final enlightenment. However these are more than prayers; they are solemn aspirations or vows (skr./pâli: *praṇidhâna*), to which both the inscription on the temple-wall and the persons present bear witness. At the higher religious level, such a vow corresponds to that of a *bodhisattva* according to Mahâyâna usage.[28]

The idea persists that the amount of merit gained depends upon the worthy status of the receiver. Thus the primary object is the 'Threefold Gem', the Buddha, his Doctrine, the Religious Community. To offer images of the Lord Buddha, to repair those broken, to lacquer and gild them are all works of great merit. To arrange for instructive religious gatherings and the reading of sacred scriptures reinforces the Doctrine and is also a work of great merit. To attend to the needs of the monastic orders with donations of everyday necessities, such as food and clothing or articles of general use is equally meritorious. Of supreme merit is the founding of a whole monastery with its *vihâra*, subsidiary buildings, provisions for the monks etc. This is usually the work of kings who hope thereby to counteract the effects of the evil acts of statecraft and warfare. Lesser folk must be content with the building of single shrines or stûpas or the planting of bo-trees (*Figus religiosa*). One of the more frequently mentioned acts of merit in these inscriptions is the freeing of slaves. One or more slaves may be freed at the same time; but their social position depends upon the decision of their previous master. Greater merit is gained by the master if they are fit to enter the religious life. Mme Saveros Lewitz refers to three states of liberty, defined by the terms *ñom*, *brei* and *barnâsram*. The term *ñom* seems to refer to those who are released into some form of service of a religious establishment. It is probably related to the term *khñum* (slave) thus suggesting a servile status of relative freedom. The term *bârnâsram* (= skr. *varṇa*, meaning caste, plus *âśrama*) suggests that the released slave (previously outside the social system) is received back into society, given maybe a low social status but fully free in a religious sense. In the section 'Influences from India' in Chapter 1, I have already stressed that there was no well-defined caste system in Cambodia similar to that of India. Thus the term *varṇa* (caste) implies no more than the kind of social

216. A small Buddha image (38 cms in height) probably older than the 16th century, as indicated by the condition of the wood at the base, local opinion and the lack of Thai influence.

stratification as described in that section. A slave was outside the social system, but on his release could be brought back into it. The term *brei* is a curious one, probably related to the same term, meaning forest or jungle, and thus by implication corresponds to our word jungly or wild, referring specifically in a Cambodian context to the local hill-folk, who were in fact often forced into slavery. Maybe such a slave is now free to return to his previous way of life, and as such he would remain outside the social system but as a free man. One may perhaps assume that a slave was freed not only in accordance with his master's wishes, but also in accordance with the slave's original status. Thus slaves of debt, who were previously free men, might well be freed into the condition of a fully free man 'liberated and exonerated as an *anak jâ*' (*vruoc jrâh anak jâ*). The main concern of the donor is normally the amount of merit that will rebound to him- or herself, but we may hopefully assume that there were masters who regarded these enslaved dependents with affection and wished them well for the future. But in this respect I note a modern practice, how old I do not know, of expecting to gain merit from the release of birds, which have been encaged and sold for this very purpose. How many die with broken wings or otherwise, seems to be a matter of no concern to the donor.

As a form of selflessness, the merit gained could be transferred by a suitable aspiration or vow to others, members of one's own family, deceased persons, or more generally to the sufferers in hell. At the same time it will be noted that no such mercy is shown towards those who deliberately effect the annulment of the vow.

I quote a few examples of these 'vows', as inscribed on temple-walls, translating them from the French version of Saveros Lewitz.

> *The* uk-ñâ *Samarasangrâm and the lady Ep, the* uk-ñâ *Bejrasamgram, the* cau *Jayâdhipati and the lady Brah, the* cau bañâ *Tejojay and the lady Ras', the* cau bañâ *Samâsangram and the lady Am, the* cau *Tas, the* anak samtec *Moks, the ladies Sa, Nung, Mas, Kî, the* cau *Kaev, the* cau *Som, the* cau *Râj, all these persons filled with faith and joy have agreed with the* uk-ñâ *Samarasangrâm to cultivate the field of merit by liberating some slaves in the year Śaka 1539 (=AD 1617), the year of the Serpent, Tuesday, second day of the waxing moon of the month Âsâḍh 2.*[29] *Present were the* mahâsangharâj anak brah *Dhammakkhett*, anak brah *Sugandh*, anak brah *Mahâmangal, the* anak brah *Râjarocisamûh, the* anak brah *Atuajettth, the* anak brah *Brahmaratna, the* anak brah *Dhammakây, the* anak brah *Buddhâram, the* anak samtec *Moks, the* anak brah *Dhamma-ariy, the elders great and small and monks as witnesses for Samarasangrâm. Filled with faith he accomplished the meritorious act of liberating the children of female Toy and male Suk, the girls named Ap and Tî. They were liberated as 'country class' and placed in the charge of* anak samtec *Moks for their maintenance. In future if anyone contests this action, even the future Buddhas, as numerous as grains of sand, cannot save him. May he be born five hundred times in the* pañcânantarik *hell, unable to free himself and return to our world.*
>
> *Futhermore in Śaka 1549 (= AD 1627), the Hare Year, Tuesday, when the first day of the waxing moon of Âsâḍh-2 was barely out of the month of Âsâḍh-1, the* uk-ñâ *Samarasangrâm and the lady Ep prepared pious offerings and invited the religious community for the consecration of Buddha-images. Then happy in their faith, they meditated on the law of impermanence, realizing that they had reached the last stage of their life. With their hearts filled with thanks, they arranged for* anak *Samana-ariy to enter the religious life, so that he would become by ordination a true monk, completely freed. Moreover they released the woman Kaen, the daughter of* anak *Samana-ariy, a son the woman Kaen named Dhan, and they were liberated as 'country class'. As foremost of our witnesses we name the Omniscent Buddha, our Lord', followed by a long list of witnesses, religious and lay. The ceremony closes with the same oath as before.*

I quote a less complex one:

> *Having planted these sacred fig-trees, I by name Ratnamahâbodhi, desiring perfect enlightenment, have (made) this statue of the Buddha. O you, pious folk, of serene spirit and possessing perfect knowledge, join with me with joy in order to obtain complete beatitude. Triple homage to the Threefold Refuge, vast incomparable, immense, yet firmly fixed in a single thought, direct and convinced. With heart perfectly holy I join my ten fingers in homage to the feet of the Lord, inconceivable, immense, abundant, spacious, incomparable, full of force and activity. Like the Bodhisattvas of the past, concentrated and confident in their desire for Buddhahood, the Elder Srî Ratnamahâbodhi has planted six sacred fig-trees, the venerable Nisrayamuni one, the monk Ratnâlankar one, the monk Indramoli one, the monk Çandaçûla one, the monk*

> *Dhammamangal one, the monk Khmau one, the monk Devaçûlâ one with the pandits Brahm, Krây, Thâ, Uv, Sâgar. (The Elder) has made a statue of the Buddha (in) nirvana* (text incomplete*).*

Another inscription records how three married couples left their village and made a difficult crossing of the Tonle Sap in order to visit relatives at Angkor (Mahânagar). Then together with others they performed various ceremonies, honouring the Buddha-images and the ordination of two youngsters, followed by a great ceremony in the gallery, where the monks recited the *paritta* (prayer for protection) and read from the Abhidhamma and the Vessantarajâtaka.[30]

Of special interest is a very long inscription at Angkor dated AD 1701, by a high official (*uk ña*) named Jaiya Nana.[31] In illustration of his aspirations for the future, Jaya Nana refers to several literary works in Pâli which presumably were well known at the time among higher ranking and educated Khmers. Our supplicant prays that he may have the perfection of decisive wisdom like the Bodhisattva Dhanañjaya Paṇḍita who solved the difficult riddle of the sprite (*yakṣa*) Nandîyakkha, thus saving the life of a king. This is a curious popular jâtaka known in local Pâli (Thai and Cambodian sources), named after the hero of the story. Jaiya Nan also prays thus: 'May I have power, magical potency, and authority as I wish. May I have the ability to create as effectively as the holy one, the holy Lord (Îśvara), who created the Lady Bhagavatî'. Here the reference is to a popular tradition in southern Thailand concerning a goddess Nâng Bhogavatî (= Lady Bhagavatî), a creation of the Lord Śiva, who wishes to perform the perfection of charity (*dâna*) and thus sacrifices her own body in order to create the whole physical world. Furthermore Jaiya Nana prays that 'he may have property and wealth, gold, silver and valuable gems, luminous, precious jewels along with silken cloths and weaves, carpets, filling the house, soft beddings, magnificent canopies, like Jotika Setthî'. This gentleman of fabulous wealth was resident at Râjagriha during the lifetime of Sâkyamuni Buddha. However he later abandoned the world and became an *arhat.* He is seemingly not named in the *Tripiṭika,* but is known from a commentary of the *Dhammapada,* a popular Buddhist collection of moralizing verses. As Mme Saveros Lewitz fairly observes, such aspirations are often more materialistic than religious.[32]

Similar inscriptions dating to the 16th century are also found on the 13th century Khmer temple of Athvea in Siem Reap, which likewise had been taken over by a Theravâda monastery.[33] It was probably during the same period that the Bakheng and the Baphuon were both converted into Buddhist sanctuaries. This practice became quite general, perhaps even more so in Thailand than in Cambodia itself, for one scarcely finds an ancient Khmer temple there which is not already enclosed within a Theravâda monastery.

These developments seem to coincide with the arrival of the first Europeans in Cambodia and with their descriptions of Angkor. The most substantial account is that of Diogo do Couto (*c.*1543-1616) who was the official Portuguese chronicler at Goa and it may be based upon a report of a Capuchin monk who visited Angkor in 1585-86.[34] Whether it is in fact the earliest is doubtful, since it refers to the subjugation of Cambodia to Siam as having happened later, and how could the original writer foretell this? But it is certainly the most carefully composed. It begins with the usual assumption that Angkor was discovered by chance, in this case by a king (unnamed) who in 1550 or 1551 was out hunting elephants. He had the whole area cleared and was so impressed by the magnificent city that was thus revealed, that he promptly moved his whole court there. Another account, that of Gabriel Quiroga de San Antonio, published in 1604 states that this city was discovered in 1570 by Cambodians who were out hunting rhinoceros. There is no doubt that the city referred to is Angkor Thom; it may well have been much overgrown by the 16th century, but Angkor Vat was surely known. Villagers worked their fields in the vicinity as nowadays, and historical allusions quoted above assert that the Angkor region had to be defended just like other parts of the kingdom. Thus there were often troop movements in the area. It seems probable that the interest shown in Angkor Vat by King Satha or possibly his predecessor first drew the attention of resident Europeans to the existence of Angkor Vat and Angkor Thom, and they were struck with amazement by what they saw, just as Henri Mouhot was struck with wonder when he rediscovered it all in the mid-19th century. Interesting as they are in themselves, these accounts do not have the historical significance of the inscriptions quoted above.

217. (above) Towards the end of the 16th century some major Angkor temples, such as Vishnuloka (thus becoming Angkor Vat), the Bakheng and the Baphuon were adapted to Buddhist usage. The west side of the Baphuon was transformed into an enormous Buddha in the lying posture of entry into nirvâṇa, 100 metres long.

218. (below) Vat Athvea in Siem Reap, built probably as a Buddhist temple in the early 13th century; it may well have remained ever since as the core of a Buddhist monastery although the earliest Buddhist inscriptions there date from the 16th century.

219. (right) The roof of a modern shrine, Vat Athvea; such structures being very fragile compared with stone.

220. (below) As explained in the text, several Buddhist monasteries were founded in the vicinity of the later chief cities (mainly Lovek and Oudong), but also (at least from the 16th century) in the vicinity of the important temples of the Angkor period, which were regarded as sacred sites. They often retain the same name from earlier times, but since nothing built of the more fragile materials of these later times survives more than a hundred years, these monasteries are continually being renewed. An illustration of any of these might do, but I choose the one built on the east approach to the Bakong. Note also Plate 110, p. 101, of Phnom Wan.

Chapter 7

The 17th to the 19th Century

Historical Summary

Up to the end of the 16th century Cambodia, although much reduced in size since the grandiose period of the 12th to 13th centuries, was still a power to be reckoned with in mainland South-East Asia. Thus it proved itself capable of holding its own on many occasions against Siamese pretensions of suzerainty. These were reasserted with the return of Soryopor (1602-1616) from exile in Ayuthaya together with his younger son Outey. He brought order throughout the country and built a new palace known as Lovek Em facing Phnom Penh across the Mekong. Siamese customs and court-dress were adopted, which caused a small rebellion. Siamese troops again entered the country but on this occasion withdrew rapidly, seemingly content that all remained under their control. Soryopor was not crowned until 1613 and a few years later he abdicated in favour of his elder son Chey Chettha, who had meanwhile been allowed to return from exile in Ayuthaya. After the death of his father in 1619, Chey Chettha married an Annamese princess, whom the King of Annam had sent him together with impressive presents, hoping thereby to gain influence in Cambodia. He moved from his palace at Lovek Em to Oudong, which remained the primary city of Cambodia until the 19th century. As the result of his cordial relations with Annam he agreed to the setting-up of a customs post at Prei Nokor (now Saigon) and at other Annamese settlements in the area. By agreeing to this he probably hoped to counteract the continuing Siamese pressure on the country. He seems to have been temporarily successful, since the same year he was able to repel Siamese attacks both from the north and from the sea, namely in the province of Bantây Meas, whence they were driven back to their boats. However this involvement of Annam in Cambodia's affairs proved to be disastrous, as the country was later victimized by both the Siamese from the north and the west and by the Annamese (later known as the Vietnamese) from the south and the east, as will be seen below.[1]

On the death of Chey Chettha the crown-prince (*obareach*) his brother Outey, assumed the title of 'regent' (*obayoreach*) and arranged for Prince Poñea To, the son of Chey Chettha, then only twenty-six years old, to be crowned as Srei Thomma Reachea. It seems that he had already left the monastic life before his father's death with the idea of organizing a campaign to win back territory from the Siamese in the Khorat area. Soon after his coronation he embarked upon this, but seems to have been generally unsuccessful. On his way back he stayed in Angkor, finding his uncle, the regent there, with his court. His uncle had taken as wife a young lady named Ang Vodey, who had earlier been betrothed to Prince Poñea To, now King Srei Thomma. They had clandestine meetings both at Angkor and on the return to Oudong, which could not be concealed for long from his uncle. The couple fled, but they were pursued and killed. The regent Outey, still in charge of events, arranged for a son of Chey Chettha to be crowned king as Ang Tong Reachea, but he died after a short reign and was succeeded by the eldest son of the regent, namely Ang Non. This enraged the third and remaining son of Chey Chettha, namely Prince Chan, who conspired with a group of Malays and Chams to assassinate both his cousin Ang Non and his uncle, the regent Outey.[2] Crowned as Satha Reamea-'thipadei (= Lord Râma) he was soon at war with the Dutch as the result of robbing one of their ships on the Cambodian coast, for which he refused to make amends. During the negotiations, he married a Malay wife, accepted the religion of Islam, taking the name of King Ibrahim. This doubtless pleased his Malay and Cham supporters,[3] but was certainly not agreeable to his own Khmer subjects. However the Dutch were repulsed, and failing to reach any agreement with King Ibrahim, finally withdrew their trade from Cambodia. Eventually Prince Saur, aged twenty-six, and Prince Ang Tân, aged eighteen, sons of the former regent Outey, decided to take up arms against the King. A younger brother of Ang Non, namely Ang Em now entitled *Kevhvea* (see below concerning this title), remained on the side of King Ibrahim, alias Satha Reamea-'thipadei, although he had murdered his father. Princes Saur and Tân were supported by the Queen Mother, wife of the former regent, whom he had married as a princess from Annam. The Annamese welcomed the opportunity of gaining more control of Cambodia, sent adequate forces, which resulted in the capture of King Ibrahim, who was imprisoned in an iron cage and taken to Quang-binh (on the frontier between Tonkin and Annam), where he did not survive very long.[4] In return for their help, the Annamese demanded a yearly tribute, and claimed that all prisoners taken in the campaign should be theirs, while all Annamese resident in Cambodia should have full rights of possession of their land. Ang Saur now became king (1656-1671) and seems to have dealt harshly with Malays and the Chams who regretted the loss of their Muslim king. Thus in connivance with them, the king's nephew, Ang Chey (son of Ang Non) arranged for his assassination. However he in turn was killed at the instigation of the widow of Ang Saur. On the death of Ang Saur, his younger brother Ang Tân together with his nephew, Ang Non (son of Ang Em who had previously supported Ibrahim) went to seek Vietnamese help. In the meantime Ang Chi, who as the eldest son of Ang Saur had a fair claim to the throne, became king. Ang Tân, arriving with Vietnamese troops, would have been content with his succession, as Ang Chi was his own nephew. However learning of the arrival of Vietnamese forces, Ang Chi suspected an attempt to dislodge him, so he promptly took up arms against his uncle. A disastrous war, during which Ang Tân died, seems to have continued until the death of Ang Chi, who was succeeded by his younger brother Saur, crowned as Chey Chettha. Although he managed to prevail against Ang Non (Ang Tân's nephew and associate) who fled to Annam, the feud did not end. Ang Non returned, established himself in Phnom Penh, and continued a campaign against Chey Chettha in Oudong, even carrying off the Queen Mother when Chey Chettha was absent. Although Chey Chettha managed to free his mother from captivity, the war between the two princes lasted until the death of Ang Non in 1691. Thus for more than twenty years the country was ravaged by this futile warfare between members of the same royal family. Traders left Phnom Penh for Ayuthaya, where conditions were more conducive to business, and thus foreign commerce suffered. In the meantime the Vietnamese had occupied Prei Nokor (Saigon) and thereafter Cambodia was cut off from the Mekong River route (except with their consent) until the French occupied Saigon in 1862.

Thus Cambodia was not only enfeebled by this vicious antagonism between two branches of the royal family, but also by their inviting the intervention of the Annamese and allowing them to claim rights on Cambodian territory. (It will be recalled that the Annamese had already absorbed Champa in the 15th century, thus becoming the neighbours of Cambodia on the south-eastern flank.) Another cause of Cambodia's internal problems was the lack of any well-established law of succession. The crown prince might have a primary claim, but a regent who is some cases was more powerful than the actual king (such as the *obhayoreach* Outey) might also name a successor of his own choice, and even arrange to have the reigning king seized and killed. The term for a king is straightforward, either *sdach* or *luong*, although longer honorific titles would normally be used. However next to the king there is the title *obhayoreach* (a term corresponding to Sanskrit *ubhayarâja*), translatable as 'king in a double sense' and usually referring to a king who has abdicated but may still hold power. It was often held by a 'regent' who ruled in place of a young monarch not yet old enough to be formally crowned. This institution could cause much trouble, especially if overused, as will be illustrated below. The normal title for the heir to the throne is *obareach* (Skr. *uparâja*), but there is another title that a king may bestow upon any prince whom he especially favoured. This is *kevhvea* best translated perhaps as 'Brilliant'. (It seems to be a compound of the Khmer/Thai word for crystal and a Thai word for sky.)

Chey Chettha, who became king in 1675 at the age of nineteen, retired to a monastery in 1688 in favour of a nephew, thus becoming *obhayoreach*. Assuming power the same year, he ruled until 1695, when he abdicated again in favour of the same nephew Prince An Yang Outey, who was duly crowned king at the age of twenty-three, but he died the next year, and Chey Chettha assumed power for the third time. In 1699 he abdicated again, this time in favour of a prince named Ang Im, on whom he had bestowed the title of *Kevhvea* because of his success in a war against the Annamese. Chey Chettha had been renovating a monastery, founded by King Chan in 1534, and in 1701 he took the robes of a monk there. The same year he resumed his authority as king but only for one year, just long enough to deal with an upstart rebel. Then yet again he entered the religious life just for three days in favour of his eldest son, the *obareach* Srei Thomma. Since he was only twelve years old his consecration was postponed. Then in 1705 this young prince abdicated in favour of his father, the *obhayoreach*, who now became king for the fifth time. In 1706 King Chey Chettha abdicated yet again, and his son Srei Thomma was duly crowned king at the age of seventeen. Now it is not surprising that *Kevhvea* Ang Im who had been 'king' for a short time in 1700-

1701, waited for the first opportunity to replace Srei Thomma. He found his opportunity in 1710 when a Loatian group which had settled in Cambodia rose in revolt. He promptly took their side, arranged for a force of 20,000 Annamese to arrive from Cochinchina (South Annam) which he further reinforced by 10,000 tribal people, with whom he was probably already in contact. King Srei Thomma together with a very young son and his younger brother managed to escape to Ayuthaya.

Kevhvea Ang Im now became king in 1714. Threatened by a Siamese army, which demanded his abdication in favour of the deposed Srei Thomma, he managed to come to terms, promising his submission. It seems almost useless to continue this disastrous story much further, but only thus can one realize the ruinous state of the country when the French arrived on the scene a century later. The country was invaded from all sides, by the Siamese from the north and from the sea, by the Annamese from the south and also by a Chinese 'pirate-baron' named Mac Cuu, who now occupied Cambodian territories bordering on the Gulf of Siam, recognized as his by the court at Hue. In such warfare all parties supported the various claimants to the throne, sometimes changing sides as may suit their advantage, with no one giving any thought whatsoever to the ever-worsening state of the country. Between Poñea Yat, who took the decision to abandon Angkor in 1431 and the reign of Ang Duong (1847-1860) there were thirty-eight reigns, and very few of these began without internal fighting and foreign intervention

Srei Tomma, who ruled for a short time (1701-1702) and again from 1706-14 and then was ousted by the Prince Ang Im (see above), regained the throne in 1738 after the usual contentious vicissitudes and was recrowned at Oudong.[5] His eldest son succeeded him in 1747 but was soon assassinated by his young brother. A cousin, Prince Ang Tong then became king, but he was opposed by Ang Chi, (son of Ang Im) who claimed the title of king. After yet more contentions Ang Tong regained the throne in 1756 and was eventually succeeded by his nephew Ang Tân (1757-1775). The fall of Ayuthaya to the Burmese in 1767 did not lessen the pressure from the Siamese side. The new ruler, Taksin was determined on the continuing submission of Cambodia. After failing in a direct attack from the north, he invaded again by sea, debarking at Kampot and then advancing towards Oudong. He brought the young prince Ang Non, a grandson of King Srei Thomma, as claimant to the throne of Cambodia. Ang Tân fled to Annam. Later, when Ang Non's Thai supporters abandoned him because of the threat of another Burmese attack at home, Ang Tân was able to re-establish himself in Oudong, but the southern provinces remained under Ang Non. In 1775 Ang Tân invited Ang Non to succeed him, thus putting an end to this division of the country. Ang Non was crowned as Reamea-'thipadey (= Râmâdhipati 'Lord Râma'), the third king with this title. Ang Tân's action seems to be a rare case of magnanimous statesmanship. He was now effectively 'regent' *(obhayoreach)* but because of ill health, he played no part in the intrigues and murderous events that followed. These seem to be the work of high officials who had been faithful to him, primarily the *uk-ña* Sou, who wanted a descendant of Ang Tân to replace Ang Non. First the crown-prince was killed with the excuse that he was plotting against the king. Ang Tân himself had no part in this, and ill as he already was, he soon died. Ang Non made himself unpopular by agreeing to send an expeditionary force in support of a campaign which Taksin was waging against Laos, mindful that it was the Siamese who had effectively brought him to power. This led to large-scale desertions, to reprisals by the king and then to a well organized uprising against him. A high official, So, governor of Kampong Svay Province, which had been the centre of the trouble, joined the rebels. So was subsequently executed for this and his two brothers Peang and Ten were severely punished, but freed on condition that they brought the revolt to an end. This was made difficult by the mother of So, a great lady named Chumteav Lâng, who sent emissaries all around campaigning against Ang Non. Another important player in this affair was a high official named Mou, who was the elder brother of So, Peang and Ten. He had served under Ang Tân, now under Ang Non, but was not slow in joining the family feud against his new master. The king (Ang Non) then led a quickly recruited army against Mou and his family, and unaware that So was in league with Mou's family, he left him in charge at Oudong together with another high court official named Ben, who in his sentiments seems to have remained faithful to the memory of Ang Tân and so was not trusted by So and Mou. In accordance with an earlier arrangement made by Mou with the Vietnamese, So now called upon their assistance. One part of the Vietnamese forces easily occupied Oudong, pillaging the monasteries and the villages all around. Ang Non's four children were put to death presumably at So's instigation. The other part easily defeated the king, who was also killed on Mou's orders. Mou now appointed himself regent (*obayoreach*) and Prince Ang Eng, son of Ang Tân, aged seven years, was crowned king.

Ben, who allowed all this to take place without protest, was summoned to Thonburi by Taksin, who first punished him for his negligence but then kept him in reserve for an imminent Siamese invasion of Cambodia in order to put an end to this continuing interference by the Vietnamese. The land-army reached Angkor but was disheartened by the loss of its commanding general, while the attack from the sea was frustrated by the Chinese 'pirate baron' mentioned above, who took the side of the Cambodians. Another army was sent, and it had already reached Oudong, when the generals learned of a successful revolt against Taksin and so hastened back to Thonburi. The commanding general, Chao Phaya Chakkri was acclaimed king of Siam, thus founding the Chakkri dynasty, which continues to the present time. One of his first acts was to move the capital across the river from Thonburi to Bangkok. Meanwhile the usual intrigues continued in Cambodia. So who had been in charge of the Cambodian forces, now conspired with Ben, who had returned to Cambodia with the Siamese army, and together they murdered the regent Mou. Then Ben turned the tables on So, put to death his old enemies, even murdering his associate So and declared himself chief minister. Threatened by a superior force mustered by Mou's younger brother Ten, Ben retreated to Battambang and then to Siam, taking with him the young king Ang Eng, his two aunts and three sisters. He was well received by King Râma I, who took the three princesses as his wives and duly arranged for Ang Eng to be crowned King of Cambodia in Bangkok, thus asserting his sovereignty over Cambodia. As for Ben, he made him governor of the province of Battambang (including Angkor), which was still an integral part of Cambodia, as though it were his to give. (It thus remained the property of Ben and his successors, until the French retrieved it for Cambodia in 1907.)

For a while Cambodia was divided into two with Ben holding power in the north, and Ten, son of Mou, still in control in the south thanks to Vietnamese assistance. However the situation to the south was complicated by the fact that a local princely family (Nguyen) was asserting its independence against Hue and King Râma I saw it in his interest to support their independence against Annam while dealing with Ten's occupation of southern Cambodia. As so often on other occasions, Cambodia was being ruined by wars fought by others on Cambodian soil. However Ten was captured and brought to Oudong, where Ben was at least theoretically master of the whole kingdom, but local uprisings and frequent pillaging occurred here and there, and famine seems to have been widespread. Ben was ferocious and brutal in dealing with those who caused him trouble, but on this occasion he spared Ten from execution and exiled him to Bangkok. Ben remained subservient to Siam and even deported thousands of unfortunate Khmers as slave-labourers to work on the reconstruction projects of Râma I.

In 1794 the King of Siam authorized the return to Cambodia of Ang Eng, who had been crowned King of Cambodia in Siam, but this changed the wretched condition of the country in no way. Ben, who had already been given Battambang Province, and another high official, Kan, who had been given Siem Reap (Angkor) by Râma I in 1793, took up residence there and promptly offered their allegiance to Râma I, who readily accepted it. Totally unable to defend his rights, Ang Em made the journey himself to Bangkok to beg for their return. Disappointed in this fruitless personal mission, he died soon after he got back to Oudong.

Râma I confirmed Siam's hold on Cambodia by ordering that Ang Em be cremated in Bangkok, and allowing that his son, Prince Chan, only ten years old, should succeed him with a high official, named Pok, acting as regent. Deprived of its major northern provinces, Cambodia had now become a mere dependency of Siam. During the reign of Ang Chan Outey Reachea (1806-1834) the heavy hand of Siam, first of Râma I and then of Râma II (from 1809 onwards) maintained Cambodia and its king in a constant state of subugation. If the king wished to discipline any high official or governor of a province, such as the governor of Kampong Svay Province, this person could flee to Bangkok for protection. It seems that Râma II even encouraged the king's brother, Ang Snguon, as a pretender to the throne, and with no reliable forces of his own to defend his position, Ang Chan called upon the help of the court of Hue. This inevitably strengthened still further the position of the Vietnamese in the country, thus provoking the inevitable reaction from the Siamese side.

In 1829 the Siamese attacked Laos and laid waste Vientiane. After that they invaded Cambodia again in order to assert their sovereignty, but their fleet arriving from the south was totally lost in a storm, while Annamese intervention eventually forced their total withdrawal. King Ang Chan Outey Reachea died in 1834, and the Vietnamese were now in control of the country. As he had no son, the Annamese placed a young daughter of his, Ang Mei, on the throne, while the real power lay with the Annamese resident, who now set about turning Cambodia into a province of Vietnam. All court officials had to wear Vietnamese dress. The provinces were reorganized and Vietnamese officials controlled the Cambodian governors. The resident now went even further, trying to replace the Theravâda Buddhism of Cambodia with the partly Confucian-style Chinese Buddhism of Vietnam. Monks were driven from their monasteries, sacred bo-trees were cut down and the small stûpas serving as mausoleums were destroyed. He sent the Cambodian ministers to Hue, saying that the king wanted to decide the future of Cambodia with them, and soon afterwards even the Queen herself and the other princesses. The regent Ang Em (brother of the deceased Ang Chan) arrived in Phnom-Penh in response to a letter sent him by the Vietnamese resident, who pretended that he had supervised the election of the Queen Ang Mei only as a temporary measure until a Cambodian prince was old enough to reign. Fortunately the regent's young brother Prince Ang Duong remained in Bangok, for soon after the regent's arrival where he was greeted with enthusiasm by the suffering Khmer populace, he was imprisoned in a cage and sent to Hue. There was thus now no doubt of the Vietnamese intentions, and little encouragement was needed on the part of a few leading Cambodians for the whole country to rise up in fury against them. Meanwhile a message was sent to Bangkok, beseeching the king to restore the Cambodian monarchy. Presumably this was the moment for which he had been waiting. An army advanced from Battambang and another arrived by sea. The whole country was now the scene of warfare between two enemies who had the satisfaction of fighting on foreign soil to the utter devastation of Cambodia and the ruin of its people.[6] Finally the harassed Vietnamese, realizing that it was impossible to hold their own in Cambodia, agreed to a truce. The royal hostages in Hue were returned in exchange for Vietnamese prisoners. The royal sword was returned and so in 1847 Prince Ang Duong was eventually crowned King of Cambodia at the age of fifty-two in the presence of high Siamese and Vietnamese officials.

The reign of Ang Duong (1847-1860) was one of relative peace. Some madcaps claiming magical powers gathered a band of credulous followers and raised a revolt, which was fairly easily put down. More serious was a revolt of Chams and Malays in the Kampong Cham area. Together with the Malays the Chams represent the main Muslim population in Cambodia. The cause of the trouble remains unknown, but the king was furious at the seeming ingratitude of this foreign community, and quelling the revolt in person, he reallocated these families along the banks of the Tonle Sap, where they could be more easily controlled. Apart from these troubles Ang Duong was able to devote much of his time to works of peace and reconstruction. His own palace at Oudong had to be rebuilt, and he also raised defensive earthworks around the town. He built a road from Oudong to Phnom Penh and then on to Kampot, thus encouraging overseas trade, which was hampered on the Mekong river route by the Vietnamese hold on Saigon. He reorganized the administration of the provinces and established new ranks and titles. He introduced a new silver coinage (*prak bat*) as the older one had practically disappeared with the warfare that led to his accession. A man of profound religious faith, he did his utmost to restore the fortunes of Buddhism in the country by encouraging the rebuilding of monasteries and schools. He asked the King of Siam (Râma IV) to assist with the provision of qualified monks and Buddhist texts, and it is thus that the reformed sect of the Dhammayutika found its way into Cambodia. Relations with Siam remained generally good, so long as King Ang Duong maintained a subservient attitude, but any suggestion of independent action would bring a stern rejoinder.

It was clear to him that the only hope for the future of Cambodia lay in procuring a powerful protector who could restrain the pretensions of his powerful neighbours, and his thoughts turned to the French, who were already involved in punitive expeditions in Vietnam first at Da-nang (Tourane) on the east coast and later at Saigon (1857-60), provoked by the systematic persecution of Catholic missionaries in Vietnam. In Cambodia by contrast these missionaries were welcome guests, although the Khmers were too attached to their own religion to become converts. At the same time these French prelates were willing to assist Ang Duong in making contact with Paris through the French consul in Singapore. In 1856 a French plenipotentiary, named Monsieur de Montigny arrived in Bangkok to discuss trading agreements with the Siamese government, and it was arranged that he would then travel on to Kampot where he would meet King Ang

Duong. Seemingly quite unaware of the confidential nature of the proposed meeting with the King of Cambodia, he tactlessly let it be known in Bangkok that this was his intention. The result was a stern letter from Râma IV to King Ang Duong, forbidding him under dire threats from attending this meeting. There can be little doubt that Ang Duong had been hoping for a form of French protection against both his more powerful neighbours, but in the letter which he subsequently sent to Napoleon III he expressed the more limited hope that the French would assist him in regaining the southern provinces occupied by the Vietnamese.[7] Such wording would cause less offence in Bangkok, even though any form of French intrusion in Cambodia would be resisted by Râma IV.

The French campaign in Cochinchina leading to the treaty with the Court of Annam in 1862, enabled the Cambodians to harass Vietnamese settlers on their southern frontier, but the death of Ang Duong in 1860 and the ascension to the throne of his eldest son Norodom, aged twenty-six, soon led once more to internal strife in Cambodia. Râma IV had already recognized Norodom's right to the throne, and it seems strange that he permitted Norodom's two younger brothers to return to Cambodia. This soon caused trouble, as the youngest of the three princes, Prince Votha, only nineteen years old, was hoping to gain the throne for himself. With the usual intrigues he managed to raise a substantial body of supporters, and King Norodom was so hard pressed that he retreated to Battambang, and the commanding general of Prince Votha's forces even occupied Oudong. The Chams and Malays who had been forcibly moved from Kampong Cham Province to the area around Lovek by King Ang Duong now decided to take the part of King Norodom and the rebel-general had to retreat to Phnom Penh. Here he came upon a gun-boat which the French Catholic mission has obtained from Cochinchina for their own protection, but he seems to have interpreted its presence as French support for King Norodom. Perhaps it was thus interpreted by Râma IV who arranged for Norodom to reach Oudong via Kampot, and sent an army through Battambang direct to Oudong. Thus by 1862 Norodom was once more secure on his throne, but even more bound to Siam for the support which had been given him.

The French, who had now replaced Vietnamese authority on Cambodia's southern frontier, were concerned about this obvious controlling interest of Siam in their neighbour's affairs, and in 1863 Norodom was induced by formal treaty to accept French protection. This obviously displeased the Siamese court and when Norodom asked for the royal insignia, which were all in Bangkok, his request was refused. He thus arranged for a provisional form of coronation to be performed in Oudong without them. However, learning that the French treaty with Cambodia has finally been ratified in Paris, Râma IV gave way and Norodom was finally crowned in Oudong with all the insignia brought from Bangkok in the presence of French and Siamese high officials. But the transfer from Siamese and Vietnamese protection to French protection was not yet complete. Fearful that the French might not establish themselves permanently in Cochinchina, Norodom made a secret treaty for protection with the Siamese court. This was discovered in Saigon in 1867 resulting in much embarrassment on the part of the Siamese, who claimed that this treaty had been initiated before the French agreement with Cambodia was known. At this time the French consul in Bangkok, who knew nothing of the true situation regarding these territories, signed a treaty according to which the French authorities recognized the Siamese claim to provinces of Battambang and Siem Reap, and this was ratified in Paris before the French authorities in Saigon realized what a serious mistake had been made. King Norodom was furious about this unfortunate action. Here was France claiming to be Cambodia's protector giving away large parts of Cambodian territory which was not theirs to give. They were not restored to Cambodia until 1907 in accordance with another treaty between France and Siam. King Norodom moved the capital from Oudong to Phnom Penh in 1883, imposing new taxes for this purpose, which made him unpopular. This might well have led to further uprisings in the country, but due to the French presence Cambodian kings now remained secure on their throne. His brother Sisovath, on whom their father had bestowed the title of *Kevhvea*, was later recognized as crown-prince (*obareach*) under French pressure and eventually succeeded Norodom in 1904. Prince Votha who had caused so much trouble in the early years of Norodom's reign withdrew with his followers to Sambor in the far north-east of the country, awaiting an occasion to try once more to gain the throne. This never came and he died in 1891.

Temples and Palaces

As the result of the internal wars and invasions recounted above, little remained from the past when the French began to interest themselves in Cambodia from the mid-19th century onwards. We read above that when Soryopor returned from exile in Ayuthaya at the very beginning of the 17th century he built a palace at Lovek-Em across the Mekong from Phnom Penh not far from the earlier 'capital' of Srei Santor. Meanwhile Phnom Penh seems to have remained an important trading centre so long as commerce was not disrupted by warfare. However, Soryopor's son Chey Chettha (1616-1625) moved his official residence to Oudong, which remained the recognized capital city of Cambodia until Norodom formally moved it to Phnom Penh in 1883/4. It had already served as the chief city of Ang Chan Outey Preachea (1806-1834) on his return from Saigon where he had been seeking Vietnamese help against the pretensions of Siam, and it remained the capital under the terrible Vietnamese occupation of 1835-47, when Oudong suffered accordingly. The Vietnamese built a fort at Phnom Penh, which was later dismantled by Ang Duong, who re-established the capital again at Oudong. Thus it remained a royal residence even after Phnom Penh became the recognized capital, and the unhappy Queen Ang Mei who had been put on the throne by the Vietnamese, passed her last years there. Nothing remains of any of the royal residences because of the general destruction carried out by the Khmer Rouge (1975-79). The oldest surviving construction in Phnom Penh appears to be an Angkor-type stone tower, which was later transformed into a stûpa when Vat Uṇṇalom was founded on the site by Poñea Yat in the 15th century.[8] The importance of Phnom Penh as a trading port must have given impetus to the founding of other such shrines, including the famous Vat Phnom. According to local legend it was founded by a lady named Dong, who had the mound raised to build a shrine in the 15th century for some ancient Buddha-images in wood, which she had discovered floating in the river. The great stûpa on the summit may date to the 17th century and the small *vihara* built on the site with its pleasing wall-paintings probably to the early 20th century. The finest remaining set of wall-paintings in Phnom Penh are those of the Râmâyana epic which cover the walls of the courtyard around the Silver Pagoda in the royal palace. The royal palace itself, built entirely in Thai style, was built by the French in the 20th century.

In the vicinity of the royal sites mentioned in this and the previous chapter ancient monastic foundations are still to be found, but as already observed above, no such actual building is older than the 19th century. Since they have been continually rebuilt, all earlier wall-paintings are lost. In her admirable study of post Angkorian iconography, Madelaine Giteau (*Iconographie du Cambodge*) refers to some which were already undergoing destruction in the late 1960s, and now even fewer will still be in existence. One remarkable set, again of the Râmâyana epic, happily survives at Vat Bo in Siem Reap.

Many *vihâras* have been rebuilt since the early 1990s, replacing those destroyed or damaged by the Khmer Rouge and the art of wall-painting has come into its own again, but the earlier skill seems to have been lost and the colours are garish. A fairly good set, portraying the life-story of the Bodhisattva Vessantara decorates a courtyard of the *vihâra* near the great Bakong stûpa at Ruluos The main scenes painted on many temple-walls represent the life of Sâkyamuni Buddha, usually beginning with his appearance in the country of the Sâkyas as son of King Suddhodana and Queen Mahâmâyâ. He is represented as entering the womb of his mother as she dreams of a small white elephant descending upon her from the Joyful Heavens. The account then continues in separate scenes up to his entry into nirvâṇa, the incineration and the sharing out of the holy relics. This life-story follows the Theravâda account, which spread through all the Buddhist countries of South-East Asia, namely Burma, Thailand, Cambodia and Laos. So far as Cambodia and Laos are concerned, Thai style tends to predominate in the later ones, the only ones that survive. Other scenes often depicted are those of Sâkyamuni's previous lives, especially the supposed last one before he appeared on earth to manifest the state of buddhahood to his disciples, namely the story of Prince Vessantara who excels in the virtue of unlimited generosity. This is the final one of a set of ten, but the other nine are seldom represented by more than a single scene.[9] In the traditional Pâli collections there are far more than these, 500 and

221. (p. 203, top left) No substantial buildings of stone seem to survive from the later capital cities of Lovek and Oudong, except this one stone temple, recently destroyed by the Khmer Rouge at Oudong.

222. (p. 203, top right) View of repaired stûpas at Oudong.

223. (p. 203, bottom) Wood was preferred not only for building purposes, but also for sculpture. Thus stone images become rare. A broken stone image of a lying Buddha on a hill-top in Oudong.

224. Vat Uṇṇalom, Phnom Penh.

more, and to these can be added several 'apocryphal' rebirth-stories, such as those named in the very long Angkor inscription dated AD 1701 (see Chapter 6). When scenes from the Buddha's life appear together with rebirth-stories, his life is depicted in an upper series with the rebirth-story depicted below. One may note that the same arrangement applies also on the first platform of the great stûpa of Borobudur. Here the sculptured scenes were based on Sanskrit sources, but Sâkyamuni's life-story and many of the rebirth-stories are practically identical.

Throughout the 16th and 17th centuries and well into the 18th the importance of Angkor Vat (previously known as Vishnuloka), is attested by the many inscriptions recording donations, already mentioned in the previous chapter. There also exists a 17th 'guide' to the bas-reliefs. [10] However as noted above, from the last years of the 18th century onwards, Angkor as well as Battambang became effectively subject to Siam. Although Angkor Vat continued to be occupied as a Theravâda monastery, maybe with Thai inmates as well as Khmers, contact seems to have been generally lost by the Khmers in the rest of the country which was now constantly involved in invasions and internal warfare. It is significant perhaps that European visitors to Angkor during the 19th century, mainly French, usually travelled there from Bangkok, and not from Oudong or Phnom Penh, as had certainly been the case in the 16th century. This loss of contact from the Khmer side seems to have resulted in general ignorance concerning the earlier Khmer history of Angkor, which was even attributed popularly to another race of people or even to mythological giants.

Buddhism and Pâli

When the French began to establish some order in their Indo-Chinese colonial empire, they noted the existence of two Buddhist groups within the Cambodia *sangha* (religious community): the *Dhammayutika-nikâya* (literally: 'the assembly which holds to the Dharma') and the *Mahâ-nikâya* ('the great assembly'), who were by no means unified in their practices.[11] The first derived directly from the Thai efforts at regulating Buddhist religion, first in their own country and subsequently in Cambodia, while the second must have far more complex antecedents by no means exclusive to Cambodia.[12]

It must be noted that even in Thailand despite the efforts of Râma I to bring some order into the practice of Buddhism following upon the social and religious chaos which engulfed the country as the result of the fall of Ayuthaya in 1767, unorthodox forms of Buddhist practice, in dress, in monastic discipline and in various ritual practices continued to have a substantial following. Some of these practices probably had far earlier antecedents, deriving from adaptations of the more regular Theravâda practice, presumably going back to the time when these communities were still active in northern India up to about the year 1300. As explained above, there is no separate Mahâyâna Buddhist 'sect', as still seems to be commonly believed. Those who gradually accepted Mahâyâna teachings in India from about the 1st century AD onwards were all adherents of the earlier *srâvaka* sects, generally remaining faithful to the *Vinaya* (monastic disciple). It would have been surprising if no Theravâda monks had succumbed to this development, which affected so profoundly other early religious sects, notably the Sarvâstivâdins.

However first one should emphasize the strength of conventional Theravâda Buddhism, as witnessed by the many devotional inscriptions already mentioned above. These include references to the copying of Pâli texts from the *Tripiṭika* and related works, which were deposited at that particular monastery in order to perpetuate the teachings of the Buddha.[13] They also witness the profound religious sensibility of ordinary Khmers, who appear to be well instructed in the moral teachings of Buddhism. But more than this, they also reveal a precise knowledge of the technical terms relating to the more mystical religious life. In the introduction to his thesis, *Le Manuel des maîtres de kammaṭṭhân* Olivier de Bernon quotes the professed aspirations of Queen Srìsujâtâ according to the inscription (IMA 2 of AD 1577), referred to above (see p. 190, Ch. 6).

> *I wish to hear the items of the eternal Dharma which are the 37 'factors of enlightenment'.*[14] *I wish to withdraw from the world and take the (Buddhist) robe, to receive full ordination (in accordance with the formula) 'Come O monk' and at the same time to have my head shaved, to know truly what is the core of the 'fourfold purification' (viz. the code of discipline, the constraint of the senses, approved means of existence and the four necessities for a monk). Then I want to practice the thirteen 'privations'* (dhûtanga), *apply myself to meditation of the forty 'special topics'* (kammaṭṭhân), *which produce the fruits of arhatship together with the fourfold analytical knowledge. I wish to enter into nirvâṇa at the same time as the noble (Future Buddha) Maitreya.*[15]

In all Buddhist countries ever since the first efforts were made to codify the teachings of Sâkyamuni there has been an inevitable tension between the supposed authority of the written word and the practicalities of the quest for nirvâṇa or 'enlightenment', as the goal may be variously defined. It must also be noted that there could never be any one universally agreed orthodoxy, as the various Buddhist orders, as they separated, were always free to make amendments, deletions and additions as the ever-growing sacred literature was copied and recopied. The Mahâyâna developments, with which we are not concerned here, created a vast extra literature, rewriting the philosophical and ontological theories of the earlier schools. We have already sketched above the manner in which the whole Theravâda tradition was brought into order primarily through the efforts of certain kings of Ceylon, Pagan, Sukhothai, Ayuthaya and Bangkok, since it is quite normal for rulers in settled times to attempt to regulate the life of religious communities, of whom they regarded themselves as the overseers. All such attempted re-ordering of the life of the monks involved a vast amount of scholastic activity, primarily in Pâli, the sacred language of Theravâda Buddhism. Special schools were set up (scarcely however in Cambodia during its later troubled centuries) in order to encourage monks to learn Pâli so that they may read and recite the texts in the original language. Other religious practisers, intent on the religious life for its own sake, have little or no use for such scholastic activities. Their primary need is a religious master who gives practical instructions stage by stage, based on notes of instruction, which would have been passed from one religious master to another. Olivier de Bernon notes that many such manuals were in use in Cambodia up to the 1960s, but they were already suffering the effects of official suppression by the 'orthodox' party, identified with the *Dhammayutikanikâya*, while the state of chaos to which the country has been reduced since 1970 and the deliberate destruction of monastery libraries by the Khmer Rouge has resulted in the loss of some 95 per cent of all Cambodian religious literature. Thus to give a coherent account of Buddhism in Cambodia during the 17th to the 20th centuries would seem to be an impossible task. The unsettled conditions in the country certainly suggest that the practice of the Buddhist religious life resulted from personal decision and the choice of a trusted religious teacher.

The accession of Ang Duong to the throne in the mid-19th century led to the restitution of the Buddhist way of life, the reconstruction and repair of monasteries that had suffered disastrously under the Vietnamese occupation of 1835-47 and the subsequent Siamese invasion that drove them from the country. Despite the brutality in warfare, which seems to have been sadly typical of the contenders, Thailand practised the same form of Buddhist religion and once peace was restored Ang Duong could count upon the assistance of Râma IV in his effort of restoration.[16] The French occupation hindered the continuing strengthening of Buddhist institutions in no way, for although Catholic priests might still hope for religious conversions, the Khmers were so strongly committed to their traditional ways of life of which the Buddhist religion was an intrinsic part, that they gained no success whatsoever.

With the accession of Norodom at the beginning of the 20th century the French administrators could turn their attention to the development of state education, but this interfered little with the operation of the local monastery-schools, especially in the countryside, where Khmer children would not only be instructed in Buddhist teachings but also in the reading and writing of the Khmer language. One notable difference in educational matters between Vietnam and Cambodia is that whereas the French succeeded in establishing a romanized system of writing Vietnamese (Quoc-ngu), a similar effort to impose a romanized form of Cambodian (Khmer) was vigorously opposed, primarily because it would have destroyed the traditional monastic form of education. Thus the Khmer script, like the Thai one, remains still in force. French-sponsored education was of benefit to the wealthier classes, who saw the advantage of joining the French administrative system and even welcomed the opportunities of higher academic training, thus aspiring to scholarships in Paris. Thus Buddhism continued to flourish undisturbed in the country up to 1970 when Prince Norodom Sihanouk was deposed as Chief of State and a ruinous civil war developed between the republican government of General Lon Nol and the encroaching communist forces. These rapidly gained the upper hand, leading directly to the terrible régime instituted by Saloth Sar (Pol Pot) and Ieng Sary, both of whom had enjoyed French scholarships in Paris! One is bound at this point to anticipate these events of the late 20th century because apart from creating a condition of universal misery, they resulted in the total eradication of all outward signs of Buddhist religion and the destruction of some 95 per cent of Khmer literature, mainly Buddhist in content. Thus in writing of Buddhism as it was practised from its restitution in the late 19th century onward, one's main source is recent Buddhist practice as reconstituted over the last two decades of the 20th century.

In accordance with early Buddhist Indian practice (and the similar climate of mainland Indochina) the two major Buddhist festivals relate to the monks' retreat during the monsoon season (Pâli and Khmer: *vassa*). The retreat begins on the first day after the full-moon of the Indian month of Âśâḍha (June-July), when a special candle is lit in every monastery which must be kept burning throughout the retreat. It is preceded up to the full-moon day by festivities, offerings to the monks, prayers for the departed and sermons. It ends three months later with the full moon of the month of Âśvina (September to October), which is an occasion for even greater festivities for the layfolk, who set little carved boats carrying a candle and a stick of incense floating wherever they can on streams and lakes.

A more solemn festival of great importance for all families relates to the offerings made to departed family members on a festival known as the general offering of *pinda* (pronounced 'bin' in Khmer) balls of spiced rice such as were traditionally offered to ancestors in India from ancient times. This festival lasts fifteen days and it is mainly a joint offering of food to the monks on the part of the whole community when they are expected to circulate daily with their begging bowls (*pâtra*). However on the fifteenth day a special feast is offered to them at midday, and after that the various families visit the small shrines, usually in the monastery precincts, where they leave food-offerings and artificial currency notes for the benefit of their deceased relatives. Such a practice would seem to be in contradiction to the Buddhist belief in the inevitable process of rebirth, which remains fundamental in normal after-death ceremonies, since on those occasions the monks are called to pray for a satisfactory rebirth for the person concerned. But popularly it is believed that if one is remiss in making such regular offerings to their deceased relatives, especially parents, these deprived 'consciousness-ghosts' are liable to bring misfortune upon the family concerned. It may be interesting to note in passing that the term used is a combination of the Khmer term for ghost (*kmouch*) and the Sanskrit/Pâli term for 'consciousness' (usually assumed to be the primary of the five aggregates of personality, namely consciousness, bodily form, feelings, perceptions and impulses). For Buddhism generally such a concept of 'conscious-ghosts' or 'spirits of the dead' is scarcely orthodox.[17] However it is in accordance with the earlier Brahmanical practice of the Angkor period as also with Chinese Confucian custom. Some food-offerings, balls of cooked rice, are also left for the *neak-tâ* (literally 'the old folks' but referring to local spirits, especially those who haunt the paddy-fields and who are besought to ensure good crops. This festival takes place during the second half (the dark fortnight) of the month of Bhadrapada (August-September), corresponding approximately to the 1st to 15th September in the western calendar, thus just before the planting season.[18]

Towards the end of the monsoon season there is yet another important festival when the monks are supplied with new sets of robes (skr./ Pâli: *kaṭhina*). This lasts for two days with processions around the monastery bearing the intended gifts, sermons by the monks, and the usual feasting. One may note the total dependence on the monks upon the laity, from the king himself downwards for their practice of religion and for their livelihood. From the historical sections above, it will have been noted how often rulers withdraw to a monastery of their choice, either for repose or for political reasons. The same occurs at all social levels when old age approaches, while of all the youngsters to go to the local Vat for their primary education some will remain as practicing monks. Apart from the gaining of merit, which plays so important a part in the layman's practice of his religion, the monks will be called upon for such family ceremonies as name-giving, purification ceremonies, wedding and funerals.

Few monasteries can have gained power and wealth, as was the case of mediaeval Europe or of Tibet until some fifty years ago, except in the case of certain royal foundations. It seems also unlikely that they became centres of great scholarship, for only a small minority of Khmer scholars (paṇḍita) mastered the intricacies of Pâli syntax and grammar, a language totally different in its whole structure from Khmer, but here there could be notable exceptions where royal interest was involved.[19] Whereas during the Angkor period Khmer prelates, whether Brahmanical or Buddhist, as well as many rulers and high officials, mastered the use of the Sanskrit language and its various forms of versification to perfection, from the 14th century onwards Sanskrit was neglected and Pâli was used for religious manuals and as a necessary language of convenience for administrative purposes. Ang Duong, who was a notable scholar, arranged for the codification of the official 'royal court language' (*râjasabd*), which had deteriorated over the recent troubled times, by introducing Pâli terminology for the parts and attributes of the human body.[20] More popularly a kind of hybrid language developed as a combination of Pâli and Khmer, as already noted in the case of the many votary inscriptions.[21] As is well known, Pâli has been used to create a vast number of modern terms, again the work of the pandits, thus supplementing the many earlier terms, already derived from Sanskrit. However apart from the more popular words, many of these remain incomprehensible to the majority of Khmers, although listed in the great Khmer Dictionary, first published by the Buddhist Institute in 1938.

Indigenous Works

By far the most important texts in Khmer are those relating to the Cambodian version of the Indian Râmâyana epic, known as the Riemker which is the Khmer pronunciation of the Sanskrit spelling *Râma-kîrti* ('Fame of Râma'). It was certainly well known during the Angkor period, as proved by its representation on so many stone-carvings, especially in the north-west corner pavilion and along the west (front) side of Angkor Vat, but no early literary version survives. The original Sanskrit Râmâyana is attributed to a Vedic sage named Vâlmîki who is represented in the text as a contemporary of the events recounted, as centred in the city of Ayodhya, capital of Kosala, where Râma was born as one of the four sons of King Dasaratha.

The general setting of the whole story suggests some historical core in pre-Aśokan India, but it may have been committed to writing as an extended epic poem about the beginning of the Christian era. In any case some chapters were added later and more popular versions soon became current. The source for the 'Angkor version' is unknown, but presumably received directly from India as transmitted by Brahman scholars. The partial form in which it is known in its later Khmer versions probably derives from Thai sources, but has been further elaborated within Cambodia itself. There were also shorter more popular versions such as those compiled for the performances of the royal ballet. It is interesting to note that the several scenes preserved in the stone carvings of Angkor Vat and elsewhere correspond well enough to the literary versions known today. Thus in the north-west pavilion, there is a scene of Râma gaining his wife Sîtâ at a concourse of heroes at the court of King

225. Two monks and the decorated walls of Vat Bakong.

Janaka in the neighbouring state of Mithilâ. Later when Râma is due to be consecrated as crown-prince, his step-mother extracts a promised boon from the king and urges that her son Bharata should succeed to the throne and that Râma should go into exile for fourteen years. Although Bharata himself protests, Râma insists that these supposed promised conditions are maintained and thus goes voluntarily into exile in the forest together with his wife Sîtâ and his devoted brother Lakśmana. The latter displeased the evil king Râvaṇa of Lanka (supposedly the island of Ceylon) by disfiguring his sister Surapanakha when she persisted in trying to win Râma for herself. Râma made the feud even worse by killing her two demon-brothers who came to avenge the insult. Râvaṇa now decides to abduct Sìtâ and entices the two brothers away from their hermitage by getting one of his followers to transform himself into a deer, which Râma tries to capture, followed by Lakśmana who thinks he hears his brother calling for help.

The scene of Râma killing the deer is shown on a plaque in the south-west pavilion of Angkor Vat. Ravana now appears to Sîtâ in the form of a Brahman and easily induces her to step outside the magic circle with which Lakśmana has surrounded her for her safety. He flies off with her to the Isle of Lanka and the rest of the story is concerned with her rescue. There is no doubt that the story became a very popular one because of the army of monkeys led by the chief Hanuman who assists in this great enterprise. This comes about by chance when Râma becomes involved in a dispute between two monkey-kings Bâli and Sugrîva, in which the latter prevails thanks to Râma's support. This scene also appears in the south-west pavilion, and a famous and massive sculpture of the two brothers struggling together may be seen in the National Museum, Phnom Penh (brought from Koh Ker). Râma and Lakśmana are shown making an alliance with the monkey-king Sugrîva in a scene depicted in the north-east angle pavilion. In the same place there is also a scene of Râma and his brother making a further alliance with the demon Vibhîsana who thus betrays his brother Râvaṇa. Hanuman's secret visit to Sîtâ while in captivity in Lanka is also illustrated there, as well as Râma and his brother battling with the terrible monster-demon Kabandha. Many of these scenes are reproduced in Vittorio Roveda, *Sacred Angkor*, especially pp. 141-61. As is well known the whole of the great battle of Lanka is depicted in detail along the west (front) side of Angkor Vat.

With the defeat of Râvaṇa and the regaining of Sîtâ one might expect the story to come to a happy end, but a later chapter was added to the Indian version, which develops the unhappy theme of a violent quarrel between Râma and Sîtâ, relating to a drawing which she made innocently of Râvaṇa. She flees to the forest and lives in Vâlmîki's hut with her two sons, who resist the approaches of Lakśmana and his brothers. Sîtâ refuses to relent and forgive Râma for his lack of trust in her, declaring that she will return to Ayodhya only when she hears of his death. He feigns death in order to induce her to come, but when she finds him still alive, she disappears into the land of the nâgas and Râma is left disconsolate. This strange addition to the story is preserved in Khmer in the second of two separate manuscripts, as translated by Judith Jacob.[22] The substance of this is preserved in popular performances in Râma's rejection of Sîtâ until her purity is attested by her passing through a sacrificial fire. This scene and the succeeding one of the royal pair returning in triumph to Ayodhya is likewise illustrated in the north-west pavilion at Angkor. It is also represented on a stone plaque that has been recently uncovered on the Baphuon.

226 & 227. Scenes from the Vessantara-jâtaka, as painted at Vat Bakong.

226. (above) The Bodhisattva gives away his royal father's precious white elephant.

227. (below) Sent into exile by his enraged father, he leaves the palace with his wife and two children.

There was also a popular religious literature consisting of the *jâtaka* or previous life stories of the Buddha, precisely those that have already been described as frequently decorating the temple-walls. As mentioned above, these represent a common stock of traditional Buddhist stories, deriving ultimately from canonical sources, but these have been augmented by the adaptation of local legends and 'fairy-stories' to Buddhist themes, thus producing an even larger popular literature. While the scholarly Pâli versions were certainly known to the better educated, this whole literature developed as a largely oral tradition so far as ordinary folk were concerned. By far the most popular of all these 'previous birth' stories is the story of the Prince Viśvântara (Pâli: Vessantara) who strained the patience of the King, his father, by his lavish generosity, and, eventually exiled together with his wife to a life of asceticism in the jungle, he even gives away their two children to a Brahman beggar who asks for them as servants, and in some versions even his wife as well. The story ends happily, since those who made such extreme demands of the Bodhisattva were the gods in disguise, who were merely testing the limits of his unstinted gift-giving. Thus the children and wife are restored and the Bodhisattva returned to rule righteously in his father's kingdom. It is interesting to note that this story was as well known during the Angkor period as was the story of Râma, and that the scene of the giving away of the two children appears on several Angkor temples (see Chapter 5). During the later Theravâda period the story of Vessantara vies in popularity with the story of Râma, who is likewise conceived as an emanation of Buddhahood.

Scholarly monks and even lay rulers also produced sets of moral verses or rules of conduct, referred to under the general term of Chbap (= Lore/Law). They are interesting in terms of the norms of social behaviour, especially as regards social ranking, but scarcely great literature.[23] One such writer of these verses was King Srei Thomma Reachea (ruled 1627-1631), who was killed on the orders of his jealous uncle Outey. There is also a long tradition of love-songs and love-stories, of which the most famous *Tum Teav* tells of the vicissitudes of the romance of Tum, a monk-novice who is also a travelling entertainer, and the beautiful girl Teav, with whom he falls in love. As so often the story ends in tragedy like that of Srei Thomma Reachea.

228. Vat Bo in Siem Reap.

229 & 230. Scenes from the Râmâyana epic as painted on the internal walls of Vat Bo.(Photographs by Tom Sarœun.)

229 (above) Scene i. Angkut (a monkey-prince) and Hanuman (chief of Râma's monkey army) go to get extra forces from (the monkey-king) Mahâjambu (see Judith Jacob, Reamker, *page 119 ff.).*
Scene ii. Râma assembles his officers and orders Hanuman and Angkut to open the way.

230. (below) Scene i. Angkut kills the guardians of the four portals (of the city of Lanka).
Scene ii. He brings a (threatening) message (from Râma) to Râvaṇa.

EPILOGUE—THE 19TH TO 20TH CENTURY

Despite the continuing literary activities in aristocratic circles, the abject condition of ordinary illiterate Khmers in the 19th century led some European travellers to wonder whether they could really be the same people as those who had built Angkor and the other similarly impressive ruins. Henri Mouhot, 'the rediscoverer of Angkor', who travelled widely in Thailand as it then was (thus including Angkor) from 1859 to 1861, suggested that they may have been two different peoples, one the creators of this earlier civilization (perhaps from China or India!) and the other being later invaders who destroyed it. Apart from Angkor itself, he visited ancient Khmer sites in the region of Battambang, and incidentally adduces sufficient linguistic evidence, even at this early stage of scholarly research, to suggest that they were one and same people, namely Khmers.[24] As already shown above, back in the 16th century Angkor was certainly not forgotten by the royal court at Lovek. Manuscript evidence refers to certain repairs carried out on Vishnuloka (soon to become known as Angkor Vat, as Theravâda monks settled there), and up to the mid-18th century devotional inscriptions continued to be inscribed on its walls. However by the 19th century when the French arrived on the scene, memory of the past seems to have been generally forgotten. Angkor Vat and a few other important sites in Angkor Thom were certainly not abandoned, since communities of monks continued to reside there, but the historical connection seems to have been lost, and the villagers who lived in the vicinity assumed that these strange buildings were the work of giants of the past. One might refer to a Khmer literary compilation of the 19th century, entitled the 'Buddha Damnây' or 'The Prophesy of the Buddha'. This is based upon the supposedly historical prophecy of the Sâkyamuni Buddha, as known from early historical accounts, that his doctrine would endure only 5,000 years. This has been adapted to explain the steady decline of the kingdom from its glorious past under a mythological king named Puddam Vans and subsequent catastrophes, beginning with capture of Lovek by the Thais in 2000 BE which would correspond to AD1457[25] (actually c.1594). There is no connection whatsoever with Angkor, which was certainly known to exist, but with no general memory of its great past.[26] The name of the king Puddam Vams may represent a vague connection with the last great Khmer king, Jayavarman VII, but it is relevant to note that he emerged as a known historical figure only in the mid-20th century thanks to French researchers, primarily George Coedès and Philippe Stern.

In fact much more had been known earlier in rather limited European circles, thanks to the reports of Portuguese and Dutch adventurers of the 16th century at a time when Khmer kings, ruling from Srei Santhor or Lovek, remained fully conscious of their earlier connections with Angkor.[27] There was thus no doubt that they represented one and same people. However by the 19th century much had been forgotten, not only by the Khmers themselves, but also in Europe. Here, the great event of the French Revolution had occurred followed by the long Napoleonic wars, creating a psychological break with the past. Also the French has lost most of their overseas possessions in India and North America and the British had enough to do elsewhere in Asia to hold their own colonial possessions. After the Napoleonic wars they colluded with the Dutch in the exchange of fortified trading posts in the Malay archipelago, and mainland South-East Asia (usually referred to as Indochina) remained unclaimed by any colonial power. French interest in the area derives ultimately from a treaty signed at Versailles in 1787 between Louis XVIth and the ruler of Cochinchina who thus with some limited French assistance was able to regain his throne and eventually to establish a new imperial dynasty based at Hue, then the Vietnamese capital. Better known as Gia Long (1802-1820), he remained grateful to the French missionary bishop, Pigneau de Béhanime (1741-1799) who was instrumental in arranging this treaty. Tourane (now better known as Da-nang) and the nearby island of Poulo-Condore thus became a French stronghold. However, Gia Long's successors instituted a severe persecution of Catholic missionaries and of local converts, resulting in armed Franco-Spanish intervention on their behalf. By a peace treaty signed in 1862 the French gained control of the three eastern provinces of Cochinchina.[28] The following year a treaty was signed with King Norodom, making Cambodia, which had suffered from Vietnamese and Thai incursions, a protectorate of France. A later treaty

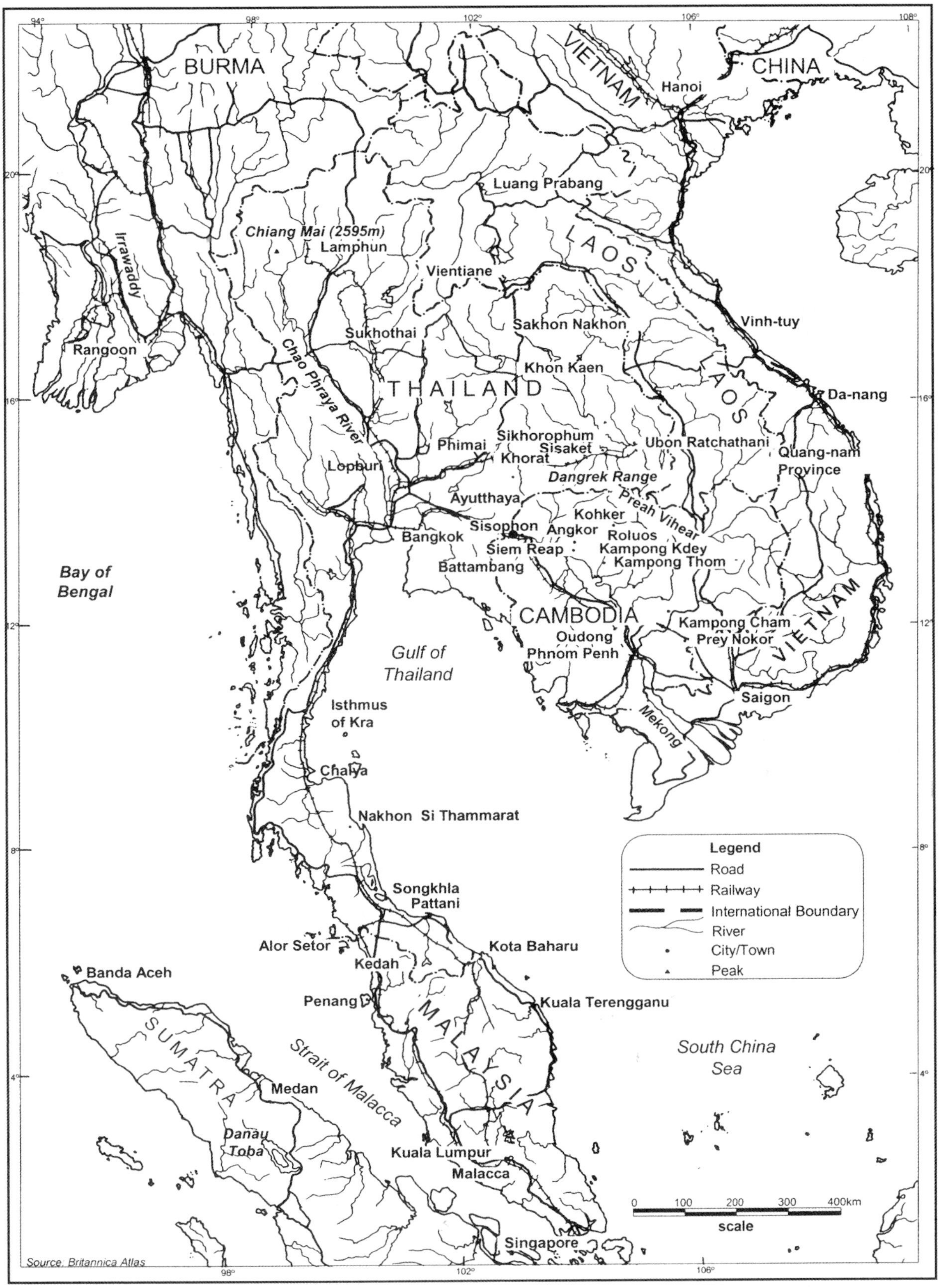

Map 10. Present-day Cambodia.

of 1884 secured French control also of Annam and Tongking.

However, owing to the refusal of King Norodom to have his royal prerogatives tampered with, it was practically impossible to carry out effective administrative reforms until his death in 1904.[29] Within this context one may quote Henri Mouhot's impressions of similar social conditions in Thailand written around the year 1860:

> *Between the two kings (the second one usually being heir to the throne) and the people there are some twelve orders of princes, several classes of ministers, five or six of mandarins, then for the forty-one provinces of the kingdom, an endless series of governors and under-governors, whose incapacity and extortions surpass whatever one can imagine and would seem to justify my missionary friend Bruguierie, who claims that the Siamese word* sarenival, *which we translate as* governor *means literally 'devouring the people'. The functionaries are paid insufficient, badly controlled and never supervised; the consequence is easy to imagine, they are all extortioners. The King knows this, but closes his eyes, maybe because of the excessive number who ought to be punished, or maybe because such matters are not worth his attention. The provinces are the milch-cows of the governors, who force the people to give everything which they can possibly surrender. The ordinary people are divided in Siam as slaves, gentlemen and those who pay tribute. Some tribute reaches the coffers of the king, and as for rest he does not worry himself.*[30]

I quote also his observations concerning Battembang in the mid-19th century:

> *The province of Battambang has been subject to Siam for almost a century. The people have tried to revolt several times and even to surrender themselves to the Annamites who twenty years ago took possession of the rest of Cambodia, but they were repulsed by the Thais as far as south of Phnom Penh. Since this time Cambodia has suffered no more attacks except from Cochinchina, but it remains subject to Siam. Apart from the war in which France is now engaged against the empire of Annam, it is probable that the last hour would have struck for the little kingdom of Cambodia, of which the most likely destiny is to disappear and become assimilated to its neighbours. ...*
>
> *The majority of the population of Battambang is Cambodian, and as farmers they have their paddy-fields behind their houses, and although subject to a foreign country for nearly a century, they have retained their own ways of life, while the present (Thai) administration allows them the same freedom as the rest of Cambodia, even exempting them from the taxes and impositions which ruin the other provinces. This special favour creates a relative prosperity at Battambang, where the inhabitants enjoy a certain condition of well-being, of which one is at once aware* (Mouhot, *Voyages dans le royaumes de Siam*, p. 175).

The French conquest of Cochinchina and the subsequent protectorate established in Cambodia left the frontiers as they were until 1907 when a treaty with Siam allowed for the return of the provinces of Battambang and Siem Reap (Angkor) to Cambodia.

In 1873 another French explorer, Louis Delaporte, who had earlier taken part in the French mission of exploration of the upper reaches of the Mekong River in 1866-68,[31] set out on an official mission to explore the wonders of Angkor. With a gun-boat and a steam-launch he reached Phnom Penh by river-routes and was well received by King Norodom. Continuing by river-routes to Stoung, he then travelled overland with buffalo-carts to the impressive temple of Preah Khan of Kampong Svay. Then continuing eastwards for a further eighty kilometres he reached the 10th century temple-citadel of Koh Ker with its surrounding subsidiary temples. All these sites were buried in the jungle, but with official support he had followers enough to clear the way for the making of sketch-maps, drawings and plans.[32]

He notes the same miserable conditions, although he is more detailed in his observations. Thus he mentions the existence of a Chinese agent as tax-collector in the fisheries, who maintains at the same time an opium and gambling den.

> *The royal treasury gains enormous revenues, but for the people it is sheer ruin, for it is superfluous to state that the dice absorb regularly the pay of the miserable coolies, often also that of their masters, and often also the actual person of some fishermen who play until they are reduced to slavery* (Delaporte, *Voyage au Cambodge*, p. 45).

When visiting Koh Ker, which is certainly a remote region, he notes that the local people were eating a kind of root, similar to a taro. Eaten fresh it is poisonous, but they know how to remove its poisonous qualities by soaking. He adds:

> *The use of this gross kind of food illustrates their incredible misery into which these people have fallen, either as the result of the last civil war or*

of the exactions of the mandarins. Most of the population would prefer to live as savages in the forest rather than continue labouring for fruits which are not theirs. Such is their poverty that, as soon as money became known, the few families who might possess a bar of silver (value 80 francs) hide it carefully and would part with it for nothing in this world. But most of the people have never even seen money (p. 95).

Both these travellers were royally entertained by the King and were well aware of the difference of life at court-level.

I do not attempt to estimate the success of French efforts in the succeeding period to restore some better order in the administration of the country, except perhaps to observe that there was little time to achieve as much as was in fact achieved after the death of King Norodom in 1904 and during the compliant reigns of Kings Sisovath and Sisovath Monivong—merely thirty-five years before the outbreak of the Second World War, when Cambodia, under Japanese occupation, was nominally subject to the Vichy French government. It is perhaps significant that with Japanese agreement, Thailand was then able to reclaim the provinces of Battambang and Siem Reap (Angkor), which however were correctly returned to Cambodia immediately after the war. A notable event of the 'Vichy period' was the crowning of King Norodom Sihanouk at the age of eighteen as King in 1941, who thus comes to preside over Cambodian affairs in some quite extraordinary way until the present day, whether as King, or Chief of State or in exile as the best-known spokesman on behalf of his country. Controlled from 1945 onwards from Saigon and Paris, he managed to gain independence for Cambodia in 1953. This came about when the French were engaged in their desperate war in Vietnam, resulting eventually in the division of the country, Communist in the north and pro-Western in the south. The Communist incursions which led to the full involvement of the United States in war with Vietnam, affected Cambodia adversely, where the King remained generally opposed to the introduction of democratic reforms at such a dangerous time. In order to secure direct control of affairs he abdicated the throne to his compliant father and declared himself Chief of State. Attempting to keep Cambodia neutral in the war, he displeased both the USA and Thailand, which was co-operating fully with the American forces. This however did not prevent increasing Communist incursions into the country and he was forced to give limited facilities to the Vietnamese. His situation became untenable and in 1970 he was deposed while abroad in France by the General Assembly which he himself had brought into being as a move towards a slightly more democratic form of government. Since that time chaos has engulfed the country, leading to even greater miseries than before.[33]

However by this time the French had surveyed most of the ruins of Khmer temples, not only in Cambodia, but also in neighbouring Thailand, as demonstrated by the compendious works of Étienne Aymonier (*Le Cambodge*, 3 vols. Paris 1900-04,[34]) and of Lunet de Lajonquière (*Inventaire descriptif des monuments de Cambodge*, 3 vols. Paris 1902-11). The École française d'Etrême Orient, which was founded in 1898 (corresponding in many respects to the Archaeological Survey of India founded by the British about the same time), became responsible for the Angkor site in 1907 and thus remained the main administrative organization for all the research-work and care and maintenance of archaeological sites up to 1975 when the occupation of Phnom Penh by the Khmer Rouge put an end to all such cultural activites.

Over much the same period a new form of literature, namely the modern novel, was gradually developed by the Khmers themselves, following Western patterns. I quote from a recent work on this subject by Klairung Amratisha:

The reform of education from the informal schooling in the Vat to the French-styled lycée had a great influence on the birth and development of modern literature. Modern schools, especially the Franco-Cambodian schools in the cities, had created a new urban class, a class of western-trained people. They had a chance to study French philosophy and literature, such as the works of Montesquieu and Jean Jacques Rousseau, as well as the slogans of Liberty, Equality and Fraternity. It is interesting to note that among the earliest novelists none were from high-class families or had been educated abroad. Unlike the upper class they maintained close contacts with ordinary people, even though they were fluent in French, lived mainly in the cities and enjoyed the convenience of material goods from the West. Therefore although adopting a different form of writing, their subject matter was their own environment and their own society.[35]

The growth of Khmer nationalism, which seems to have developed during the Second World War when the French administration was subjected to Japanese control, gave further impetus to the writing of novels in the Khmer language which generally date from

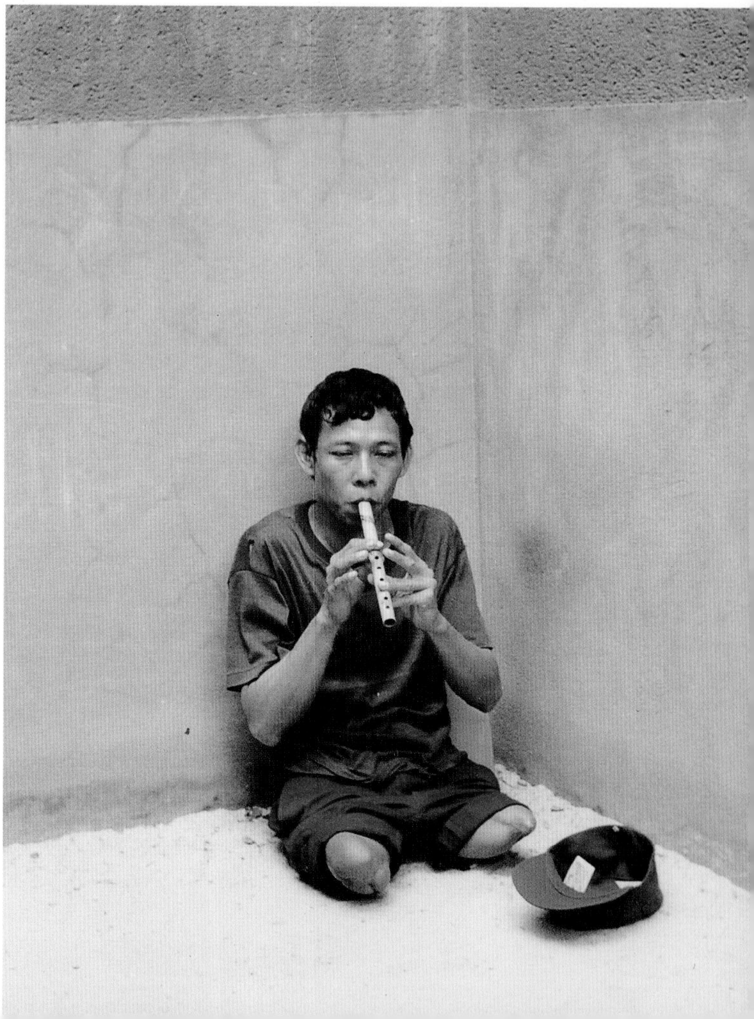

this period. About the same time the first Khmer dictionary, sanctioned by royal decree in 1915, was finally produced in 1938 by the recently formed Buddhist Institute. The impetus for this essential work came from the great French scholar George Coedès, then head of the EFEO, although at the same time French efforts to persuade the Khmers to accept a form of romanized script proved unsuccessful. Now for a short period of some thirty years we note the first blossoming of Khmer modern literature corresponding to the modern literatures of neighbouring countries, such as Thailand, Vietnam and Indonesia which were already further advanced. However due to the disasters that have afflicted the country since 1970 and especially the utterly destructive Khmer Rouge period this important development has been totally undone, leaving the country with no established authors and no general educated reading public. The country has been ravaged by warfare of one kind or another for nearly thirty years, while the Khmer Rouge régime during a period of barely four years destroyed all the bases and all the amenities of civilized life, both Cambodian and French, schools and monasteries, medical and administrative service, neglecting roads and railways, and worst of all, wiping out a whole generation of educated and cultured people, whether layfolk or monks. All must be restarted, presumably beginning with the personal stories of horrendous suffering under Pol Pot and his henchmen.

At the same time the 'civilizing mission' of the French has been largely undone, although French remains the language of government and diplomatic language. So far as the administration is concerned the country returned to a situation not very different from that described by Henri Mouhot and Louis Delaporte 150 years ago. However, added to the numbers of the deprived are the numerous ex-soldiers, whether from government or Khmer Rouge ranks who are now no longer required, and so are abandoned with little or no pay, many of them lacking limbs. Meanwhile some of their commanders have made fortunes out of illicit forestry or the mining of gems, and now often succeed in extorting land from the traditional village owners by making good use of the still corrupt legal system. The government lacks funds to pay the administrative services, the police, school and university teachers, hospital staffs, anywhere near enough to live on, so that they are forced to seek money by other means, whether by seeking other forms of work part-time or by bribery whenever their official position renders this possible.

What could possibly remain of French administrative and social efforts, even where these had proved successful? Apart from the endemic corruption, what can be expected of the present Cambodian legal system, when French norms and all legal training together with all other forms of education were wrecked by the Pol Pot régime, and then reformed on a Vietnamese model during the following years of Vietnamese occupation? However it is certainly due to the French occupation that Cambodia has emerged from all its sufferings as a fully recognized independent country including the earlier lost provinces of Battambang and Angkor. And it is also thanks to many French adventurers and scholarly administrators that the past history and impressive culture of the Khmers has been made known to the present generation of Cambodians, and indeed to anyone else who is interested in the fate of this small country. Since 1990 the EFEO has returned and continues its research and preservation interests, nowaday assisted by various archaeological missions from other countries. The essential work of cultural reconstruction is thankfully encouraged by the present Cambodian government, notably the Ministries of Culture and of Foreign Affairs. However it will be a long time before any form of modern Khmer literature can be developed, although attempts in this direction have now begun. There is no adequate reading public, and the sign of this is the absence of book-shops, replete with local literature and translations of Western scholarly works, so plentiful in the neighboring countries of Thailand, Vietnam, Singapore and Indonesia.

Much has been irrevocably lost. While Thailand has made such impressive progress over the last fifty years in the rediscovery and preservation of early sites (including those of the Khmers), Cambodia during this same period has neglected and then often destroyed the results of earlier French efforts at preservation. Where remote sites such as Koh Ker and Preah Khan of Kampong Svay had been cleared of the jungle, sketch-maps, plans and photographs taken, the jungle has taken total possession once

231. (top left) Monks blessing offerings of rice presented by villagers.(Photograph by Suthep Kritsanuvarin.)

232. (top right) A wood-carver at work. (Photograph by Suthep Kritsanuvarin.)

233. (bottom left) Ancient eaves carved in wood (scarcely more than a hundred years) at Vat Bodhi Bantây Chey.

234. (bottom right) A legless beggar.

235. (top row, left) A procession of monks going to a ceremony near the Bayon.

236. (top row, right) A group of small stûpas in Vat Bodhi Bantây Chey near Siem Reap. Khmer Buddhism during the Angkor period leaves no trace of the cult of the stûpa, and there was certainly nothing to compare remotely with great stûpa of Borobudur in Central Java. However with the coming of Theravâda Buddhism, the stûpa comes into its own again. Although kings of the Lovek and Oudong periods certainly built stûpas, nothing of any note has survived, except the one at Vat Phnom in Phnom Penh. Stupas (known as çaetday from skr. *çaitya) nowadays serve mainly as memorials to the deceased in the courtyards of the monasteries.*

237. (2nd row, left) Recent paintings on the roof of a crematorium, same monastery.

238. (2nd row, right) A white elephant bearing a small stûpa amongst other stûpas in grounds of Vat Aranya Sokor.

239. (3rd row) A village house.

240. (left) Schoolboys at play in their school-grounds at Ban Bir near Prakonchai (Thailand) where there happens to be a Khmer 13th century hospital chapel. (Photograph by Suthep Kritsanuvarin.)

more. Meanwhile over the last thirty years rampaging soldiers have looted these sites, reducing them to an even more ruinous state. If one wants to visit such places, it is upon these earlier maps and descriptions that one must depend for guidance. One thus notes the changes for the worse that have come about in the meantime.

One remarkable national achievement since the total destruction of religion during the Khmer Rouge period (1975-79) and the restrictions imposed during the Vietnamese occupation (1979-89) is the rebirth of Buddhism in Cambodia since 1990. This is entirely a popular development, unassisted by government funds (of which there are none to spare) and unassisted by foreign aid. It is the villagers and townsfolk themselves, and sometimes more wealthy people anxious for merit, who have provided the funds for the rebuilding of monasteries and thus encouraged the reforming of Buddhist communities. A few elderly monks who have survived have played the main constructive part in re-establishing the religious life of the country which within the short space of some twenty years already forms the essential part of the daily life of most Khmer families much as it used to thirty years ago.[36] But at the same time it seems that the brutality of the Khmer Rouge excesses has left their mark on a younger generation, many of whom are capable of vicious actions with no regard for the teachings of their religion. As a foreigner living in the country one normally learns of this dark side of the Khmer character from news reports in the local papers[37] (and what other national character lacks its dark aspect?). Otherwise the Khmers are a courteous, tolerant and cheerful people, staunch and reliable. An early French Resident, who lived here from 1886 to 1913, subsequently writing the best available account of Cambodian civil and religious festivals, namely Adhémard Leclère, presented his work, published in 1916, thus:

> *to the Cambodian people who are a good people and who were once a great nation I dedicate this book where I recount how I have encountered them at all the moments of their lives.*[38]

242. (p. 220 top) A view of Phimai across the lake. (Photograph by Suthep Kritsanuvarin.)

243. (p. 220 bottom) A picnic in the grounds of Angkor Vat. (Photograph by Suthep Kritsanuvarin.)

241. (below) A group of monks as tourists at Phimai. (Photograph by Suthep Kritsanuvarin.)

Endnotes

Abbreviations and their meanings used in this section may be found on p. 237.

Chapter 1

[1] Concerning these people who now have no country to call their own, see Guillon, *The Mons, a civilization of Southeast Asia*; also Brown, *The Dvâravatî Wheels of the Law and the Indianization of South East Asia*.

[2] See O'Reilly, 'Excavations in NW Cambodia'.

[3] See Higham and Thosarat, *Prehistoric Thailand from early settlements to Sukhothai*, especially pp. 91-171, which covers admirably the bronze and iron-age settlements. Concerning Sri Thep, see pp. 180-182 and Briggs, *The Ancient Khmer Empire*, p. 30.

[4] See Pelliot, 'Le Fou-nan', p. 266 for the full context; also Wheatley, *The Golden Khersonese*, pp. 14-25. He identifies Chin-lin as a small state on the Gulf of Siam and the three other names he places as ports along the coast of the peninsula. In order to place this and the following excerpts concerning Funan in a well argued context, refer to Jacq-Hergoualc'h, *The Malay Peninsula*, p. 95 ff.

[5] These abbreviated translations are quoted from Wheatley, *The Golden Khersonese,* pp. 48-49. Because of an earlier version of this legend, namely that the royal lineage of Funan had already been founded by an Indian Brahman, named Kauṇḍinya, armed with a magic bow, which he shot into the boat of a dragon-princess who came out to meet him, the Kauṇḍinya named in the quotation above is sometimes referred to as the second Kauṇḍinya. However they may well be one and the same, as recorded rather differently in a legendary and in a possible quasi-historical version.

[6] For the inscription, see Coedès, 'Stèle de Baray Occidental' v. A 2.

[7] Vickery, *Society, Economics and Politics in pre-Angkor Society,* p. 151 ff. *Mratâñ* like *poñ* is another early title for important persons. In both cases the prefix k- seems to have an intensifying effect; *añ*, originally a pronoun meaning 'self' or 'I myself' appears to enhance respect with the implied meaning of 'his true self'.

[8] This process can be traced in a useful book by O'Flaherty, *The Rig Veda, an Anthology*. An essential work relating specifically to Cambodia is that by Kamaleshvar Bhattacharya, *Les religions brahmaniques dans l'ancien Cambodge*.

[9] For most lay Buddhists the acquisition of merit, best achieved by their material support of the monks, tends to be an end in itself in that they hope thereby to achieve a better rebirth in some future life.

[10] For far more detailed accounts see my *Indo-Tibetan Buddhism,* especially pp. 44-79.

Chapter 2

[1] See Coedès, *The Indianized States,* pp. 59-60. The quotation is taken from Pelliot, Le Fou-nan, p. 269.

[2] See Vickery, *Society, Economics and Politics*, pp. 70-71 for this item of historical construction. Also see below under 'Angkor Borei'.

[3] See Coedès, *The Indianized States*, p. 17. The main source is Malleret, *L'archéologie du Delta du Mékong*. For a résumé of essential matter see Coedès 'Fouilles en Cochinchine'. See especially J.C.M. Khoo, *Art & Archaeology of Fu Nan, Pre-Khmer kingdom of the Lower Mekong Valley.*

[4] Amarâvati, one of the most important ancient sites in south-east India, thriving from the 2nd to the 11th century, first under the Andra and later the Pallava dynasty (*c.*600-900), was one of the main sources of Indian influences in South-East Asia. Concerning Cham art and architecture see Guillon, *Cham Art*, and Vandermeersch and Ducrest, *Le Musée de Sculpture Cam de Da Nang.*

[5] See Coedès, *The Indianized States*, pp. 42-45 and Hall, *A History of South-East Asia*, pp. 28-29.

[6] See *Études épigraphiques sur le pays Cham* de Louis Finot, Édouard Huber, George Coedès et Paul Mus, réunites par Claude Jacques, pp. 1-7.

[7] *Études épigraphiques*, p. 79 ff.

[8] *Études épigraphiques*, p. 254 ff.

[9] See Coedès, *The Indianized States*, pp. 57 and 65. Vickery (*Society, Economics and Politics,* p. 73) following Claude Jacques rejects this interpretation, partly on account of the script but also because no known Cham king could rightly claim such a title. Script is a doubtful argument. But this king does not claim such a title. He asks that it might be bestowed, and he hopes for this favour from the god of a sacred mountain, which was sacred to the Chams and identified as Śiva with the typical Cham title of Bhadreśvara.

[10] Quoted from Ma Tuan-lin, *Ethnologie des peoples étranges*, p. 483.

[11] See Coedès, *The Indianized States*, pp. 65-66. For his source material see 'Le site primitif de Tchen-la', and 'La stèle de Wat Luong Kau près de Wat P'hu'. For an archaeological description of what still remains today,

see Freeman, *A Guide to the Khmer temples in Thailand and Laos*, pp. 200-207. The whole area has been investigated by a number of archaeological missions, most recently by the Italian Lao/UNESCO mission, directed by Patrizia Zolese of the Lerici Foundation.

[12] See Coedès, 'La Stèle de Prah Khan d'Angkor', verse 6.

[13] Coedès, 'Inscription de Bâksei Camkrong, vv. 13-15. The text continues: 'Thereafter came the kings of whom the foremost was Rudravarman etc.' and there is no suggestion that they had any direct connection with one another.

[14] This is first suggested by Briggs, *The Ancient Khmer Empire*, p. 39, and more firmly by Vickery, *Society, Economics and Politics*, pp. 38-40. See also his pp. 80-81.

[15] See Chandler, *Facing the Cambodian Past,* pp. 119-35.

[16] See Coedès, *Indianized States*, p. 65. He quotes from Pelliot, 'Le Fou-nan', p. 272, noting incidentally that *ch'ali* probably represents Sanskrit Śrî and not *kṣatriya.*

[17] Pelliot, 'Le Fou-nan', p. 295.

[18] For precise details relating in the process of its reconstruction from its previously ruined state see the article of Mauger, 'L'Âsram Mahârosei'.

[19] I note that the main collections of Khmer sculpture are in the National Museum, Phnom Penh and at the Musée Guimet in Paris. A major work with selected items from these two museums is *Angkor et dix siècles d'art Khmer*, and the English version: *Angkor and ten centuries of Khmer Art.*

[20] For a plan and description of this temple see Lunet de Lajonquière, *Inventaire descriptif, I*, pp. 3-7.

[21] For these inscriptions see Barth, 'Ang Chumnik', and Coedès, 'Stèle brisée de Kdei Ang'. The site is described by Lunet de Lajonquière, *Inventaire descriptif, I*, pp. 53-54.

[22] See Bruguier, 'Les vestiges archéologiques du Phnom Trotung'.

[23] I have given a fuller survey of all these events in my *Asian Commitment,* pp. 357-409. For a good account of how the very existence of Śrîvijaya was discovered, see Jacq-Hergoualc'h, *The Malay Peninsula*, pp. 233-55.

[24] There is evidence that a son of Îśânavarman, named Śivadatta ruled at Jyeṣṭhapura in the area north of Chanthaburi in Thailand beyond the present Thai-Cambodia frontier. See Vickery, *Society, Economics and Politics,* p. 338. A grandson of his, named Harṣavarman may have ruled much further west in the region of U Thong, 90 km west of present-day Ayuthaya. See Brown, *The Dvâravatî Wheels*, pp. 22-24 and 49 ff. It seems that this last-named set up a *Śiva-linga* in this area of Dvâravatî Buddhist culture, thus emphasizing the basic general difference between Mon culture, largely Buddhist, and Khmer religious interests, primarily Śaivite so far as the rulers were concerned.

[25] See I-tsing, *A record of the Buddhist religion*, p. 12. According to a footnote by the translator Takakusu 'Poh-nan (Kuo) 'is "Siam" but also includes part of Cambodia'. As Siam (Thailand) has no place on the Indochina mainland in this early period, he can only mean Cambodia. However Poh-nan is clearly an alternative spelling of Funan.

[26] See Vickery, *Society, Economics and Politics,* p. 330 and note 24 just above.

[27] See also Briggs, *The Ancient Khmer Empire*, p. 33, pp. 53-55, and especially Vickery, *Society, Economics and Politics*, pp. 341-66.

[28] See *Handbook for travellers in India*, p. 366.

[29] See Vickery, *Society, Economics and Politics*, pp. 357-66.

[30] See Coedès, 'Stèle de Baray Occidental' v. A 2.

[31] Coedès, 'Piédroits de Vat Khnat', p. 56.

[32] See Coedès, *Indianized States*, p. 94, and especially Vickery, *Society, Economics and Politics*, pp. 267-8 and pp. 379-81. He lists the several inscriptions from this area, dating from 624 onwards, pp. 103-4, suggesting a form of succession with *poñ* leadership going back to the early 7th century.

[33] See Coedès, *The Indianized States,* p. 93, deriving from Abû Zaid Hasan, *Voyage du marchand arabe Sulaymân en Inde et en Chine, rédigé en 851, suivi de remarques par Abû Zaid Hasan (vers 916).* This story connects very well with the tradition concerning Jayavarman II's coronation ceremony designed to free the country from subservience to Java. The name Zâbag derives from *jâvaka,* and by implication refers to Śrîvijaya. See Chapter 3, 'Jayavarman II'.

[34] Concerning 'Java' see note 7, Ch. 3 below. I note that Vickery (*Society, Economics and Politics*, pp. 386-93) rejects the whole idea of such an invasion, and also denies (with perhaps insufficient evidence) that Chenla tends to disintegrate during the early part of the 8th century, thus discounting the Chinese view of Chenla as having fallen apart into at least two separate parts.

[35] A good brief description of this site in English is in Briggs, *The Ancient Khmer Empire*, pp. 74-75. Recently a thorough study has been produced by Tranet, *Sambaur-Prei-Kuk, monuments d'Içânavarman (615-28).* His work replaces earlier descriptions, all in French, e.g., Frédéric, *Sud-Est Asiatique, ses temples, ses sculptures*, pp. 245-60; Lunet de Lajonquière, *Inventaire descriptif, I*, pp. 225-36, and Parmentier, *L'art khmer primitif*, pp. 44-92 and thirty-five plates.

[36] For all such references see Coedès, 'Inscriptions de Sambor Prei Kuk'.

[37] Kâla or Mahâkâla, the god of time (or eternity), became a popular protective divinity often set up by the entrances to Hindu and Buddhist shrines in India, and his presence seems to be ubiquitous on ancient lintels in Cambodia from the 9th century onwards. He was equally popular in Central and East Java. The decorative lintels of this pre-Angkor period have been divided into three styles named after typical early sites: 1. the Sambor Prei Kuk style of the 7th century; 2. the style of Prei Kmeng (now a total ruin near the western end of the West Baray) in the first half of the 8th century; 3. the style of Kampong Preah of the second half of the 8th century, but the *kâla*-mask seems to have been neglected in the cited examples. See also Boisselier, *Le Cambodge*, pp. 146-57. The main work on the subject is that by Smitthi Siribadra and Mayuree Veraprasert: *Lintels: a comparative study of lintels in Cambodia and Thailand*. However these styles often overlap one another.

[38] A recent study of these has been made by Tranet in his Volume 3 of the Sambour-Prei-Kuk series (1998-99), financed like the earlier two volumes by the Toyota Foundation.

[39] Available maps of Cambodia are so inadequate that it is perhaps best to explain how one reaches this site. Crossing the new bridge at Kampong Cham one follows the road eastwards towards the Vietnamese frontier. About half way along this road some 10 km beyond the town of Suong, there is a monastic entrance on the right into which one turns, driving southwards for a further approximate 15 km.

[40] For a brief account see Briggs, *The Ancient Khmer Empire*, p. 33, or more usefully Lunet de Lajonquière, *Inventaire descriptif, I*, pp. 134-7 and Parmentier, *L'art khmer primitif*, pp. 204-8.

[41] For a general plan see Lunet de Lajonquière, *Inventaire descriptif, I,* pp. 142-55, and for the relevant inscriptions Coedès, 'Inscriptions de Prâh Thât Prâh Srei'.

[42] See Barth, 'Ang Chumnik'.

[43] For a detailed description see Parmentier, *L'art khmer primitif*, pp. 197-200.

[44] See Lunet de Lajonquière, *Inventaire descriptif, I,* pp. 176-9 and Coedès, 'Stèle de Sophas'.

[45] See Trouvé, who excavated the site, 'Ak Yom'. For the inscriptions see Coedès, 'Inscriptions de Prâsât Ak Yom'.

[46] This too was excavated by Trouvé, revealing an inscription which refers to a grant of a palanquin and a piece of land to the shrine by Jayavarman III (here named as 'the king who had gone to the abode of Vishnu'). See Coedès, 'Piédroit de Prâsât Prei Kmeng'.

[47] See Marchall, 'Le degagement de Prâsâd Kok Po'. Its founder was presumably Nivâsakavi, the *guru* of Jayavarman III, thus making it the last of this group. See Coedès & Dumont, 'Les inscriptions du Prâsâd Kok Po'.

[48] Both of these temples are described in Freeman, *Khmer Temples in Thailand*, pp. 127-31 and 174-5.

[49] See Vickery, *Society, Economics and Politics,* pp.111-2, 126-7 and p. 192.

[50] See Finot, 'Lokeçvara en Indo-Chine'.

Chapter 3

[1] Coedès and Dupont, 'Les stèles de Sdok Kak Thom, Phnom Sandak et Prah Vihâr'. One may note also the discourse of Coedès, 'La fondation de la royauté angkorienne et les récentes découvertes archéologiques au Phnom Kulên'. For a description of this 11th century site of Sdok Kak Thom (which may mean the 'Great Reed Lake'), see Freeman, *Khmer Temples,* pp. 132-5.

[2] Śivâśrama, an important religious house, was founded jointly by Śivasoma, a learned guru, and Vâmaśiva of the Śivakaivalya line, who both served under Indravarman. They both received the title, first Śivasoma and then Vâmaśiva, of 'Lord of Śivâśrama'. In the present context the name would refer more properly to Vâmaśiva.

[3] See Coedès, *Indianized States*, p. 97 and Briggs, *The Ancient Khmer Empire*, p. 81. The source is Barth and Bergaigne, 'Phnom Sandak', especially pp. 344-5.

[4] For the inscription see Coedès, *IC V*, pp. 32-34. Concerning Preah Thiet Preah Srei see Chapter II, 'Other Early Sites'.

[5] For the inscription see Coedès, 'Piédroits de Lobok Srot', and for a wider discussion see Vickery, *Society, Economics and Politics*, pp. 393-408.

[6] See Groslier, *Indochine,* p. 87.

[7] Better known probably are the references to Sumatra, known as Java by such intrepid travellers as Marco Polo and ibn Battuta in the 13th to 14th centuries. See 'Java' in *Hobson-Jobson*, pp. 454-6. However, the name is used so widely that it could refer to almost any part of the Malay archipelago.

[8] A reference to this bridge, referred to as Spean Praptös, will be found in Lunet de Lajonquière, *Inventaire descriptif,* I, pp. 269-71. Restored during the 1960s, it is the largest (approximately 80 m long and 12 m wide) and by far the most impressive of several other far smaller ones (of which only scant foundations remain) along the route from Siem Reap to Kampong Kdei. See also Bruguier, 'Les ponts en pierre du Cambodge ancient'.

[9] For Coedès' identification of Kuṭi and other sites associated with Jayavarman II, see his article 'Les capitales de Jayavarman II'. In the text of the Sdok Kak Thom inscription Kuṭi is described as *pûrvadigviśaya,* translatable as 'a district in the eastern direction'. Vickery identifies this with the Pûrvaviśaya of several inscriptions which he places in the north-west or the

Battembang region *(Society, Economics and Politics,* pp. 400-404). See also notes 16 and 31 just below.

For archaeological evidence of the Angkor site as Kuṭi, see the article 'Kuṭîśvara' by Marchal; also Finot, 'Inscriptions d'Angkor', especially pp. 354-63. Now only the brick walls of the central shrine of the original set of three are still standing. It is still known by the educated as Kodi Purah (the old temple compound), but local villagers who use it as a site for cremation refer to it as *dop-kmouch* = the haunted wood.

[10] See Lunet de Lajonquière, *Inventaire descriptif, I*, p. 263, and especially Stern, 'Hariharâlaya et Indrapura'.

[11] See Briggs, *The Ancient Khmer Empire,* for diagrams showing the position of these temples

[12] 'Les sites archéologiques de la région du Bhnam Gûlen (Phnom Kulen)'. Their work was brought to a sudden end as the result of the revolutionary coup d'état in March 1970, which deposed Sihanouk. Since then until very recently there has been no assured peace in the country and thus this area, like many others, has remained inaccessible. I visited Phnom Kulen in December 1998 and was sad to note the wanton destruction that has overcome this site, as elsewhere in Cambodia. All potentially moveable pieces, unearthed and even cut away from the surrounding rock, have been carried off by the occupying soldiers for eventual sale in the art and antique shops of Bangkok. The upper course of the River, known as Kbâl Spean ('Bridgehead') has happily suffered much less, as many of the stone-carvings are under water and those inscribed on the surrounding rocks are cut in such shallow relief that their removal is impracticable. Boulbet and Dagens refer to an inscription of 1054 recording the decoration of the site with 1,000 small *lingas* by a minister of Sûryavarman I in 1054, while another records the ceremonial visit of Udayâdityavarman II in 1059 and the erection of a golden *linga.* Phnom Kulen was maintained as a sacred royal city up to the time of Jayavarman VII (1181-1219), and later it was taken over by Theravâda monks, like other important royal sites. Now the army (already responsible for so much looting of ancient sites) controls the whole area, insisting that the Cambodian Government gave it the land in 1998. (See *The Cambodian Daily*, 4/12/01, p. 15.)

[13] Coedès identifies Janapada as a site now known as Prâsâd Khna, in the Kampong Thom province. See 'Le site de Janapada', p. 8. See also Vickery's further comments, *Society, Economics and Politics*, p. 383. Prâsâd Khna now presents itself as a group of ruins, once a Śaivite ashram. See Briggs, *The Ancient Khmer Empire*, p. 130 for a description and for his sources, Aymonier, *Le Cambodge*, vol. 1, pp. 47-53 and Lunet de Lajonquière, *Inventaire descriptif,* I, pp. 240-242.

[14] Vickery proposes a possible 'family-tree' that would link him with Jayavarman I *(Society, Economics and Politics*, pp. 389-90).

[15] See note 5, Ch. 3 above.

[16] The logistics of Jayavarman II's progress north, first Kuṭi, then Hariharâlaya, then to the NW, then back to Hariharâlaya and Phnom Kulen surely places Kuṭi (in the eastern region) east of the Great Lake, where as pointed out in the text there were already many well established Khmer settlements. I am surprised at Vickery's insistence that this 'eastern region' was somehow NW of the lake. He writes on p. 394 (*Society, Economics and Politics*): 'Of course a name such as "eastern district" must have in origin referred to a location east of something, but in the time of Jayavarman II it can hardly have been Angkor, which did not yet exist.' Surely this is a spurious argument. Yaśovarman's city of Yaśodharapura had not yet been founded, but the Angkor region was well known at least from the reign of Indradevî, and there were already numerous temples there, many of which have already been named above. It would be strange indeed if the Khmers did not recognize this part of their territory, east of the Great Lake as anything other that their 'eastern region'.

[17] See Coedès, 'Nouvelles precisions sur les dates d'avènement de quelques rois des dynasties angkoriennnes'. Jayavarman would have had a very long life indeed, if he arrived in Cambodia as a young man some time before 770, the year of the first inscription where his name probably appears, and then lived until 850, but see Jacques, 'La carrière de Jayavarman II'. The difference in date depends on the correct interpretation of a Khmer phrase in an inscription (K.521) dated 850, referring to Jayavarman III. 'He reigned at 16 years' or 'he had reigned for 16 years'. As the latter is almost certainly correct, one arrives at 850 minus 16. See Vickery 'Resolving the Chronology and History of 9th Century Cambodia', specifically p. 19.

[18] See the article by Jacques, 'Les noms posthumes des rois dans l'ancien Cambodge'.

[19] An excellent review of this Devarâja 'problem' can be found in an article by Woodward, 'Practice and Belief in Ancient Cambodia: Claude Jacques'.

[20] See Boulbet and Dagens, 'Les sites archéologiques', pp. 42-43 and their illustrations, nos 121-3.

[21] The names of most of these ancient temples are local nicknames, of which the original meaning is now lost. However the name 'Sacred Bull' refers to the three stone images of Nandin, Śiva's mount, which face the three shrines.

[22] See Briggs, *The Ancient Khmer Empire*, pp. 103-4, and his source, Seidenfaden, 'Complément à l'inventaire descritif des monuments de Cambodge pour les quattre provinces du Siam oriental', esp. pp. 62-64.

[23] The source of the local name of Lolei remains unexplained unless one accepts the suggestion of Coedès

that it is an abbreviated deformation of Hariharâlaya, once the name of the whole city.

[24] Agastya, who appears frequently on Brahmanical sculptures from now on, was a north-Indian Brahman who is renowned as a missionary to South India, thus becoming the 'patron-saint' of the Tamils.

[25] I draw attention to an interesting article by Moore, 'The temple of Preah Ko and the city of Hariharâlaya'.

[26] Concerning such religious sects see Basham, *The Wonder that was India*, p. 328 ff.

[27] For the text of the inscription see Coedès, 'La stèle de Tep Pranam' and Bergaigne, 'Stèles du Thnal Baray'. Unfortunately Coedès' Sanskrit version of this Buddhist inscription omits those parts where the text is identical with the inscriptions of the various non-Buddhist orders. For these sections one must refer to Bergaigne's earlier work.

[28] See the section 'Buddhism and the Devarâja cult' in the next chapter.

[29] One may contrast this with the situation in Nepal where until the Gorkha conquest of 1768, both *âcârya* and worthy bhikṣu (*ba-re*) under the tolerant Newar kings were accorded the rank of quasi-Brahmans. See my *Indo-Tibetan Buddhism,* pp. 375-7.

[30] See Coedès, 'Inscriptions de Phnom Sndak'.

[31] For references see Briggs, *The Ancient Khmer Empire*, pp. 105 and 112. The relevant inscription is K.878, Coedès, 'Piédroit de Prâsâd Kuk Pradak'. I note that Vickery (*Society, Economics and Politics*, pp. 401-2) cites the text of this inscription to argue that Pûrvadiśa ('eastern region') must be logically in the north-west simply because it is named in association with two other places in that region, but this is no satisfactory argument as it might just as easily be elsewhere, namely east of the Great Lake. One may refer back to note 9, Ch. 3.

[32] See Bernon 'Note sur l'hydraulique théocratique angkorienne', in which he sets down the arguments against this assumption that these lakes were used for irrigation purposes. The leading opponents are W.J. van Liere, Kenneth Hall and Philip Scott, who maintain that there is no evidence of such a use, and that these reservoirs served solely a religious purpose. But see Dumarçay's contrary view in *Angkor et dix siècles d'art Khmer*, pp. 93-100. I too would maintain that they were used both for religious and æsthetic purposes by the rulers and the aristocracy and for various practical purposes, including irrigation, by the ordinary people. The primary interest of some monarchs, such as in the case of Jayavarman VII and the Jayataṭâka (see below), may well have been æsthetic/religious, but I doubt if any ruler, however tyrannical, could impose such an enormous task upon subjects who suffered already from excessive impositions regarding the many temples they had to build, unless there were also some benefit for themselves, not to mention the general prosperity of the country. The situation probably resembled that of the great early cities of Anuradhapura and Polonnaruwa in Ceylon, where these artificial lakes were popularly known as 'tanks' (from Portuguese: *tanque*). I quote from Brohier (previously of the Survey Dept of the Government of Ceylon), *Seeing Ceylon*, p. 3: 'We can but glean shadowy impressions of the vital part these *tanks* played in beautifying the Mahamega or royal pleasure gardens, by filling the bathing pools with water, by providing for the communal needs of the population, and finally by passing the water down to irrigate the rice-fields in the suburbs of the capital.' With little change of phrase these words might well apply to Angkor.

[33] The story of the 'Churning if the Ocean' (skr. *samudra-manthana*) is a popular theme for carvings on Khmer temples, the best known example being on the south side of the east gallery at Angkor Vat. It depicts the legend of how the gods and the demons churned the ocean to regain valued items, primarily the elixir of life, lost during a great primaeval flood. Vishnu metamorphosed as a turtle (*kûrma*) at the bottom of the sea, served as the basis for the churning-stick for which Mount Mandara was used, while the serpent Vasûki served as the churning rope. The story is told in the *Bhâgavata Purâna*, which relates 22 such incarnations (*avatâra*) of Vishnu.

[34] Hall, pp. 144-6, quotes extensively Groslier, *Angkor et le Cambodge au XVIe siècle d'après les sources portugaises et espagnoles.* I note that as part of his argument Groslier quotes appositely Stern, 'Diversité et rhythme de fondations royales khmères', where quotations from several inscriptions attest to the primary importance of maintaining these large reservoirs. My brief quotation is from Groslier, pp. 116-7.

[35] Coedès, *IC IV*, pp. 88-101.

[36] Coedès, 'Inscriptions de Prâsât Kravan'.

Chapter 4

[1] The date of 928 derives from an inscription from Prâsâd Neang Khmau in Bati district (Ta Keo). See Coedès, *IC II*, pp. 32-34. For the relevant inscriptions from Koh Ker itself, see Coedès, *IC I*, pp. 47-71. See also Coedès 'La date de Koh Ker'.

[2] Louis Delaporte, *Un voyage en Cambodge*, pp. 96-97 with a plan on pp. 392-3. One may compare this description with that given by Lunet de Lajonquière, who visited the site some 30 years later, *Inventaire descriptif,* vol. 1, pp. 371-80. He counts up to 12 shrines arranged in parallel rows north to south. A good description in English is available in Briggs, *The Ancient Khmer Empire,* pp. 117-21.

[3] The massive stonework relates it clearly to Koh Ker, so early 10th century is surely more accurate.

[4] For some fine illustrations especially of the lintels see Smitthi Siribhadra, Elizabeth Moore and Michael Freeman, *Palaces of the Gods*, pp. 85-97.

[5] An inscription of Śaka 812 (AD 890) refers to ceremonial arrangements for the sacred fire, ordered by Yaśovarman (889-910) and threatens with the torments of hell those who transgress the commands of Indavarman and Yaśovarman; see Saveros Pou, *Nouvelles Inscriptions du Cambodge*, vol.2, pp. 84-85. For later inscriptions which bring us to the 11th century see Coedès, *IC VI*, pp. 296-9 and Coedès, *IC VII*, pp. 63-70.

[6] For the inscription see Coedès, *IC V*, pp. 297-305. For a detailed description of the site see Freeman, *Khmer Temples*, pp. 98-111 and *Palaces of the Gods*, pp. 266-305.

[7] See Coedès, *IC I*, pp. 73-142.

[8] See Glaize, 'Angkor', p. 158, and other more recent 'Guides'.

[9] The temple of Kok Po preserved important inscriptions referring to the main events of the reign of Jayavarman V. See Briggs, *The Ancient Khmer Empire*, p. 142 and for his source, Coedès and Dupont, 'Les inscriptions de Prâsâd Kok Po'. It has already been mentioned that the last inscription of Ak Yom is dated 1001.

[10] See Lunet de Lajonquière, *Inventaire descriptif*, I, pp. 202-8 and Tranet, *Sambaur-Prei-Kuk*, 3, pp. 195-205.

[11] See Coedès, *Indianized States*, pp. 116-7; and especially Coedès, 'Inscriptions de Bat Chum'.

[12] For the relevant inscriptions see Coedès, *IC I*, pp. 143-57. The section quoted below comes from verses i to iv and then xii to xxix, Sanskrit text on pp. 148-50. Coedès' French translation, pp. 152-4. See also his article 'La date du temple de Bantay Srei'.

[13] A detailed description will be found in *A Guide to the Temple of Bantay Srei*.This is a translation by J.H. Stape of a joint work by Finot and others, *Le temple d'Içvarapura*, EFEO, 1926. For a later reference to this temple see below beginning Chapter 6.

[14] See Coedès, 'Inscriptions de Vat Prah Einkosei', and 'Une réplique de la stele de Prah Einkosei: la stèle de Prâsâd Komphus'.

[15] See Finot, 'Sek Ta Tuy', and 'Prâsâd Trapang Çong (for Khyang)'.

[16] Concerning Vat Sithor one may refer to Lunet de Lajonqière, *Inventaire descriptif*, I, pp. 167-9, and more substantially to Étienne Aymonier, *Le Cambodge*, vol. I, pp. 60-70. Apart from the inscription nothing ancient of note seems to remain on this site. For the Sanskrit edition and French translation of this inscription see Coedès, 'Un document capital sur le bouddhisme en Indochine, le stèle de Vat Sithor'.

[17] The preferred school of Buddhist philosophy is thus that of Yogaçâra or 'Mind Only' (*Çittamâtra),* representing the latest and 'Third Turning' of the Wheel of the Doctrine, as promulgated by the Bodhisattva Maitreya and the Sage Asanga (5th century AD), to whom the basic text of the *Madhyântavibhâga* was believed to have been revealed by the Bodhisattva Maitreya. See my *Indo-Tibetan Buddhism,* pp. 94-116. This work has been translated with the English title as given above by Theodore Stcherbatsky in *Biblioteca Buddhica,* vol. 30, Moscow/Leningrad 1938, reprinted in Calcutta 1971. The *Tattvasamgraha,* as referred to above, is an 8th century work by Śântarakṣita, and the commentary was the work of his pupil Kamalaśîla. The text is available in the *Gaekwad Oriental Series, vols XXX and XXXI*, edited by E. Krishnamacharya, with the translation in the same series, *vols. LXXX and LXXXIII*, by Ganthanatha Jha. It may be interesting to note that these favoured Indian scholars played a leading part in the famous debate held in Lhasa towards the end of the 8th century concerning which form of Buddhism was to be followed. See my *Indo-Tibetan Buddhism,* pp. 431-6.

[18] These are the Four Rites of pacifying, prospering, subduing and destroying, commonly referred to and still practised in tantric Buddhism. See my *Indo-Tibetan Buddhism*, pp. 238-40; also my *Buddhist Himâlaya,* pp. 257-62.

[19] These are the inscriptions of 'Phnom Sandak and Prah Vihâr' (Coedès, *APKh I*, pp. 245-65) included in the article by Coedès & Dupont, relating in the first instant to the inscription of Sdok Kak Thom, q.v.

[20] See his *Account of the Buddhist religion as practised in India and the Malay archipelago,* p. 10. It is often assumed, quite wrongly, in books on Buddhism, that Buddhists of a Mahâyâna persuasion rejected all the earlier teachings including the ancient rules concerning monastic discipline. Please see my comments on 'Continuity in Buddhist Monastic Life' in *Indo-Tibetan Buddhism,* pp. 305-15. The *Mûla-sarvâstivâdin* group (where *mûla,* 'root' means effectively 'fundamental') appear on the scene as a later development from the earlier *Sarvâstivâdin* group, one of the four main groups into which the early divulging Buddhist sects came to be traditionally arranged (see I-tsing, *A record of the Buddhist religion*, pp. xxii-xxiii). They may have developed as a recognized group during the 4th to 5th century AD using pure Sanskrit for the promulgations of their partially revised scriptures. They were thus open to the strong Mahâyana influences which were then in vogue in India, and their *Vinaya* must have presented itself as the most suitable one for use by communities of monks which were then readily adopting as 'Buddha-Word' the Mahâyâna treatises of such renowned scholars as Nâgârjuna, Aryadeva, and still later those of Asanga and Vasubandhu of the *Yogâcâra* or *Cittamâtra* ('Mind Only') philosophical schools. It came to be widely used

in Central Asia and thence in Tibet, as well as throughout South-East Asia until the Theravâdins won over the Indo-Chinese mainland.

[21] Concerning the ephemeral king see Coedès, 'Une nouvelle inscription de Jayavîravarman à Prah Ko'. Briggs (*The Ancient Khmer Empire*, p. 148) repeats the interesting theory of a Dutch scholar, F.D.K. Bosch, that the future king Udayâdityavarman (still in his mother's womb) and his elder brother Narapativîravarman were taken to East Java by their mother, the elder sister of Jayavarman V, who feared for their lives at the Angkor court. He then identifies the future King Udayâdityavarman (whose earlier personal name is unknown) with a Javanese prince Udâyana who married Queen Mahendradatta of Bali, becoming known from inscriptions (dating from 989 to 1001) as King Dharmodayâvarmadeva. It is thus suggested that this ruler (of presumed Khmer origin) returned to Angkor on the death of Jayavarman V together with his elder brother Narapativîravarman in order to claim the throne. An inscription of Udayâdityavarman from Prâsâd Khna of 1001 (see Coedès, 'Une inscription d'Udâyadityavarman I'*)* names Narapativîravarman as his general in Cambodia. Udayâdityavarman disappears from the Cambodian scene in 1003, presumably returning eventually to Bali, where the name Dharmodayavarmadeva appears again on Bali edits in 1011. Bosch suggests that his brother Narapativîravarman continued the struggle against Sûryavarman, ruling under the name of Jayavîravarman, finally losing his life in this war. However he is still known as Narapativîravarman in an inscription which he seems to have erected himself, recording his dedication of a golden image to Vishnu 'in his own image' which he set up at Prâsâd Khna.

[22] See Coedès, *IC V*, pp. 200-201.

[23] See his article 'The Khmer empire and the Malay peninsula', especially pp. 283-4. He assumes that the Khmers maintained close associations with the Bandon region of the Malay Peninsula after the demise of Funan's sea-power, until Śrîvijaya gained control in the 8th century. Furthermore a king of Tâmbralinga, known by the Chinese as To-hsi-chi, who sent an embassy to the Imperial court in 1001, married a Cambodian princess, their son being Sûryavarman. He notes two little-known inscriptions in praise of Sûryavarman, both from Barth, 'Prea Kev' (pp. 97-117) A, vv. 9-17, but nothing conclusive may be deduced from these.

[24] See Coedès, 'Inscription of Robang Romeas'. This records the setting up of a *Śiva-linga* by a certain Someśvarapaṇḍita, and the granting of territories, one of which had been obtained by the royal favour of Sûryavarmadeva. Concerning the site of Robang Romeas, see Tranet, *Sambaur-Prei-Kuk*, 2, p. 273-7.

[25] See Coedès and Dupont, 'Les stèles de Sdok Kak Thom etc.' already quoted above; for this quotation, vv. D.45-50, see Coedès, *APKh II*, p. 201 for the Khmer text and pp. 233-4 for the French translation. *Valabhi*, which Coedès leaves untranslated here, means in Sanskrit a 'pinnacle or raised building or a extra roof-structure'.

[26] An inscription (Coedès, *IC II*, pp. 29-30) dated 1019, refers to territory and personel given to Sûryaparvata, the god of Chisor, by Sûryavarman I. Two more inscriptions (*IC III*, 148-56) dated ?1015 and 1017 refer to gifts by a monk Śivâcarya for the founding of a monastery as authorized by the same king. A later inscription *(IC II*, pp. 137-9) dated 1116 refers to donations to the god Sûryaparavata by an ascetic of the royal household.

[27] See Coedès, *IC III*, pp. 3-24; two other inscriptions, *III*, pp. 122-5 and *IC VI*, pp. 287-92, refer to various donations and arrangements presumably in the vicinity during the reign of Udayâdityavarman.

[28] For the inscription see Coedès, *IC III*, pp. 26-28. Concerning these two temples and also Phnom Banon, see Lunet de Lajonquière, *Inventaire descriptif, III*, pp. 427-44, and Aymonier, *Le Cambodge*, II, pp. 287-302 (English version: *Khmer Heritage in the old Siamese Provinces of Cambodia*, pp. 97-96).

[29] See Coedès, 'Piédroit de Banan'.

[30] See Aymonier, *Khmer Heritage in the old Siamese provinces,* pp. 79-84, and my '*Khmer Civilization and Angkor*, p. 61. I must add that the photograph of the 10-armed tantric divinity in the same book (first edition) p. 62, is misplaced. It comes from the temple of Narai Jaeng Vaeng (see below) and must therefore be an image of Śiva.

[31] For an inscription, which is undated and incomplete, giving names of personnel, see Coedès, *IC III*, pp. 126-7.

[32] See also Roveda, *Preah Vihear*, pp. 82-83.

[33] See Coedès, *Indianized States*, p. 136, where he quotes as his source R.C. Majumdar, *Annual Report on Indian Epigraphy* (1949-50), p. 4.

[34] For detailed descriptions of these three temples see Freeman, *Khmer Temples,* pp. 214-8.

[35] They were described at the beginning of the 20th century by Aymonier. See *The Khmer Heritage in Thailand*, Phnom Wan, pp. 126-33; Phimai, pp. 140-147; Muang Tam and Phnom Rung, pp. 156-61. His observations have mainly historical value, as these temples have since been magnificently restored by the Fine Arts Department of the Government of Thailand. One may note that all these great 'temple-fortresses' are 'bantay' according to Khmer terminology, but in Thailand all ancient Khmer temples are referred to as *prâsâd*. See the Glossary.

[36] The source for this is a Cham inscription dated 1056. See *Études épigraphiques*, pp. 125-7

[37] Barth, 'Inscription de Preah Ngok'.

[38] To distinguish separately a list of Khmer names with no certain break between them, strung together in a Sanskrit verse is no easy task. I reproduce them as listed by Barth but inserting hyphens: Deva-khpal-khpas, Gñang-lam, Poh, Spot, Khmoññ, chief of Avadhyapura (possibly for Âḍhyapura). The verses translated here are nos 17-25 on side B.

[39] *ibid*, side C, v. 17 ff.

[40] Coedès and Dumont, 'Les stèles de Sdok Kak Thom etc.' vv.D. 82-85. See Coedès, *APKh II*, p. 203 Khmer text, and p. 241 French translation.

[41] *ibid.* vv. 120-124. See Coedès, *APKh II*, p. 197 for skr. text and p. 213 for French translation.

[42] See Aymonier, *Le Cambodge*, vol. 2, pp. 420-21. A more detailed description is given by Lunet de Lajonquière, *Inventaire descriptif*, vol. 3, pp. 248-52.

[43] Coedès, 'Piedroits de Nam Van'.

[44] See Coedès, 'La stele de Palhal'.

[45] See Barth, 'Lovek'.

[46] See Coedès, 'La date d'avènement du Harṣavarman III: l'inscription de Prâsâd Sralau'.

[47] See Aymonier, *Khmer Heritage in the old Siamese provinces*, pp. 195-200.

[48] See Coedès, 'Nouvelles données chronologiques et genéalogiques sur la dynastie de Mahidharapura'.

[49] To trace any of these routes with certainty or to locate a place-name such as Phumi-chhoen on existing maps is well-nigh impossible. I note that the sizeable town of Tbeng Meanchey appears to be the capital of Preah Vihear Province, and thus is locally referred to as Preah Vihear. Yet both places are marked as separate on existing maps. The actual fortress temple of Preah Vihear is some 80 km further north on the crest of the Dongrek range. All such distances given here indicate a straight line on the map from one place to another and thus take no account of the actual ground covered. E.g. the actual distance by road from Tbeng Meanchey to the foot of Preah Vihear summit, which we covered in February 2000 was nearer 145 km and not 80.

[50] Louis Delaporte, who reached the town of Stoung by negotiating narrow and difficult rivers, followed from there of necessity this overland route to reach Preah Khan. With buffalo-drawn wagons the journey took five days. We covered the same route, a mere 50 km, with a four-wheel drive vehicle in about five hours. For his description of the ruins of Preah Khan see his *Voyage au Cambodge*, pp. 57-89.

[51] It this respect it is interesting to note that there are three badly preserved inscriptions on the central sanctuary. One of these on the south tower (K.707) has a date corresponding to AD 997 and pays homage to Vishnu and Śiva (in fact Hari and Śankara) and refers to Jayavarman (V) and the Brahman Śivâcârya. The inscription on the central tower (K.706) again pays homage to Śiva and praises a king (name missing) but probably Jayavarman V, since Śivâcarya in named again as making substantial gifts to Bhadreśvara. This has a date that may correspond to 1003 (or 1013). The one on the northern tower has a date corresponding to AD 1019 but it is too badly ruined to make any sense. See Coedès, *IC V*, pp. 216-21. All that one deduces from this is that others were interested in Preah Khan before Sûryavarman I had anything to do with it.

[52] Louis Delaporte, who seems to have been the first to note this inscription gives a translation (*Voyage au Cambodge*, pp. 411-2) which he attributes to M. Aymonier. But a totally revised text and translation is given by Finot in 'L'Inscription de Preah Khan'. I am also grateful to my friend Kamaleswar Bhattacharya (see his article 'L'état actuel des travaux sur les inscriptions sanskrites du Cambodge') for drawing my attention to a strange error in Finot's translation and also resolving other problems in this text.

Chapter 5

[1] By this time the Syam (from which name Siam derives) had already occupied the upper Chao Phraya Valley, and were well known to their Burmese, Khmer and Champa neighbours as auxiliary troops (as in the present case) or as slaves.

[2] For Sûryavarman II's interest in this site see Coedès, 'Stèle de Wat Ph'u'.

[3] Concerning the Mahîdharapura dynasty, see Coedès, *Indianized States*, pp. 152-4, and 'Nouvelles données chronologiques et genéalogiques sur la dynastie de Mahîdharapura'.

[4] For a detailed description and some fine photographs see Freeman, *Khmer Temples*, pp. 70-89 and *Palaces of the Gods*, pp. 229-65.

[5] One may refer to a brief article by Finot, 'Dharmaçâlas au Cambodge'. This contains a sketch-map showing the 'rest-houses' later built along this route by Jayavarman VII. The road and the precise number of stages are mentioned in the Preah Khan inscription. See Coedès, *APKh II*, p. 160.

[6] For the inscription see Coedès, 'Epigraphie du temple de Phimai'. Coedès recalls that this Vîrendrâdipativarman is one of the high dignitaries who figures in the grand procession on the carved panels of Angkor Vat and thus is closely associated with Sûryavarman II.

[7] The divinities, of which Vajrapâni's maṇḍala is composed, are listed in the long introduction to the *Sarva-tathâgata-tattva.sangraha, facsimile reproduct-ion* by Lokesha Chandra and myself, New Delhi 1981, p. 49. I have translated the full account of this triumph over the great Hindu gods, as recounted in this important

tantra, in my *Indo-Tibetan Buddhism*, pp. 136-41.

[8] See Freeman, *Khmer Temples*, pp. 145-50, and *Palace of the Gods*, pp. 134-45.

[9] See Freeman, *Khmer Temples*, pp. 170-173.

[10] See Freeman, *Khmer Temples*, p. 93 and pp. 96-97.

[11] This site was noted by Aymonier. See *The Khmer Heritage in Thailand*, pp. 178-9.

[12] For the inscription, see Coedès, *IC VI*, pp. 281-3.

[13] See Har Dayal, *The Bodhisattva Doctrine*, pp. 80-164.

[14] Roveda, *Sacred Angkor*.

[15] These are later 16th century additions. See Chapter 6, p. 188.

[16] I note that Bhandari, *Saving Angkor,* pp. 151-3, refutes this theory vigorously. He adduces a rather surprising theory for the anticlockwise direction of the friezes; namely that since the Indian *devanagari* script is written from left to right, so art and sculpture must be likewise 'read' left to right. If this were so, all such temples with friezes or a series of paintings would be expected to conform to his rule, and they patently do not. He argues also that no one in the Hindu tradition builds a funeral temple, because the physical remains must be returned to the natural elements. Thus one may well question whether the king's Brahmanical entourage would have agreed to such a procedure. This is a valid point. He suggests also that this great shrine faces west because this is a more convenient approach for a ceremonial procession from Angkor Thom of which the centre was still the Baphuon. In this respect it is fair to point out that other important Khmer temples face directions other than the usual east, simply for reasons of convenience. Preah Vihear faces north while Ta Muen Thom and Phimai face south.

[17] I retain the usual popular spelling of this name, although phonetically I would prefer to write Beung Mia-lia. A long â in Khmer spelling in some consonantal formations is pronounced as 'ia' phonetically. In English this might sound as 'ea' as in hear or 'ie' in bier.

[18] See Coedès, 'Note sur l'iconographie de Beng Mâlâ'.

[19] Concerning this Yaśovarman see Coedès' article on the Mahîdharapura dynasty (see note 3 above), p. 307 ff. where there a discussion of this strange attack by the Daitya Râhu and the identity of the prince who came to his rescue. See also Briggs, *The Ancient Khmer Empire*, p. 206. He suggests that Indrakumâra was a son of Jayavarman VII.

[20] See 'La grande stèle du Phimânâkas', Coedès, *IC II*, pp. 161-81. There is no date, but the text refers to the treachery against Yaśovarman and the war with the Chams, as well as the foundation of both the great temples of Preah Khan and Ta Prohm at Angkor. Thus it is datable to the end of the 12th century.

[21] Inscriptions were found at these four shrines. See Coedès, *IC IV*, pp. 207-53. Since the NW inscription was never finished and because of other scribal defects, he suggests that the walls, like the Bayon, were not completed until after Jayavarman's death.

[22] Avalokiteśvara, the Lord who looks down (in compassion) is by far the most popular of bodhisattvas throughout the whole Mahâyâna Buddhist world, while he remains well represented in the earlier period in lands where Theravâda Buddhism now prevails. (Strangely in China and thus elsewhere in the Far East, where his name was correctly translated as Kuan-Yin, he was popularly treated as 'Goddess of Mercy', thus feminine in aspect.) As for his origins, it is probably correct to regard him as representing the future Sâkyamuni, who still as a bodhisattva looked down *(avalokita)* in compassion on the world from the Tuśita Heaven before finally resolving to accept rebirth in order to show the way to salvation to all living beings. At the same time he is often referred to as *Lokeśvara* (Lord of the World), a title which usually applies to Śiva, especially in Khmer texts.

[23] See Dagens, Bruno, 'Étude sur l'iconographie du Bayon (frontons et lintaux)'.

[24] I note from Maurice Glaize's excellent guide-book, *Les monuments du groupe d'Angkor*, p. 141, that the name Palilay derives from 'Pârilyyaka', the name of the forest near Kosambhi, where this event is said to have taken place.

[25] See Glaize, *Les monuments du groupe d'Angkor,* pp. 129-30, and Giteau, *Iconographie du Cambodge post-Ankorienne,* pp. 113-6.

[26] See Coedès, 'La stèle de Prah Khan d'Angkor', vv. 33-35. The verses selected are: 32-36 and 72-77. In this context the 'Lotus-Eyed' is presumably Vishnu, although this would be a more suitable epithet for Varuṇa, god of the Waters. The three 'Watering places' (*tîrṭha*) are the three lakes mentioned just above in my text.

[27] Having recently measured it, we find it just 6.4 m square. John Sanday, who first noted this, has also drawn my attention to the traces of the depicting of Buddhist imagery and also traces of colouring on some walls in the inner shrines. See his article 'The Triumphs and Perils of Khmer Architecture' in *Angkor and ten centuries of Khmer art.* I note that the French edition, *Angkor et dix siècles d'art Khmer*, translates the title of this article as 'L'architecture Khmer, un colosse aux pieds d'argile'.

[28] Coedès, 'La stèle de Ta-Prohm'.

[29] See Victor Goloubew, 'Le cheval Balaha'.

[30] See Finot, 'Inscriptions de Mi-song, no. 24', *Études épigraphiques sur le pays Cham*, p. 152 ff. and specifically pp. 156-7. (The 32 marks of perfection, e.g.

well-set feet, long fingers, soft skin, long ear-lobes etc. were regarded as the outward signs of Buddhahood or of a world-conqueror. See my *Indo-Tibetan Buddhism*, p. 32.)

[31] See Finot, 'Inscriptions de Mi-song, no. 11', *Études épigraphiques sur le pays Cham*, and specifically p.89.

[32] See Freeman, *Khmer Temples,* pp. 238-40, noting that he laments the ill-conceived work of restoration, which gives an inadequate idea of the original.

[33] I first visited this haunting and suggestive site with Vutthy in January 1999. A succinct description of Bantay Chmar (meaning the 'Fortress-temple of Cats', obviously a local nickname) is available in Freeman, *Khmer Temples,* pp.136-41. Of importance is the article by Groslier, 'Étude sur le temps passé à la construction d'un grand temple khmer'. I note also the article by Coedès, 'Quelques suggestions sur la méthode à suivre pour interpréter les bas-reliefs de Bantay Chmar et de la galerie extérieur du Bayon'.

[34] Some good illustrations of these many images of Hevajra can be seen in the catalogue of the exhibition *Angkor et dix siècles d'art khmer.* There is also an article by Wibke Lobo, 'L'image de Hevajra et le bouddhisme tantrique', pp. 71-78, but apart from a general description of tantric Buddhism, it adds little precise information concerning the rôle of Hevajra in Cambodia, simply because information is lacking. She suggests that Hevajra may have been referred to as *Vajrin* in Cambodia. However all the contexts in which the name Vajrin appears on inscriptions clearly relates this name to Vajrapâṇi, just as the abbreviated name Lokeśa refers to Avalokiteśvara. The two abbreviated names often occur together, as may be shown from some of the extracts quoted above. It may seem superfluous to mention in this note my edition of the *Hevajra-Tantra,* London Oriental Series 1959, and several later editions, but I take this opportunity of drawing attention to my later discourses on Hevajra, to be found in my *Indo-Tibetan Buddhism,* especially pp. 248-62 and other briefer references to be found in the index.

[35] See Chirapat Prapandvidya, 'The Sab Bâk inscriptions: evidence of early Vajrayâna Buddhist presence in Thailand'.

[36] See Hall, *A History of South-East Asia*, p. 85.

[37] See Trouvé, 'Le Prasat Tor', and for the inscription, Coedès, 'La Stèle de Prâsât Tor'.

[38] See Coedès, *Indianized States*, p. 173.

Chapter 6

[1] See Briggs, *The Ancient Khmer Empire*, p. 238 for this reference, noting that the king is Indravarman II, not III. See v. 13 of the Mangalârtha inscription, reference in following note.

[2] See Finot, 'Le temple de Mangalârtha'; also included in Finot, *Guide to the Temple of Bantay Srei,* inscription 10, pp. 84-89, verse 13.

[3] See Ishizawa and Marui, 'La découverte de 274 sculptures'.

[4] See Briggs, *The Ancient Khmer Empire*, p. 251; see also Finot, *Guide to the Temple,* inscription 5, pp. 78-82, v. 12.

[5] G. Coedès, 'La date d'avènement de Jayavarman Parameśvara'. For the inscription see Bergaigne, 'Inscription d'Angkor Vat'.

[6] See Coedès, 'La plus ancienne inscription en Pâli de Cambodge'.

[7] For my quotations from this important document I use the English version, first published by the Siam Society in Bangkok 1987, 3rd ed. 1993, entitled *The Customs of Cambodia* by Chou Ta-kuan, *translated into English from the French version of Paul Pelliot of Chou's Chinese original by J. Gilman d'Arcy Paul.* Pelliot's first French translation was published in the *BEFEO II*, pp. 123-77. An amended version by him was published as *Mémoires sur les coutumes du Cambodge de Tcheou*, Adrien Maisonneuve, Paris, 1951.

[8] By Siam only Sukhothai might be intended, but such an attack seems unlikely. See also Wyatt, *Thailand,* p. 58 and note 16, Ch. 6 below.

[9] A detailed study of the Khmer army, based on these carvings has been made by Jacq-Hergoualc'h, *L'armament et l'organization de l'armée khmère.*

[10] See Coedès, *Indianized States*, pp.184-5. Also Hall, *History of S.E. Asia,* p. 70. Wyatt, in *Thailand,* p. 51, argues that a Thai ruling family was established there by the mid-13th century.

[11] See Coedès, *Indianized States,* pp. 208-9, and Wyatt, *Thailand*, pp. 47-48.

[12] See Coedès, *Indianized States*, pp.177-8. The source for this is Pe Maung Tin and Luce, *The Glass Palace Chronicle of the Kings of Burma,* a partial translation of the *Hmannan Yazawin*, London, 1923, Rangoon reprint 1960, p.142.

[13] See Coedès, *Indianized States*, p. 208 for references regarding these embassies sent by Lopburi. Concerning Mongol intrusions into this part of S-E Asia following upon the accession of Kublai Khan as Emperor of China, effectively from 1263 when he founded a new capital at Peking, see primarily Coedès, *Indianized States,* pp. 169-88: 'The repercussions of the Mongol Conquests'. One may also see Wyatt, *Thailand*, pp. 42-43 with reference to the collapse of the Burmese kingdom of Pagan, and especially pp. 48-49 where the Thais themselves were concerned. Fortunately for Cambodia, Champa succeeded in beating off Mongolian attacks, 1281 onwards. See Hall, *History of S.E. Asia,* p. 208. Mongol attempts directed at suzerainty over Java were equally

unsuccessful; see my *Asian Commitment*, Ch. X, p. 406.

[14] See Wyatt, *Thailand*, p.65 ff. I note also Fouser, *The Lord of the Golden Tower*. Although concerned specifically with King Prasat Thong (1629-1656), it provides a useful survey of the earlier cultural dependence of Ayuthaya upon Angkor.

[15] One such has been translated by Doudard de Lagrée and edited by Grenier, 'Chronique royale de Cambodge'. Two other recessions have been interpreted by Moura in *Le Royaume de Cambodge*; they have also been used by Leclère in his *Histoire du Cambodge*, Paris. A critical study of the whole *genre* has recently been made by Vickery, *Cambodia after Angkor*. Another detailed study has also been made by Khin Sok, *Chroniques royales du Cambodge*.

[16] See Coedès, *Indianized States*, pp. 236-7, and Wyatt, *Thailand*, pp. 68-69. However Briggs in a well argued article, in which he checks Khmer, Ayuthayan and Chinese sources, 'Siamese attacks on Angkor before 1430', insists that there was no Siamese occupation and sacking of Angkor before 1430, although the two capital cities were constantly at war.

[17] For Vickery's slightly variant account see *Society, Economics and Politics*, pp. 492-3.

[18] See Chandler, *A History of Cambodia*, pp. 77-78, concerning 'The shift from Angkor to Phnom Penh.'

[19] See Khin Sok, *Chroniques royales*, pp. 174-5. See also his *Le Cambodge entre le Siam et le Vietnam (de 1775-1860)*, p. 30.

[20] For a discussion concerning the validity of this date see Khin Sok, *Chroniques royales*, pp. 45-49.

[21] See Briggs, 'Spanish Intervention in Cambodia'. Also see Groslier, *Angkor et le Cambodge au XVIe Siècle*, pp. 24-26 and 34-62.

[22] According to Khin Sok's genealogical table of Khmer kings (*Le Cambodge entre le Siam et le Vietnam*, back-folder) he is listed as Barom Reachea V, because he applies the numeration to other intervening kings. It would seem that such numeration becomes confusing in that all Khmer kings merit this title (*=Paramarâja*) whether formally attached to their name or not.

[23] See Groslier, *Angkor et le Cambodge*, p. 56

[24] These events are recounted in Moura, *Le Royaume du Cambodge*, pp. 57-58 and dated to 1590-91, but they must have occurred somewhat later.

[25] See also Bhandari, *Saving Angkor*, pp. 90-93. For a detailed discussion of the carvings see Madelaine Giteau, *L'iconographie du Cambodge*, pp. 93-111. She notes in detail the discrepancies in the iconography of the major figures. Thus Agni is conventionally seated on a ram, not a rhinoceros, as here. Enthroned on Kailâsa, Śiva should appear in all his glory, not as an ascetic as might be suitable in a forest scene. She notes also the particularities of the garments and ornaments, some of which might suit 16th century usage.

[26] See Saveros Lewitz, 'Textes en Khmer moyen: inscriptions modernes d'Angkor 2 & 3'.

[27] See Saveros Lewitz, 'Les inscriptions modernes d'Angkor Vat'.

[28] See Har Dayal, *The Bodhisattva Doctrine*, p. 64 ff.

[29] Concerning these lunar months, see note 18, Ch. 7. In this particular year the month of Âsâḍh *(skr.* Âṣâḍha) will have been doubled as a 13th month to compensate for the accumulating discrepancy between the lunar and solar year.

[30] I quote from Saveros Lavitz, 'Inscriptions modernes d'Angkor', pp. 113-6, pp. 102-3 and pp. 226-8. Apart from the titles, the curious term *brei* rendered here as 'country class' must be noted as well as the term for the lowest hell, translatable as 'fivefold immediate' and according to André Bareau probably synonymous with the Avîci Hell, where those guilty of the five heinous sins, matricide, patricide, killing a saint (arhat), wounding a Buddha or creating schism, suffer immediate punishment. For similar texts see Aymoner, *Le Cambodge*, vol.3, p. 291 ff. Also Saveros Lewitz, 'Inscriptions modernes d'Angkor', pp. 101-21 and 221-47. A full list of her publication of these inscriptions (also under the name of Saveros Pou) will be found in her *Nouvelles Inscriptions du Cambodge*, vol.1, p. 124. These are followed by her *Nouvelles Inscriptions du Cambodge*, vols 2 and 3.

[31] See Skilling, 'Some literary references in the *Grande Inscription d'Angkor* (IMA 38)'.

[32] For her translation of this text (no. 38) see 'Inscriptions modernes d'Angkor'.

[33] See Aymonier, *Khmer Heritage in the old Siamese provinces*, pp. 208-11.

[34] This text was first noticed by Professor C.R. Boxer of the University of London, who reported it at the 23rd International Congress of Orientalists held in Cambridge in 1954. A French translation together with other contemporary accounts is available in Groslier, *Angkor et le Cambodge au xvi siècle*, pp. 64-89.

Chapter 7

[1] This situation continued until the French formally annexed Cochinchina, the southern part of Annam (largely filched from the Cambodians by the Vietnamese during the previous two centuries) from the control of the Annamese court in Hue in 1862. The whole of Annam became a French protectorate in 1883. The last king of Annam, Bao Dai, was recognized as emperor of all Vietnamese, but was deposed in 1955. French sources continue to use the name Annam (deriving from Chinese An-nam = 'Pacified South'), but since winning their prolonged wars of independence against France and the

USA, Vietnam has becomes the established name of the now unified country.

[2] These and succeeding events are covered by an account by a Dutchman, Gerard van Wusthok, *Récit succinct de ce qui s'est passé de curieux aux Indes orientales, dans le royaume de Cambodge, entre les années 1635 et 1644*. See Leclère, *Histoire du Cambodge*, p. 343.

[3] It will have already been noted that the Chams were present in large numbers in Cambodia, ever since their country had been finally wiped off the map by the Vietnamese (namely the kingdom of Annam) in 1471. Over this period the Chams, a coastal people, were largely converted to Islam at the time that the whole of the Malay archipelago was likewise converted. Thus they readily consorted with the Malay traders in Cambodia, since they were their fellow co-religionists.

[4] According to Khin Sok's account, *op. cit.*, p. 35, the king of Annam, angry that the Khmers had turned against the Vietnamese who had gone to help them, ordered the release of Ibrahim but he died on the way to Annam. However there is no essential contradiction here. The order for his release came too late.

[5] It is interesting to note that one of the last recorded inscriptions at Angkor Vat (dated AD 1747) set up by a high official (*Uk-ña*) named Vongsa Aggraj gives some details of the troubled reign of this king. See Chandler, *Facing the Cambodian Past,* pp. 15-21: 'An eighteenth century inscription from Angkor Wat'.

[6] Apart from the Chronicles, this terrible story of the Vietnamese occupation is told in a separate work by a monk-official named Pich with the title of Batum Baramey, 'Perfection of the Lotus-flower', edited and translated by Khin Sok, *L'annexation du Cambodge par les vietnamiens au XIXe siècle d'après les deux poèmes du vénérable Bâtum Baramey Pich.*

[7] See Osbourne, *The French Presence*, p. 28 and note 48 on p. 296.

[8] See Bernon, 'Le plus ancien edifice subsistant de Phnom Penh: une tour angkorienne sise dans l'énceinte de Vatt Uṇṇalom'.

[9] For an English translation of these stories see Wray, Rosenfeld and Bailey, *Ten Lives of the Buddha.*

[10] See Pang, 'Lpoek Angar Vat', in Aymonier, *Textes Khmers*, extract 2.

[11] The founder of the Dhammayutika-nikâya was Prince Mongkut (1804-1868) of Thailand, who during the reign of his elder half-brother, Rama III, devoted himself entirely to the religious life, gradually creating this reformed religious order (by about the year 1830). On ascending the throne in 1851 he modified some of the changes, primarily those of monastic dress, in accordance with popular demand. See Wyatt, *Thailand,* pp. 175-91. The 'reformed' Dhammayutika order was introduced into Cambodia by King Ang Duong (1847-1860) but it probably proved less acceptable in Cambodia than in Thailand.

[12] The most recent studies carried out on 'unorthodox Buddhist practices' in Cambodia are those by François Bizot under the general title of *Recherches sur le bouddhisme khmer*, notably *Le figuier a cinq branches*, and *Le don de soi-même*. I draw attention again to Kamla Tiyavanich, *Forest Recollections*, which provides an important incidental account of the varieties of Buddhist practice encountered by these monks on their wanderings, which certainly included the Khmer districts of Sisophon and Battembang. It also draws attention to the widespread belief in the potentially malevolent operations of local spirits and the need for their propitiation by 'spirit-doctors' to the general detriment of the practice of Buddhism.

[13] See Saveros Pou, *Nouvelles Inscription du Cambodge*, I, 'Inscription du monastère de Tâ Tok (K.292)', pp. 58-65. Note also the improved version by Bernon, 'Une relecture de l'inscription K.892 provenant de Vatt Tâ Tok'.

[14] These represent a composite set of various conventional groups covering the whole practice of the religious life. There are inevitable duplications. They include the 'four applications of mindfulness' (with regard to the body, feeling, thoughts and phenomena), the 'four exertions' against evil influences, the 'four wonder-working powers', the 'five faculties' (viz. faith, energy, mindfulness, concentration and wisdom), the 'five powers' (a variable list, e.g. meritorious works, patience, exertion, meditation and knowledge), the 'five constituents of enlightenment' (mindfulness, discernment, energy, rapture, serenity), and finally the 'noble eightfold way', viz. right views, right intention, right speech, right action, right livelihood, right effort, right mindfulness and right concentration. See Har Dayal, *The Bodhisattva Doctrine*, pp. 80-164.

[15] Bernon, 'Une relecture de l'inscription K.892', pp. 24-25.

[16] See Khin Sok, *Le Cambodge entre le Siam et le Vietnam,* pp. 134-7.

[17] See my *Indo-Tibetan Buddhism*, pp. 19-22 on personality as 'non-self' and later entries in the index on 'consciousness' (*vijñâna*).

[18] The Sanskrit names of the months are: Çaitra (March – April), Vaiśâkha (April – May), Jyaiṣṭha (May to June), Âṣâḍha (June–July), Śrâvaṇa (July–August), Bhadrapada (August – September), Âśvina (September – October), Kârttika (October – November), Mârgaśîrṣa (November – December), Pauṣa (December – January), Mârga (January – February) and Phâlguna (February – March).

[19] I note the cases of two great prelates who lived during

the reign of King Norodom, namely Sanghareach Teang and Sokuntheathipadei Pan, quoted by Khin Sok, *Le Cambodge entre le Siam et le Vietnam,*, pp. 269-71.

[20] See Saveros Pou, *Nouvelles Inscriptions*, I, pp. 126-7.

[21] See Saveros Pou, *Nouvelles Inscriptions du Cambodge*, pp. 118-32, 'Le Pâli au Cambodge'.

[22] See Jacob, *Reamker (Râmakerti), the Cambodian version of the Râmâyana.* For a French translation, interpreted as tantric symbolism, see Bizot, *Râmaker ou l'Amour symbolique de Râm et Seta.*

[23] See Saveros Pou and Philip N. Jenner, 'Les Cpap ou "codes de conduite" khmers', *BEFEO 62* ((1975), pp. 369-94, and later volumes, up to *BEFEO 70* (1981), pp. 135-93. See also the short article by Chandler, 'Normative Poems (Chbap) and pre-Colonial Society', in *Facing the Cambodian Past,* pp. 45-60. See also the short article on Cambodian literature by Judith Jacob in Dingwall, *Travellers' Literary Companions*, pp. 154-75.

[24] For his personal account of his travels see *Voyage dans les royaumes de Siam, de Cambodge, de Laos*, as extracted from his journal and correspondence by Ferdinand de Lanoye, first published in 1868 and now reprinted by Éditions Olizane, Geneva.

[25] Assuming AD 2003 corresponds to 2546/7 BE. The year 543/4 BC is accepted as the conventional date of Sâkyamuni's final nirvâṇa in the Theravâda countries of South-East Asia, noting that the Buddhist year begins in April. However a corrected version of this Theravâda tradition would date the final nirvâṇa around about 480. This is more in accord with Mahâyâna sources which suggest various dates about a century before the reign of the Emperor Aśoka, thus about 380 BC at the latest. Much scholarly work has been spent on this question, yielding no firm result. See the article by Ruegg, 'A new publication on the date and the historiography of the Buddha's decease'. Since it is asserted traditionally that Sâkyamuni lived to the age of 80, his date of birth is a simple calculation with no independent value of its own.

[26] See the article by Bernon, 'Le Buddh Damnây, note sur un texte apocalyptique khmer'.

[27] See the last paragraph of Chapter 6.

[28] There is no other suitable name for the southern part of Vietnam known by the French as *Cochinchine.* The name was already in general use by the Portuguese in the 16th century. The Malays knew this region as Kuchi (possibly derived from Annamite Kuu-chön) and –china was attached to distinguish it from Kuchi (Cochin) in India. See *Hobson-Jobson*, p. 226.

[29] Note the report which the Governor of Indochina, Le Myre de Viliers, sent to the French Minister of the Colonies in April 1882 concerning King Norodom's lavish court, quoted by Osbourne, *The French Presence in Cochinchina and Cambodia*, pp. 201-2

[30] Translated and quoted from Mouhot, *Voyages dans les royaumes*, pp. 1-2.

[31] See the chapter by Osbourne 'Francis Garnier (1839-1873) explorer of the Mekong River'.

[32] The account of his journey, *Voyage au Cambodge*, including that of a tour of his colleague M. Faraut to the Battambang area, first published by the Librarie Delagrave in 1880, has been reprinted by Maissonneuve & Larose, Paris 1999. He also took back to Paris an important collection of large pieces, which are now on display in the Musée Guimet in Paris. Although this may be regarded by some as reprehensible, we must note that they would otherwise have been lost irretrievably on account of the looting and destruction which has since taken place, especially over the last 30 years.

[33] A succinct account will be found in Chandler, *A History of Cambodia,* p. 204 ff. A far more detailed account with numerous personal case-histories is that of Vickery, *Cambodia 1975-1982.* The best personal account is that by Bizot, who was himself a prisoner of the Khmer Rouge in 1971, *Le Portail.*

[34] An English edition of some parts of his work is now available, namely *The Khmer Heritage in the old Siamese provinces of Cambodia,* and *The Khmer Heritage in Thailand.*

[35] See Klairung Amratisha, *The Cambodian Novel*, p. 60 ff. One may hope that this excellent work with its detailed survey of modern Khmer literature may soon be published in book form.

[36] A recent article by Bernon, 'Le rituel de la 'grande probation annuelle' (*mahâparivâsa*) des religieux de Cambodge', serves to illustrate the great progress which has been made and the popular following for the institution of even supplementary religious ceremonies which might seem to have been almost forgotten.

[37] One may note for example the week-end edition (1-2 November 03) of *The Cambodian Daily*, pp.4-5, which gives a survey of recent vicious crimes for which the perpetrators have not been brought to justice. I mention from personal experience the case of our motorcyclist-companion Chok who may be seen in an illustration on p.29. He disapppeared some two years ago. He was found a week later tied against a tree in the forest near Sambor Prei Kuk. He had been blindfolded and then shot. The only known motive for this butally staged crime was to steal his motorcycle.

[38] Leclère, *Cambodge: fêtes civiles et religieuses*. For a brief account of his life and numerous other publications see Tranet, 'Adhémard Leclère: Sa Vie, ses travaux', *Seksa Khmer 7* (1984), pp. 3-33.

Glossary

Abhidharma, 'Further Dharma', the third part of the Pâli and other early Buddhist canons. It comprises primarily philosophical disquisitions on the nature of phenomenal existence (*samsâra*) and its relationship to nirvâṇa, but includes also quasi-historical accounts of the Buddha's life-time.

Agastya, a north-Indian Brahman, renowned as a missionary to South India, thus becoming the 'patron-saint' of the Tamils. His seated cross-legged image appears on many temples, often replacing earlier small Buddha-images.

Aparṇâ, a Himalayan nymph, known as the 'mountain-self-born' (Açalâtmajâ) who becomes the spouse of Śiva. She is also known as Parvatî (from *parvata*, skr. for mountain, with the feminine î ending.) See also Bhagavatî.

Apsara (*skr.*), a celestial maiden.

Arhat, meaning literally 'worthy', is a term used to define the highest state of perfection as might be obtained by a Buddhist monk according to the teachings of early Buddhist sects, including the Theravâda. He has attained nirvana and will be reborn no more. See Mahâyâna.

Ashram, a hermitage (*skr. âśrama*).

Bantay (Khmer: bantây), a temple-fortress.

Baray, a term referring to artificial lakes, as built at Angkor, which may be derived from skr. *pârâyana,* suggesting a vast space.

Bell (*skr.* ghaṇṭhâ), a bell. See vajra below.

Bhagavad, the lord, referring to Buddha in any Buddhist context.

Bhagavatî, the lady, usually referring to the spouse of Śiva under whatever name she may be known, e.g. Aparṇâ, Devî (the goddess), Gaurî, Parvatî, Umâ, or in her fierce manifestation as Durgâ.

Brah (Khmer), holy or sacred. Pronounced as Preah in modern Khmer, it occurs in many sacred place-names or titles. The literary spelling Brah is retained for the title Brah Guru in my text.

Brahmanical, referring to all that pertains to the traditions and teachings of learned Indian Brahmans. The term may be contrasted with Hindu, referring to all the later accretions of Indian popular religion, which had little or no influence in Cambodia, notably the whole Indian caste-system. Thus the ancient Khmers readily accepted Brahmanical traditions, but it may be misleading to refer to their religion as Hindu.

Bodhisattva (*skr.*), a human or supernatural being intent upon the acquisition of enlightenment (*bodhi*). Used in the following contexts:
i. of Sâkyamuni previous to his enlightenment. He is the Bodhisattva *par excellence,* and since there are many legendary stories of his having been born as a virtuous animal, the term would still apply in such non-human cases;
ii. of monks and layfolk of the Mahâyâna tradition whose goal is final enlightement;
iii. divine beings, often portrayed as human in previous births, who have achieved a state of supernatural existence, but delay their entry into final enlightenment (Buddhahood) so that they may continue to assist suffering living beings, viz. such as Avalokiteśvara, Maitreya and Vajrapâni.

çaitya (*skr.),* (Pâli çetiya, pron. çaetday in Khmer), a shrine of various kinds, but often referring to a stûpa.

çaṇḍi, a term commonly used in Java referring to ancient Buddhist or Bhahmanical shrines. Its derivation seems to be unknowm, but I would take it as a nazalized version of the previous term. There is no semantic connection with *skr*, çaṇḍa, meaning fierce, and Çaṇḍikâ, a fierce goddess, identified with Durgâ.

Çittamâtra (*skr.*), 'Mind-Only' or 'Mere Thought', the definitive school of Buddhist philosoply. See Yogaçâra below.

Devarâja, see 'Note on the Devarâja' in Chapter 3.

Gandharva (*skr*), a celestial musician.

Gopura (*skr.*), an ornate entrance to a palace or temple, often built of stone.

Hînayâna (*skr.*), the 'inferior way' of Buddhist practice, according to the followers of the Mahâyâna, the 'superior way'. A more polite term is Śrâvakayâna. See below.

Hindu, In its widest sense this term means simply Indian, as in Hindustan, the name for India. In a more restricted sense it refers to Hindu religion as opposed to Islam, and so one would scarcely refer to an Indian Muslim as Hindu, although he is certainly Indian. In a religious sense the term includes all indigenous religious systems from the early Brahmanical period (see Brahmanical) down to the popular Hinduism of later days, which embrace many local cults and practices more or less adapted to Hindu traditional customs. One essential aspect of Hindu religion is the strict caste-system, which makes life even more miserable than need be for those who are excluded from higher social rankings. Although Khmer inscriptions make a clear distinction between aristocrats and common folk, it is misleading to refer to the Brahmanical religion, as fostered by the ancient Khmer rulers, as Hindu. It is even misleading to define Khmer temples as Hindu, as distinct from Buddhist, as is done in many popular guide-books. The proper term is Brahmanic. In the wider sense of the term Hindu, all Khmer temples, whether Brahmanic or Buddhist, are subject to Hindu influence.

Homa (*skr.*), a Brahmanic sacrifical burnt offering, primarily of clarified butter, which was later adopted in tantric Buddhism.

Jâtaka (*skr.*), a 'rebirth-story', usually recounting the exploits of the future Buddha Sâkyamuṇi in his previous lives, often as a virtuous animal, as noted above under Bodhisattva.

Kâla (*skr.*), time or the god of time, often appearing as a fierce mask above doorways; see Mahâkâla below.

Kauravas, descendents of Kuru, See Pânḍavas.

Kinnara (*skr.* literally: 'what! a man?), a celestial sprite, an imp.

kuḍu, architectural term referring to a small decorative circular device usually embracing a human face.

linga, a phallic symbol representing Śiva; it appears in many names, e.g. Lingaparvata (Linga Mountain) above Vat Phu, or Lingapura (Linga Citadel), ancient Khmer stronghold near the same site.

Madhyamaka, lit. 'middle way' an important Buddhist philosophical system, which maintains a middle way between assertion and denial. See my *Indo-Tibetan Buddhism*, p.81 ff.

Mahâkâla, a fierce protective divinity.

Mahârshi, a great sage; see rishi.

Mahâyâna, the 'Great Way' of Buddhism. This represents the later phase of Buddhist developments from the early centuries AD onwards, based upon the philosophical theories of the Madhyamikas and the later ones of the Yogaçâras. It includes a whole new range of *sûtras* (doctrinal treatises) which proclaim the transcendence of the Buddha and the practice of the way of the Bodhisattva as the ideal religious life, thus treating as inferior the earlier goal of arhatship. It had a strong following in mainland South-East Asia up to the 13th century, when it was gradually replaced by the Theravâda. It also disappeared from India about the same time, largely due to devastating Muslim invasions. It survives now in Tibet, Mongolia and China, and may be said to flourish in Japan.

Maṇḍala, a circle. It may refer to the circle of four continents around the central Mount Meru of Indian tradition, a circle of shrines round a central major shrine, a circle of divinities around a central divinity. In symbolic form it often serves as the place for tantric ritual.

Maṇḍapa, the vestible which opens out towards the central shrine of a temple.

Mantra, a 'spell' to invoke a chosen divinity, often representing the feminine aspect of a male divinity. E.g. the 'spell' of Avalokiteśvara is *oṃ mânipadme huṃ*, referring to the Lady of the Jewel-lotus, namely Târâ, the 'Saviouress'.

Meru, the central mountain of Indian tradition, usually identified geographically as Mount Kailasa.

Mudrâ (*skr.*), a hand-gesture, as used to distinguish the attitude of any particular divinity, e.g. to differentiate the Five Buddhas of Mahâyâna tradition.

Nâga, a serpent.

Nâṛâyana, an epithet (from *skr.* nara = man) of the primeval man (*purusa*), applied to Visnu especially as the primal being from whose navel Brahmâ is born on a lotus-stalk, a common motif on Khmer stone carvings.

Nyâya (logic), an Indian philosophical system.

Pânḍavas, the descendents of Pânḍu. The feud between these five brothers and their rivals, the Kauravas provides the main theme of the great Indian epic, the Mahâbhârata. The great battle of Kurukśetra is carved on the walls of Angkor Vat.

Pâśupâta, a follower of Paśupati (Lord of the Herds), a title of Śiva.

Perfection of Wisdom (*skr.* Prajñâpâramitâ)
i. the name given to a collection of early Mahâyâna sûtras (discourses) which denounce the Abhidharma of the Srâvakas and propound a doctrine of absolute relativity.
ii. the Great Goddess of Mahâyâna Buddhism who symbolizes this Perfeçtion of Wisdom.

Prâsâda (*skr.*), temple, as used of many Khmer temples. One may contrast 'Bantay', properly used of a temple-fortress, such as Bantay Chmar. However in Thailand all such great temple-fortress are known as Prâsâda, e.g. Prâsâd Phimai, which in Cambodia would certainly qualify as a 'bantay'.

Preah, see Brah.

Pura (*skr.* a citadel), occurring in many Khmer place-names.

Rig Veda (*skr*. ṛg-veda), literally 'knowledge of the ṛc, sacred verses', namely the first of four such Brahmanical compilations of ancient knowledge (Veda).

Rishi (*skr*. ṛṣi), an Indian sage.

Śaka, this Indian era widely used in South and South-East Asia, begins in AD 78 about the middle of March.

Skanda, leader of Śiva's hosts again the enemies of the gods, thus a god of war.

Śakti, (*skr*. lit. power or potency), the feminine partner of a Hindu god, and later also of a tantric Buddhist one. Here the term is applied to Aparṇâ, spouse of Śiva.

Śambhu (*skr*. benevolent), one the names of Śiva.

Sâmkhya (lit. enumeration), an early Indian philosophical school.

Somasûtra (*skr*.), the stone channel leading from the yoni along which flows any liquid which is poured over the linga. It is thus sanctified as 'soma' the elixir of the gods.

Śrâvaka (*skr*. literally 'one who listens'), usually referring to the early disciples of Sâkyamuni, and by extension to all later Buddhists who reject the Mahâyâna teachings.

Stûpa (*skr*.), in the early period an earthen mound raised over sacred Buddhist relics, later a ornamental shrine, large or small depending upon the circumstances, patterned symbolically according to the relevant period.

Sûtra (*skr*. literally 'thread'), a thread of discourse, a didactic compilation treating of religious teachings.

Tantra (*skr*. literally a 'loom' or 'warp from a loom'), a Hindu or Buddhist text of complex ritual, the primary intention being the self-identification with one's chosen divinity and thus the acquisition of his supernatural powers.

Tantric, an anglicized adjectival form of the term.

Taṭâka, a lake.

Theravâda, 'Way of the Elders'. Theravâdin, 'a follower of such a way'. Note e.g. Sarvâstivâdin in the Index. The first serious split in the order of monks founded by Sâkyamuni is said to have occurred at a Buddhist Council held at Vaiśâli about 160 years after his death. Some monks were accused of introducing new theories and doctrines (which would in fact lead eventually to the development of the Mahâyâna). They appear to have been a majority for they were known as the Mahâsangha, the 'Great Community', while those who claimed to remain true to the original doctrines were known as Theravâda (*skr*. Sthaviravâda), way of the elders. Later splits duly occurred, but the Theravâda, thanks to a secure position eventually secured in Ceylon, has since come to represent the main religion of South-East Asia.

Toraṇa (*skr*.), an ornamental frontispiece raised above a lintel.

Upâsaka (*skr*. lit. 'one who sits close'), a committed lay Buddhist; -â (fem.) = a nun.

Vaiśeṣika (*skr*. lit. discriminating), an Indian philosophical school.

Valabhi, a raised section or tower of some kind.

Vajra, a 'thunderbolt' such as the weapon of Jupiter in classical tradition. In Hindu tradition it is the weapon of Indra, god of the storm and of war. In the Mahâyâna it becomes the weapon of Vajrapâni (lit. 'Vajra-in-hand') who may be regarded as a later form of Indra.

Vajrâçârya, a fully qualified master (*skr*. âçârya) of Buddhist tantric teachings.

Vat (Thai: Wat), the more recent S-E Asian term for a monastery. It derives from Pâli vatta (and is so written in Khmer with double t), which means 'self-controlled' as well as a monastic establishment.

Veda 'knowledge', e.g. the Four Vedas. See Rig Veda.

Vihâra (*skr*. lit. 'a place of rest'), in early Buddhism it refers to the parks which were often placed at the disposal of Sâkyamuni and his disciples by wealthy donors; thus it comes to mean 'monastery' and especially the main temple-hall of a Buddhist monastery. It appears in the name of Preah Vihear (spelt *Brah Vihâr*).

Vinaya (*skr*. discipline), the first part of all Buddhist canons, giving rules for the ordering of a monastic community, as attributed to Sâkyamuni himself.

yakṣa, a local divinity, often of natural phenomena; these creatures serve as attendants on Kubera, god of wealth. Popularly they are often regarded as harmful demons.

Yogaçârya (skr. lit 'the practice of yoga'), a philosophical school of Mahâyâna, also known as Çittamâtra (q.v.), attributed to the Bodhisattva Maitreya (the future Buddha) who revealed this teaching to the Indian sage Asanga (5th century AD). Together with the Madhyamaka (q.v.) it provides the basic philosophy for Mahâyâna Buddhism.

Yoni (*skr*.), female sexual organ, the dish-like receptacle with a lip on which the linga stands.

Bibliography

Abbreviations

AFAO Association française des Amis de l'Órient.

APKh Articles sur le Pays Khmer, by George Coedès, 2 vols, EFEO, Paris 1989 and 1992.

ASEANIE Sciences humaines en Asie du Sud-Est, Editions du Centre d' Anthropologie Sirindhorn, Bangkok.

BIPPA Bulletin of the Indo Pacific Prehistory Association.

EFEO École française d'Extrême-Orient.

BEFEO Bulletin EFEO.

CEFEO Cahiers EFEO.

East and West, Journal of IsIAO (formerly ISMeO), Rome.

IC Inscriptions du Cambodge, by George Coedès, 8 vols, EFEO 1937-1966.

IJHA International Journal of Historical Archaeology.

ISC Inscriptions sanscrites du Cambodge, Études asiatiques, Académie des Inscriptions et Belles Lettres, Paris.

JA Journal Asiatique, Paris.

JPTS, Journal of the Pali Text Society.

JRAS Journal of the Royal Asiatic Society.

JSAS Journal of Southeast Asian Studies.

JSS Journal of the Siam Society.

Abû Zaid Hasan, *Voyage du marchand arabe Sulaymân en Inde et en Chine, rédigé en 851, suivi de remarques par Abû Zaid Hasan (vers 916)*, trans. and ed. by Gabriel Ferrand, Paris, 1922.

Ang Choulean, see Molyvann.

Angkor et dix siècles d'art Khmer, Réunion des Musées Nationaux, Paris 1997, English version: *Angkor and ten centuries of Khmer Art*, National Gallery of Art, Washington, 1997.

Aymonier, Étienne, *Le Cambodge*, 3 vols, Paris, 1900-1904; An English edition is now available of some parts of Aymonier's work. See *The Khmer Heritage the old Siamese Provinces of Cambodia*, and *The Khmer Heritage in Thailand*, translated by W.E.J. Tips, White Lotus Press, Bangkok, 1999;

— *Textes Khmers*, Saigon, 1878.

Bareau, André, *Les sectes bouddhiques du Petit Véhicule*, Paris, 1955.

Barth, Auguste, 'Ang Chumnik' *ISC*, Paris, 1885, pp. 51-60, 64-72;

— 'Hanchei inscription' *ISC*, Paris, 1885, pp. 8-21;

— 'Inscription de Preah Ngok' *ISC*, Paris, p. 140-172;

— 'Lovek' *ISC*, Paris, 1885, pp. 122-40;

— 'Prea Kev', *ISC*, Paris, 1885, pp. 97-11;

— and A. Bergaigne, 'Phnom Sandak', *ISC*, Paris, 1893, pp. 331-46.

Basham, A.L., *The Wonder that was India*, London, 1954, reprint New York, Macmillan & Co., 1959.

Beal, Samuel, *Si-yu-ki, Buddhist Records of the Western World*, London, 1884, reprinted in Delhi, 1969.

Bergaigne, A., 'Inscription d'Angkor Vat' *ISC,* Paris, 1885, pp. 560-588;

— 'Stèles du Thnal Baray' *ISC*, Paris, 1885, nos 56-60, pp. 413-525.

Bernon, Olivier de, 'A propos du retour des bakous dans le palais royal de Phnom Penh' in *Études thématiques 6, Renouveaux religieux en Asie,* EFEO, Paris, 1997, pp. 33-58;

— 'Le Buddh Damnây, note sur un texte apocalytique khmer' *BEFEO 81*, 1994, pp. 83-96;

— 'Note sur l'hydraulique théocratique angkorienne' *BEFEO 84*, 1997, pp. 340-348;

— 'Le plus ancien edifice subsistant de Phnom Penh: une tour angkorieene sise dans lénceinte de Vatt Uṇṇalom' *BEFEO 88*, 2001, pp. 248-60;

— 'Une relecture de l'inscription K.892 provenant de Vatt Tâ Tok', forthcoming in *Palm-Leaf and Stone*, Bangkok, ?2004 or later;

— 'Le rituel de la "grande probation annuelle" (*mahâparivâsa*) des religieux de Cambodge', *BEFEO 87,* 2000, pp. 473-510.

Bhattacharya, Kamaleswar, *Recherches sur le vocabulaire des inscriptions sanskrites du Cambodge*, EFEO, Paris, 1991;

— *Les religions brahmaniques dans l'ancien Cambodge*, EFEO, Paris, 1961;

— 'L'état actuel des travaux sur les inscriptions sanskrites du Cambodge' *JA*, 1997, pp. 301-9.

Bizot, François, *Le don de soi-même*, EFEO, Paris, 1981;

— *Le figuier à cinq branches*, EFEO, Paris, 1976;

— *Le portail*, La table ronde, Paris, 2000;

— *Râmaker ou l'amour symbolique de Râma et Seta*, EFEO, Paris, 1989.

Black, John, *The Lofty Sanctuary of Khao Phra Vihâr*, the Siam Society, Bangkok, 1976.

Boisselier, Jean, *Le Cambodge,* Paris, éd. Picard, 1966;

— *La statuaire du Champa*, EFEO, Paris, 1963.

Boulbet, J., *Le Phnom Kulen et sa région*, EFEO, Paris, 1979;

— and B. Dagens, 'Les sites archéologiques de la région du Bhnam Gûlem (Phnom Kulen)' *Arts Asiatiques 27*, special number, Paris, 1973.

Briggs, L.P., *The Ancient Khmer Empire*, Transactions of the American Philosophical Society, new series, Vol. 41, Philadelphia, 1951, reprinted 1962, 1964. Recently reprinted in a new edition by White Lotus Press, Bangkok, 1999;

— 'The Khmer empire and the Malay peninsula', *Far Eastern Quarterly 9*, 1950, pp. 256-305;

— 'Siamese attacks on Angkor before 1430' *Far Eastern Quarterly 8*, 1948, pp. 3-33;

— 'Spanish Intervention in Cambodia' *Toung Pou* 39, 1949, pp. 132-60.

Brohier, R.L., *Seeing Ceylon*, Colombo, 1965.

Brown, Robert L., *The Dvâravatî Wheels of the Law and the Indianization of South East Asia,* Brill, Leiden, 1996.

Bruguier, Bruno, *Bibliographie du Cambodge ancien,* 2 vols, EFEO, Paris, 1998;

— 'Les ponts en pierre du Cambodge ancien' *BEFEO*

87, pp. 529-51;
— 'Les vestiges archéologiques du Phnom Trotung' *Proceedings of International Conference on Khmer Studies 1996*, Phnom Penh, pp. 475-86.
Chakravati, Adhir, *Royal Succession in Ancient Cambodia*, Asiatic Society Monograph xxvi, Calcutta, 1982;
— *The Sdok Kak Thom Inscription: a study in Indo-Khmer civilization*, Calcutta, 1978.
Chandler, David P., *Facing the Cambodian Past*, Silkworm Books, Chiang Mai, 1996;
— *A History of Cambodia,* Westview Press, Boulder, also Oxford UK, 1993, and Silkworm Books, Chiang Mai, 1994;
— see Mabbett.
Chirapat Prapandvidya, 'The Sab Bâk inscriptions: evidence of early Vajrayâna Buddhist presence in Thailand' *JSS 78/2*, 1990, pp.10-14.
Coedès, George, *Articles sur le pays Khmer*, EFEO, Paris, 2 vols, 1989 and 1992;
— *The Indianized States of South-East Asia* in the English edition as published by the East-West Center Press, 1968 (since 1971, known as the University Press of Hawai). From the original French: *Les états hindouisés d'Indochine et d'Indonésie*, Paris, 1948, reprinted by Editions E. de Boccard, Paris, 1964;
— *Inscriptions du Cambodge*, 8 vols, EFEO 1937-1966;
— 'Les capitales de Jayavarman II' *BEFEO 28*, p. 117ff. *(APKh I*, pp. 127-37);
— 'La date d'avènement de Jayavarma Paramesvara' *BEFEO 28*, pp. 145-6;
— 'La date d'avènement du Harṣavarman III: l'inscription de Prâsâd Sralau' *IC I*, pp. 221-6;
— 'La date de Koh Ker' *BEFEO 31*, p. 10ff. (*APKh*. pp. 214-20);
— 'La date du temple de Bantay Srei' *BEFEO 28*, pp. 289-96;
— 'Un document capital sur le bouddhisme en Indochine, la stèle de Vat Sithor' *IC VI*, pp. 195-211;
— 'Epigraphie du temple de Phimai' *BEFEO 24*, p. 345ff. (*APKh I*, pp. 81-88);
— 'La fondation de la royauté angkorienne et les récentes découvertes archéologiques au Phnom Kulên' *CEFEO 14*, 1938, pp. 40-48 (*APKh II*, pp. 277-85);
— 'La grande stèle de Phimânakas *IC II*, pp. 161-81;
— 'Inscription de Bâksei Camkrong' *IC IV*, pp. 88-101;
— 'Inscription de Prâsât Nâng Khmau' *IC II*, pp. 32-34;
— 'Une inscription d'Udâyadityavarman I' *BEFEO 11*, 1911, pp. 400-404;
— 'Inscription de Vât Ek' *IC III*, pp. 26-28;
— 'Inscriptions de Bat Chum' *JA 12*, 1908, pp. 213-54;
— Inscriptions de Nom Vân' *IC VII*, pp. 263-70;
— 'Inscriptions de Phnom Sandak' *IC VI*, pp. 89-90 & pp. 249-50;
— 'Inscriptions de Prâh Thât Prâh Srei' IC V, pp. 32-34;
— 'Inscriptions de Prâsât Ak Yom' *IC V*, pp. 57-59;
— 'Inscriptions de Prâsât Ampil' *IC V*, pp. 200-201;
— 'Inscriptions de Prâsât Bâset' *IC III*, pp. 3-24 & 122-5;
— 'Inscriptions de Prâsât Kravan' *IC IV*, 68 to 76;
— 'Inscriptions de Prâsât Robang Româs' *IC V*, pp. 191-197;
— 'Inscriptions de Sambor Prei Kuk' *IC IV*, pp. 3-35;
— 'Inscriptions de Vat Prah Einkosei' *IC IV* pp. 108-39;
— 'La légende de la nâgi' *BEFEO 11*, p. 391ff. (*APKh II*, pp. 1-3);
— 'Note sur l'iconographie de Beng Mâlâ' *BEFEO 13(2)*, pp. 23-26;
— 'Une nouvelle inscription de Jayavîravarman à Prah Ko' *IC I*, pp. 189-94;
— 'Nouvelles données chronologiques et genéalogiques sur la dynastie de Mahîdharapura' *BEFEO 29*, pp. 297-330;
— 'Nouvelles inscriptions de Koh Ker' *IC I*, pp. 47-71;
— 'Nouvelles precisions sur les dates d'avènement de quelques rois des dynasties angkoriennnes', *BEFEO 43*, pp. 12-16;
— 'Piédroit de Banan' *IC VII*, pp. 40-41;
— 'Piédroit de Prâsât Kuk Pradak' *IC V*, pp. 88-90;
— 'Piédroit de Prâsât Prei Kmeng' *IC IV*, pp. 64-5;
— 'Piédroit de Sâk'on Lâk'on' *IC VI*, pp. 281-3;
— 'Piédroit de Vât Bâset' *IC VI*, pp. 287-92;
— 'Piédroits de Lobok Srot' *IC II*, pp. 92-95;
— 'Piédroits de Nam Van', *IC VII*, pp. 63-70;
— 'Piédroits de Vat Khnat', *IC VII*, pp. 50-57;
— 'La plus ancienne inscription en Pali de Cambodge' *BEFEO 35*, pp. 14-21;
— 'Quatres nouvelles inscriptions de Bantây Srei' *IC I*, pp. 143-57;
— 'Quelques suggestions sur la méthode à suivre pour interpréter les bas-reliefs de Bantay Chmar et de la galerie extérieure du Bayon' *BEFEO 27*, p. 71ff. *(APKh, II*, pp. 229-39);
— 'Une réplique de la stèle de Prah Einkosei: la stèle de Prasad Komphus' *IC I*, pp. 157-86;
— 'Le site de Janapada d'après une inscription de Prâsâd Khna' *BEFEO 43,* pp. 1-16 (*APKh I*, pp. 334-7);
— 'Le site primitif de Tchen-la' *BEFEO 18,* p. 1ff. (*APKh I*, pp. 53-55);
— 'Stèle de Baray Occidental' *IC IV*, pp. 54-63;
— ' Stèle brisée de Kdei Ang' IC VII, pp. 3-19;
— 'La stèle de fondation de Pre Rup' *IC I*, pp.73-142;
— 'La stèle de Palhal' *BEFEO 13 (VI)*, pp. 27-36;
— 'La stèle de Phnom Bantây Nâng' *IC II*, pp. 202-6;
— 'Stèle de Phnom Rung' *IC V*, pp. 297-305;
— 'La stèle de Prah Khan d'Angkor' *BEFEO 51*, pp. 255-301 (*APKh II*, pp. 119-66);
— 'La stèle de Prâsât Tor' *IC I*, pp. 227-49;
— 'Stèle de Sophas' *IC VI*, pp. 10-11;
— 'La stèle de Ta-Prohm', *BEFEO 6*, pp. 44-85 (*APKh II*, pp. 11-52);
— 'La stèle de Tep Pranam' *JA 1908* March/April p. 203, Sept/Oct p. 253;
— 'Stèle de Wat Ph'u' *IC V*, pp. 288-95;
— 'La stèle de Wat Luong Kau près de Wat P'hu', *BEFEO 39*, pp. 209-20;
— 'Les stèles de foundations de Prâh Ko et Bakong', *ICI I*, pp. 17-36;
— 'Stèles des prâsât crung d'Ángkor Thom' *IC IV*, pp. 207-53;
— and Dupont, P. 'Les inscriptions du Prasad Kôk Pô' *BEFEO 39*, pp. 379-413;
— 'Les stèles de Prâ Ko et de Bakong' *IC I*, pp. 2-35;
— 'Les stèles de Sdok Kak Thom, Phnom Sandak et Prah Vihâr' *BEFEO 43*, p. 56ff. (*APKh II*, pp. 167-265).
— and Dupont, P. 'Les inscriptions du Prasad Kôk Pô' *BEFEO 39*, pp. 379-413;
— 'Les stèles de Prâ Ko et de Bakong' *IC I*, pp. 2-35;
— 'Les stèles de Sdok Kak Thom, Phnom Sandak et Prah Vihâr' *BEFEO 43,* p. 56ff. (*APKh II*, pp. 167-265).
Dagens, Bruno, *Les Khmers*, Les Belle Lettres, Paris, 2003;

— 'Étude sur l'iconographie du Bayon (frontons et linteaux)' *Arts Asiatiques*, 1969, pp. 123-67;
— see Boulbet.
Dalsheimer, Nadine, *Les collections du musée national de Phnom Penh*, EFEO, Paris, 2001.
De Martini, G.F., *A New and Interesting Description of the Lao Kingdom*, based on *Delle missioni dei padri della compagnia di Gesu nella Provincia del Giappone*, 1663, N.A.Tinassi, Rome and on an extract published as *Relation nouvelle et curieuse du Royaume de Lao*, 1966, Gervais Couzier, Paris, translated by Walter Tips and Claudio Bertuccio, introduction by Luigi Bressan, Bangkok, 1998.
Delaporte, Louis, *Voyage au Cambodge*, first published by the Librairie Delagrave in 1880, reprinted by Maissonneuve & Larose, Paris, 1999.
Dingwall, Alastaire, ed., *Travellers' Literary Companions, S-E Asia*, Print Publishing, UK, 1994.
Ducrest, see Vandermeersch.
Dumarçay, Jacques, 'L'hydrolique khmère' in *Angkor et dix siècless d'art khmer*, pp. 93-100.
Études épigraphiques sur le pays Cham de Louis Finot, Édouard Huber, George Coedès et Paul Mus, reunies par Claude Jacques, EFEO, Paris, 1995.
Ferrand, Gabriel, see Abû Zaid Hasan.
Finot, Louis, 'Dharmaçâlas au Cambodge' *BEFEO 25*, pp. 417-22;
— 'L'Inscription de Preah Khan' *BEFEO 4*, pp. 672-5;
— 'Inscriptions d'Angkor' *BEFEO 25*, pp. 289-407;
— 'Inscriptions de Mi-song, no. 24' in *Études Épigraphiques du Pays Cham*;
— 'Lokeçvara en Indo-Chine' *Études asiatiques, 1*, EFEO, p. 235;
— 'Prasad Trapang Çong (for Khyang)' *BEFEO 39*, p. 292;
— 'Sek Ta Tuy' *BEFEO 28*, p. 46;
— 'Le temple de Mangalârtha à Angkor Thom' *BEFEO 25*, pp. 393-406.
Finot, Parmentier et Goloubew, *Le temple d'Içvârapura*, Mémoires archéologiques, EFEO, Paris 1926, transl. by J.H. Stape, *A Guide to the Temple of Banteay Srei*, White Lotus Press, Bangkok, 2000.
Fonteyn, Jan, *The Sculpture of Indonesia*, National Gallery of Art, Washington DC, 1990.
Fouser, Beth, *The Lord of the Golden Tower*, White Lotus Press, Bangkok, 1996.
Frédéric, Louis, *Sud-Est Asiatique, ses temples, ses sculptures*, Paris, 1964;
— see Nou.
Freeman, Michael, *A Guide to Khmer Temples in Thailand and Laos*, River Books, Bangkok, 1996;
— see Jacques, Claude;
— see Moore, Elizabeth;
— see Smitthi Siribhadra.
Gilman d'Arcy Paul, J., *The Customs of Cambodia by Chou Ta-Kuan, translated into English from the French version of Paul Pelliot of Chou's Chinese original*, first published by the Siam Society, Bangkok, 1987, 3rd ed. 1993. Pelliot's first French translation was published in the *BEFEO II*, pp. 123-77. An amended version by him was published as *Mémoires sur les coutumes du Cambodge de Tcheou Ta-Kouan*, Adrien-Maisonneuve, Paris, 1951.
Giteau, Madelaine, *Iconographie du Cambodge post-Ankorienne*, EFEO, Paris 1975.
Glaize, Maurice, *Les monuments du groupe d'Angkor*, Adrien-Maisonneuve, Paris, 1963; new edition 1993, entitled simply *Angkor*.
Goloubew, Victor, 'Le cheval Balaha' *BEFEO 27*, pp. 223-38. See also under Finot.
Grenier, François, 'Chronique royale du Cambodge' *JA 18*, 1871, pp. 36-85 and *JA 20*, 1872, pp. 112-44.
Groslier, Bernard P., *Angkor et le Cambodge au XVIe siècle d'après les sources portugaises et espagnoles*, Paris, 1958 (English translation in preparation: Orchid Press, Bangkok, 2004);
— *Indochine, carrefour des arts*, Albin Michel, Paris 1961;
— 'Étude sur le temps passé à la construction d'un grand temple Khmer' *BEFEO XXXV*, pp. 57-68.
Guillon, Emmanuel, *Cham Art*, River Books, Bangkok, 2001;
— *The Mons, a civilization of Southeast Asia*, English translation from the French by James V. Di Crocco, The Siam Society, Bangkok, 1999.
Hall, D.G.E., *A History of South-East Asia*, Macmillan Press, London, 1955 and numerous reprints of which the 1994 edition is to hand.
Handbook for Travellers in India, Pakistan, Nepal, Bangladesh and Sri Lanka, ed. by Rushbrook Williams, publ. by L.F. John Murray, London, 1978. This is an entirely new edition, in effect the 22nd of the much earlier *Handbook for Travellers in India*, first published in three parts, 1859-83. It was published as a single volume in 1892 with numerous reprints up to the time of the World War II.
Har Dayal, *The Bodhisattva Doctrine,* Kegan Paul, London, 1934.
Higham, Charles, *The Civilization of Angkor,* Weidenfeld & Nicolson, 2001;
— 'The Ban Chiang Culture in wider perspective' *Proceedings of the British Academy*, *LXIX*, 1983, pp. 229-61;
— and Rachie Thosarat, *PrehistoricThailand from early settlements to Sukhotai.*
Hirth, Friedrich and Rockhill, W.W., *Chau Ju-kua, his work on the Chinese and Arab trade in the twelfth and thirteen centuries,* St Petersburg, 1911.
Hobson-Jobson, see Yule.
I-tsing, *A record of the Buddhist religion as practised in India and the Malay Peninsula, AD 671-695*, translated by Takakusu, Oxford, 1868.
Ishizawa, Yoshiaki and Marui, Masako, 'La découverte de 274 sculptures et d'un caitya bouddiques lors des campagnes de fouilles de 2000 et 2001 au temple de Bantay Khei à Angkor', *Arts Asiatiques*, 57, 2002, pp. 206-17.
Jacob, Judith, *The traditional literature of Cambodia*, OUP, London, 1996;
— and Kuoch Haksrea, trans., *Reamker, The Cambodian Version of the Ramayana*, RAS, London, 1986.
Jacques, Claude, 'La carrière de Jayavarman II' *BEFEO 59*, pp. 205-20;
— L'emplacement d'Aninditapura & La carrière de Jayavarman II' *BEFEO 59*, pp. 193-220;

— 'Les noms posthumes des rois dans l'ancien Cambodge' in *Fruits of Inspiration,* eds. Klokke, M and Erbert Groningen van Kooij, Forsten, 2001, pp. 191-8;

— (ed.) *Études épigraphiques sur le pays Cham* de Louis Finot, Édouard Huber, George Coedès et Paul Mus, EFEO, Paris, 1995;

— and Michael Freeman, *Angkor, Citadels and Palaces*, River Books, Bangkok, 1997; French edition: *Angkor, Résidences des dieux,* Éd. Olizane, Geneva, 2001.

Jacq-Hergoualc'h, Michel, *L'armement et l'organisation de l'armée khmère*, Paris, 1979;

— *The Malay Peninsula; crossroads of the Maritime Silk Route*, Brill, Leiden, 2002;

— 'Une cité-état de la Péninsule Malaise: le Lankasuka' *Arts Asiatiques*, 50, 1995, pp 47-64;

— 'Un exemple de civilisation de ports-entrepôts des Mers du Sud: le Sud Kedah (Malaysia) Ve–XIVe siecles' *Arts Asiatiques*, 47, 1992, pp. 40-48;

— 'Temples brahmaniques de l'ancien Tambralinga' in *Les apports de l'archéologie à la connaissance des anciens états en Thailande*, Silpakom University, Bangkok, 1995;

— in cooperation with Tharapong Srisuchat, Thiva Supajanya and Wichapan Krisanapol, 'La région de Nakhon Si Thammarat du Ve au XIVe siècle' *JA*, 1996, pp. 361-435;

— 'Archaeological Research in the Malay Peninsula' *JSS 85*, 1997, pp. 121-32;

— with T. Supajanya & W. Krisanapol, 'Une étape maritime de la route de la soie: la partie méridionale de l'isthmus de Kra au IXe siècle' *JA*, 1998, pp. 235-320.

Khin Sok, *L'annexion du Cambodge par les Vietnamiens au XIXe siècle d'après les deux poèmes du vénérable Bâtum Baramey Pich*, You Feng, Paris, 2002;

— *Le Cambodge entre le Siam et le Vietnam (de 1775-1860)*, EFEO, Paris 1991;

— *Chroniques royales du Cambodge (de Baña Yat à la prise de Lanvaek),* EFEO, Paris, 1988;

— *La Grammaire du Khmer moderne*, éd. You Feng, Paris, 1999.

Khoo, J.C.M. (ed.), *Art & Archaeology of Fu Nan*, Orchid Press, Bangkok, 2003.

Klairung Amratisha, *The Cambodian Novel, a study of its emergence and development*, presented for the degree of Doctor of Philosophy of the University of London (School of Oriental and African Studies), 1998.

Leclère, A., *Cambodge: fêtes civiles et religieuses*, Imprimerie nationale, Paris, 1916;

— *Histoire du Cambodge*, Geuthner, Paris, 1914.

Lewitz, see Saveros.

Lunet de Lajonquière, É., *Inventaire descriptif des monuments du Cambodge*, 3 vols, Paris, 1902-11.

Mabbett, Ian and David Chandler, *The Khmers*, Blackwell, Oxford, 1995.

Marchal, Henri, 'Kutîśvara' *BEFEO 37*, pp. 333-46;

— 'Le dégagement de Prasad Kok Po' *BEFEO 37*, pp. 361-78.

Mauger, Henri, 'L'Asram Mahârosei' *BEFEO 36*, pp. 65-95;

— 'Preah Khan de Kampong Svay', *BEFEO 39* (2), pp. 197-220.

Molyvann, Vann (editor), Ang Choulean, Eric Prenowitz & Ashley Thompson, *Angkor, a manual for the Past, Present and Future*, Apsara, publication of the Cambodian Government, 1996. A French version was published in 1997.

Moore, E., 'The temple of Preah Ko and the city of Hariharâlaya' in *Studies and reflections of Asian art and archaeology: Essays in honour of HSH Professor Subhadras Diskul*, Bangkok, 2538 (=AD 1995).

Moore, Elizabeth, with Philip Stott, Sriyavudh Sukhasvasti and Michael Freeman, *Ancient Capitals of Thailand,* Asia Books, Bangkok, 1996;

— and Anthony Freeman, 'Circular sites at Angkor: a radar scattering model' *JSS 85*, 1997, pp. 107-19;

— see Smitthi Siribhadra.

Mouhot, Henri, *Voyages dans les royaumes de Siam, du Cambodge, du Laos*, as extracted from his journal and correspondence by Ferdinand de Lanoye, first published in 1868 and now reprinted by Éditions Olizane, Geneva, 1999.

Moura, Jean *Le Royaume du Cambodge,* 2 vols, Paris, 1883.

Ma-tuan-lin, *Ethnographie des peuples étrangers à la Chine*, French translation by Marquis d'Hervey de Saint-Denis, Geneva, 1883.

Nou, Jean-Louis and Louis Frédéric, *Borobudur*, Paris and Rome, 1994.

O'Flaherty, Wendy, *The Rig Veda, an Anthology*, Penguin Books Ltd., 1981.

O'Reilly, Dougald, 'Excavations in NW Cambodia' *Siksâcakr, Bulletin of the Centre for Khmer Studies, no.3*, Siem Reap, July 2001, p. 31.

Osborne, Milton, *The French Presence in Cochinchina and Cambodia*, first published by Cornell University 1969, reprinted by White Lotus Press, Bangkok, 1997;

— 'Francis Garnier (1839-1873) explorer of the Mekong River' in Victor T. King (ed.), *Explorers of South-East Asia, Six Lives*, Kuala Lumpur, 1995.

Palaces of the Gods, see Smitthi Siribhadra.

Parmentier, H. *L'art Khmer primitif,* 2 vols of text and plates, Paris, 1927;

— 'Complément à l'art Khmer primitif' *BEFEO XXXV*, 1935.

Pelliot, Paul, 'Le Fou-nan' *BEFEO III*, p. 263ff.

Pisit Charoenwongsa and Subhadradis Diskul, *Thailand*, Nagel Publishers, Geneva/Paris/Munich, 1978 (in the *Archaeologia Mundi*).

Prenowitz, Eric, see Molyvann.

Pou, see Saveros.

Rawson, Philip, *The Art of Southeast Asia*, London, 1967 and later editions.

Rooney, Dawn F. *Angkor, an introduction to the temples*, Odyssey Publications, Hongkong, 1994 and later editions.

Roveda, Vittorio, *Khmer Mythology*, Bangkok, 1997;

— *Preah Vihear*, River Books, Bangkok, 2000;

— *Sacred Angkor: The Carved Reliefs of Angkor Wat, photography by Jaro Poncar*, Thames Hudson (London) and River Books, Bangkok, 2002.

Ruegg, D. Seyfort, 'A new publication on the date and the historiography of the Buddha's decease' *BSOAS 62*, 1999, pp. 82-87.

Sakar, H.B. *Cultural Relations between India and Southeast Asian Countries*, Delhi, 1985.

Saveros Lewitz, 'Inscriptions modernes d'Angkor' *BEFEO 59*, 1972, pp. 101-21 and 221-49;

— 'Les inscriptions modernes d'Angkor Vat' *JA 260*, 1972, pp. 105-29;

— 'Textes en Khmer moyen: inscriptions modernes d'Angkor 2 & 3' *BEFEO 57*, pp. 99-126.

Saveros Pou, *Nouvelles Inscriptions du Cambodge*, vol. 1, EFEO, Paris, 1989;

— *Nouvelles Inscriptions du Cambodge*, vols 2 and 3, EFEO, Paris, 1996;

— and Philip N. Jenner, 'Les Cpap ou "codes de conduite" khmers', *BEFEO 62*, 1975, pp. 369-94.

Seidenfaden, Erick, 'Complément à l'inventaire descriptif des monuments de Cambodge pour les quattre provinces du Siam oriental' *BEFEO 22*, pp. 55-99.

Skilling, Peter, 'The advent of Theravâdin Buddhism to mainland South-East Asia', *JIABS*, 20, 1, 1997, pp. 93-107;

— 'Buddhism in Cambodia in the Early Period', Paper read to the EFEO in Phnom Penh, early February 1997;

— 'A Buddhist inscription from Go Xoai, Southern Vietnam and notes towards a classification of *ye dharma* inscriptions', in *80 pi satsadachan dr. prasert na nagara: ruam bot khwam wichakan dan charuk lae ekasanboran* [80 Years: A collection of articles on epigraphy and ancient documents published on the occasion of the celebration of the 80th birthday of Prof. Dr Prasert Na Nagara], Bangkok, 21 March 2542 [1999], pp. 171-87;

— 'A citation from the *Buddhavamsa* of the Abhayagiri school' *JPTS XVIII*, 1933, pp. 165-75;

— 'Dharmakîrti's Durbodhâloka and the literature of Śrîvijaya' *JSS 85*, 1997, pp. 187-94;

— 'Some literary references in the *Grande Inscription d'Angkor* (IMA 38)' *Aseanie 8*, 2001, pp. 57-66.

Smitthi Siribhadra and Mayuree Veraprasert: *Lintels: a comparative study of lintels in Cambodia and Thailand*, Siam Commerical Bank, Bangkok, 1989.

Smitthi Siribhadra, Elizabeth Moore, Michael Freeman, *Palaces of the Gods, Khmer Art & Architecture in Thailand*, River Books, London, 1992.

Snellgrove, D.L., *Asian Commitment: Travels and Studies in the Indian Sub-Continent and South-East Asia*, Orchid Press, Bangkok, 2001;

— *Buddhist Himâlaya*, Cassier, Oxford, 1957, reprinted by Himalayan Bookseller, Kathmandu, 1995;

— *The Hevajra Tantra*, 2 vols, OUP, London, 1959 and later reprints;

— *Himalayan Pilgrimage*, Cassirer, Oxford, 1961; first American edition by Prajña Press, Great Eastern Book Company, Boulder, 1981; later editions by Shambhala Publications, Boston;

— *Indo-Tibetan Buddhism*, Serindia Publications, London 1987, reprint Orchid Press, Bangkok, 2004;

— *Khmer Civilization and Angkor*, Orchid Press, Bangkok, 2000;

— 'Borobudur: Stûpa or Mandala' *East and West*, 46, 1996, pp. 477-83.

Stark, Miriam, 'The transition to history in the Mekong Delta: a view from Cambodia' *IJHA*, 1998;

— and Bong Sovath, 'Recent research on emergent complexity in Cambodia's Mekong' *BIPPA, The Melaka Papers*, vol.5, Canberra, 2001.

Stern, Philippe, 'Diversité et rhythme de fondations royales khmères', *BEFEO 44*, 1954, pp. 649-87;

— 'Hariharâlaya et Indrapura' *BEFEO 38*, pp.175-97 and eleven plates.

Stott, Philip see Moore, Elizabeth.

Stuart-Fox, M. and Bunhaeng Ung, *The Murderous Revolution*, Orchid Press, Bangkok, 1986.

Subhadradis Diskul, M.C. (editor and contributor), *The Art of Srîvijaya*, UNESCO, 1980;

— see Pisit Charoenwongsa.

Thompson, Ashley, see Molyvann.

Tranet, Michel, *Sambaur-Prei-Kuk, monuments d'Içânavarman (615-28)*, vol. 1, 1995-96, vol. 2, 1996-97, vol. 3, 1998-99, financed by the Toyota Foundation and printed in Cambodia (no other details given);

— 'Adhémard Leclère: Sa vie, ses travaux' *Seksa Khmer 7*, 1984, pp. 3-33.

Trouvé, G. 'Ak Yom' *BEFEO 38*, p. 530ff.;

— 'Le Prasat Tor' *BEFEO 35*, pp. 207-32.

Tiyavanich, Kamala, *Forest Recollections, Wandering Monks in 20th-century Thailand*, Silkworm Books, Chiang Mai, 1997.

Vandermeersch, Léon and Jean-Pierre Ducrest, *Le Musée de Sculpture Cam de Da Nang*, AFAO, Paris, 1997.

Vickery, Michael T., *Cambodia after Angkor*, a dissertation presented to Yale University as a Ph.D. Thesis, 2 vols, December 1977;

— *Cambodia 1975-1982*, Allen and Unwin, Singapore, 1984, 1985;

— *Society, Economics and Politics in Pre-Angkor Cambodia*, Tokyo, 1998;

— 'Resolving the Chronology and History of 9th Century Cambodia' in *Siksâcakr, Bulletin of the Centre of Khmer Studies*, Siem Reap, no.3, July 2001.

Wheatley, Paul, *The Golden Khersonese, Studies in the historical geography of the Malay Peninsula before 1500*, Kuala Lumpur, 1961;

— *Impressions of the Malay Peninsula in Ancient Times*, Singapore, 1964.

Winstedt, R.O., *A History of Malaya*, Singapore edition, 1962.

Wiseman Christie, Jan, 'Trade and State formation in the Malay Peninsula and Sumatra' in Kathirithamby-Wells J. and John Villiers (eds), *The Southeast Asian Port and Polity, Rise and Demise*, Singapore University Press, 1990.

Woodward, Hiram W., 'Practice and Belief in Ancient Cambodia: Claude Jacques' Angkor and the *Devarâja* question' *JSAS 3 (2)*, pp. 249-61.

Wray, Elizabeth, Clare Rosenfeld and Dorothy Bailey, *Ten Lives of the Buddha*, Weatherhill, New York & Tokyo, 1972.

Wyatt, David, *Thailand*, Yale University Press, New Haven, 1982.

Yule, Henry and A.C. Burnell, *Hobson-Jobson, a glossary of colloquial Anglo-Indian words and phrases*, John Murray, London, 1903, new edition by William Crooke, Munshira Manoharlal, Delh, 3rd ed., 1979.

Appendix
Chronology of the Khmer Kings

Śrutavarman and his son **Śreṣṭhavarman** (not firmly established epigraphically), said to have founded the city of Śreṣṭhapura in the early 6th century AD near Vat Phu.

Bhavavarman, son of Vîravarman, of the city of Bhavapura, assumes power at Angkor Borei, thus succeeding Rudravarman, the last king of Funan;

and his brother **Çitrasena > Mahendravarman**, second half of the 6th century;

Îśânavarman, founder of Îśânapura, during first half of the 7th century;

Bhavavarman II around the middle of the 7th century;

Jayavarman 1 during the second half of the 7th century;

Queen Jayadevî, early 8th century. She is known from an inscription of 713. A period of uncertainty follows.

Jayavarman II probably begins his campaigns to reunite the country about 770; he is crowned 802, establishes Hariharâlaya and Mahendrapura (Phnom Kulen) as his capital cities; dies 834/5;

Jayavarman III 834/5 – 877;

Indravarman I 877 – 889;

Yaśovarman I 889 – 900 or later; he founds Yaśodharapura (Angkor);

Harṣavarman I 900 or later – 922/3;

Îśânavarman II 922/3 – 928;

Jayavarman IV 928 – 942, reigning from his capital at Chok Gyargyar (Koh Ker);

Harṣavarman II 942 – 944;

Râjendravarman 944 – 968, reigning from Yaśodharapura (Angkor);

Jayavarman V 968 – 1001;

Udayâdityavarman I 1001 – 1002, ousted by Jayavîravarman, who is ousted *c.* 1006. A long contest;

Sûryavarman I contesting the throne 1002 onwards which he gains about 1010; self-acclaimed as the legitimate ruler, he is usually dated 1002 – 1050;

Udayâdityavarman II 1050 – 1066;

Harṣavarman III 1066 – 1088, possibly followed by a claimant to the throne;

Jayavarman VI 1080 – 1107, a usurper who gains power in the north, while Harṣavarman is still ruling in Angkor;

Dharaṇîndravarman I 1107 – 1113, who succeeds Jayavarman VI in the north;

Sûryavarman II 1113 – 1150, who reunites the whole country; (Dharaṇîndravarman II)

Yaśovarman II 1150 – *c.*1165;

Tribhuvanâdityadeva (usurper) *c.*1165 – 1167;

the Cham invasion

Jayavarman VII 1181 – 1219/20;

Indravarman II 1219/20 – 1243;

Jayavarman VIII 1243 – 1295;

Śrîndravarman (= Indravarman III) 1295 – 1307;

Śrîndrajayavarman 1307 – 1327;

Jayavarman Parameśvara 1327 – ? One may note that Parameśvara is his posthumous name; thus he might well be known as Jayavarman IX. He is the last king mentioned in a Sanskrit inscription at Angkor.

Thereafter there is a gap until we come to the first king named in the Cambodian Chronicles These are supposed to begin from the year 1346. They were prepared by a minister appointed to the task by royal command in the first half of the 19th century in order to replace those destroyed by earlier wars. They depend partly on the Annals of Ayuthaya but are also a concoction of hearsay and legend. Up to the 19th century all dates remain unconfirmed.

The details of these later kings who were still ruling at Angkor are compiled mainly from G. Coedès, *Indianized States*, pp. 236-7. One may also refer usefully to L.P. Briggs, *The Ancient Khmer Empire*, pp. 251-7. I have tried to produce some coherence in the accounts, but my list inevitably remains provisional. As will be noted here some of these kings are also mentioned in Chinese records but the names are seldom firmly identifiable.

Nippeanbât (= *Nirvânapada*) – a posthumous name 1346 – 51

Lampong-râja 1352, but Râmâdhipati of Siam is said to have occupied Angkor in 1352 and placed a Thai prince on the throne. Lampong-râja fled to Laos and may have soon regained his kingdom with the help of his brother.

Sûryavamṣa Râjâdhirâja, brother of Lampong-râja, 1357 – *c.*1377

Paramarâma, a son of Lampong-râja *c.*1377 – *c.*1380

Dhammâsokarâjâdhirâja, brother of Paramarâma (known in Chinese records as Chao Ponhea Kambuja) *c.* 1380 – ?

Râmesuan of Siam is said to have occupied Angkor in 1393 and placed a son of his on the throne but he is soon assassinated.

[See D.K.Wyatt, *Thailand*, p. 69 where he says that this event is unconfirmed. Note also that L.P. Briggs in a well argued article, in which he checks Khmer, Ayuthayan and Chinese sources, 'Siamese attacks on Angkor before 1430', *Far Eastern Quarterly 8* (1948), pp. 3-33, insists that there was no Siamese occupation and sacking of Angkor before 1430, although the two capital cities were constantly at war.]

Samdach Chao Poñea (presumably = Dhammâsokarâjâdhirâja) continues to rule until 1405, when his death is announced in Chinese sources, and he is succeeded by Chao P'ing-ya, who may be identified with Cho Poñea Yat.

Chao Poñea Yat, who later took the glorious name of Sûryavarman and he may also have received the posthumous name of Nippeanbât = *Nirvânapada*) 1405 – ?, but note the 12 year discrepancy below. During his reign the decision was made in 1431 to move to the South.

The later kings of Srei Santhor, Lovek, Oudong, Phnom Penh, deriving largely from Kin Sok, *Le Cambodge entre le Siam et le Vietnam*, EFEO, Paris 1991.

Poñea Yat (1417 – 63, but note the unresolved discrepancy of 12 years just above);

his eldest son: **Norea Reachea**, [Naṛâyana râja] (1463 – 1468);

his brother, **Râmâ-'thipdey Srei-reachea** [Râmâdhipati Srîrâja] (1468 – 1486)*,
his brother, **Thomma Reachea** (1476 – 1504)*,
their nephew, son of Norea Reachea, **Soriyor** (1476 – 1486)*,
* These three kings were ruling different parts of the country at the same time;

his cousin, **Sokontor**, son of Thomma (1504 – 1512);

his son-in-law, a usurper, '**King Kân**';

Ang Chan, Barom Reachea, younger brother of Thomma (1525 – 1567);

his son, **Bâraminda Reachea** (1567 – 1579);

his son, **Satha Mohinda Reachea** (1579 – 1595);

his younger brother, **Poñea An** (1595 – 1600);

his nephew, youngest son of Satha, **Poñea Ñom** (1600 – 1602), never crowned;

his uncle **Soryopor**, brother of Satha and elder brother of Poñea An (1602 – 1616);

his son, **Chey Chettha** (1616 – 1625);

his younger brother **Outey** (1626 – 1627, but Chey Chettha continues in power as 'regent');

his nephew, son of Chey Chettha, namely Prince Poñea To, crowned as **Srei Thomm Reachea** (1627 – 1631), killed on orders of Outey;

his brother, second son of Chey Chettha, **Ang Tong Reachea** (1631 – 1635);

a cousin, **Ang Non**, son of Outey, who still holds power; (1636 – 1638);

his cousin, the third son of Chey Chettha, Prince Chan, who kills both Ang Non and Outey; he is crowned as Satha Reamea-'thipadei, later becomes a Muslim, known as **King Ibrahim** (1638 – 1655);

his cousin, **Ang Saur**, brother of Ang Non (1656 – 1671);

his nephew **Ang Chi**, son of Ang Non (1671 – 1675);

his younger brother, (another) Ang Saur, crowned as **Chey Chettha** (1675 – 1695);

his nephew, **An Yang Outey** (1695 died very soon);

Chey Chettha returns to power (1696 – 1699);

A distant cousin, *kevhvea* **Ang Im**, son of last-mentioned Ang Non (1700 – 1701);

Chey Chettha returns to power again (1701 – 1702);

his eldest son, **Srei Thomma** (1702 – 1705);

Chey Chettha returns to power again (1705 – 1706);

Srei Thomma again (1706 – 1714);
his cousin *kevhvea* **Ang Im again** (*c.* 1714 – 1738 with contentious interludes);
Srei Thomma again (*c.*1738 – 1747);
his son, another **Ang Im** (Srei Thomma Reachea) (1747 – 1748 murdered);
a cousin **Ang Tong** (1748 – 1757 with contentious interludes);
a nephew **Ang Tân** (1757 – 1775);
a grandson of **Ang Non** (brought from Siam by Taksin) (1775 – 1779);
a son of Ang Tân, Ang Eng, crowned as **Norea Reamea** [= Naṛâyan Râma] (1775 – 1796);
his son **Ang Chan Outey Reachea** (1806 – 1834);
his daughter **Ang Mei**, as chosen by the Vietnamese (1835 – 1847);
her uncle, younger brother of Ang Chan, **Ang Duong**, installed by Râma III of Thailand (1848 – 1860);
his son **Norodom** (1860 – 1904);
his half-brother **Sisovath** (1904 – 1927);
his eldest son, **Sisovath Monivong** (1927 – 1941);
his nephew, **Norodom Sihanouk** (1941 –).

Index

A

Âṣâḍha, n. a lunar month 206, 232(18)
Âdibuddha 173
Âdityavarman 173
Aśoka 207, 233(25)
Âśram 20, 21, 36, 41, 57, 191, 234
Âśvina, n. a lunar month 206, 232(18)
Aśvins, divine horsemen 30
Agastya, an Indian sage 56, 225(24), 234
Agni, god of fire 15, 42, 142, 231(25)
Ak Yom 39, 47, 223(45), 226(9), 241
Akṣapada, epithet of Vedic rishi Gotama 80
Akṣobhya, Buddha 173
Amarâvati, pl.n. 15, 168, 221(4)
Amarendrapura 47, 59, 83
Amrîmad Amrâta 38
Anavatapta, lake 160, 161
Ang Chan Outey Reachea 199, 200, 202
Ang Duong 198, 200, 201, 202, 205, 207, 232(11)
Ang Em 196, 199, 200
Ang Im 197, 198
Ang Mei 200, 202
Ang Non 196, 197, 198
Ang Saur, king (1656-71), 197
Ang Saur, prince, becomes King Chey Chettha, q.v.
Ang Tân, son of Outey 196-7, 198
another Ang Tân (king 1757-75) 198, 199
Ang Vodey 196
Angkor Borei 2, 4, 15, 19-23, 41, 85, 88, 221(2)
Angkor Thom 58, 61, 109, 110, 117, 136, 146-164, 174, 175, 193, 212, 229(15)
Annals of Ayuthaya 183
Annam 196, 197, 198, 199, 201, 212, 214, 231(1), 232(3)
Âḍhyapura 21, 22, 98, 228(38)
Arab sources 24, 46, 222(n.33)
Arabia 4, 7
Aranyaprathet 40, 44
Aravindahrada 98
Athvea 193, 194, 195
Âtmaśiva 71, 80
Avalokiteśvara 12, 14, 15, 17, 41, 83, 85, 110, 120, 146, 148, 149, 156, 157, 160, 161, 162, 163, 167, 168, 171, 172, 229(22), 230(34), 234.
avatâra 12, 21, 225(33)
Aymonier 76, 99, 215, 224(13), 226(16), 227(38, 30), 228(42,47,52), 229(11), 231(33), 232(10), 237
Ayuthaya 1, 96, 127, 179-189 *passim*, 196, 197, 198, 202, 204, 205, 222(24), 231(14,16)

B

Ba Phnom 19
Babor, pl.n. 188, 189
Bakheng 19, 58-59, 60, 62, 65, 72, 99, 193, 194
Bakong 47, 51-57 *passim*, 195, 202, 208, 209
Baksei Chamkrong 16, 61-62, 70, 72
Bali 85, 227(21)
Ban Bung Ke 56
Bangkok 1, 2, 123, 199, 200, 201, 204, 205
Banon, Phnom 89, 227(28)
Bantay Ampil 86
Bantay Chmar 5, 145, 166, 168, 170, 230(33), 235, 238
Bantay Kdei 47, 146, 154, 155, 157, 161, 171, 175
Bantay Prei 146, 154, 162
Bantay Prei Nokor 34-35, 36, 44
Bantay Samre 139-140
Bantay Srei 65, 78, 81, 84, 175, 176, 226(12, 13), 230(2), 238
Bantay Thom 162, 163, 164
Baphuon 58, 65, 97, 98, 99, 146, 178, 193, 194, 208, 229(16)
baray(s), see lakes, artifical; also East B, West B.
'Baray Group' 39, 56, 72, 99
Barom-reachea 186
Baset, Prâsâd 65, 88
Bat Chum 65, 74-77, 84, 85, 226(11), 238
Bati 165
Battambang 2, 47, 50, 59, 65, 88-93, 166, 180, 184, 186, 189, 199, 200, 201, 204, 212, 214, 215, 217, 233(32)
Bayon 58, 99, 139, 146, 148-152, 160, 166, 171, 172, 173, 175, 177, 178, 218, 229(21), 230(33), 238
Ben, an official 198, 199
Beng Mealea 86, 110, 121, 139, 144, 166
Bernon de xv-xvi, 190, 205, 232(8,13, 15), 233(26,36), 237
Bhadragiri 59
Bhadraniketana 44, 97, 98, 99
Bhadrapaṭṭana 88
Bhadravarman, a Cham king 15
Bhadreśvara 15, 16, 37, 59, 71, 109, 221(9), 228(51)
Bhâgavata(s), religious sect 57
Bhaiṣajyaguru 168, 180
Bhavâlaya 45, 60
Bhavapura 22, 70, 85
Bhavavarman 19, 21, 22, 23, 35, 36, 37
bhikṣu (monk) 57, 225(29); see monk/s
Bhrigu, an Indian sage 15
Bhûpatîndrapaṇḍita 174
Binh-dinh 15, 121
Blas Ruiz 187
bo-tree 152, 186, 191, 200
Bodhisattva 11, 12, 22, 41, 82, 110, 117, 122, 146, 157, 162, 163, 166, 168, 171, 172, 181, 188, 191, 192, 193, 202
Borobudur 22, 46, 204
Brah Guru (pron. Preah Guru), priestly title 56, 59, 78, 98
Brahmâ 11, 12, 15, 17, 26, 30, 41, 42, 57, 67, 76, 89, 94, 99, 100, 105, 109, 119, 134, 152, 164, 171, 174, 188, 235
brahman 12
Brahmanical 10, 11, 15, 26 etc. See the Glossary
Briggs 86, 221(3), 222(14,35), 223(40), 224(11,22), 225(31), 226(9), 227(22,23), 229(19), 230(1,4), 231(16,21), 237
Buddha-images 41, 116, 130, 138, 149, 188, 189, 190, 192, 193, 202, 234
Burma/ Burmese 4, 6, 9, 10, 121, 157, 168, 169, 174, 178, 180, 183, 198, 202, 228(1), 230(12), 240

C

Çampeśvara 71
Çaṇḍi 20, 22, 53, 59, 144
caste 10, 191, 234, 235
Çaturmukha (Çatomukh) 71, 183, 184
Ceylon 9, 86, 178, 180, 205, 208, 225(32), 236, 240
Chaiya 10, 93, 170
Cham / Chams 6, 9, 10, 24, 182, 187, 197, 228(36), 232(20)
Champa 1,4,10, 13, 15, 16, 23, 24, 71, 98, 121, 166, 168, 182, 187, 197, 228(36,1), 230(13), 232(20)
Chan, Prince, then King 184, 185, 186, 188, 189
Chan, Prince, becomes King Satha-reamea-'thipadei (= King Ibrahim) 196-7
Chan, Prince, becomes King Ang Chan Outey Reachea 199, 200, 202
Chanthaburi 23, 184, 186, 222(24)
Chao Phraya, river or valley 93, 180, 182, 228(1)
Chau-say-tevoda 135-7, 139
Chau Srei Vibol 99 100
Chenla 14, 16, 19, 21, 22, 24, 222(34)
Chey Chettha, son of Soryoport 196, 202
Chey Chettha, King (formerly Ang Saur), a son of Outey 196, 197
Chiang Mai 178, 182
China 4, 6, 7, 9, 14, 24, 178, 212, 229(22), 230(31), 235
Chinese 1, 2, 6, 9, 10, 14, 15, 16, 19, 23, 24, 25, 51, 67, 136, 152, 176, 178, 182
Chisor, see Phnom
Chok Gyargar 43
Chok Phlâng 86
Chou Ta-kuan 152, 176, 177, 178, 180, 230(7)
Chronicles 182, 183, 184, 188, 189, 232(6)
Churning of the Ocean 61, 89, 141, 142, 146, 152, 225(33)
Çitrasena 19, 44
Çittamâtra 82, 226(17), 234, 236
Cochinchina 198, 201, 212, 214, 221(3),